To Tony;

50/50
Chance to Live

In the Grips of Death

May God's anointing be evident in all your directives.

A 'New Autobiography'

In Christ's love,

by

Johnnie R. Jones

Johnnie R. Jones

PS - Thx Sheryl, for your participation in my spiritual legacy.

Copyright © 2009
Johnnie R. Jones
All Rights Reserved

Library of Congress Control Number:
2008909220

ISBN: 978-0-615-25836-2

S-Y-D Publications
316 Hwy. 78 N.
Blue Ridge, TX 75424
972-752-5611

Printed in the USA by
Morris Publishing
3212 E. Hwy. 30
Kearney, NE 68847
1.800.650.7888

Dedicated to the Armed Forces of the United States of America

For me, the Air Force was a maturing and life-directing experience. I would highly recommend a tour of duty in the service of our Armed Forces. Many pages in this book give my military story, revealing the people and events that changed my life for the better.
To all involved, I dedicate this story.

and

Dedicated to my Grandchildren,

to whom I pray my journey of life will give them lasting pleasure and confidence in their own legacy.
I love you!
(see back of book for pictures!)

Contents

Introduction – 1970 – A Tattoo?...7

The 1950s
1951 – In the Beginning...8 ✢ 1955 – 50/50 Chance to Live #1...8

The 1960s
1960 – Key West, Florida...12 ✢ 1961 – 50/50 Chance to Live #2...14 ✢ Pawn Shops and Poverty...15 ✢ Tobacco Road...16 ✢ A 50/50 Chance at Religion #1...17 ✢ Elementary Schools in Sharon and Whitmell Communities...18 ✢ 'Puppy' Love...19 ✢ Damaged Goods: Teenagers!...20 ✢ Duke University Medical Center...22 ✢ Life on a Farm – Dry Fork, Virginia...25 ✢ Tunstall High School: Eighth Grade and Girls?...27 ✢ Ninth Grade and Girls!...27 ✢ 1967 – Hard Working Man...28 ✢ 1969 – 50/50 Chance to Live #3...29 ✢ The Job of My Dreams...32

The 1970s
1970 – Marriage or Military?...34 ✢ Lackland AFB, San Antonio, Texas...38 ✢ Surgery, Military Style...46 ✢ Basic Training...51 ✢ Air Force Academy?...56 ✢ Parade Rest!...58 ✢ Military Madness...66 ✢ Chanute AFB, Rantoul, Illinois...70 ✢ Drugs Anyone?...72 ✢ Vietnam, Please...73 ✢ Rosendale, Wisconsin...74 ✢ Hawaii?...76 ✢ Home for Christmas...77 ✢ Will You Marry Me?...81 ✢ 1971 – Hickam AFB, Honolulu, Hawaii...85 ✢ Waikiki Beach!...87 ✢ First Impression is a...?...89 ✢ First Day on the Job...92 ✢ Wedding Bells?...100 ✢ A 'Monkey Wrench' in Life...102 ✢ A 50/50 Chance at Religion #2...104 ✢ A 50/50 Chance at Religion #3...114 ✢ Singing Flashback: 1961...119 ✢ Moment of Truth...120

1973 A.D. – A New Creation...122
Roller Coaster Christianity...127 ✢ A 'Call' Into the Ministry...132 ✢ 'Aloha' Also Means 'Goodbye'...135 ✢ Danville, Virginia...140 ✢ Carswell AFB, Fort Worth, Texas...142 ✢ College in Texas?...147 ✢ AWOL...Happy Holidays?...154 ✢ In the Grips of Death #4...157 ✢ Dallas Baptist College, Dallas, Texas...161 ✢ Diane Leroy...167 ✢ Marriage Derailment?...184 ✢ February 1, 1975 – Wedding Bells...189 ✢

Welcome Jenny Carol Jones! – February 6, 1976...193 ✢ North Wilmer Baptist Church, Wilmer, Texas...201 ✢ Welcome Timothy Aaron Jones! – September 29, 1977...209 ✢ Glen Hill Baptist Church, Ringgold, Virginia...214

The 1980s
1980 – Gospel For Asia Missions – Back to Texas...223 ✢ Gateway Baptist Schools Administrator – Back to Virginia!...232 ✢ 1981 – Back to Texas, Again!...235 ✢ The Dallas Transit System...239 ✢ A Knife in My Back...In the Grips of Death #5?...239 ✢ Southwestern Baptist Theological Seminary, Fort Worth, Texas...249 ✢ First Baptist Church, Roxton, Texas...254 ✢ North Star Baptist Church, Anderson, Alaska...256 ✢ Adjunct Professor for Wayland Baptist University...259 ✢ Back to Texas, Once Again...265 ✢ Spring Hill Baptist Church, DeKalb, Texas...272

The 1990s
1990 – Alta Vista Baptist Church, Pasadena, Texas...277 ✢ Register Tapes Unlimited, Inc., Houston, Texas...291 ✢ Garden Villas Baptist Church, Houston, Texas...295 ✢ A Writer and Photographer for the *Pasadena Citizen*...302 ✢ First Baptist Church, Blue Ridge, Texas...303

The 2000s
2007 – Shingles and Post Herpetic Neuralgia...308 ✢ Mission Trip – Back to Alaska!...308 ✢ Medical Disability or Retirement?...313 ✢ Life Goes On...315

Family Tree...317 ✢ **Postscript...320**

Additional Writings by the Author...324

Having surveyed the selection of used cars, little Johnnie Ray left the lot, confident he had chosen the most economic vehicle available.

What is a 'New Autobiography' genre?

In her book, *Your Life as Story*, Tristine Rainer describes the New Autobiography as
> a late twentieth-century liberation of the established genre of writing...It is new because it is written as a self-discovery rather than self-promotion. It is new because it beholds the individual's life, not through Puritan mandates of moral edification, nor twentieth-century credos of materialistic success, nor twentieth-century formulas of reductionist psychology, but through the cohesion of literature and myth. Stylistically it is new because it employs storytelling devices, such as scenes and dialog, that are borrowed from fiction (© 1997, Jeremy P. Tarcher/Putnam, New York, NY; pg. 10).

The New Autobiography genre allows me to walk into my past life with a mixture of non-fiction and fiction with no intention of distorting the factual accounts of my history. The New Autobiography genre adds a more dramatic effect to actual events. I have distributed numerous manuscripts to many of those mentioned in the story, asking for corrections and clarifications. My apologies to others I could not get in touch with prior to this publication. Some names are changed due to time. – JRJ

Introduction – 1970: A Tattoo?

I stared momentarily at the shirtless engraver as he motioned for me to take a chair. His arms, neck, and torso were like neon signs in the night shining forth in tattoo ads. My friend, Air Force Sergeant Frank Thompson, wanted to "introduce" Airman Day and me to the indelible world of body art. Both Frank and the engraver stood before me with arms, chests, and backs covered in sculptures of women, insignias, dragons, and snakes. They were proof that one's body can survive the multiple stitching of a dye-cast needle. I hesitated.

"Look here at this baby," said Frank while rolling up his left sleeve, flexing his bicep. He revealed a beautiful sculpture of Diamond Head Crater, located a few miles from where we stood. We were at a tattoo parlor on Hotel Street in Honolulu, Hawaii, a street with numerous "off limits" facilities for military personnel.

"Jonesie, the women love this one!" He showed me his other arm with an eagle and a flag insignia.

"Do you have one with a heart that says 'Mother' on it?" I asked,… Frank rolled his eyes.

"Oh that's an old one," the engraver responded. "I haven't done that in a long time. Let me look in my books and see. While I'm looking, perhaps you guys would like to watch a movie?" With that question, he immediately stepped over to a curtained entryway and revealed a small, darkened theater as the back portion of his parlor with seating for about twenty-five, more or less. A few heads silhouetted the room. From a distance I could see an adult movie projected onto a screened wall.

"I think we'll pass on that for now," said Frank. "I've got bigger plans for us tonight!"

"Bigger plans?" I thought. *"Surely with none of these female creatures on Hotel Street!"*

I began to wonder how much peer pressure my dad went through when he got his "Mother" tattoo, the one I had engraved in my mind since childhood. My dad was a World War II Navy veteran who served on the USS Randolph in the Pacific. I remember, as a boy, how I admired the tattoo on his freckled arm, indelibly engraved through his bushy red hair. And, man, was he strong! My older brothers, Joe, Gary, and I would sometimes gang up on him and try to wrestle his arm to the table. It wasn't until Joe and Gary began to get older that I saw those two, together, put his arm down; but on my own I never could.

That was many years ago in Danville, Virginia, my hometown. But now it is the spring of 1970 and I'm an Airman First Class, serving at Hickam Air Force Base in Honolulu. I'm fresh out of tech school, starting my first tour of duty, a young man of 19 years, and trying to follow the steps of my daddy and my two older brothers. I'm a long ways from home, making decisions that may scar my life forever.

But Hawaii? Why am I here? This place was not my first choice for military assignment—not even second! I had put in for Vietnam, the place where my high school buddy was serving. I wanted to go fight the Viet Cong with him! 'Nam was where the action was and I wanted to be right in the middle.

I was not afraid of dying. In fact, I had been in the grips of death three times already. My mom tells me that I was a preschooler when my first encounter of a 50/50 chance of survival occurred. These death-defying encounters were only a part of the circumstances that allow me to be standing here, in Hawaii, about to make my "manly" decision on a tattoo. My story began many, many miles ago, about 4700 of them...

1951 – In the Beginning...

The first man I ever met slapped me. He then turned to my mother and said, "It's a boy!" That was on June 28, 1951 in Danville, Virginia. I was born to Wallace Allen Jones and Mildred Ruth Burke Jones. Both worked for the Dan River Cotton Mills. I am the middle child of five: two older brothers, Joe and Gary, and a younger sister and brother, Sandra and Ricky. Mom says I weighed in as the heaviest of the siblings. She also remembers missing a family fish fry. Her mom, my Granny Burke, said that fried fish wasn't good for nursing mothers.

My mother says she named me, Johnnie Ray, after a contemporary singer of that day. Obviously, I did not object to it at the time. My first home was a small wooden-framed house, located on my Great-Uncle Hort Gerrells' farm on Tunstall Road in the Sharon community near Danville. I have no recollection of living there, but did see it time-to-time in an uninhabitable condition while growing up.

1955 – 50/50 Chance to Live #1

"I'm sorry, Mildred, but Johnnie must be quarantined for at least a week." This was the statement made to my mom by Dr. Robert McNeely when I was four years old. According to her, I had rheumatic fever—I was one sick little puppy. My dad had to give me two units of blood through an immediate transfusion. It was not uncommon for a child to die of such diseases. I was given a 50/50 chance of survival. Several weeks passed and I survived, thanks to a mom who stayed by my side and a dad who had blood to spare.

My earliest recall of a home was not our own. It was at Pawpaw and Granny Burke's farmhouse on Tunstall Road in the Sharon community. I remember bouncing on a bed upstairs with a cousin named Junior. Not long after that, I remember seeing my uncle and aunt, Marvin and Betty Haymore, sitting in the front living room, Betty sitting in Marvin's lap crying. Their son, Junior—my bed-bouncing buddy—had just died of the croup. I have only a faint image of his face sketched in my mind, but I remember playing with him.

My dad was a good man and served in the Navy during World War II. Although he served his country well, his military experiences led him into alcoholism. This occurred before I was born, so I only knew Daddy as an alcoholic—a very passive alcoholic. He was no disciplinarian. In fact, I cannot recall a single incident of my dad lifting a disciplinary finger toward me or my brothers and sister. It was my mom who would say, "Go pick me out a switch," and send me out of the house to find my own personal switch with which she would administer a whipping.

Daddy loved his alcohol. He also had undying love for hunting rocks. I guess my mom and us kids were third on his list of loves. Although I cannot recall him ever saying that he loved me, I know he did, but the effect of alcohol has a way of clouding the affection a family needs. Regardless, I loved my dad and grew up wanting to be with him.

I was the middle of five children.

I grew up hunting rocks with Daddy. Rock hunters were called "rock hounds" because they always kept their heads down to the ground. Many weekends were spent walking with Daddy, our heads down, kicking through the soft dirt along a field somewhere on a back road in Virginia, searching for some treasure in the rough. I loved rock hunting with my dad; it was peaceful and I always got a soda or some ice cream at our local beer joint before we rock hounds lit out onto a fresh mineral scent. We'd spend hours hunting rocks, finding a flint arrowhead or some other interesting specimen that always produced a low-keyed whistle as Daddy studied the find.

I loved my dad. He died in 1982. I inherited his genes in our family. Not only was I his shape—short and round—I also championed his passivity. My passivity became a tremendous resource for a quality in life called, patience. As a preteen, I could go into the woods and sit on a log or stump and remain so still, that the squirrels in the surrounding trees would forget I ever came into their playground. In time, out they came, playing and jumping across tree limbs right in front of me. Sometimes I carried my brother's single-shot 22-caliber rifle. That's all I needed, because I was so still I could flick a pre-planted rock or acorn to the opposite side of a tree and watch the squirrel slide around the trunk to my side, sometimes within a yard or two. Yeah, I shot a few; but most the time I preferred watching them get caught by my patience.

We lived miles away from any town in what was called the "sticks," most of my growing years. Entertainment consisted mainly of homemade games with my brothers and sister, such as kick-the-can, freeze tag, and capturing "Lightning" and June bugs. Lightning bugs made great skin spots on our bodies and June bugs were a treat to fly from a string tied to its leg. Many an hour was spent just lying on the ground in the woods, listening to the wind gently blowing through the treetops. It was a place where many dreams were born.

Miles of wooded terrain surrounded our country home on Pawpaw Jones's farm. Our "running" water came from a spring-fed hole in the ground that we "ran" to, if we were in a hurry. The trees down by the creek were loaded with large vines that were always a treat to ride. I remember once we were enjoying some "Tarzan" rides, swinging out across the creek. Daddy came down from the house to gather a couple buckets of water from the spring.

The old house on Pawpaw Jones' farm.

"Hey Wallace! Come give it swing," said my cousin Ronnie Pruitt. Daddy grinned and shook a "no" with his head as we each took turns swinging over the creek.

Ronnie's brother, Jimmy, the biggest of the crowd, grabbed the vine and took off.

"Wallace, if it can hold me, it can hold you."

After safely landing, Jimmy handed the vine to Daddy. He dropped his buckets, grabbed the vine, and took off running toward the creek bank. Off he went, gliding gracefully across the indented creek bed. As he was making his return voyage across, the vine broke and down he went, right in the middle of the creek, stumbling around in the knee-deep mire. We began rolling on the ground laughing and hollering. What a sight!

We boys were always building forts and small "cabins" in the woods, using the small pine seedlings throughout the area. We would also build dams on the creek and create our own personal swimming holes that we shared with an occasional snake or two, being careful to keep our distance from the water moccasins. We built a small bridge across the creek bed to help us get to the spring. The bridge resembled a makeshift ladder consisting of slender pines, held together with rungs from additional dead tree pieces. It was a treat for us to cross the creek with a pail or two of spring water.

Now Daddy was a bit larger than all us boys. He came down to our pool to get us to bring some water over the creek. I guess we were having too much fun, because he watched us a bit, then carefully walked over the suspended bridge to the spring. It seemed secure enough, but the additional weight of the spring water was just a tad bit more than the bridge's load limit. "Crack!" came the sound and down through the poles he went, landing securely on his feet in the creek, still holding both pails in his hands. Daddy wasn't too happy over the situation, but, once again, there was sheer joy and laughter from us kids.

We had a small green snake that was curious enough to "walk" us down our road a small distance as we headed to the school bus stop. It was a treat for us to look for him when we returned from school, and, usually, we'd find him hanging out on a small bush. Then one day he was gone. I believe it was the following weekend that our mom mentioned to us to be careful down the road a bit, because she had killed a green snake that was following her. Sandra cried as we told Momma that the snake was our pet. She had no idea that we had befriended the reptile.

Our house was framed in wood with some type of brick-impressed composite, which was wrapped over the wood. The house was very old and had its leaks and squeaks. One day, Momma heard something out of the ordinary in the front wall.

"Wallace, there's something in the wall," she said.

"Ah, you're just hearing things...probably the house shifting."

"No! I know there's something in this wall. Go out there and check it out."

Now Daddy was a slow starter, but mom's persistency got him to finally go outside. We kids went with him for the external inspection. After studying the wall a bit, Daddy looked at Gary and said, "Go get me the hoe."

In a matter of seconds, Gary came back with the hoe. Daddy took it and began pushing against the covering. As he pushed, the wall began moving. He pushed harder. At the top of the composite a large black snake began pouring out like black tar. The snake came down onto the porch right in front of Daddy. We seemed to jump up simultaneously and screaming every time he whacked that snake with the hoe. He finally chopped its head off.

I was about halfway across the front yard before I stopped and began to carefully make my steps back toward the porch. Dad was looking at the 6-foot catch and was still studying the wall when I made my way back onto the porch. He took the hoe and once again pushed hard on the wall. I thought he was trying to push the covering back against the wood, but out poured another long black snake. Once again, we kids scattered like tightly racked billiard balls that were solidly hit by a pool shark.

One day Daddy's foot began to bother him. I remember it was swollen and had a red spot on the bottom, near the big toe. He soaked it a lot in Epson salt and treated it as best as could be done. Daddy worked on his feet as a weaving loom fixer, so it wasn't too many days before he had to go to see Dr. McNeely. He began poking around to Daddy's much discomfort.

"There's something in there, Wallace. Have you stepped on something recently?"

"No, not that I can recall."

Dr. McNeely numbed the area and began digging deeper into the infection. It wasn't long before he pulled out a portion of a glass bottle top. It looked liked part of an old Wildroot or Vitalis bottle neck.

Daddy brought his newly found treasure home and kept it with some of the rock "jewels" he had found. After a lengthy reflection of his past, he remembered running down the hill to the creek as a boy and stepping on a broken bottle. It was a bloody event that was bandaged at home. That was twenty-seven years prior to this encounter. The dime-sized curved glass had been imbedded in his foot all that time.

1960 – Key West, Florida

Dan River Cotton Mills shut down for a week each summer. This was vacation week, which usually meant our annual trip to Virginia Beach. It was the highlight of our year, renting an efficiency beach cottage with a kitchen, riding the ocean waves on an air mattress, or fishing off the pier with Daddy. What a thrill for us country kids.

I'm not sure why, but one year Dan River took two weeks off. Daddy's brother, Uncle Robert, was in the Army and stationed in Key West, Florida. Robert had married my mom's sister, Ruby, and they also had five children—four girls and one boy—pretty much about the same age of our clan. We loved seeing our "double-first" cousins because Robert's military career kept him away from the Danville area.

The preparation for the two-week vacation was extensive. Daddy had the old '57 Plymouth serviced and bought some new retreaded tires. There were Momma, Daddy, and the five children in that car with no air conditioning. We began the trip before daylight and had driven about five miles when one of the car's wheel covers flew off and rolled into the dark brush. Daddy turned the car around and looked for the wheel cover for a few minutes. After a fruitless search, we bade the wheel cover goodbye and continued south for Florida.

I don't think Momma or Daddy realized the distance to Key West, especially with five children cooped up in such a small area. We squirmed, played, argued, and rotated the seating arrangement incessantly. We neared the Florida border about mid-afternoon. For us kids, it seemed as if we'd soon arrive at Key West. One thing that really caught our eyes was a periodic billboard advertising "7 Hamburgers for $1." We begged for hamburgers for miles, thinking Daddy would pull in at the now-famous hamburger joint. But he was a man on a mission: get to Key West by midnight! So, much to the dismay of five hungry kids—hungry for hamburgers, because we had a car full of sandwiches, chips, and cookies—we zoomed by the hamburger stand. We complained for a while, but our bellyaching was interrupted by one of our tire retreads peeling off and slapping the fender. It was only a small portion, so Daddy cut it off with his pocketknife and we continued on. (That tire never gave us a moment's trouble afterwards.)

Midnight found us in Miami. Somehow, we missed a turn and went into Miami's west side. We counted over ninety intersections with a signal. This only frustrated an already tired Daddy. After Miami came the long bridges—including the famous seven-mile bridge—over the Florida Keys. I was sitting in the front middle with an assignment to keep Daddy awake. It was hard because the "clickety-click" of the bridge sections had a hypnotic effect. Finally, we made it to Key West…about 3:00 a.m.

Key West was hot, humid, and rained on-and-off daily. It was the first experience for a young boy to see "topless" swimsuits on girls. Actually, these suits had large straps that came up the front and tied around the neck. I was still young enough to think it looked silly and can remember my mom warning my dad about staring. We had the greatest time with our cousins. They had a real large "monkey-gym" playground just across the street from their apartment and we especially enjoyed chasing the "farting" truck as it belched out a fog of mosquito repellant down the street.

Aunt Ruby was great at giving military haircuts, so Momma had us boys get one. Ruby saved me for last because she said my hair was the thickest and she didn't want to burn out her electric clippers. She cut and cut until about halfway through my hair, sure enough, her clippers stopped. She gazed at her clippers, blew out the cut hair from its blades, and pounded it in her hand a few times. Then she examined at my head.

"Well Johnnie, I guess we'll just have to leave half of your head shaved and the other half long." She looked serious and I wasn't old enough to think otherwise. But all the serious faces turned into laughter, so I knew this was only temporary. As soon as the clippers cooled down, off went the rest of my hair.

I think our two-weeks' vacation turned into about seven days because Daddy wanted to get back in enough time to rest from all the traveling. We left and headed back for Virginia. Somewhere in middle Florida, we began seeing those "7 Hamburgers for $1" billboards again. Once again, the chant began: "Daddy please can we have a hamburger? PLEASE?" This time Momma jumped into the request and her assistance got us the okay. For over a hundred miles we did nothing but drool over those hamburgers. Finally, we arrived. Daddy went in and ordered the burgers. Soon he came out with just one bag. His face had an interesting read. It looked angry and then a smile; then angry again. He gave the bag to Momma. She pulled out one of the burgers with a remark that got all our attention. (I'll clean it up a bit.)

"What? Is that it?"

We were all devastated as we looked at what seemed like bite-sized hamburger buns with a piece of hamburger meat in it. They were about one-third the size of a regular hamburger. We all got mad and fussed, but this incident has always been one of the funniest stories our family talks about when we reminisce about the "good 'ol days." We made it back to Virginia, safe and sound and full of wonderful memories.

1961 – 50/50 Chance to Live #2

I became sick in the fifth grade. My Momma took me to Dr. McNeely's office. It was an office in the basement of his house. There were no appointments; you arrived, signed in, and waited...and waited...and waited. Sometimes it would take four to six hours to see the doctor. He finally came in and began going through the list of people waiting to see him. When he got to me, he took my temperature, told my mom I probably had the flu, and sent us home.

I remember being sick all week. I vomited occasionally. Momma gave me some medicine to stop the vomiting, but I vomited it as well. For a week, I remained at home in the bed. A week later on a Monday morning, I got up and, although my body was bent over in an L-shape, I asked Momma if I could go to school. She told my dad to put me in the car—back to McNeely's office!

Fortunately, Dr. McNeely was in his office that morning and he saw me just before lunch.

"Let me see you young man." He tried to straighten my body, but I wouldn't budge. He then felt around me and pushed in on the right side of my abdomen.

"Ouch!" I began to cry. I remember the acute pain in that area of my body.

"Mildred, get him over to the hospital right now! Tell them to prep him for surgery right away. I'll be right behind you. He has appendicitis."

It wasn't the flu. My appendix had become inflamed. I vaguely recall being put sideways on a stretcher and pushed down a hallway. I cried out for Momma; she was there, but had to stop at some double doors. My next recall was after surgery, lying in a hospital bed. I remember groaning for many days, tears streaming down the side of my face, finding relief only when Momma blotted my face and forehead with a cool moist cloth. My appendix had burst during the week and its poison had invaded my body. Dr. McNeely told my parents that I had a 50/50 chance of surviving.

For three weeks I lay in the hospital, watching, as the nurse would pull a long cloth-looking tube out of my incision. It was a "poison catcher." Although I couldn't feel any pain associated with the tube, I could see the nurse as she pulled it out of the incision to change it. I screamed when it was pulled out and had to be restrained each time. Again, I survived and was finally released.

I missed over six weeks of school during that illness. My teacher was very sympathetic and gave me straight A's during that grading period—the only time I ever received straight A's on my report card.

Pawn Shops and Poverty

Daddy's alcohol kept our family about one step ahead of the bill collectors. It seemed like all our family bills were paid with the late fees already factored into the payments. Bankruptcy was always a trump card; but the ace up the sleeve was a pawnshop. I can't recall the number of times my mom's diamond ring went down Memorial Drive in Danville to be traded out for some much-needed cash. Momma always fussed about pawning her rings and warned my dad about retrieving them on time. Dad's ears would rise about a quarter inch, indicating his satisfaction in averting another financial disaster.

Daddy never lost my mom's rings, but occasionally, he lost his steps ahead of the bill collectors. This meant we would move. Sometimes we moved to another rent house. Other times we moved in with my cousins. Since there were four or more kids from most marriages among my aunts and uncles, our family mergers didn't last over a month or two.

We moved a lot. I don't recall any personal problems related to moving. My patience was my "ace" that allowed me to be friends with just about anyone. Patience, plus my ability to come up with one-liner jokes under any circumstance kept me in the midst of friendship and laughter. People liked me and enjoyed having me around.

Although we moved around a bit, our family seemed to return to our favorite house on my Pawpaw Jones's farm in the Lanier's Mill community. There were a lot of woods and a creek between our houses. We had no close neighbors. My cousins (Wayne, Jimmy, Ronnie, Steve, and Danny Pruitt) lived uphill from us about three-quarters of a mile. My Great Grandma Jones's house was between us, about a quarter mile away. She and my Great Grandpa Jones had lived in the house we were now living in. I think Great Grandpa Jones died the year I was born.

Joe and Gary, the cousins, and I helped Great Grandma Jones by toting her water from Granny and Pawpaw's house, across the creek, and up a steep hill on both sides. She had two large metal milk cans with lids that we used to carry the water. One was shorter than the other, but they were both heavy when filled with water. She always had something sweet for us to eat or sometimes gave us a penny or two. She had a large fruit-bearing mulberry tree in her yard with a cluster of mistletoe near the top. Boy did we love to gather underneath that tree, in season, and eat mulberries. They were so sweet. And in the winter, we came with Joe's rifle to bring down a sprig or two of mistletoe.

Tobacco Road

I was about five years old when we moved to the Astin farm on the Old Moorefield Bridge Road. My playmate was Janet Astin, Mr. Astin's granddaughter. I recall we played in the mud near the tobacco barns while her mother, Jean, worked as the main tobacco "stringer." A stringer was one who took tobacco leaf bundles of 3 to 4 leaves each, handed to her from a tobacco sled, and wrapped them with string, making two rows down a one-inch wide tobacco stick that was about five feet long. The sticks were hung on a wooden frame called a "horse." There were usually three or four "handers" per sled brought in from the field. These sticks were then laid neatly in a pile that would eventually be hung on some tiers in a tobacco barn.

I remember one particular day that I grew tired of making mud pies and playing with Janet. I walked up to a sled to watch Jean as she masterly strung the leaves, twisting each bundle to the stick. It was always her goal to finish the sled before the next one came from the field. This was the only way she and the handers could get a break.

Usually two handers per stringer were enough; but not for Jean. She was always "talking" to her handers: "More, more!" She had a speed and a rhythm like no one else. I think this particular day, Joe and Gary were handing her leaves. Jean kept crying out, "More, more! C'mon Joe; c'mon Gary!" That's when she looked at me.

"Johnnie, what are you staring at? Get over here between your brothers and hand me some leaves."

I was more than willing and Jean was ready for the challenge of yanking the bundles from three handers. Although I was a little short, Joe and Gary managed to fix me a small pile of leaves from which to work. I'm sure I must have slowed my brothers down a bit, but it was fun and was my official first day to work.

Several days later, at Reuben's Corner Store (Daddy's favorite beer joint), our family was sitting in the car under a shade tree waiting on my dad. Mr.

Astin came out of the store and headed for the car. He began to pay Joe and Gary for their work that week. Of course they thanked him. Then he looked at me.

"I heard from Jean that you did a pretty good job handing leaves." He handed me a dollar. "Keep up the good work," he said with a smile.

I don't recall if I responded to him, but boy was I beaming. My first dollar earned! Joe and Gary didn't think much of it, but Momma was proud of me and encouraged me to keep working. That I did and it became the first of many dollars I would earn from tobacco.

A 50/50 Chance at Religion #1

I knew some things about religion. My grandparents were Baptists and my parents were Baptists. I went to Sunday School and church in a rather irregular fashion as a child. I remember my cousin, Danny, wanted to be "saved," but did not want to go to the front of the church alone. I volunteered to go with him. With some counsel and practice from Ronnie, we went to the front of the church during an altar call. Pastor Bowman of the Mount Hermon Baptist Church was standing there, bigger than life, to receive us. He took Danny first, then me.

"Why have you come to the altar, son?"

"I want to receive Jesus Christ as my Lord and Savior," I replied, based on numerous times of practice.

"That's great son." Pastor Bowman patted me on the head and had me sit down. I was six or seven years old.

It was announced that all who came to the altar to be saved or to join the church must undergo six Sunday evenings of new members training. Apparently, an adult had to attend with the children, because I remember my mom going to several of the classes with me. I think we made it to three classes before dropping out. Why did I drop out? I don't recall; it could have been due to a drive out on a back road with Daddy hunting for rocks. I do remember Danny was baptized and I was not.

The upcoming summer found me attending Vacation Bible School at Mount Hermon church. Mister Hardy gathered a bunch of children in his pickup truck and took us to VBS. He had a wooden fence assembled around the truck bed and had placed bales of hay in the bed to give us something to sit on. He'd pick up about ten of us children before arriving at the church.

My VBS teacher was the prettiest girl I ever laid eyes on. I think her name was Ms. Merrick. She asked me if I was a member of the church.

"I don't know; I went to the altar a few months ago."

"Let me check with the office," she said.

Later that day she came to me and told me that everything was okay, so there was nothing to worry about. I think she and I both made a false assumption that day. She thought that I was a saved Christian and I thought being on the church roll made me a saved Christian—but my future actions would prove that I did not possess a genuine "converted" soul.

Elementary Schools in Sharon & Whitmell Communities

I think I attended four or five elementary schools in Virginia and North Carolina, depending on Daddy's need to move us. But Whitmell and Sharon elementary schools, in Virginia, were the two I spent most of my first six grades. Mrs. Pickeral, of Whitmell Elementary, was my first grade teacher. Most of my teachers were at Sharon: Mrs. Herndon, 2nd-3rd grades, Mrs. Booth, 4th grade, and Mrs. Mitchell, 5th-6th grades. Mrs. Mitchell was also the principal.

I have a few memories in first grade. One vague memory was some type of May Day celebration which involved colored streamers tied from a central pole. The children were dressed up in commemorative clothing and held on to a certain number of streamers as they either circled or danced around the pole. It must have been the uniqueness of the event for it to have lodged into my memory. I remember watching children participate, but I do not recall participating myself. I think we had just moved back to my Pawpaw Jones' farm.

Another First Grade memory involves the class practice words that were written on the blackboard by Mrs. Pickeral. She instructed the class to write each word three times on our paper. As soon as she completed the word list on the board, she would place her chalk down, come to my desk, take up my completed paper, and make me write them again with a warning to write slowly. Apparently she knew I had two older brothers who had already taught me how to read and write.

I have similar memories at Sharon Elementary School. The Sharon community is located on Mount Cross Road. It had but one school, Sharon Elementary. I recall it had four or five classrooms and a condemned upstairs auditorium. The school bell was hand held. The six grades had to share rooms and teachers. Our teachers would instruct one grade, give assignments, and then go to another desk on the other side of the same room to teach the other grade. Each room had its pot-bellied, coal-burning stove.

There was one story floating around that I had a distant cousin who always had a pouch of tobacco in his pocket. He let the strings of the pouch hang out for clout. One of the teachers—I think the story tied it to Mrs. Mitchell—became irritated at his tobacco pouch, grabbed it by the strings, and threw it into the coal stove.

The next day, my cousin came back with another pouch in his pocket, the strings dangling. The story goes that when Mrs. Mitchell saw the pouch, she grabbed this one as well and threw it into the stove. Only this time the pouch was full of gunpowder.

"BOOM!"

Fortunately, the school didn't burn down, but it sure made a mess of one room. My cousin spent a few weeks away from school.

'Puppy' Love

It was the fifth grade that I encountered my first love. At the time, it seemed everyone had a girlfriend—everyone except me. Mandy Scearce was a cute sixth grader and I was a fifth grader. That grade difference was not a good match, but someone—I think it was my brother Gary—suggested I write her a love letter. With counsel, I crafted a beautiful love letter: "Dear Mandy, I love you. Do you love me? Please check the box below. Love, Johnnie Jones." I drew two boxes below the letter, one large box beside the word, "YES," and a smaller box beside, "NO." I was proud of my ingenious work of art.

The next morning, when I arrived, I had someone deliver the note to Mandy before school started. I remember when the opening bell rang, I quietly went to the fifth grade part of our room. What I saw next has never left my mind. There were several girls standing around Mandy's desk as she sat there…crying.

Crying? I wondered what the problem was. At that moment, Lee Ann Carter gave me a glaring look. I was the problem. I couldn't believe it. I had visions of my love letter producing a smile and, perhaps, a return note even if she planned to check the "No" box. I was not prepared for Mandy's tears. It confused me and I felt miserable. I got up from my desk and told Mrs. Mitchell that I didn't feel well and asked permission to go to the restroom.

The restroom was outside on the edge of the schoolyard, strategically located at the top of a sloping hill. It had three walls, with an offset entryway, to cover the view from the school. There was an open-air area with a long urinal trough. Enclosed was a three- or four-hole john. I paced the urinal area, trying to understand how a love letter could make someone cry. There wasn't much time for me to sort this confusion of mine out, but somehow, in that outhouse, I made a life-changing decision. I decided, then and there, that I would never make anyone cry again. I made a decision to become a funny person. I will begin to make people laugh.

About that time Gary Green came running down to the outhouse.

"Mrs. Mitchell said for you to get back to class now."

"Okay; you betcha!"

I returned with a big smile on my face. I was a new man—uh, boy. Later, I got word from several reliable sources that Mandy did not love me or even like me, and that I was not to write her again. I smiled. *"No problem,"* I thought to myself. I had a new mission in life now.

From that day forward, I began to follow the steps of my cousin, Ronnie Pruitt. Ronnie was the funniest guy around and always had a crowd laughing. I was proud to be kin to Ronnie because it gave me special recognition around him. He and Jackie Jones (another of my cousins) were the closest of friends. They were also the biggest and funniest guys in the sixth grade.

I was ten when Ronnie offered me my first cigarette. We were resting in a tobacco field on my Pawpaw Jones's farm. Ronnie instructed me that to keep from coughing twenty-one times, I needed to inhale the smoke deeply. I did as instructed and became an immediate celebrity because I didn't cough a single time. However, the "twenty-one cough" experience did come the next morning when I snuck a cigarette from my parents and went to our outhouse down by the yard's edge. I didn't inhale deep enough and out came the coughs. I know I counted twenty-one of them, just like Ronnie said, but I never told anyone.

I "borrowed" a pack of cigarettes from my parent's stock. I remember my mom accusing my dad of smoking too much because their weekly supply of cigarettes was down. I never confessed. I hid them along the house foundation rocks. My brother, Gary, found them. He came to me with the stash.

"I found these under the house. Did you hide them there?"

"No. I didn't do it."

Gary looked at me suspiciously, and looked back at the cigarettes. Then he turned toward the house.

"Maybe Daddy set them down while mowing the yard the other day."

Whew! I didn't get caught and Gary never brought it up again. Being the third of five children, I had to learn how to negotiate for things and positions around me. It contributed greatly to my patient, passive nature.

Damaged Goods: Teenagers!

I had a reputation of being clumsy while growing up. I don't know why, but my drinking glass seemed to be more top-heavy than most. One summer day in my eighth-to-ninth grade year I was helping Mr. Gibson pull his tobacco crop. This particular field just happened to be next to his watermelon patch. About mid-morning we tobacco "pullers" took a break and raided the patch. I think it was my buddy, Ricky Payne, who pulled out his pocketknife and cut a big slice for himself. He threw the knife to me and I, in turn, began cutting a slice. To stabilize the melon, I tucked it between my knees and using my right hand, proceeded to cut my slice from the bottom up. About midway up the melon, the knife blade slipped out of the rind, causing a deep stab into my left wrist. The pain was quick and severe, and a spew of blood sent everyone scattering. I remember rolling around for a while in the dirt, screaming at the top of my lungs. Rick's dad, Ben, was nearby.

"Y'all throw him into the (tobacco) sled and lay him down. Johnnie, keep pressure on the cut!"

Ben drove us to the tobacco barn. Lying there on top of the tobacco, the sled being pulled by an old tractor, I tried to sneak a peek at the cut, but the blood continued to spurt out of the puncture. My left hand seemed to be numb, but I wasn't moving it or touching any part of it. I wondered if I would pass out. When we arrived at the barn, Ben announced the problem and proceeded to put me in his truck. One of the ladies told him to stop first because old man Gibson was there. He was Mr. Gibson's dad. They ran to get him and he walked over to me, sitting on the passenger side, in Ben's truck.

"Let me see your hand son," he said. He looked at the stabbed area. The spurt had reduced to a small, pumping stream of blood coming out of a deep indenture in my left wrist, with obvious layers of flesh, surrounded by the black, sticky tar-like substance that comes from raw tobacco leaves. Once seen, Mr. Gibson turned away and walked away toward the backside of the tobacco barn. I wasn't told then, but later it was revealed to me that Mr. Gibson had a gift of prayer that could stop bleeding. The stories were told to me about how he saved a mule from bleeding to death by his gift.

Ben shut my truck door and headed away from town toward his farm where my family lived. While traveling, I took another glance at the wound; it stopped bleeding completely. I remember looking into my wrist, marveling at the different layers of flesh with small, white-looking tubes.

I'm not sure, but it seems that my dad got in the truck with Ben and me, and we three headed for Danville, to the hospital's emergency room. I was still conscious and will never forget the beauty—the purity—of that place. Everything was so clean and all the attendants were wearing white. I was filthy, with tobacco gum and sweat stains all over my clothing. I remember being afraid I was going to get something or someone dirty. But that didn't last long.

"Let me see your hand, young man," said a beautifully clean and clad black lady. She looked like an angel. I stretched out my left hand carefully. "Sit here." She pulled another chair next to mine and with a stainless steel tray nearby, began to wash my wrist and hand. I flinched at first, expecting pain, but there was none. That didn't seem to bother her as she proceeded to scrub the area around the wound. By the time she was finished, her beautiful white gown was as black as my hand and wrist.

"I'm sorry I got you dirty." She looked at me and smiled.

"That's what we're here for," she said, as she rolled the tray away to another room. The doctor came, looked at the wound and put about five stitches in it.

"It should heal nicely in about a couple weeks," he said to me and my dad. "Take him to your doctor then and he'll remove the stitches."

Days passed and my wound began to heal. But, for some reason, the feeling did not return to my hand. I'm serious when I say that I couldn't feel a thing, just beyond my left wrist to the tips of my fingers. My doctor saw me several weeks later. He removed the stitches and began sticking my fingers and hand with a pin.

"Let me know when you feel anything," he said. Nothing, absolutely nothing was felt until he neared the center of the palm. "Sometimes the feeling takes awhile to return. Come back in about a month and we'll look at it again."

I don't recall when the next visit occurred. What I do recall is the instant popularity I received by being wounded. Instead of pulling the tobacco leaves off the plants, I now became the one-handed tractor driver. Wow, this was neat!

My buddy, Ricky, wasn't fully convinced of my numbness. He thought I was "pulling" an act. One evening at my house, we were boiling hotdogs on top the oven range. Ricky began to taut me about my "act."

"You're just pretending so you don't have to work in the fields."

"Oh yeah? How much will you give me if I stick my finger in this boiling hotdog water?"

"Fifty cents."

I took my middle finger, and after deliberately pointing it in his face, I stuck it down into the boiling water. I began to stir the hotdogs in the water with my finger.

"Enough?" I asked.

"Enough," he responded, and handed me my fifty cents.

Although the finger blistered and eventually peeled off a layer of skin, I never felt any pain from the experience.

Duke University Medical Center

About six months later, my parents took me to Duke University Medical Center, in Durham, North Carolina. An important doctor—Goldner, was his name—came into my room. I know he was important because there were four or five interns with him and everything he said was being recorded. Doctor Goldner ordered a number of x-rays and tests. After what seemed an eternity, he came back, by himself, to talk to my parents and me.

"Your son appears to have completely severed one nerve and injured another nerve. If you'll notice, his lack of use of this hand has caused several muscles to atrophy; look here."

He compared my hands. Sure enough, the muscles in my wounded left hand had shrunk between my thumb and index finger and on the side beside my little finger. In fact, all my fingers had a bend in them, looking as if I were grasping an egg.

"Try and pinch me," said Doctor Goldner. I couldn't; I had no strength to even pinch the good doctor.

"If we don't do surgery to repair this nerve damage, I'm afraid your son will lose all use of his left hand."

Momma and Daddy looked at each other in a way I'd never seen before. "Whatever you say needs to be done, doctor, do it," said Momma. Daddy shook his head in approval. The doctor wrote out two prescriptions and handed them to my mom.

"The hospital will call you with the surgery schedule. In the meantime, this medical clay and apparatus will help strengthen his hand and straighten out his fingers."

We walked out of the room and into the hallway. Momma and Daddy began discussing the ability to pay for the prescriptions.

"He can use a rubber ball to squeeze," said Daddy.

"But this is clay," said Momma. "Maybe this will be better. We've got to get this apparatus anyway, so we may as well get them both."

Daddy and I headed to the car as Mom headed to another area of the hospital to get the prescriptions filled. I felt guilty. I knew we were poor and I did not like costing my parents any money. Daddy got him a beer out from under the car seat as we waited for Momma. She appeared about thirty minutes later, noticeably shaken.

"Oh Wallace, I'm sick! Look at this!" She was showing him the receipt. The clay cost about $5.00 and the apparatus was about $15.00. Twenty dollars was a lot of money back in the mid-sixties.

"Take it back," said Daddy.

"We can't. It's non-returnable."

There was a moment of silence and then they both turned, at the same time, to look at me in the back seat.

"You'd better use this stuff!"

I'm sure they said it together, because it resounded in my mind. I took the bag and opened the apparatus. It looked weird. It had two metal rods about four inches apart. It slipped over my knuckles and several rubber bands put enough tension on the rods to cause me to extend the knuckle joints of all my fingers when I opened my hand. Interesting, I thought.

Then I opened the bag of "medical" clay. It was very pliable and looked familiar. I showed it to my mom.

"Silly putty!" she shouted. "They charged us five dollars for a container of silly putty!"

And she was right. The clay bounced like silly putty and it copied newspaper print just like silly putty. At that time, silly putty cost about sixty-nine cents. It was a medical lesson to be learned.

My surgery began many trips from Danville to Durham. My hand became a study project of the hospital. Papers were signed to reduce the costs of follow-up visits. Every stage of the procedures was photographed and documented.

The surgery was performed. The feeling in my hand increased, but the nerve sensory was all messed up. I could feel sensation in my fingers, but my brain was giving me false locations. If I touched my index finger my little finger and thumb would feel it. Everything in my fingers was out of whack. Doctor Goldner would give us an explanation.

"Two main nerves were cut—one completely severed," he explained. "What I did was to find each end of the nerve and splice it together. It's like splicing a telephone cable with a thousand smaller lines inside and trying to get the same little lines to match up. Quite impossible; but, enough sensation should return to keep him from total uselessness of the hand.

"Look at his wrist. See that small lump? That is the nerve endings that did not join. When I touch that area, what do you feel?" He tapped it.

"Ouch!" I responded. "I feel pins and needles throughout my hand."

"Exactly. Your brain is receiving signals from those nerve endings that think they're out there in your hand. That area will always be sensitive, so be careful not to hit it or damage it. You will have limited feeling in that hand, but enough to give you usefulness with it.

"Now the muscles have died between your thumb and index finger and outside your little finger. This is due to non-usage. I want to do some skin grafts and replace the muscle tissue at both locations. This will give your hand more mobility."

We left this meeting. I think this was about the sixth visit to Duke University Medical Center. It would be our last as I got used to the numbness in my left hand. I remember about a year later, my dad came to me and asked me to open and close my left hand.

"You going to be okay with this?"

"Sure Dad. I can grip pretty well with it and I'm right handed."

"We don't think our insurance will cover any more surgeries on your hand."

"I'm okay, I don't need any more surgeries."

That was the last discussion on repairing my hand. I was a patient, passive young man, just like my dad. My nature allowed me to adapt pretty easily in any situation and my hand never prevented me from doing anything I set out to do, except sports. My poor performance, due to the imbalance of strength and feeling in my left hand caused me to turn away from school sports.

Life on a Farm – Dry Fork, Virginia

Our rental house on Ben Payne's farm.

Ricky Payne and I were best friends for most of my high school years. He built a small "cabin" down in the pasture, below our house. I helped him some. He decided to paint the front bright red. We were busy doing so when, all of a sudden, their bull began to snort and make all kinds of noise. He galloped toward the cabin and us. We jumped into the cabin, holding the door closed through the crack around it. The bull charged right up to the door and stopped. He snorted a bit and began smelling our fingers. Then he galloped back up the hill toward the barn, stopped, and looked back at the cabin.

"He's going to knock this thing down, Johnnie," said Ricky. "Let's make a run for that tree by the fence."

He didn't have to say it twice. We broke for the fence line and so did the bull. I was the first to the tree, grabbing a limb as quick as possible. Ricky was hollering.

"Go, Johnnie, GO!"

He literally pushed me up the tree as the bull arrived, just missing him. The bull then ran down to the cabin, snorted a bit and ran back up and into the barn. I guess the old saying that bulls don't like the color red is true.

One Christmas, I received the most beautiful bicycle I ever dreamed of. It had a second seat over the rear chrome fender. It had a center console with a headlight and horn. I mean this was a "Cadillac" of a bike. I thought this bike would make me the leader of the pack as we boys rode through the countryside. But Ricky was not to give up his position without a challenge. On the second or third day after Christmas, we pedaled several miles down to Uncle Tom and Aunt Judy's house. It was dark as we headed back home, which was what we planned since I had a new headlight to guide us.

The closer we got to home, though, the less we needed a bicycle light. I still wanted to lead, but Ricky would have none this "second fiddle" stuff. He took off for the lead and I challenged him. Somehow, we got a little too close to each other and my front wheel locked into his rear axle bolt. Sparks flew as the spokes in my wheel began to pop out of their sockets. I steered for the ditch and slid into the soft dirt. What a mess! My new bike was no longer new, but crippled by the collision. I carried it about a half-mile to Ricky's basement to assess the damage. It didn't look good.

"What am I going to do?" I was brokenhearted.

"Wallace ain't going to ever get you something nice for Christmas," said Ricky. He never was one to mince with words.

My brother, Gary, studied the bent wheel. "Let's call Tom." Now Gary usually didn't ride with us, but this time I was glad to have my older brother's opinion.

"Yeah!"

Tom Gibson was my uncle. He had married Judy, my mom's younger sister. We called him. He said to find some more spokes and he'd be up in about thirty minutes or so. Now Tom was an auto mechanic, but we believed he could fix anything. If anyone could fix my mess, Tom could; and maybe Dad didn't have to know about the accident.

Tom worked on my wheel for over an hour. Slowly, but methodically, the wheel began to take a straightened spin. It was amazing.

Tom stopped. The wheel was about ninety-five percent straight.

"Johnnie, I could try to do a little more, but it may get worse. I think I better stop at this point."

The older spokes didn't shine like their newer counterparts, and the wheel still had a little side movement, but I was so happy to be able to get back onto my bike and ride it again. I thanked Tom and never told my dad, although several weeks later he did comment about how something didn't look right about my wheel. I think he knew, but he never mentioned it again and I never revealed the accident to him.

As I grew into my teenage years, I found that there was a dark side to my passive nature. I let other people make decisions for me. For example, I did not like what alcohol did to my dad; I didn't even like the taste of beer. But, given the opportunity, I would go out with friends and drink beer throughout my teenage years. With me, there was no problem with peer pressure—it was peer control, complete control. For example:

"Hey Johnnie! You wanna run that thing through the quarter mile down 58?"

"Sure."

And off I'd go, knowing my dad's old 1960 Dodge Matador could never win a quarter mile drag race on Highway 58. But that didn't matter because I knew I could bury the speedometer needle past the 130 mph mark after the quarter mile. And that was the thrill my buddies and I sought.

One night some guys passed my buddies and me going home—I mean they blew the doors off my Matador.

"Let's catch those [bleeps] said one of my riders. "In Johnnie's tank?" came a response from someone else. "Never."

"Oh yeah? Watch this."

I turned off my headlights and sped up the Mount Cross Road. With taillights in front and moonlight above, I sped up one of the most crooked roads in the area. Less than three miles later the car ahead of me experienced the "sonic boom of the midnight rider." I had a reputation in that monster of a car. I drove it so fast that I could make the windshield wipers slide up onto the windshield, perpendicular to the road. I drove it up into the woods once and cut a new trail over to a pond. A tree stump tore the side up pretty bad; but, with my friends, I did dumb things.

Tunstall High School: Eighth Grade and Girls?

I attended high school at Tunstall High, in Dry Fork, from 1964 through 1969. Neither my dad nor mom graduated from high school. I suppose that is why I was not too concerned about graduating. Girls liked me in my eighth grade—not as a boyfriend, but as a confidant. I figured it was my ability to listen that attracted them. They especially liked to talk to me about other boys. I became a mediator for several shaky relationships. Some of the upper classmen at school came to me asking for help—secretly, of course, because they would not want others to know they talked to a lower classmate of my caliber. But that never bothered me. I felt important that I was sought after by some of the best in our school.

Up through my eighth grade, I was a chubby boy. I always had to wear "husky" sized pants. That would change during the summer between my eighth and ninth grade. It was then that Ricky Payne, our mutual friend, Woody Gibson, and I would ride our bicycles nearly every day for about eight miles, one way, to Brown's Esso gasoline station on Highway 41. We rode primarily to be together, away from the mundane scenes of the farm and the chores that went with it. This was also the summer I cut my wrist while cutting a watermelon. This accident occurred in Woody's dad's tobacco field. That summer was a turning point in my life.

Ninth Grade and Girls!

My first day at school in the ninth grade was definitely different with the girls.

"Who are you?" one girl asked.

"What'dya mean, 'Who am I'? I was in two of your classes last year."

"No, really, who are you? You definitely were not in any of my classes."

"That's Johnnie Jones; don't you remember?" another girl said.

"Oh my! You mean that fat boy, Johnnie Jones? No way!"

All of my fat had burned off that summer. Now I was a slim and trim bicycle-riding machine. Now, the girls were far more interested in me than just mediating their relationships.

1967 – Hard Working Man

I already had a job as an assistant manager of a Shell gasoline station on Riverside Drive. I had worked there since I was a sophomore. Eugene R. Gunn, Jr. ("Junior") was the station manager. His dad ran West Main Shell.

Junior Gunn was probably my first real encounter with a man who had a religious conviction about things. He was the funniest adult I ever met and always had a group of men hanging around the Shell station telling jokes and laughing. I remember him running Shelby Ford, another assistant manager, back and forth from the rear office to the public phone booth by the edge of the parking lot. Junior called the pay phone from the rear office. Shelby heard the phone ringing from a distance. He finally answered the thing.

"Hello?"

"Is this Gunn's Riverside Shell?" Junior asked, pretending to be someone important.

"Yes; who is this?"

In disguise, Junior explained that he needed to speak to Junior, but was getting a busy signal at the station. Could Shelby relay a message to him?

"Hold on." Shelby, a bit irritated, walked across part of the driveway to the rear of the station to find Junior.

Junior pretended to be on the rear office phone with someone else who was equally important. So he sent Shelby back and forth from both phones relaying messages. It took three or four trips before Junior burst out laughing. It was quite a joke on Shelby and Junior loved to tell it on him.

Junior became a moral steering mechanism in my life. He counseled me about dating and premarital sex. He brought his Bible to work. I had no Bible, except maybe a small Gideon's New Testament tucked away in a drawer at home. I was in the prime of my life and did not see a need for church or religion.

Ricky Payne got a similar job at North Main Phillips 66. Although we were still close friends, he and I began to hang out with different guys due to our job associations. I do remember that there was a time that Ricky became ill. His illness made him lethargic and, we found out, slow to respond to situations on the road. He drove a VW Beetle, with an air-cooled, rear engine and the gas tank up front. I was riding with him to Nor-Dan Shopping Center once. We stopped at a T-intersection. Coming our way was a large '54 Ford. It belonged to a neighbor near our home, so Ricky proceeded to pull out in front of the car. But the car did not turn; instead, it continued to go straight. Ricky stopped in the intersection, but it was too late. The Ford clipped the front of his VW and mangled the front badly. The VW gas tank was pushed up next to our knees, but fortunately did not burst. What we did not know was that our neighbor had sold his '54 Ford just a week prior, which is why it did not turn at the intersection.

Rick's dad, Ben, was not happy with Rick and his inability to wait for the intersection to be cleared, but it was an understandable mistake. The VW was repaired and all seemed to well for a few months. But once again Ricky and I were heading into town in his freshly painted and repaired VW, when a truck pulled out ahead of us. The truck managed to straighten up in our lane when Ricky started to pass it. Just as the pass began, I noticed a left turn signal flashing on the truck. Sure enough, the truck began to turn left into a field. The front bumper of the truck grabbed the VW at the seam of the passenger door, ripping the rear side right off the car. I looked down and saw the road and VW frame below my seat. Ricky was furious, but the damage had been done.

Although I attended Vacation Bible School several summers, my next serious encounter with church was during my dating years, starting in the ninth grade. Mrs. Monk would sometimes remind me to take her daughter, Dana, to church as a part of our Sunday night date routine. I think I took her several times to Sharon Baptist Church. I remember the preaching at the church was intense at times, but I managed to keep my mind on the most important thing…my date. Dana was a majorette at our high school and played in our school band. Dana and I dated for four years with only a few break ups. I loved her and she loved me. We both knew right from wrong, yet it was a challenge to remain a virgin during those high school years… …but we did. How? The best I can recall is that I did not want to disappoint my mom. She had been disappointed in my dad's love for alcohol, so I was determined not to be another source of disappointment for her. I never told that to Dana or my mom.

My school, my job, and Dana kept me busy during my high school years. I gained a lot of friends by working at the Shell station. Riverside Drive was the main cruising strip in Danville and many guys would pull in for gas and a quick car wash. Although Junior had to charge for the use of the wash pit, I usually discounted it after dark as long as the guys did their own washing. I also became very proficient in installing new eight-track cassette players with rear speakers.

1969 – 50/50 Chance to Live #3

It was at Gunn's Riverside Shell where I met a new friend, Larry Eanes. Larry lived just up the street on Mount Cross Road. Larry had another friend, Charles Branch, who worked the shoe store near my gas station. Sometimes Charles would close his store and come over to the Shell station. Charles came from a very religious family. He never cursed like the others and me, but he always wanted to fit in. One night, Charles showed up in the passenger's side of a new Dodge Super Charger. The driver was a friend of his.

"Hey Johnnie, look at this thing. It's a 4-speed!"

"Nice." (Turning to his friend.) "What's it packing?"

"A 340, 4-barrell; 325 horses."

"That's a lot of horsepower for a short body."

"Yeah, It'll break traction in all four gears."

"I wouldn't doubt it."

"So David and I are going out to chase some girls tonight; you're going to join us after work, aren't you?"

Now Charles and I went cruising a lot after I closed the station at eleven. He had an old family clunker, so we'd cruise in my '64 Ford Fairlane. Tonight, however, was a bit different.

"Well, man I'd love to but…"

"But what Johnnie? Look at this car; man we're gonna get the chicks tonight!"

Charles got excited easily and I could tell he was really excited about tonight's cruise.

"You guys go on. My mom's been sick and she asked me to come home tonight to watch a scary movie with her. I think I'll go spend some time with her."

"That's okay; we'll probably need the extra room for the girls any way," said Charles.

We all had a good laugh, then David and Charles sped away, headed westbound on Riverside Drive. It wasn't long before they came back. Charles jumped out of the car, so excited.

"Johnnie, you just gotta feel the power in this thing!"

"Tell you what: y'all come by tomorrow at closing and we'll cruise till midnight…and I'll buy the gas."

"Sounds great to me," said David.

"Okay, but don't say I didn't warn you when we drive by with all the girls."

"Now Charles, you'll save one for me, want you?"

Charles' face lit up with a grin from ear to ear.

"You bet! I'll get the names and addresses and we'll have a blast!"

This time, as they left the station, David gave me a demonstration of the power of his vehicle. Sure enough, it burned rubber in every gear as it disappeared up Riverside. And, sure enough, about thirty minutes later they drove by with girls screaming out the window.

"Johnnie! Johnnie!"

I wondered if I had made the right choice. It was 10:30 on Friday night, and I was going home to be with my mom? I pushed it out of my mind as I prepared to shut the station down. At eleven, I got in my car.

✦ 50/50 CHANCE TO LIVE ✦ 31

"*Left turn and I go home; right turn and I head out looking for Charles and David,*" I thought. I turned left and headed up Mt. Cross Road. Tomorrow will be another day to redeem myself with them.

I don't remember the movie Mom and I watched. It was over about 1:00 a.m. and we went to bed. The next thing I remember, she was waking me up in the middle of the night.

"Johnnie. Johnnie."

"Yeah, what is it? You okay?"

"Yes; Larry Eanes just called. Do you know a Charles Branch?"

"Yeah, he's a friend of ours."

"He was killed in a car wreck about an hour ago. Larry said for you to find him in the morning."

I didn't say another word. Mom went back downstairs to bed.

I lay there rehearsing the evening in my mind: "Charles? Dead? Surely I'm dreaming. No, not Charles; he's was the nicest guy in our crowd. He didn't curse, and he didn't even smoke. Man, he went to church every Sunday!"

I woke up about 6:00 a.m., got dressed, and headed for Larry's. Larry and his whole family were up when I arrived. Larry's sister, Sandra, ran over to me crying.

"Oh Johnnie, Johnnie; this is so terrible!"

We hugged as I looked at Larry. His eyes were as bloodshot as beets. He didn't say a word. After what seemed an eternity, Larry got up from his chair.

"Come on Johnnie."

"Larry, y'all be careful now," said his dad, Joe.

We got into Larry's GTO and headed for Riverside Drive. Charles was probably Larry's best friend. We turned westbound on Riverside. I broke the silence.

"Where'd it happen?"

"Up here at the WDVA curve."

WDVA were the call letters for a country radio station in town. When we came into the curve, up ahead at the crossover, you could see the tire skid tracks, the utility pole charred and broken, and a large burn area in the median. The alleged report was that a truck crossed from a side street in front of David's car.

"They were probably speeding Johnnie. Who was this David guy anyway?"

"I don't know much about him Larry. They came by about ten o'clock last night trying to get me to go cruising with them. I had promised my mom that I'd come home and watch a movie with her."

Larry had stopped in the crossover, staring at the place where his best friend had just died. He turned to me with tears rolling down his face.

"Johnnie, you should have been in there with them. You probably would have died with Charles last night."

"Nah; I'd of been in the back seat. Probably would have been thrown out."

I was always the optimist. I sat there envisioning myself trying to help pull Charles and David out of that burning vehicle.

Next, Larry and I headed for Charles's home. We arrived and walked inside. Charles, Sr. and his wife were sitting at the table. Larry and Mr. Branch embraced as they both cried.

"I asked him to come home Larry. He said he met a new friend and wanted to ride around with him for a while. Larry, I don't even know this boy who was driving; do you know him?"

"No; I never met him. Johnnie said they were just cruising when he shut his Shell station down."

"Larry, they say the driver's name was David. He got thrown out of the car. Somehow, Charles ended up in the back seat and was pinned in. He got burned alive—oh Larry, I pray he didn't suffer!"

I didn't hear much more after that. The back seat was where I would have been if I had chosen to go with them. If I had been with them, maybe Charles would have survived and I would have been pinned in that back seat. After a while, Larry and I left.

"That should have been me, Larry. I should have been in the back seat and Charles in the front."

"You don't know that Johnnie. He was thrown into the back. You both would have probably died together."

Maybe so, but it still didn't soften the pain of losing someone that close. Charles's funeral was held a few days later and he was buried in a small church graveyard near Pilot Point Mountain in North Carolina.

"When Charles was just a young boy, we drove down the highway by Pilot Point Mountain," said his dad. "When he saw a graveyard by a church, he said, 'Daddy, that's the most beautiful place I've ever seen. When I die, I hope I can be buried here.' I'm going to fulfill that request."

The Job of My Dreams

Larry was drafted into the army during my senior year. He went to Vietnam as a machine gunner on a tank. I wanted to go to 'Nam as well, but Dana had other plans for us. She wanted us to get married. We discussed it many times, but the issue was finances. I had to finish school in order to get a better job.

It was during my senior year that the manager of the J. C. Penney's Auto Center began trading at our gas station. Fred Hawkins was his name. He was big with a mouth to fit his size. I could not believe what was happening. You see, Penney's Auto Center was where my uncle, Tom Gibson, worked as a mechanic. He was the man I always wanted to be like. I had dreams of working at Penney's because I wanted to be near Tom. I wanted to be an auto mechanic just like him.

Now I was rubbing shoulders with Fred, listening to and trying my best to out-laugh him at his jokes. One day, while running the Shell station by myself, Fred came by.

"You plan on pumping gas all your life or do you want a job with a future?"

"I don't know; what'd you got in mind?"

"I have an opening for our gas pumps at Penney's that, if you're good at it, will open the door for you to do some other things in the shop. What does Junior pay you here?"

Fred was pushy.

"I do okay; 'bout $75 to $80 a week."

"Seventy-five to eighty a week? You come work for me and I'll give you $100 to $125 a week...how's that sound?"

"The $125 sounds better." He laughed.

"Come down by the store tomorrow and let's fill out the paperwork."

He shook my hand and was gone. I sat there sort of stunned. Did I just get hired for the job of my dreams? I ran to the phone and called my mom. She was out of work for some surgery or something. I told her the good news. Wow! Me, Johnnie Jones, working for Penney's Auto Center! Boy that sounded great. And a raise to boot! That's when I called Dana.

"Does this mean we're going to get married, Mr. Jones?"

Oops. I forgot that part of my life.

"Well, it's just a trial basis right now; we'll have to wait and see."

I lied. Trying to please everyone really made me over extend my commitments. I wanted to please my mom, Dana, Fred...and what about Junior Gunn? I'll have to tell him tomorrow why I'm late for work.

The paperwork at Penney's went well and I was to begin the following Monday. I went to the Shell station afterwards.

"Junior. I have to tell you something. I'm starting to work next Monday for Penney's Auto Center."

Junior put on his sheepish smile. A car pulled up to the pumps. Normally, whether I was on the "clock" or not, Junior would always say, "Would you get that car for me, please?" Not this time; he walked out and began waiting on the customer. I stood there looking around, wondering what next to say to a good man who I had just disappointed.

Junior did not want to talk about it. He said a few words about going to the bank, jumped into his truck, and left me with the station. I worked the rest of the evening and began closing at eleven. Junior showed up.

"How was business tonight?"

"Fine; pretty steady."

"Johnnie, I need you to stay with me here at the station. Shelby's going to open up another Shell station on Memorial Drive and I'm afraid my dad is going to need me more at his station. Johnnie, if God calls me into the ministry, you'll have to manage this store while I'm gone."

I sat there a bit startled. I didn't think Junior would let me go easily, but his announcement about a "call into the ministry" was something I had never heard before.

"What do mean, Junior? What are you talking about?"

"I think God may be calling me into the ministry and if I go I'll need you to be here for me and my dad."

Junior was known for his alibis and his tall tales, so I did not take him too seriously with his announcement of a "ministry." In fact, I don't recall him ever referring to a ministry again. I was torn between two drives: one to please Junior and the other to fulfill my dream of becoming a mechanic alongside Tom. Which one should I take?

Goodbye Junior—hello J. C. Penney's!

1970 – Marriage or Military?

The pressure was mounting from Dana to set an engagement date and an eventual marriage. The Penney's job was working well. I spent a lot of time throwing new tires onto the second floor storage area. I felt a twinge of pain occasionally, but I never complained. It was good physical labor. Junior got over my leaving him and enjoyed my visits at the Shell station. Larry Eanes' family invited me over to their house to read the letters they were getting from Larry in Vietnam. They were awesome, especially the war pictures he sent. I was pumped!

Shorty worked the gas pumps with me at Penney's. He was the serious type and spoke very straight forward with lots of colorful adjectives. He enjoyed his job, but managed to complain a lot. I set out to cheer him up as much as I could. He was talking to a couple of ladies once, by the auto center's doorway. There was a stack of new tires beside him. I took off at full speed, running right toward him, screaming my head off and dove head first into the stack of tires. With my head beneath and my feet and legs wobbling back and forth, I heard him tell the surprised ladies, "Ah, pay no attention to him; he's just a little crazy sometimes." But I got a laugh out of him and that was his favorite story to tell for many months.

Randy Holly was a salesman for the auto center. He was a gentleman. I couldn't get over how he remained so calm and so well dressed at all times. Randy was another religious influence in my life. He talked about faith in

God and taking his mother to church. I began to like being around him, for he was so kind and so positive about life. And he was single with no intentions of marrying. This intrigued me. Why would a man of his stature, in his forties, not want to marry?

Shorty was always trying to talk trash with Randy—you know, messing with women and such. I remember one reply from Randy I'll never forget.

"Oh Shorty, I've had my opportunities with the ladies. I had one lady tell me that if any man deserved her body, it was me. I told her I wasn't interested in her body—just her tires."

We all had a good laugh over that statement. But I knew Randy was different. He was genuine in his faith and his love for his mother and their church. I found myself going to church with Randy and Mother Holly often. She was such a sweet and kind lady.

Dana was a different story though. She was getting very impatient with my unwillingness to take her hints at engagement. It was obvious I was not ready for marriage. I did not like the thought of the full responsibility of rent, food, bills, etc. I told her I wasn't ready, so we didn't see each other for a while. She told me to stay away and think about. That was okay, because I had plenty of things to do and there were lots of girls at Randy's church.

It wasn't long before Dana began calling me. Of course, I went over to see her again…and again. I was too passive and too kind to be hard with her. I couldn't decide what to do…then it hit me. I would lie and tell her I got drafted. Now how would I do that?

The next day I went to the large postal building in Danville. My brother, Joe, was in the Army and Gary had just joined the Navy. Both had communicated that it was the pits. But I liked water and thought, *"What the heck; I'm choosing the Navy."* I went to the second floor of the postal building; it was about noon. The armed services offices were all side-by-side. The Navy office was closed for lunch, but the Air Force office still had a gentleman inside. He was about to get his hat and coat when he saw me looking in.

"Hi. My name is Staff Sergeant Thompson of the United States Air Force. What's your name, Airman?"

"Johnnie…Johnnie Jones, sir."

"Airman Jones. How do you like the sound of that title? You know, you'd look good in dress blues."

"Well, my brother is in the Navy and I wanted to talk to a Navy recruiter."

"He's gone to lunch; but tell you what. Come with me and I'll buy you lunch and we'll talk about flying for the Air Force."

Sergeant Thompson talked a full hour, telling me all about the Air Force. By the time he was finished, I was ready to sign on the dotted line. I wanted to become a jet engine mechanic. I had to come back on my day off to be tested. The test would tell if I had the intelligence to enlist. That test would either save me or send me back into the arms of marriage. "Airman Jones"…that title sounded nice.

I can keep a secret, but I had to tell my mom and the Eanes' about my plans. Mom just stared at me. Joe was in Italy, about to be finished with the army, Gary was somewhere in the Pacific Ocean, and now here I am telling her that I was enlisting into the Air Force. I assured her that I would probably fail the test and stay home. She wasn't too sure about that.

I took the test. Several days later I received a call from Sergeant Thompson.

"Airman Jones, congratulations; you passed the mechanical part of the test with flying colors. But I need you to come down to the office; I want to show you something."

In less than an hour, I was sitting in the recruiter's office.

"Johnnie, you passed the mechanical good enough to become a jet engine mechanic. But you also passed all four areas, and look at this: your electrical grade is high enough to get you in electronics. Johnnie, trust me on this: jet engine grease is the nastiest stuff you'll ever get your hands into. The smell not only stays on your body, but your clothes as well. Women do not like the smell of jet engine grease, no sir; I want you to sign up in electronics—that's the field that's going places, Johnnie."

I believed every word he said. I signed up to go to Roanoke, Virginia in two weeks for a physical. Now I had my alibi for Dana…DRAFTED!

Dad drove me to the bus station for my trip to Roanoke. When I got on the bus I discovered another young man my age headed for the same physical. I remember us talking about all the things we had heard about the physical we would undergo the next day: doctors making you bend way over to look at you, square-shaped needles used in very sensitive areas—stories like that that never came true. I remember us getting a bite to eat just outside the bus station and then walking several blocks to the hotel. My friend told me to speed up our walk. We got into our room before he showed me out of our window a man who had followed us from the restaurant. I guess that was my wakeup call to the big city.

The next day I joined a couple hundred other men as we were lined up wearing only our underwear. As we inched down the line, men would tell us to do certain things.

"Open your mouth; say ahh."

"Drop you drawers, turn your head, and cough." I did. "Again please." I did again; in fact this man made me cough three or four times with his finger stuck into my groin area. It was painful, but I wasn't about to show any discomfort. I remembered the stories from my two cousins, Wayne and Jimmy Pruitt. They both failed this same examination due to being flat-footed (I think).

"Young man, step out of the line. Wait over here." This didn't sound good. Several men came over to talk to me.

"Mister Jones, you have a hernia. You cannot pass this physical. What branch of service have you enlisted in?"

"The Air Force, sir."

They talked among themselves for a moment, then called another man over and talked with him.

"Mister Jones, I'm Staff Sergeant Brown with the United States Air Force. The doctors tell me that you have a hernia. Normally, we would fail your examination and send you back home. But the Air Force has what we call a MedREP enlistment program; this stands for Medical Remedial Enlistment Program. It is designed to help men like you to enlist by providing you with minor surgery at the basic training site at Lackland Air Force Base in San Antonio, Texas. After your surgery, you will be assigned light duty on the base until you are fit to enter into basic training. Would you like to continue your examination as a MedREP candidate?"

The decision was a no-brainer to me because I knew I did not want to return to Danville with my "escape" plan robbed from me due to a minor surgery. After all, the Air Force was going to pay for the surgery.

"Yes sir, I would like to continue the exam."

"Fine. Get back into the line over there and I'll get the paper work started."

Staff Sergeant Brown walked me back to the line ahead of the hernia testing area. The rest of the examination didn't seem to matter very much after that. In fact, the MedREP marking at the top of my paper work seemed to make all the examiners a little more relaxed with me.

When I finished my exam, I put my street clothes back on and was sent to another room with about fifty or sixty men. A man came in and told us to raise our right hand and repeat after him. What we pledged was some type of allegiance to serve our nation faithfully.

"Congratulations men. You have passed your physical examination and have been inducted into the United States military. You are instructed to go back to your recruiter for your scheduled departure dates for basic training. Good luck and may God bless you."

Was that it? I stepped out of the room to head for the exit.

"Airman Jones? Please step over here."

It was Staff Sergeant Brown again.

"Here are the extra papers you need to sign concerning the MedREP program. You are instructed to give these to your recruiter tomorrow. Now get out of here and head for the bus station."

The bus station was several blocks from the building. I remembered that there was a bus leaving in the mid-afternoon for Danville. I ran to the station. My bus was closing its door as I ran up to it. The driver let me in and off I went. My traveling companion was in the back of the bus smiling at me. He had failed his exam due to some medical reason. But I was now the property of the United States Air Force. It was April 7, 1970. I would leave for San Antonio, Texas in two weeks.

No one seemed to be happy that I was leaving—no one, except Larry Eanes' dad, Joe. He was happy that I would be somewhere out there supporting the safe return of Larry. He was proud of my decision.

Fred Hawkins—my boss—wasn't happy; nor was Dana. And my mom didn't like it either. My dad didn't say much. But I had done what I felt was the best decision for me. Besides, I wasn't ready for the alternative.

My final two weeks as a civilian were busy. I had a lot of family and friends to visit and I had a car to sell, my '64 Fairlane that I had purchased about a year ago.

I loved my car. It began as a faded beige, six-cylinder engine, 3-speed standard shift on the column. I paid four hundred dollars for that "diamond in the rough." Now it was a metallic gold, 289 cubic inch V-8, with a three-in-the-floor Hurst shifter. I also installed extra springs and air bags to lift the rear of the vehicle, and replaced the rims with Hurst mag wheels. It was a beauty, and it sold for eight hundred dollars. Now I was ready to go.

Dana was still mad at me, but I did manage to go by her place to say my goodbyes to her and her family. Her mom had written a poem for men in the Air Force. She gave me a copy and asked me to come by when I had some leave-time and was in town. Dana was quiet and a bit distant; however, when I began to head for my car, she followed me and gave me a kiss.

"You better come back and see me, Mister Jones."

1970 – Lackland AFB, San Antonio, Texas

The bus ride from Danville to Roanoke was a long one. I had my official papers to give to the military authorities in Roanoke. I spent a few hours at the military offices and then was placed on a bus to head out to the airport. There was a military charter flight headed non-stop to San Antonio. My destination: Lackland Air Force Base.

When the flight arrived at San Antonio International Airport, there were a group of military training instructors waiting for it.

"Young men, stand over here against the wall until your name is called. You are now the property of the United States Air Force and you will follow my commands. Is that understood?"

"Yes sir," came a lack-luster reply.

"I can't hear you!"

"Yes sir!"

The training instructor—called T.I.—didn't like the response, but continued to bark commands to prepare us for the trip over to Lackland. All of us Virginians were to begin basic training together, with the exception of one—me. At the base, the bus pulled into a parking lot beside some long buildings. Once on the base, the T.I.'s language got a little clearer.

"Alright, everyone get off the [bleeping] bus, now! Where's the [bleepity-bleep] MedREP? Stand there in the aisle, Airman, and don't move until told to; do you understand?"

"YES SIR!" I shouted. He stood there and looked me over for a moment. A slight grin came on his face.

"Welcome to hell, Airman." Then turning to the driver, "Take this piece of [bleep] over to the MedREP barracks; make sure he enters the building before you leave him. Is that understood?"

It was about 11:00 p.m. when I was turned over to the MedREP guard. I relaxed a little as I realized the guard was a fellow airman like me. With a flashlight, he took me down a hallway, opening a few room doors along the way. Finally, he found an empty bed.

"In there Airman. Put your stuff by the window and try not to wake the others."

I quietly slid my suitcase under the table by the window and climbed onto the top bunk. There were four beds in the room. I pulled the covers down and tried to get comfortable. Having begun early in the morning for this trip, it didn't take much settling in to cause me to fall asleep. I remember seeing a clock in the entranceway. It was 12:30 a.m.—1:30 a.m., Eastern Standard Time.

At 4:30 a.m., the guard threw open the door and turned the lights on.

"Get up, get up!"

"What? I just fell asleep," I thought. I looked up at the ceiling, thinking maybe I could get a second opinion on whether I should move. But I began to hear things below me that made me look down. I'll never forget what I saw. There were two men on the floor underneath their beds. What was going on? That's when I was discovered.

"Hey, who's this? Oh no, not another roommate! [Bleep] Listen Airman and listen carefully; if you want to be able to go to breakfast this morning, you'd better follow my instructions very carefully. Do you understand?"

I was getting used to the "do you understand?" phrase.

"Yeah, yeah; I understand."

"Then get out of your [bleeping] bed and tighten up the covers now. We have to be out on the sidewalk in formation in less than twenty minutes. Did you pull your covers down? Oh [bleep]! Get up and out of the way—quick!"

I slipped down from the end as I watched my roommate tackle my bed and reconstruct it as if no one had ever slept in it. In fact, as I looked at the other beds, I discovered he and the other guy had slept on top of the covers, using a bath towel as a covering. They both got underneath my mattress, between the springs, without touching the bunk below, and made sure the sheets and wool covers were aligned properly and tucked in tightly. They took my suitcase and threw it into a locker, then used the towel covers to wipe the floor for any dust particles I may have brought in on my shoes. Next, they threw their towels into their dirty clothes bag, neatly tied at the end of each bunk.

"Don't ever sleep under the covers again; do you understand? Now get dressed and get outside for roll call."

It was 4:55 a.m. now. Another airman in charge began to give the orders for the day.

"Airman Smith, Brown, Rosenberg, Tilley; you are assigned to the restrooms today. Airman Goodman, Johnson, McAllen, and Eastman, you take the hallways."

The orders continued until everyone in the barracks had a duty assigned, except one.

"Rosenberg, you'd better stick with the new guy today to keep him from screwing up the rest of us, understood?"

"Yes sir," came Rosenberg's reply. Rosenberg was one of my roommates. He seemed to be a gentler airman than my other roommate.

We were dismissed and began to walk, single file, down the sidewalk, toward the highway. I had no idea where we were headed and no one was talking. Rosenberg began to speak quietly to me.

"What's your name, Airman?"

"Johnnie, Johnnie Jones. And yours?"

"David Rosenberg, but the others call me Rosie. Where's home Johnnie?"

"Danville, Virginia."

"Oh. Is that near D.C.? I'm from D.C."

"Nah, it's at the opposite end of Virginia. Sorry. Say, Rosie, where're we headed?"

"Breakfast is at the hospital across the highway. Wilford Hospital; that's where you'll get operated on and that will be where you work each day as you recuperate from surgery."

"You've had surgery?"

"Sure. Everyone in our barracks is here for hernia surgery as a part of the MedREP program."

"How long will I be in MedREP?"

"Nine weeks, if you're lucky. Some stay a week or two longer. It depends on your body and its ability to heal correctly."

Rosie began to give me the details of our daily routine. We shave and shower at night before bed. A wool blanket is placed over all the windows at 10:00 p.m. to give the appearance that the lights are off. The Military Police (MPs) patrol outside the barracks to ensure the lights are out. At 4:30 a.m., we wake up; at 4:55, we are dressed and in formation, ready for our after-work cleaning details. Breakfast begins at 5:30 a.m. We walk over before daylight so that we don't have to watch the cars for a commissioned military officer; otherwise we'll have to watch the road and salute all commissioned officers cars. That's why we walk over in the dark.

After breakfast, there's a break room in another part of the hospital where we can sleep for about an hour, as long as no one else comes in. At 7:00 a.m., we report for our day shift at the hospital. We are assigned different floors of the hospital for light duty. At the end of our shift, we go back to our barracks for a few hours of free time. Finally, we do our assigned cleaning details at the barracks; then we have a few more hours off."

"That's it?"

"That's it."

"What about weekends?"

"There are no weekends here, Johnnie. You have the same schedule every day for as long as you're in MedREP."

"How long have you been here, Rosie?"

"Three weeks, two days, eight hours, and twenty-five minutes."

I sensed the detailed time response was from an inner longing to move on in this routine.

"Are all the guys in our barracks as friendly as our roommate?" I asked sarcastically.

"Oh Michaels? Don't mind him; he's from upstate New York. He's a bit more structured than most of the guys. His detailed attitude comes in real handy for our weekly inspection."

"Weekly inspection? Oh, oh."

"Yes. Our barracks are used to train new T.I.s on how to inspect barracks. It gets pretty interesting sometimes, but our Sergeant usually helps control the trainees. They love to cuss us out—practice, I guess. You learn to take it and keep going. Just don't take any of it personally. It's an ego thing—a reputation a T.I. must have."

Rosie helped me through the breakfast line. This was my first encounter with "S.O.S." It was thick gravy with sausage chunks, poured over several pieces of toast; thus the name, "[Bleep]-on-Shingles."

After breakfast, Rosie escorted me to the break area where we caught another hour of rest. After that he took me back to the barracks to meet our sergeant. Sergeant Evans had an upstairs office. No one could enter without proper protocol, so Rosie gave me some pointers on how to approach him.

"Just knock loudly once and wait for him to say, 'Enter.' You then walk up to his desk at ninety-degree angles and stop right in the middle of the front of his desk. You salute him with your right hand and keep your left hand down beside your leg and say, 'Sir, Airman Basic Jones reporting as ordered.' Do not lower your salute until after he salutes you. If he receives your visit he'll say, 'At ease airman,' and ask you a reason for your visit. That's when you give him your orders and wait for his instructions. Even though he's not a commissioned officer, for basic training purposes we must salute all commissioned and non-commissioned Training Instructors as commissioned officers."

That sounded easy enough. I went to my room—shoes off this time—and got my paper work ready for my first encounter with Sergeant Evans. About 9:30 a.m. I went upstairs and knocked once on the closed office door.

"Enter," came the reply. I opened the door and proceeded to make my awkward ninety-degree turn, tripping once over my own feet.

"Sir, Airman Basic Johnnie R. Jones reporting for duty...I mean, as asked."

Boy did I ever mess up my approach. I stared just over Sergeant Evans' head, bracing internally for a royal chewing out.

"Where're you from Airman Jones?"

"Danville, Virginia, sir."

"Airman Jones, when you reply to an officer, you always begin with the word 'sir' and end with the word 'sir.' Do you understand?"

"Sir, yes sir!"

"You also do not give an officer your full name, just your rank and last name. Now go back outside my door and try it again."

I turned to leave.

"Airman Jones, who dismissed you?"

Oops. Now I'm going to get it.

"No one, sir."

"What?"

"Sir, no one, sir," I shouted.

"That's more like it. Now when I salute you and say 'you're dismissed,' you then take your right foot and place it behind the heel of your left foot and spin around 180 degrees for a proper exit. Now get outside and try it again."

"Sir, yes sir!"

I saluted him and he saluted me; then I spun around, but not quite 180 degrees. I walked out of his office and tried again. The second time was acceptable and the sergeant received me. He reviewed my paper work, filled out some requisition forms, and called the dorm guard into his office.

"Guard, find Airman Basic Rosenberg and send him in here."

In no time, Rosie was knocking at his door, making a flawless approach to the sergeant's desk.

"Airman Basic Rosenberg, you have been given a temporary assignment to take Airman Basic Jones to get his clothing—and make sure he gets a haircut. You will be responsible for keeping him out of trouble until he learns the ropes of military protocol. Do you understand?"

"Sir, yes sir."

"Now both of you get out of my sight. Airman Basic Jones, report to me again in the morning, same time, in military uniform. You're dismissed—oh, by the way Jones, you ever heard of Chesapeake, Virginia?"

"Sir, yes sir," I replied with a grin. "Every summer, going on vacation to Virginia Beach, my family drove right through Chesapeake."

"That's where I'm from," said Sergeant Evans. He smiled back. "I'm expecting a fellow Virginian to make me proud of his progress, so don't disappoint me."

"Sir, yes sir!"

Without further words, Rosie and I left the room and headed straight to our room.

"Whoa; I can't believe what just happened," said Rosie.

"What?"

"He smiled—did you see that—he smiled! Sergeant Evans has a reputation of being one of the meanest T.I.s on base. I thought he was more stone than human. I can't believe we got out of that mess without a chewing. I think he likes you, Jonesie."

"Maybe. Everybody likes me, Rosie, because I know how to make people smile."

The rest of the day was filled with walks all across the base, picking up clothing, filling out papers, and getting a picture identification card. We then went to a tailor to get my name and insignia sewed onto my uniform.

"Wow, this is great," I said. "Let's hurry back to the dorm so that I can change."

"Nope; not without a haircut. You can't walk around the base in uniform with long hair. The MPs will get us for sure."

One of the base barbershops was located at Wilford Hall. Rosie suggested we go there because it was time to eat supper.

"Come on in Airman," said the barber. "What'll it be?"

"Just leave the ears," said Rosie as he pointed me to the chair.

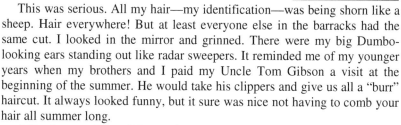

This was serious. All my hair—my identification—was being shorn like a sheep. Hair everywhere! But at least everyone else in the barracks had the same cut. I looked in the mirror and grinned. There were my big Dumbo-looking ears standing out like radar sweepers. It reminded me of my younger years when my brothers and I paid my Uncle Tom Gibson a visit at the beginning of the summer. He would take his clippers and give us all a "burr" haircut. It always looked funny, but it sure was nice not having to comb your hair all summer long.

Adjusting to military life wasn't very hard. All you had to do was learn to say "sir" in front of all your questions and constantly clean everything you touched in your barracks. Besides your personal space, you were assigned a portion of the general dorm to keep spotless. I remember especially the bathroom detail. We took sponges and bleach and got down on our knees and scrubbed the floors with pure bleach. Boy, did it burn the eyes and nostrils.

But everything I saw was spotless; I mean you could eat off the floors of that barracks.

"Attention dorm," cried the guard. "We are under inspection!"

I learned quickly that that meant some rookie T.I.s were approaching the barracks. All airmen in the barracks had to stand at attention at the foot of their bunks. We stood there and waited…and waited…and waited. Finally I heard the men next door cursing about some dirt found in the room. I took a quick glance around ours—spic and span, I concluded. But was I in for a shock. Our door swung open. Two T.I.s started looking us over.

"You [bleeping] airmen think you have a spotless room?"

"Sir, yes sir," replied Michaels. I was glad Michaels was there.

"Well let's take a look." The T.I.s began opening our personal drawers looking for a miss-folded handkerchief or tee shirt. Nothing was out of place. Then they took the actual drawers, which were built into the walls, and pulled them out of the walls off of their guides. Underneath the drawers were all kinds of dirt, dust, and building residue left behind from the time the barracks were built. It was awful.

"You called that spotless airman? You guys live in nothing but filth. Now get down there and clean all that out. That's an order airman!"

They walked out and slammed the door. Michaels stared at the drawers in a state of shock. Rosie walked over to the exposed drawer openings and looked in.

"[Bleep!] You can see from one end of the room to the other under here. Surely they don't mean for us to clean all that!"

Michaels' neck was red hot. He headed for the door and disappeared. I reached into my dirty clothes bag, found a towel and went to the latrine down the hallway. After dampening the towel, I came back to the room and began wiping the exposed wood under the guide rails of my drawer. Oh man; with just one wipe of the towel, it became dirty black. I began a second wipe when the door opened again.

"ATTENTION," cried Rosie.

Sergeant Evans came walking into our room with Michaels and our dorm chief. I stood at attention with my dirty towel. Evans looked at the drawers and through the openings. Then he looked at my dirty towel and me. He left as quickly as he came in.

Within a minute or two the chatter began circulating down the hallway.

"Come here guys, quick," someone cried softly. We all tiptoed down the hallway to a window. Outside on the sidewalk was Sergeant Evans talking nose-to-nose with the two inspecting T.I.s. Evans was hot. He was using words I'd only heard about that were bad. Both of the rookie T.I.s were frozen at attention as Evans verbally ripped them down one side and then the other. He pointed them to the parking lot and followed them to their car, continually cursing them out as they got into their vehicle. When they pulled out onto the road, Evans was still hurling superlatives in their direction. Wow! I had never witnessed anything like this before.

About thirty minutes later a dorm meeting was called. The dorm chief assembled us in the game lounge. Sergeant Evans appeared.

"Attention!"

"At ease, men. Today I authorized an unannounced inspection. You know these things can happen. But the T.I.s went a little too far in pulling out the drawers in the walls. You do not have to clean underneath those drawers. However, I expect to be written up as interfering in an authorized inspection. Therefore, I expect a second inspection to occur within a day or two from the base commander. This means that if I'm to get off the firing line, this next inspection must be flawless. Today is Friday. I expect the visit will occur Monday or Tuesday. Every one of you must devote your entire weekend to cleaning this barracks from top to bottom, from one end to the other. There can be no mistakes. Do you understand?"

"Sir, yes sir," came a resounding response.

"Okay; go get your supper and get back here for detail."

"Sir, you can count on us," said the dorm chief.

Sergeant Evans left the meeting and left the barracks. The dorm chief took the floor.

"Okay guys, you heard what we must do. Sergeant Evans went out there and kicked some fresh T.I. [bleep] for us. Now it's our time to shine. No one goes for supper. We're going to clean this [bleeping] building until midnight, then start again at 0800 hours in the morning. Start with your rooms, then come by here for your cleaning assignments."

Clean. I began to hate the word. Everything looked so clean already. Why risk messing up what was already clean? But no one else was thinking as I. In my room Rosie and Michaels had begun reorganizing their clothing in the drawers. I began doing the same. We organized, straightened, swept, mopped, and polished. Every bolt on our bed ends was checked for tightness and conformity.

In the barracks, all the walls were washed; some were even painted. Blinds were taken down and cleaned. Even the blind strings were given a dose of white shoe polish. The light fixtures and electrical plug outlets were disassembled, checked for cracks or blemishes, and cleaned. At the end of each hall, was a grated door with a large fan behind it. The door was cleaned as well as the fan.

By Sunday afternoon every conceivable item in that barracks was cleaned. The dorm chief performed several mock inspections. One word: perfect. Now came the wait. Monday, nothing; Tuesday morning, nothing; Tuesday afternoon: "Attention dorm! We are under inspection."

Here they came: six T.I.s and Sergeant Evans. Everyone stood at attention beside their beds and waited…and waited…and waited. This inspection was taking longer than normal. They never came into our room, but you could hear an occasional conversation in the hallway. Finally the "all clear" call was announced.

"Whew," said Rosie. "I wonder how it went?"

"I don't know, but I have sweat trailing down my back," I responded.

Michaels left the room as if on a mission. He came back a few minutes later with a smile on his face.

"Only one demerit! Dust on a hall fan blade. The T.I. put on a white glove and stuck his hand through the louvers and found a speck of dust...can you believe that?"

I could only think of how nit-picky the military seemed to be. I had heard that everything had to be kept in tip-top shape, but this seemed incredibly ridiculous. We were, however, under a medical restrictive order. What else could we do?

Surgery, Military Style

My surgery came during my second week. The doctor gave me a spinal block, so I spent the entire surgery telling jokes. The doctor kept looking over the sheet at me; I could tell he was grinning. They put me in a room with three other men. One man was a captain with the same surgery I had. Another guy was a retired man with a leg amputation. He was a chain smoker. I remember him because when his doctor came in and saw this guy smoking, the doctor became a little irritated.

"If you don't stop smoking immediately," said the doctor, "I'll be amputating your other leg in six weeks."

The guy put out his cigarette and didn't say a word. After the doctor left, the guy lit up another cigarette, cursing the pain he was experiencing. I lay in my bed, patiently waiting for the feeling to return to my legs. A nurse came to my bed.

"Can you wiggle your toes?"

I tried and they moved just a little. She left. About an hour later a male nurse came in.

"Airman Jones, it's time to stand you up."

I tried to move my legs. No movement.

"I can't move my legs, sir."

"I'll help you."

He reached underneath me and swirled me sideways, allowing my legs to drop to the floor. Then he lifted me up and stabilized me on my feet. This was not good.

"I'm seeing black. I can't see beyond the window. Now I can't see you."

As I began to fall, he pushed me toward the bed. As soon as I went horizontal, the lights began to come back on. I nearly passed out.

"We'll try again in about an hour," the nurse said.

"Take your time; I'm not going anywhere." I lay there wondering, "Why the rush?" Soon I fell asleep.

"Boom!" I woke up to a large blast. Then came another: "Boom!" What was going on now? Without the nurse's help, I slid off the side of my bed to see out of the window. I checked first to see if I was going to pass out. Nope; everything remained its color. I hobbled over to the window. In a field about two hundred yards east of the hospital fence was a field sprinkled with round barrels in a mesh of barbed wire spread all across the field. Some of the barrels were smoking. Then, from another barrel came another "boom!" I looked around and saw my smoking roommate wake up and light up another cigarette.

"What is going on over there," I asked him.

"Field training. That's where you'll go later in your basic training. In about an hour, the first squadron will show up and all hell will break loose."

Sure enough, at 0800 hours, the explosions began. This time they were more numerous with rapid-fire gunshots. I managed to walk over to the window to watch. There were men on their bellies sliding underneath the barbed wire with some sort of stick in their hands, representing a gun. When someone got near a barrel, an explosion would occur: "boom!" The explosions seemed to increase the speed of those scooting on their bellies. It produced a scary thought in my mind about my future. I made my way back to my bed.

"Don't let it scare you Jones," said the captain. "They've never lost an airman yet."

"But why do folks in the Air Force have to go through that?"

"Well, you have to think of the bigger picture. Airplanes get shot down and sometimes they crash land behind enemy lines. You have to be trained for survival under any and all circumstances. That field is one part of a large obstacle course that everyone must go through. You will climb tall walls, swing over water pits, and roll all over the ground in full gear."

"Wow. I never realized all the things you have to do in basic training. My recruiter never told me of this!"

The old smoker next to me laughed. "Don't trust any thing anyone tells you, son. They'll feed you a line of bull [bleep] just to get you to sign on the dotted line. If you want my advice, get out under a medical discharge as soon as possible or you'll be headed for 'Nam in no time."

"That's where I want to go. I have a best friend in 'Nam. He's a gunner on a tank. I'm going to fly over him and drop some bombs so he'll get a better shot at the enemy."

He laughed again. "Son, you're already in the hospital; you're damaged goods. You'll never get out from behind a desk somewhere. You'll be a pencil-pusher for the real soldiers."

"Don't listen to him, Jones," said the captain. "You concentrate on being the best airman in your flight; learn the ropes and you'll do just fine. Always remember that the training is designed to break you down mentally and emotionally. Basic training is for the purpose of weeding out those who collapse under pressure. Your instructors will give you hell, but they will not hurt you. Only *you* can hurt you."

I didn't like "Smokie," but the captain was a neat man. He really helped me to see the bigger picture and I resolved within myself to become a trusted airman.

My day nurse was a second lieutenant; Connors was her name. She looked like an angel, so it wasn't hard to show her how well I was improving. I made her laugh a lot with my one-liners. Once, I had her crying with laughter when the doctor came in. She quickly straightened up and left the room. The doctor checked me out and stared at me for a moment.

"Airman, you're being discharged to your medical barracks today. Everything is fine with you, but I need to ask you one question."

"What's that, sir?"

"Did you eat the canary or was it that nurse?" He smiled as he walked out the room.

I walked back to the barracks, carrying a small medical release bag with some instructions for Sergeant Evans and some meds. I figured I'd get a week of relaxation, then maybe some light duty around the barracks.

"Airman Jones," said Evans. "Tomorrow morning you will have bed rest. I want you to go back to Wilford Hall for lunch, and then report in at the administrator's office. Take this letter with you and give it to the secretary."

Okay; so much for a week of relaxation. The next day I slept in while the others were doing the daily morning routine. After lunch, I reported to the hospital's administration office.

"Have a seat, Airman."

"Yes Ma'am." I waited for about a minute.

"Tomorrow morning at 0800 hours, you will report to the fifth floor, Wing G. Be ready to do some light detail."

"Tomorrow? I just got out of the hospital yesterday."

She smiled. "Welcome to the Air Force. This letter authorizes me to put you to work tomorrow. If you have a problem with that, I suggest you report back to your commanding officer. That is all, Airman."

I wanted to give her a sarcastic "snap-to-attention" salute, but I still had a bandage over my incision and tightening my muscles hurt. Plus, she was a civilian. I left wondering about my being in the Air Force and if this was going to be just like Smokie described. I went to my floor where I had recovered. Smokie was preparing to be dismissed and the captain had already left.

Smokie was in his usual happy mode: "[Bleep] leg! I hate this God-forsaken place."

"Just don't go to any [bleep]-kicking parties until you get a handle on those crutches."

Smokie didn't laugh at my one-liners. He was a bitter man and blamed the world for his problems. I left the ward. Dropping by the nurse's station, I saw the second lieutenant. Her eyes lit up and she gave me a hug. We visited a moment and then I left.

"Hey Jonesie!" It was Rosie. "You get your assignment?"

"Yeah; fifth floor, Ward G."

"Oooo; that's the cancer floor. I went there for a day, but got sick."

"Sick? What do you mean?"

"Well, everybody smelled bad and it was so depressing. I threw up on the first bed I was told to strip down and fumigate. Ha! That was the best thing that happened to me, and I got transferred to the admin's office for filing detail."

"Ugh," I thought. *"This is going to be hell."* Word spread pretty fast in the barracks about my assignment; and so did the stories about that God-awful Ward G. I lay awake on my bed that night thinking about what I should do—could do—to get out of my assignment. *"Why me?"*

The next morning, I arrived five minutes late. I thought perhaps my tardiness would get me the boot. I reported to the nurse's station.

"Ma'am, I'm Airman Basic Jones reporting for duty."

"Oh, hello Airman Jones," said a middle-aged female sergeant. "I'm Staff Sergeant Pender, the head nurse for day shift. May I see your reporting papers?"

I handed them to her.

"Umm, light detail for a few days, then medium. Great. I'm so glad to have you and I hope you will like working with us. Come and let me show you some of the ward."

We began walking down the hallway. Sergeant Pender seemed to be a friendly lady and the smell was no different than where I had been laid up for a few days.

"I want you to assist my patients to the treatment center in the basement. Take your time, but don't be late for their appointment. Don't let any of them talk you into going outside or anywhere besides where I send you."

"Yes, ma'am."

"You're cute. The ladies are going to like you."

And ladies they were. In fact, Ward G was nothing but women. Pender introduced me to the ladies in an eight-bed section.

"Girls, this is Airman Jones. He will be assisting you to your scheduled treatments. Treat him nice and he'll stay with us for awhile."

"Great!" "Hello young man." "He's cute!"

These were some of the comments I heard. Most of the women were my mom's age or older…and none of them "smelled" bad.

"Mrs. Thompson is your first assignment, Jones. She's due for her treatment in fifteen minutes. Julia, you ready to go?"

"With this honey? Oh yeah!"

✦ 50/50 CHANCE TO LIVE ✦ 50

I smiled. Maybe this was going to be okay after all. Mrs. Thompson looked fairly nice. She was probably in her fifties and had a nice gown on with a full head of curly hair. I helped her into a wheelchair and proceeded down to the patient elevator. We talked a bit while traveling.

"Ouch!" Apparently I hit her foot against the elevator door.

"Oh I'm so sorry; are you okay?"

"Yeah, I'm okay. Here hold this while I rub my foot."

Before I knew it she was handing me her head of curly hair—a wig! I stood there with my mouth wide open and speechless, holding her hair and staring at her baldhead. I had never seen a baldheaded woman before. She looked up at me for a moment, and then started grinning. Then the laughter started coming from behind me. All the women in Mrs. Thompson's section were watching and waiting for this joke. It was a setup!

"Give me my hair back Jonesie...and quit your staring!"

By then, one of the other women had come to my side.

"Airman Jones, we just wanted you to relax around us and not to be shocked at what you might see. Welcome to Ward G—G stands for us grooving gals. Ain't that right girls?"

The laughter turned into a popular song about "grooving on Saturday afternoon." I must say they got my goat on that one. From then on I had a lot of fun carting those ladies down to their appointments. There were about thirty ladies that I began to work with. Some of them were a pain—due in part to their cancer—but most enjoyed the presence of a man on their ward.

One lady, Gwendalyn Garcia, was a bit younger than the others. She was always talking to me about the military life and where she and her husband had been on tours of duty. One Friday, she asked me about leaving the base.

"I'm getting out for the weekend and we're going to have a party at my place. I was wondering if you could go with my husband and me? I've got some cousins that I want you to meet."

"Well, I don't think my sergeant will allow that, Gwen. I'm still a basic airman and they won't give me a pass until after I finish."

"What's your sergeant's name?"

"Evans—Jack Evans."

"Oh, I know Evans; he's been to several parties of mine. I'll give him a call."

I didn't know what to think about this proposal. Sergeant Evans usually left the barracks about an hour or two before I returned. This time, it was different.

"Jones, Sergeant Evans wants to see you in his office right away," said the dorm guard.

I knocked and did the proper protocol for entering.

"At ease; sit down Jones." Now this was a bit different. I had never been told to sit. "How long have you got left for hospital duty?"

"Sir, three more weeks, sir."

Evans got up and walked past me to shut the office door. He then walked over to the window, staring across the field toward the hospital.

"One of my drinking buddies called me to see if I could bring you into San Antonio tomorrow night. I'd forgotten about his wife's cancer and her stays at the hospital. Gwen's a sweet girl, you know?"

"Sir, yes sir."

"Relax with the 'sir' stuff for just a minute, okay?"

"Okay."

"I've been assigned to the MedREP barracks for three years now and you're the first guy that I've ever been asked by a friend to come off base with me. What's with this request, Jones?"

"I think she likes me, sir. She's got a bunch of girls that she wants me to meet. That's really all I know."

"Yeah, that's what I figured. Listen to me carefully, Jones, and this had better not be repeated outside this office; do you understand?" Evans' look on his face put me back into protocol.

"Sir, yes sir."

"Gwen has a few cousins; I've met a few of them myself. I'm a married man, you understand, so I kept my distance. Some of Gwen's so-called cousins are prostitutes. Is that what you want? Have you ever been laid before?"

"No sir! Not me."

"I didn't think so, and that's why I'm not going to let you off this base. You're different, Jones, and I'm not going to be the one to change that. Always remember, women love men in uniform. It's a symbol of protection, of security. Don't ever let your guard down and don't ever let a woman get to you through this uniform. Do you understand me?"

"Yes sir!"

"What was that?"

"Sir, yes sir!" I stood up and snapped to attention this time. Evans looked me over and then smiled.

"This conversation never happened Jones; now get out of my office."

I saluted Evans, did an about face, and left his office. I saw Gwen several weeks later. We talked briefly as she left the hospital.

"Jones, here's my phone number. Call me when you get official leave. I want to see you again."

She handed me a number scribbled on a napkin and squeezed it into my hand. I think I kept the number for a while, but eventually got rid of it. At times of loneliness I thought I was crazy for not calling her, but I could not get the image of Sergeant Evans' face out of my mind when he sat me down for a man-to-man talk.

Basic Training

The final weeks of MedREP became more intense. Sergeant Evans began to teach us how to act as if we were in regular basic training. We began exercising, jogging, and marching maneuvers. We were taught how to salute and who to salute. Each week a few of us got our papers for regular basic training assignment. That was the tough part of being in MedREP; you still had to complete the entire eight weeks of basic training.

I was ending my eighth week of MedREP when I received my orders.

"Jones," said Evans. "You ship out next Tuesday evening at 10:00 p.m. A bus will be here to pick you up and you'll join your Flight in front of your new barracks. Good luck, Jones, and make me proud that I had you for a few weeks."

Wow; nine weeks already! Rosie had left three weeks before; in fact, I had two new roommates. It was traditional to give each departing airman a few days of non-detail in the barracks. That was as close to a pass you could get in MedREP. And cigarettes came free from anyone and everyone.

Tuesday evening came and I carried my duffle bag down to the bus stop with my orders. I got on the bus and headed east to another portion of the base. The regular basic training area was off limits to us MedREPs because we were allowed to walk alone. To get caught walking alone by a normal T.I. could have meant extreme verbal and possible physical retribution, thus creating a medical emergency. The bus driver had read my orders and knew exactly where to drop me off.

"Here you are airman. Just head down that sidewalk and you'll see building 1355 on the right. Wait outside until the rest of your Flight arrives. They'll be coming in from the airport about midnight."

"Thank you, sir."

Now comes the hard part. How would I be treated? I already had my haircut and all my government issue clothes. Everything was starched nicely and folded correctly. What could possibly go wrong? As I turned the corner in the dark, sitting on the barracks' steps was a lone cigarette glowing in someone's mouth. I spoke first.

"Howdy."

No response. As I made my last turn toward the lit cigarette, I made another attempt at being friendly.

"Got a smoke?" Wrong question.

"Smoke?" said the shadow. "Who the [bleep] are you, Airman, and what are you doing here in front of my barracks?"

When he stood up, the light revealed the traditional T.I. hat. What a way to begin with my new training instructor.

"Sir, I'm Airman Basic Jones reporting from the MedREP barracks to join your new Flight, sir!"

"Stand at attention, Airman, when you address me! Let me see your orders."

He snatched them out of my trembling hands. He was short with a tan complexion and his mouth was oval, revealing all his teeth.

[There's just too much cursing involved in my T.I.'s vocabulary to put in all the "bleeps." I will sprinkle in a few just to remind you that the cursing was definitely real.]

"Ah, [bleep]! Not again! I hate you [bleeping] MedREPs, coming in and [bleeping] up my new troops. Let me tell you something Jones. Because you've already been here for nine [bleeping] weeks, I'm expecting double duty from you and crisp responses from you. Do you [bleeping] understand me?"

"Sir, yes sir!"

"Now you pick up that [bleeping] duffle bag and get your [bleep] back down to that bus stop and wait for your Flight."

I did an about face and got out of that encounter as fast as I could. Man! What was I getting into? I ran the encounter through my head a number of times wondering if I would even make it through basic training. All this cursing was still new to me.

About midnight, four or five buses turned down the lane, all stopping near me. I moved over to the light pole. A T.I. jumped out of each bus.

"All right you guys," said one of the T.I.s. [Again, too much cursing to write them all]. "Get out of the bus and line up on the other side of the sidewalk. I want rows no wider than fifteen men and go as deep as necessary."

The guys looked weird—so civilian looking! I'd forgotten what long hair looked like on a man. They were clustering together trying to figure what to do. The T.I.s were trying to out-curse each other, I think, and enjoying every minute of it. That's when I got involved, because I knew how to curse as well. I headed for the corner of the group.

"Line up against my left arm, Airman, and stick your left arm out to touch the next guys right shoulder, face forward at all times, and be still. Put your feet together and stand up straight!"

All of a sudden, lines began to be formed from my corner over and some semblance of order was being made. A T.I. looked over my way.

"Who the [bleep] are you?"

"Sir, I'm Airman Basic Jones, reporting from the MedREP barracks to join my Flight, sir!"

"Let me see your orders airman! Ah, [bleep]! He's Cruz's boy! Hey Jenkins, we got a junior T.I. over here."

Oh, oh; this is not good. Three additional T.I.s came and encircled me.

"Jones, blah, blah, blah, blah, blah!"

That's all I could make of the multiple cursing over me. They were on me like buzzards on a dead possum. Then came the sweetest sound I ever heard from Cruz's mouth.

"ATTENTION! ATTENTION!"

A hush came over the place. T.I. Francisco Cruz may have been a short Hawaiian, but he had a voice that gained attention and respect. He began chewing on the other T.I.s.

"This [bleeping] airman is mine, and his [bleep] is mine, so get your [bleep, bleep, bleep] teeth out of his [bleep]. I'm the only one who can chew on his [bleep]!"

The other T.I.s stood down from Cruz and began shuffling papers. Four flights were brought in that night. My Flight began to be formed at my corner. Cruz ordered us down the sidewalk and into the upstairs of our frame-built barracks. He then had us sit down on the floor in the middle. Instructions were given about bunk assignments and details of order and command. He made a statement that I know he repeated about five times: "You'd better give your heart and soul to Jesus, because your [bleep] is mine." It was about 1:30 a.m. when he dismissed us.

"Jones, you take this first bunk right by my office. I'm making you dorm chief."

"Sir, yes sir!" I shouted with a loud and firm voice. Then I turned to the others.

"Get in the restrooms, take a [bleep], and get in your beds now. That's an order!"

Since I already had my uniform, it was very easy to bark orders to these new recruits. Cruz went to his office, where he had a cot. I saw him at his doorway a couple times observing me. I walked into the bathroom where there was a lot of chattering.

"Who the [bleep] gave you permission to talk? This is not your private bathroom. Do you understand me? You do not talk unless you've been given permission. And you will wipe up every drop of water you allow to hit the walls, floors, or basins."

Slowly, everyone made their way to a bunk; some downstairs and some upstairs. Lights went out at 2:00 a.m. At 4:45 a.m. I woke up, right on schedule. Two men were talking in Cruz's office. At 4:55, both came out and flipped the lights on.

"Get up! Get up now! Everyone get the [bleep] up now! Jones, get these guys up now!"

"Sir, yes sir!"

I ran down each side of the middle path of the barracks where the foot of all the beds were positioned, pulling all the covers off each bunk.

"Get up, get up now!"

There were some grumbling sounds being made. Some of the guys were not responding to my commands. I looked at Cruz and he looked back at me, as if I was being tested. My passive nature was at its extreme end and apparently it was showing. Cruz took over while the other T.I. was downstairs barking orders.

"Get out of your [bleep, bleep] beds or you'll get no breakfast this morning," said Cruz. Everyone get your clothes and shoes on and form a line outside the barracks, ten wide. Jones, get out there and form your Flight."

Cruz and the other T.I. (Allen, was his last name) marched us down to the mess hall. About a half block from the mess hall Allen called out.

"Airman Basic Jones, get over here. Take this roster in and sign us up for breakfast."

I ran ahead of the group and got in the sign-up line. With a uniform on, I seemed to attract attention.

"Airman, what are you doing in uniform? Who's your T.I.?"

"Sir, Sergeant Cruz's, sir."

"Let me see that."

He jerked the paper out of my hand, looked it over, and then grunted.

"There are three more Flights ahead of you. Tell Cruz to park you guys to the left of the door, behind Doogen's Flight."

"Sir, yes sir."

I learned earlier in MedREP that a basic trainee does not ask a sergeant a question of explanation. I quickly turned around and ran off to greet my Flight just as they were turning into the mess hall drive.

"To the left Sergeant Cruz, to the left! Right behind Doogen's Flight, sir!"

Cruz stopped our Flight.

"What? Jones, come here! First of all, you do not shout at me! You run up to me and stand at attention. You then address me as Sir! Do you understand me, Jones?"

"Sir, yes sir."

"I can't hear you!"

"SIR, YES SIR!"

"And the next thing; Doogen's Flight is not even here yet. So how can we get behind a Flight that's not here yet? What the [bleep's] going on?"

I didn't answer. I was frustrated and didn't know what to say. I remembered Rosie telling me that if you say little, you get chewed on little.

"Let me see that sign-in roster."

Cruz walked away toward the mess hall, swearing every step.

After breakfast, we were marched back into the barracks. Showers and shaving were ordered, so everyone began forming lines toward the bathroom. I went to the head of the line.

"Guys, I'm Airman Basic Jones, the dorm chief. If you have a need or a problem, you come to me and I'll do what I can to fix it for you."

Just as I was finishing my impromptu speech, Cruz stuck his head into the bathroom.

"Jones, come to my office as soon as you're showered and dressed."

"Sir, yes sir." Five minutes later, I was heading for his office. I knocked on the door and made a perfect approach and introduction. T.I. Allen was present as well.

"At ease, Jones. (Allen shut the door behind me.) Sergeant Allen and I have been talking about you. You know too much protocol to be our dorm chief. We must have a dorm chief that is naïve, so that he will do only that which we instruct him. You will be our Flight runner. This means that you will march at the back left rear of the Flight. You will run ahead of us wherever we go to sign us in. You will also carry an extra canteen on your belt, full of salt tablets. Everyone must take six tablets a day. Every morning, you come into my office and review the day's schedule. You're the only basic allowed in this office. You will make sure that we are always on schedule and that we are always ahead of Doogen's Flight. Do you understand me?"

"Sir, yes sir."

"Where're you from Jones?" asked Allen.

"Sir, Danville, Virginia, sir."

"Danville, Virginia. I'm from Georgia; Cruz's from Hawaii. Did you know all these guys in your flight come from Youngstown, Ohio?"

"Sir, no sir, but I knew by their talk they had to be Yankees."

They both laughed. I squeaked out a little grin, but it quickly left when Cruz looked at me sternly.

"Jones, the next man I call into my office will be our new dorm chief. While he is in here, I want you to switch beds with him. Do you understand?"

"Sir, yes sir!"

Sergeant Allen smiled as I did an about face and left the room.

Air Force Academy?

It was June in San Antonio, Texas. HOT was the word, and it seemed like I ran most of the time from one assignment to another. The first few days were spent getting everyone in military uniforms, haircuts, and shots. Not only was I keeping us on schedule, but also managed to keep us a few steps ahead of Doogen's Flight. Cruz did not like Doogen.

About three weeks into our training, as we were returning to the barracks, Sergeant Allen spoke to me.

"Jones, you come with me."

I stood at attention beside him until Cruz walked away.

"At ease, Jones. Come walk with me to the office to get the mail."

This was a first. Mail was sort of like having gold, or in hot Texas, a cold beer handed to you. To get mail was everyone's dream come true.

"Jones, I'm leaving for the Air Force Academy next week. I've been reassigned to teach academy students military law. I've been watching you and I want you to seriously consider applying for the academy. Now I know some folks up there and I'm sure they will get you in if at all possible. Now here is my contact number in Colorado. As soon as you get to tech school, I want you to call me. Do you understand me, Jones?"

"Sir, yes sir. Sir, can I learn to drop bombs at the academy?"

"What?"

"Sir, I have a buddy in 'Nam that is a gunner on a tank. I want to help him complete his mission. That's why I joined the Air Force."

Allen smiled again.

"Jones, you are something else. If you get into the academy, you'll be able to send a hundred planes into 'Nam to blow a hole deep enough for all them [bleep's] Viet Cong to fall into."

We walked into the office where there were about six T.I.s smoking and talking.

"Gentlemen, this is Airman Basic Jones. Take a good look at him because one day he'll be coordinating our bomb runs into Vietnam."

I recognized some of the T.I.s as those who got into my face the first night. Allen wasn't there when it occurred and I don't think these guys were interested in me anyhow.

"Jones, get the mail for our guys, would you? And step outside and wait for me."

When we left the office, Allen began talking to me again as he cut diagonally across the intersection. I followed beside him, but he stopped right in the middle of the intersection.

"Jones, you know it is illegal for you to walk out here with me. Now go back to the sidewalk and walk around."

I did as I was told. He waited for me on the opposite side.

"Just because I like you does not mean you can break military law. Always remember that we are all under military law, Jones."

"Sir, yes sir."

"Got a letter from a sweetheart in that stack?"

"Sir, I haven't even looked. Besides, I broke up with my girlfriend just before I left. She's was putting a lot of pressure on me to get married and I wasn't ready for that kind of commitment."

"Well, maybe you did the right thing, but it sure is nice to get a letter with a woman's scent on it down here, don't you think?

I smiled.

"Oh yes sir; that would be nice."

Allen led me on into the office where Cruz was sitting. He looked me over for a moment, and then actually cracked a grin with all teeth showing.

"Sergeant Allen says he wants to take you with him, Jones. You want to be a teacher?"

"Sir, no sir. I want to drop bombs in 'Nam!"

"Bombs? What the [bleep's] gotten into you Jones? All these other guys want to get as far away from 'Nam as possible, and you want to go? Where did you say you were from?"

"Sir, Danville, Virginia sir."

"Listen to me Jones; put in for Hawaii and enjoy the good life of the Air Force. 'Nam is hell; Hawaii is heaven. You want to go to hell or heaven, Jones?"

"Sir, neither right now. But I do want to get my buddy out of hell as soon as possible."

Parade Rest!

Sergeant Allen left and it was one week before our major inspection. There were two weeks remaining for us to pass the parade march, to qualify at the gun range, and, of course, the obstacle course over by the hospital. Cruz was now our only T.I. and he marched us endlessly. Several guys passed out in the heat of the afternoon, so Cruz changed our marching to follow supper. After our final march one evening, he gave us a smoke break.

"Men, tomorrow we go to the gun range for practice. We will simulate shooting and cleaning our weapons. Friday, we will use live rounds. You'll have sixty shots. Fifty-six and above is considered marksman. I want ninety percent of you to qualify as marksmen. If you do, you'll get a base pass on Saturday"

"Does that mean San Antonio," asked one of the guys.

"Is San Antonio on the base?"

Cruz began laughing. We all laughed. Wow, he was human after all.

Thursday, we practiced. Friday we began marching away from the regular areas toward the main highway. As we neared the highway, Doogen's Flight fell in right behind us. We all marched about a mile to the north. I could see the hospital to the west about a half-mile away. And it seemed that we were heading for the obstacle course. Yes, there it was: tall cliffs with scaling ropes, water pits with ropes to swing over them, and the barbed wire field with the canisters. I knew what that was all about. We stopped nearby and Cruz and Doogen brought us all together.

"Men, Doogen and I have a bet going on. He's betting more of his men will out shoot us and more will pass the obstacle course next week. Now take a hard look at this course. It is full of surprises and it is meant to be a distraction. All this is necessary in order for you to become a reliable airman. If you ever fall behind enemy lines, this will save your life. You listen carefully to every instruction given to you and you will make it."

We all got back into our flights and began the march down to the gun range. It was partially wooded, mostly mesquite bushes. Doogen's Flight began picking up the march pace as they slid to our left side to pass. Cruz began the same pace. Then Doogen called for double-time march. It was sort of a trotting march. That's as fast a march we had been taught. As Doogen's Flight came beside us, all in the front line began a full-scale run. That's all it took, because everyone began to run then. Can you imagine about sixty men running full speed toward a gun range? All you could hear in the rear were Cruz and Doogen laughing and shouting: "Flight halt! Flight halt!"

We did, right at the gun stacks. Finally, the Air Force began to make sense and we were actually enjoying each other's company.

We began shooting our M-16s as instructed. I shot a 57. Some guys got more than sixty, which means someone else's shot landed on their target as well. The scores began to be tabulated. Doogen's Flight got a 90 percentile. Next came ours: 92 percent! We did it! There was a lot of shouting going on for a while.

Cruz got us back to supper and the barracks in one piece. Then we had mail call. I had gotten a few letters from my family and enjoyed hearing from them. Cruz was in charge of distributing the letters. This time he was in a very happy mood. He would smell each envelope, making like they were scented, which most were not. Then he came to one that got my attention.

"Jones, what's this?" He sniffed it for a bit. "You've been holding out on this one. Tell us about her."

"Sir, it's just my mom or sister; I got no girlfriend."

"Well if this is your momma—or sister—I want to meet her!"

He grinned as he threw the letter. It was scented! I looked at the return address: Dana Monk! Well I'll be. She wrote me a letter, after all these months. I don't remember a lot about it, other than an apology for not writing and saying that she missed our drives down Riverside Drive. She had called my mom for my address. Well, it was a delight to get her letter for such a time as this.

Cruz bid us goodnight.

"Tomorrow is Saturday. Jones will issue everyone a two-day base pass in the morning. If you don't screw up, you won't see my ugly face until early Monday morning. Be in by 10:00 p.m. and hold the noise down."

Wow. Two days of real life. What would the guys do? Most were going to write letters. I told the guys how to get to the base commissary and the base exchange for food and letter writing materials.

Me? I knew where I was going. I put on my dress khakis.

"Whoa there Jones," said my friend, Pinkston. "Where're you headed all dressed up?"

"I'm going to the hospital."

"The hospital? What's at the hospital?"

"Oh nothing much; just a descent meal for a buck and a half. And maybe a good-looking nurse or two."

"Wait just a moment; I'm going with you!"

We walked about a mile to the hospital. The first thing I did was to check out the cancer ward. There were a couple faces I recognized, but most of my ladies—including Gwen—were either dismissed or had left for the weekend. Next, I headed for the area where I had my surgery. And there she was: Second Lieutenant Connors. When she saw me, she produced her angelic smile and came over to me with a big hug.

"So good to see you, Jonesie! And look at you! How are you feeling?"

"Great! I'm doing just fine. I'd like for you to meet Airman Pinkston from Youngstown, Ohio."

"Hello, I'm Nurse Connors."

Pinkston's jaw was still a bit open. I think he was caught a little off guard by the greeting she gave me.

"What are you doing back here? Need some more surgery?"

"Oh no. We have a weekend base pass and I was wondering if I could take you downstairs and buy you lunch?"

"Well, I would love to, but…"

"Yeah, I bet you hear a lot of 'butts' up here"

She laughed.

"You know how it is up here: all work and no play."

"Okay. I guess me and Pinkston here will have to go eat alone."

"If I can sneak away, I'll come down and let you buy me a drink. If I'm not down there in thirty minutes, I won't be coming. Oh it's so good to see your smiling face again. Nice to meet you Pinkston. Bye."

We left and headed down to the cafeteria. As we came in, I saw Smokie at the elevator.

"Hey Smokie!"

"Well I'll be [bleep]. Airman Jones. What are you here for?"

"Oh just taking a break from basic training. And you?"

"Well, I'm checking in today for another amputation next week."

"You gotta quit that smoking; it's going to kill you."

He laughed.

"Gotta die sooner or later. I'd rather die smoking than live trying to quit."

The elevator door opened and he crutched his way in with his usual lit cigarette in his mouth.

"Take care of yourself, Smokie."

"You too, Jones."

Nurse Connors didn't show. On the return to the barracks, Pinkston was nothing but mouth.

"Man, Jones, you know everybody on this [bleeping] base. Do you know the base commander?"

"Sure do; but I know his daughter better."

"Don't [bleep] me, Jones!"

We both had a good laugh. When we arrived at the barracks, Pinkston was still on a verbal roll.

"Guys, you won't believe this! We've been jawing with a second leuie!"
Much disgust and disbelief was expressed.

"No, I'm not joking. Jones got a hug from the most beautiful thing I've seen on this base. It was incredible!"

Pinkston thought I had hung the moon after that day; but the glory was short lived, because we were entering our final week.

Monday was practice for the final inspection. A parade was scheduled for Wednesday morning before the base commander. Cruz worked us in the early July morning sun and in the late evening.

Each marching command was done with precision as he had us doing cuts and turns that would make any college band routine blush. The orders were like rapid fire.

"Right flank 'harch'; left flank 'harch'; double-right 'harch'; ep-two-three-four, ep-two-three-four, left, left, left-right-left; to the rear 'harch'."

We were flawless until Cruz gave us so many turns in sequence that we literally imploded. We all hit the ground laughing. Cruz thoroughly enjoyed the moment. Then he called us into a group formation.

"At ease men. Let's take a smoke break."

We all lit up—even the non-smokers puffed away.

"Men, you're about to compete in our final official inspection. You've shown me that you can march flawlessly; I'm proud of you. Tomorrow, you'll spend the day getting all the transfer forms filled out, sending you to your tech schools. We'll do a final practice tomorrow evening and then it's extra bed rest. You give me an inspection with no more than two demerits and there'll be no more training. Do you understand me?"

"Sir, yes sir!"

Tuesday was nothing but forms to fill out and videos about drugs and alcoholism. We had previously been informed as to the areas of schooling that were available. We were given three choices to make. Since I was qualified in the electrical field, I chose ammunitions (bombs), basic electrical, and aircraft electrical. Thursday, we were to get our orders.

Wednesday morning, we got suited in dress khakis. Normally, parade inspections required full blue dress uniforms; but the temperature was predicted to be near 95° Fahrenheit by noon. The parade began at 10:00 a.m. and would end about 11:30. Cruz was as nervous as we were.

"Men, time to form ranks outside. On the double!"

We ran outside and got in formation. Cruz followed.

"Remember, whatever you do, DO NOT lock your knees at attention or at parade rest. You will pass out if you do and that means demerits. Any questions? ATTENTION!"

And off we went, marching casually down the road. As we passed other barracks, several other Flights were in waiting; they were called to attention and joined in the casual march to the main parade field across the highway. As we marched, we saw several new Flights being chewed on as they were just beginning to be introduced into the military world. It was a great feeling to see how far we had come.

As we neared the parade field, we could hear the military band playing on the field. The horns and the drums were setting the cadence as we turned the corner to enter the field.

"Flight, halt!" Those words echoed through each marching flight. A brief scan over our ranks and Cruz was ready. "ATTENTION! ("Attention, attention,..." fading down through the flights) MARCH! ("March, march,...")"

We marched out onto the field to make a rectangular route that would take us by the review stands, which included the review board and the base commander. We listened to Cruz as he gave each turning command in precise order. From the rear I could see that there wasn't a head bobbing in the ranks, which was a sign of perfection. As we passed the review board, we turned our heads and saluted. Next we made a final turn to head back into the middle of the field to face the review board, from where the base commander would give his speech.

We stood at attention for the colors and then were ordered into parade rest. The commander began his speech. Ten minutes passed; then fifteen. At about twenty minutes, Airman Brown began to wobble ahead of me. He was going to pass out!

"Get Brown," I whispered loudly. "Oh [bleep]!" came a few replies.

I could hear several men beside Brown talk to him.

"Bend those knees Brown, quick!"

Brown fainted neatly in rank as he fell to his knees. Fortunately he was hidden in the ranks and hardly noticed. He sat there for a minute, sneaking a drink from a canteen I had. (Runners always carried water and salt tablets.) The canteen made it back to me, unnoticed, and Brown slowly stood to his feet with a little help from his friends. The commander ended his speech.

"ATTENTION!"

The band started again and was the first in line for a final passing. We joined in about midway and headed for the end of the field. As soon as we left the field, I broke ranks and ran up the lines to retrieve Brown. The guys pulled him out of his line and threw him in my direction, as Cruz was about to halt us. I made Brown sit down and began cooling him with a water-soaked handkerchief. He had vomited on the field.

"Flight, halt!"

Cruz came immediately to Brown and me.

"Jones! Brown! What the [bleeps] going on?"

"Sir, Brown passed out on the field; he vomited, sir."

"What!?"

"Sir, yes sir; but we were undetected."

"Jones, why didn't you come get me? You know runners can break rank."

"Not necessary, sir. We took care of our man and the review board never saw it, sir."

"You don't know that, Jones. There are parade reviewers at every corner of this [bleeping] field. Nothing gets past their eyes!"

The march back to the barracks was not as celebrative as the other flights with us. Cruz was quiet and so were we. We arrived at the barracks just in time to go to lunch. Cruz allowed us to change quickly out of our sweat-drenched khakis and back into our fatigues. He stayed in his office as our dorm chief marched us to the mess hall. As we ate, a few of us dared to speak around the table.

"What do you think, Jones? Did we fail because of Brown?"

"Man, I don't think so. I saw it all; no one saw him go down. We were in dead center of all the flights and Brown was hidden. How in [bleep] could anyone see what happened?"

"Boy, Cruz was [bleeped]."

"Yeah, but there was no way I was going to break rank and get him or Brown. We did the right thing guys. We took care of our own problem. If they can't understand that, then so be it."

"[Bleeping] yeah," was the unanimous decision around our table.

About that time a bunch of T.I.s—including Cruz—burst into the mess hall. They were each carrying a paper of the parade results.

"Two [bleeping] demerits," said Doogen.

"Only one for me guys," said another T.I.

"Cruz, what did your flunkies get?" asked Doogen.

Cruz looked mad. He walked over to our area as the mess hall became silent.

"ZERO demerits men—a PERFECT SCORE!"

That was all that was heard for a while as we went ballistic in the mess hall.

"Hip, hip, hoorah! Hip, hip, hoorah!"

Cruz was all smiles now as the other T.I.s congratulated him.

We marched back to the dorm like a parade of new cars being previewed before hungry buyers. Once inside, Cruz called us into the middle of the second floor—just like the first night when we arrived.

"Men, today you proved yourself capable of being number one. You are number one. You ranked first in the inspection and I congratulate you for a job well done. Tomorrow, you will have light duty around the barracks as you prepare for your departure next Monday. I should have your orders by tomorrow afternoon. We will assemble at that time. For the rest of the evening, you will stay inside the dorm. You're dismissed...except Jones. You come to my office."

The men began to congratulate each other as I followed Cruz. Once inside the office, he motioned for me to shut the door.

"Sit down Jones."

"Sir, yes sir."

"Dispense with the 'sir' business for a moment. What happened out there today was risky. We should have been slapped with a half-dozen demerits, at least. When an airman falls, it is your responsibility to notify the next in command. You should have come to me."

"But sir, I did what I decided was best for the Flight. We were in competition as a Flight to win first place. Brown needed help and we helped him without breaking ranks and without being detected. Shouldn't the whole be considered when a small part is detected as weak?"

"If you had been detected, the whole inspection would have failed."

"But we weren't, sir. I scanned the whole situation and made a split-second decision to act to save our [bleep]. You already set the standard high for us. If I had broke rank, your standard would have been compromised. You would not be sitting here right now in first place, but in last place. I did this for me, our men, and for you."

Cruz looked out his window, lit another cigarette and handed it to me.

"Before he left, Sergeant Allen told me that there was something about you that he liked. He said you were different. I thought he was getting soft on me because he was leaving for the academy. Jones, I didn't like you coming into my flight. You MedREPs always think you're more special than the others; always want preferential treatment. But not so with you; you took all the hell I could muster against you and you survived. In all my years of training young men, none have ever taken the risk you did today for the common good of all. I misjudged you and I want you to know that you and the men made me proud today. Keep in touch with me, Jones, and remember…"

"Yeah, yeah: 'remember, this conversation never occurred.'"

"What?"

"Oh nothing. I've heard that line a few times on this base."

Cruz responded to my grin and my extended hand with a like response. We shook hands; I put out my cigarette, and walked out of his office.

Thursday morning, we practiced saluting on the streets. Some of the men did laundry, while others prepared a few letters to announce their orders to family members.

After lunch, the long awaited time came. Cruz had our orders. We assembled upstairs.

"Men, the Air Force has decided you can leave basic training. Most of you will be reassigned to a different base. Others will be trained on this base, depending on your field assigned."

He then began to call out each man's name and announced the assignment. Each guy was congratulated, even though most of the guys' first choice was not selected. All were to leave next Monday morning. There was only one problem…

"Sir?"

"Yes Jones?"
"You didn't give me my orders."
"What?"
"Sir, my orders; I didn't receive them."
"Umm. Let me check back at the office. I'll be back."

Boy, what a letdown. I had been on this base now for seventeen weeks and I was ready to leave this hot place. Why me, again? An hour passed; then two. Finally, Cruz returned.

"Jones; into my office."

"Oh not again," I thought.

"Jones, because you were put into this Flight from the MedREP, your papers were not processed with the others. You have been assigned into the aircraft electrical school at Chanute Air Force Base in Rantoul, Illinois, but you have no shipping orders."

"Sir, are you saying I don't get to leave?"

"Oh, you will leave this barracks, but there are a few holding barracks about a block from your old MedREP barracks. You will catch a bus Monday morning and report to those barracks. There you will stay until your orders are processed."

"How long does that take, sir?"

I was visibly shaken. I was angry inside, yet I maintained my composure.

"I don't know; I've never had this happen before, Jones. But, knowing you, you will have something special to do over there...probably save someone's life or something like that."

Cruz smiled; I didn't this time. I did an about face and walked away. I could not believe the Air Force could mess up a simple order as mine. I mean, they even gave me my third choice: aircraft electrician. Couldn't they show a little kindness and get me out of this place?

I hung out in the barracks most of the weekend. Sunday was a sleep-in day for me. I wrote a few letters to home describing my dilemma and my total disgust in the whole system. I even wrote to Dana—nothing romantic, however, just the facts.

Monday morning came with about as much excitement as could be tolerated. Everyone was talking about their new assignments and leaving our old barracks. I wasn't as joyful as the others. I packed my duffle bag and headed for the bus stop. The air-conditioned buses for the trip to the airport were all in line waiting to fill up. The base shuttle was not air-conditioned. It couldn't come down our road due to the other buses, so I had to walk a long block to another stop. But that was okay; I wanted to be alone. I sat at the stop wondering, *"What next?"*

Military Madness

The bus stopped at my next home: a set of wooden barracks similar to my MedREP one. As I neared the entrance, I could hear rock music coming from a barracks window. Hum. Maybe this would be better. It was mid-morning. I saw a couple of airmen in civilian clothes in the recreation room, shooting pool, and drinking from what looked like a bottle of wine. *"Okay, so maybe this will be different,"* I thought to myself. As I entered, I saw an office door open and a sergeant walk toward me.

"May I help you?"

I dropped my duffle bag and snapped to attention.

"Sir, Airman Basic Jones reporting as ordered!"

The sergeant smiled at my response.

"At ease Airman Basic Jones. Let me see your orders. Okay, looks like you'll be staying with us for a few days at least. I'm Sergeant Randall. I'll show you your room in a moment; but first let me give you your new protocol. From here on out, you do not have to snap to attention for a non-commissioned officer. That was only for training purposes in basic. You are no longer an 'Airman Basic'—just an 'Airman.' Some of us may have more stripes on our sleeves than you, but we're the same. You only snap to attention or salute a commissioned officer. So relax."

Relax? Now that was a word I hadn't heard for some time.

"So where is everyone?"

"Oh, most are still in bed."

"In bed? What's with that?"

"Well, it's because most of the men in our barracks work through the night, just like you will."

"Doing what?"

"Cleaning the C.O. (Commissioned Officers) and N.C.O. (Non-Commissioned Officers) Clubs. They're both pretty big and messy places. The clubs close at 11:00 p.m. on weeknights and 1:00 a.m. on Saturday and Sunday mornings. You'll join one of the crews tonight and work until the place is spotless, usually until about 6:00 a.m. on weeknights and 8:00 a.m. on weekends."

"Any days off?"

"Nope. You're here only a few days at best. I need every man I can get. Sorry, Jones, but that's the way it is around here. Just remember, when you're not working, you can do anything you want and go anywhere you want as long a you are here to join your cleaning crew an hour before cleaning starts. Which reminds me; get your first stripe sewed on all your uniforms as soon as possible. That signifies that you're no longer in basic training and will keep you from getting in trouble with the T.I.s."

"Do I still have to salute them?"

"Nope. With that stripe, you are released from all commands of a T.I."

Wow, this sounded like a dream come true. There was still one item I had to ask about.

"Tell me, do airmen get paid?"

Randall laughed.

"Oh yes; you should get a large check on the first of the month. The military holds your basic training salary until you get to your training school. If you're here on the first, you should get paid."

That would be another seven days and I had no money. Up to this point, I had no need for money. But now, I could actually go somewhere and shop.

"You can bum a few dollars from some guy that's been paid, but don't forget you can only carry what you can put into your duffle bag when you ship out."

Randall showed me to my new room: two cots and no one else inside. My very own room!

"You'll be responsible to keep your room cleaned. Civilians clean the rest of the barracks. Someone else may be put into your room if they show up today or tomorrow; otherwise, it'll be next week before anyone else may come in. But you should be long gone by then. Most guys stay here about five days."

I finally began smiling again. Five days didn't sound very long, plus the relaxed atmosphere was a welcomed relief. I lay on my bed, closed my eyes, and rested for the first time in sixteen weeks.

About four o'clock I woke up. I was hungry. There was a mess hall about three blocks away, but I knew how to get to the hospital. So I began my walking plans when I remembered the shuttle bus. It was previously off limits to airmen basics, but not to an airman. I pulled out my only "civies" (civilian clothes) and tried them on. Oh no; they were about three inches too large around the waist. Seventeen weeks in the military had me slimmer than ever. I decided to slip down to the nearest mess hall and just blend in with the rest.

At about 9:00 p.m., traffic began to pick up around the recreation lounge. There were no T.I.s and everyone seemed to be enjoying the relaxed atmosphere. I shot some pool and played ping pong with some guys on my cleaning crew.

At 10:00 p.m., we were dressed in our fatigues and headed for the C.O. Club. Once it was confirmed as empty, we went into the foyer. One crewmember in charge assigned our areas and off we went. With the front doors locked, someone turned up the radio to keep the tempo rolling. The smell of cigarettes and alcohol was everywhere. The restrooms were nasty.

"Ugh," I thought. *"Why does everything have to be so clean in the military?"*

"Jones," said the crewmember in charge. "Make sure you hold those ashtrays up to the light. They must be spotless."

I had some wild thoughts on how I would clean those ashtrays, but managed to keep them to myself. *"It's only a job and it's only for a few days,"* I kept reminding myself.

Five days came and went. Still no shipping orders. I went to Randall.

"So where the [bleep] are my orders?"

"I don't know. I'll make some calls today."

I had heard some stories about the military life. It's always a "hurry up and wait" routine. It was becoming true for me. I was beginning to think I was becoming a permanent fixture at Lackland AFB. Randall found me in my room.

"Got some good news and some bad news."

"Oh I need some good news!"

"Your shipping orders to start your electrical school are ready. You're going to Chanute Air Force Base in Rantoul, Illinois."

"All right! Great! When do I leave?"

"That's the bad news: you've got another ten days here."

"What!?"

"Sorry."

"What do you mean? They can't keep me here ten more days! That's crazy! Randall, tell me you're joking; PLEASE!"

He wasn't joking. The electrical classes started every four weeks and there was no way I could arrive in Illinois early. Oh boy. I was beginning to develop an attitude. I began to have feelings of anger and disgust for the military. It was the most inefficient organization I had ever come up against. No wonder people had to be drafted into the silly thing.

About the only bright spot on the horizon was payday. On August 1st all the cleaning crewmembers went down to the office. We waited outside as the first sergeant came to us.

"Men, how's it going?"

I wasn't talking. I just wanted some proof that I wasn't in a military prison camp. The "First Shirt" (that's what they called first sergeants) began calling out names and handing out the checks. They weren't sealed, so he made remarks about how much—really, how little—money everyone was getting.

"Ooo wee, you're gonna get some cheap wine with this check!" Then came my turn: "Jones, Airman Jones?"

"Right here, sir."

He stopped smiling.

"Jones, I'm going to have to hold yours. Something is wrong with it."

"What?"

"It's way too much money; about four times too much. There must be a clerical error. If I give this to you and it's wrong, they could put you and me in jail."

Oh no, not again.

"Come with me Jones."

I followed him inside to his office. He laid the check down. It was $659.00. Wow! That was a lot. The First Shirt was on the phone. After hanging up he turned back to me.

"Go over to headquarters and the administration office. Ask for a Sergeant Hollis; he'll straighten this all out. Give him this check, do you understand?"

It was late afternoon and the shuttle buses seemed awfully hot and slow. I figured the way my luck was running, I'd have to return tomorrow to get my first check. What a bummer.

Hollis was waiting for me.

"Hi, Airman Jones. Please sit down. Now let's take a look at your billing status."

He began looking through a stack of papers and stared carefully at some cards with perforated holes in them.

"The military is using a new electrical recording system, called a computer, to figure everyone's salary now. I'm going to rerun your cards."

"A computer? What does it do?"

"It reads all these holes in each card and somehow relays it into a central computer brain which, in turn, prints out a large sheet of paper with all your pay information."

"Sounds like a waste of time and paper to me."

"Yeah, you wouldn't believe the amount of paper we go through."

I watched as Hollis went inside a temperature-controlled room and put the stack of cards on top a large machine—the computer. As the cards began to disappear, two large tape reels began turning. They spun momentarily then stopped. Hollis left the enclosed room where the six-foot tall computer was kept.

"Come with me Jones; we'll get the output reading down at the main printer."

I followed him into another room. There was another large machine, about three feet wide. Underneath was a large box with a lot of wide green and white striped paper. We stood there for a couple minutes.

"Where you from, Jones?"

"Danville, Virginia."

"Oh yeah? I'm from Minnesota. You're just now getting out of basic?"

"Two weeks ago, sir."

"Oh, I bet you're anxious to get to tech school. After eight weeks of basic, it's time to leave this hot hell hole."

"Eight weeks? Try seventeen weeks! I've been here since April 7th."

"What? How's that?"

"I came under the MedREP program. I've had surgery at Wilford Hall. That's how."

"That's it!"

"That's what?"

"That explains your large check. Not only does this check cover seventeen weeks, but also you got a pay raise after eight weeks. You're an E-2 now. Congratulations Jones!"

About that time, the printer began taking control of the noise level. Boy was it loud. The green and white paper began dancing up from off the floor and through a narrow sleeve as a ribboned arm began tracking across it, back and forth. When it stopped, Hollis pressed a button to advance the paper then pulled it across a metal bar, tearing it clean from the rest. He began walking back to his desk.

"Now let's see if my theory is correct. Hmm. Yep, there it is in black and white."

He pointed to the typed message.

"You mean 'green and white,' don't you?"

We both laughed. The check was correct and Hollis handed it to me.

"Jones, take my advice: go over to the base bank tomorrow and convert most of this to travelers checks. You're not going to be here long enough for a bank account."

"Well, I was kinda thinking about going into San Antonio with a bunch of guys and getting real drunk for a few days."

"Ah Jones, you're crazy. Remember, everybody got paid today and everybody will be drinking for the next twenty-four hours. Now go do what I told you."

And I did. But I still had some time on my hands, so a group of us decided to go into San Antonio. My spirit was down, so I wasn't on my best behavior. We found several beer drinking places, but were not allowed to drink because of our ages. Finally, we paid a guy to go buy us some beers. We managed to drink a few on a river walkway in downtown without any problems. It was particularly helpful to me, since I was so uptight about my orders.

Chanute AFB, Rantoul, Illinois

From the plane, Chanute Air Force Base looked like a spot surrounded by fields of squares. And flat; the area was extremely flat looking from the air. I began wondering how such a place could be chosen for an air force training center. I think the plane circled the base just to rub in the devastating appearance of the area. Some of the guys groaned. We landed without a hitch, loaded on a few buses, and were dropped off at the debriefing area.

Different training school representatives were there to greet us. Once again we were reminded that this was the military and that we were the lowest on the food chain.

"Attention! Airmen, form your ranks!"

Like little ducklings, we began to line up as instructed. From a distant set of barracks, I could hear a few voices repeating one word.

"Ping! Ping! Ping!"

What was that all about? A couple of the First Class Airmen in charge smiled. These guys were well groomed and not only had two stripes on their fatigues, but also a colored rope tied around one shoulder.

"You hear that Airmen?" one of the men asked. "That's the sound of your hair popping back out on your head. You'd better get used to hearing those 'pings.'"

I wondered if this charade of humiliation would ever end. It seems as if everyone in the military loved to show and to pull their rank above the lower levels: stripes, colored ropes, and now hackling.

"Ping! Ping! Ping!"

My "Rope" was First Class Charleston. He pulled about twenty of us out among several hundred.

"Form two lines and march to my command. Attention! Forward, march! Hep, toop, threep, fourp, hep, toop threep, fourp; left..., left..., left, right, left."

We marched to the east of the base toward rows and rows of barracks. We stopped in front of a lackluster building.

"Guys, we'll have a mandatory dorm meeting tonight at 1900 hours. You'll get your room assignments then. Let me welcome you to the 57th Weather and Electrical Squadron. This will be your home for the next few months. This barracks is shared by two schools: you who are training to be spark chasers on airplanes and you who will keep your heads up in the clouds, otherwise known as weathermen.

"I marched you guys down here just to remind you that you will still have to march to and from school. Except for special parade days for dignitaries, this will be the only time you march. You should have seen the Base Exchange a block from where you debriefed and we passed the mess hall coming here. There's an Airman's Club directly behind our barracks, two blocks down. You can drink all you want on the weekends, but I'll warn you that drunks will not be tolerated on Monday mornings."

"Sir, where is..." Charleston interrupted him.

"Don't call me 'Sir,' airman. I'm an airman also. You can call me Charlie. I'm in leader training. That's what this red rope indicates."

"Charlie, can we grow hair again," I asked.

Charlie laughed. "Yep. That's what all that pinging is about. You'll have to keep it off your ears and under your hat. Anything longer is not allowed. Any other questions?"

"Yeah," someone said. "Where's the women's barracks?"

A number of positive responses joined in at the same time.

"Sorry fellows. There are a couple WAFs (Women in the Air Force) in the admin building, but they live off base and are off limits. On weekends, you can head south to the University of Illinois in the Champaign/Urbana area. There's plenty of partying on Friday and Saturday nights. Make sure you go as a small group and you'll get a list, tonight, of all the 'off-limits' areas. Okay, anything else? All right, it's 1700 hours now. The mess hall just opened. Go chow down, look around, and be back here at 1900 hours."

Tech school at Chanute was a transition time for all airmen. Each school had its instructors, but the education came primarily from reading small modules and testing over the material. The instructors were there to answer questions and give us safety lectures.

The days became weeks and it wasn't long before I began looking like my old self again. When I wasn't in school, I could wear my civilian clothes. Also, since I had accumulated extra money, I rented a stereo from a local store and set it up in the window to play outside my room while the guys and I played a little tag football in the street. A truck came around the barracks selling pizza and cold drinks. The sergeant running the business would open the barracks door and holler, "Pizza, pop!"

Such was life in tech school. My two roommates were studying in the weather school. One of them, Bob Huth, became a good friend of mine. Bob was from Rosendale, Wisconsin. We enjoyed each other's company and would go to the Airmen's Club a lot. There wasn't much to do on base except listen to music and drink beer. At the dorm, some of the guys played Pinochle, a card game. They tried to get me to play, but I never had a liking for it because it required holding a lot of cards in my left hand, my "bum" hand.

Drugs Anyone?

I remember another friend, Wilson, from another set of barracks that I met at the Airmen's Club. He and I shared a love for acid rock music. Led Zepplin, Iron Butterfly, and the like were our favorites. One Saturday afternoon, Wilson invited me to his place.

"I want you to come over to my room about 9:00 tonight, Jonesie. I got some stuff that'll really make this music rock in your soul."

"What'd you mean?"

"Oh, we'll start with a little weed and see where that leads."

I had never smoked marijuana, but heard it was similar to alcohol. I was interested in knowing how it felt, but wasn't sure of how Wilson got it.

"How safe is it over there?"

"Oh, me and a few of the guys have smoked a little before. Nothing to worry about, just come on over. It'll be an experience you'll never forget."

"Okay."

After supper I hung out in my room, doing odds and ends, killing time while the time to go over to Wilson's dorm approached. About 8:00 p.m., Bob and a few others came bursting in the room.

"Come on, Jonesie, you've got to see 'Little Bit' perform on stage. She's the girl dancer I told you about from Chicago."

Now the Airmen's Club didn't allow strippers, but occasionally, a girl dancer would come and dance on stage.

"I don't know; I already told someone else I'd be at his place in an hour."

Bob would have none of this. He grabbed my arm.

"Come on now. You've got to see her. You can go visit your other friends another time."

So I went and, as usual, Bob, the others, and me drank for hours while watching Little Bit dance. Before I knew it, the club began closing. We talked to Little Bit some then went to our barracks.

The next morning was Sunday, so things were a little relaxed. I headed over to the mess hall about 9:00 a.m. for a late breakfast. When I got there, I saw another guy that lived in Wilson's barracks.

"Hey, how's it going?"

"Okay Jonesie."

"Where's Wilson?"

"Oh, you haven't heard?"

"Heard what?"

"He got busted last night. The MPs raided his room and found him and a few others smoking dope. They found some other dope in there and took them all to jail."

I sat there stunned for a moment. Once again, I had made a choice that affected my entire career. Wilson had violated military law. He didn't get court-marshaled, but the Air Force gave him an "undesirable" discharge. I never saw him again.

Vietnam, Please

About three weeks to the end of my tech school, I had to report to Admin for active duty assignment. Finally, I would get to go somewhere more permanent. The office personnel were typically undetached to us airmen.

"Your name and number please?"

"Johnnie R. Jones, ***-**-****."

"Okay, Airman Jones, looks like you're an aircraft electrician, 42330."

"That's me."

"Okay, you get to make three choices for assignments. If you don't know where you want to go, I suggest that you list three regions."

"I want to go to 'Nam."

The sergeant stopped typing and looked at me.

"You want to go where?"

"Vietnam. My buddy is over there on a tank and I want to go help him win the war."

"We're not at war over there, Jones."

"Whatever. Just put down Vietnam as my first choice."

"Okay, what's next?"

"I don't care, you tell me."

"Well, there's Thailand where a lot of 'Nam guys go for a little R&R. Then, there's Hawaii where everyone wants to go, but rookies just out of school never get Hawaii."

"Put me down for both."

"Okay, it's done. Look this over and sign below."

Rosendale, Wisconsin

School was nearing its end. It was Thanksgiving weekend ahead and I was scheduled to leave tech school on December 1st, 1970. My roommate, Bob was headed for Wisconsin for the extended weekend.

"Hey Jonesie, you want to go to Wisconsin with me?"

"Naw, I don't want to get in the way of your family time. They haven't seen you for months, you know."

"Aw come on! They won't mind. They'll love that Virginia accent of yours. I want to show you my drums and stuff."

"Are you sure?"

"Yeah! Come with me and I'll call my parents."

We walked down the road toward a cluster of payphone booths where Bob made a call to home. The parents were ecstatic about Bob bringing home a friend. So, on Wednesday evening, after class, we headed north in a rental car. Several other guys rode with us into Chicago where we dropped them off. Another guy went as far as Milwaukee before bailing out. Then it was to Fondulac, turn left, and west into Rosendale, Bob's hometown.

"Welcome to Rosendale," said Mrs. Huth, with a hug. I shook hands with Bob's dad. They were very friendly.

"Thank you for having me up. It's great just to get off base for a few days."

"Bob has told us a lot about you, Mr. Jones. He loves your jokes. Or should I call you Airman Jones?"

"You can call me 'Jonesie.' Everyone else does. But don't call me late for supper."

They all laughed.

"See there," said Bob. "I told you he was funny."

Thanksgiving Day was filled with a lot of Bob's kinfolks coming by to see him. It was refreshing to be in a real home setting. As the day wore on, the company left and Bob showed me his drum set—a full room of equipment with a stereo record player. He would put on some music and play the drums with each song.

Friday involved a little traveling around the towns of Rosendale and Fond du Lac. It was mainly a farming area with vegetable processing plants nearby. There were acres and acres of vegetable fields being prepared for spring planting.

"So what do you think, Jonesie?"

"Boring."

"Boring? Yeah, it is. But I have an idea for tonight. Let's get back home."

At home, Bob got on the phone and made a few calls. I went to his drum room and tried my touch of rhythm.

"Give it up, Jonesie, before the dogs start howling."

"So what's happening tonight?"

"We are going bar hopping with my cousin. He says he knows where we can see some girls."

So, after supper, Bob and I left for a cousin's house where we parked his car and got into his cousin's. Frank was his name. He was 22 years old and, therefore, our legal alcohol purchaser. We headed into Fond du Lac.

"Guys, if we hit these places right, we'll see more skin than you can imagine."

"All right," said Bob.

I wasn't aware that we were heading for clubs with topless dancers, but there they were. Every club we entered had a girl or two dancing either on stage or in a raised caged area. They had no tops on and very little bottoms. I had never witnessed this before, so I was taken aback when I first encountered it. We would go in, sit down, order a beer, and watch. When the girl finished her routine, Frank motioned for us to leave.

"Wow, Frank. That was awesome," said Bob. "What'd you think, Jonesie?"

"I'm definitely not in Virginia anymore. I haven't seen sacks like that since the last time I milked ol' Bessie."

Bob and Frank howled with laughter.

"We've only just begun, Jonesie," said Frank.

And he was right. I think we must have visited six more clubs in three different towns around Rosendale. With the exception of one comedy show, every dancer seemed to be disconnected with the crowd of men staring at her. The girls would dance with the music, put their tops back on, then exit into a back room, never making eye contact with the men who were whistling at them and asking to buy them a drink. Sometime around 2:00 a.m., we found our way back to Bob's house and fell into bed.

Hawaii?

We left Sunday afternoon to head back to the base. Monday was the last day of November, the day I would get my orders. I was anxious to know where my first real assignment would be.

The day began with final examinations, and then early dismissal at 2:00 p.m. As soon as I was dismissed from the ranks, I made a beeline to the Admin office.

"Okay, Airman Jones, let's see what cards were dealt to you. Now where did you put in for?"

"Vietnam, Thailand, and Hawaii."

"Okay, here's your orders; now let's see...Vietnam? Nope, you didn't get your first choice."

"What?"

"Well, it's probably because you're still a three-level. You'll still need six months of on-the-job training before they'll let you go off on your own. Now let's see...Thailand? Nope, not Thailand either—the same reason."

"Don't tell me...Hawaii?"

"Well I'll be [bleep]...ALOHA! And welcome to Hawaii, Airman Jones. You're the first guy I've ever known to go straight to Hawaii from tech school. How lucky can you get?"

"Luck? I don't want to go to Hawaii, my friend's in 'Nam. I want to go to 'Nam!"

The sergeant could see my disappointment.

"Let me tell you a little secret. As soon as you get settled in at your new location, go to your First Shirt and put in for TDY assignments all over the Asian area. They always need emergency personnel in war zones, uh, you know...to replace those that get hurt?"

I left Admin sort of disappointed. The military reasoning was hard to figure. I mean, why was there a need for me in Hawaii? I shouldn't have put it down to begin with; it was my own fault.

Tomorrow was November 30th. I would be released from my duties here at Chanute and would begin a 30-day leave time on December 1st. My orders told me to report to my new assignment quarters on January 1st, the first day of 1971. I had a dorm address at Hickam Air Force Base in Honolulu, Hawaii.

The next day was uneventful. I received my release papers and headed for my dorm to begin plans for my 30-day leave. Bob and I packed our duffle bags. His mom had driven down to take him home. She had a hotel room off base. We went out with her for supper and a glass of wine. I was intrigued at how they were so comfortable drinking together. This was new to me.

The next day, Bob and his mom offered to take me to the bus station in town.

"Thanks man; this bag is heavy for a five-block carry."

"Well that's what friends are for, you know? Say, you're going to keep in touch, aren't you?"

"Forever man, forever."

Home for Christmas

The trip back to Virginia took about 27 hours by bus. It allowed me much time to think about the future. I knew I had changed. My backwoods, country naivety had been challenged by the new world I had discovered in the Air Force. I was anxious to see my family and friends, but not sure about Dana. I sensed in her last letter that she had a renewed interest in me. And here I was, a lonely single man, coming back into the area of my high school sweetheart.

I was about 25 pounds lighter with a groomed mustache. I was a focused young man with a future. All I needed was someone to share my life with. When I got home, I called Dana.

"Hey girl, it's me."

"Johnnie? Oh my! Please don't come over here; everything's a mess, including me. Oh Johnnie, why didn't you tell me you were coming home? I can't believe this. Oh my…"

This was a typical response from Dana that meant absolutely nothing.

"I'll be over in an hour."

I hung the phone up and finished my time with Mom and Dad. I borrowed my brother's car and headed over to see Dana. Her mom met me at the door.

"Hello Airman Jones. It's great to see you again."

Mrs. Monk was always a great sight to see. She was a schoolteacher and knew how to converse with people. She also had a brother who was in the Air Force.

"Hi, Mrs. Monk. It's good to be back. So where's Dana?"

She grinned.

"Oh I think I can manage to get her out of hiding. Come on in. Dana! Dana! Airman Jones is here to see you."

She was in her bedroom, a room I was never allowed to enter.

"Tell him to go away. I don't want him to see me like this."

Mrs. Monk rolled her eyes, and then smiled at me.

"You'd better come out here and see this man."

"I don't want him to see me like this. I'm fatter now."

Dana was always conscious about her weight and was always drinking a disgusting diet soda, but as a majorette in high school—currently head majorette during her senior year—she never looked overweight.

"I'm not leaving until you come out Dana," I said.

"Come on in the kitchen, Johnnie, and I'll fix you a glass of pop," said Mrs. Monk. Pop was their word for a carbonated beverage. I knew them as Cokes or sodas.

We visited for about fifteen minutes. In addition to Dana, she had three boys and a husband, so there was plenty of catching up on the happenings of everyone. Dana finally stuck her head around the kitchen doorway. She smiled her usually guarded smile, making sure her crooked tooth wasn't exposed. That tooth may have bothered her, but it wasn't that bad to anyone else...especially me.

"Hi."

"Hello, Mister, I mean, Sergeant Jones."

"I'm not a sergeant yet; you can call me Johnnie. Hey, come out and let me take a look at you."

"Mom, could you, please?"

"I was just about to leave. The boys and me are going to the grocery store to get some things for supper. Stick around Johnnie and I'll fix you something to eat."

"Mom, please!"

Mrs. Monk smiled as she left us in the kitchen. We stared at each other for a few seconds without saying a word. Dana finally broke the silence.

"What's that thing on your lip?"

"Oh, just a mustache. It's something allowed after basic training. Do you like it?"

"I'm not sure just yet. It makes you look much older."

We talked "stuff" for about an hour. That's when Mrs. Monk returned. The boys came in with her, carrying the groceries, making lots of noise, and annoying Dana.

"You're staying for supper, aren't you?" asked Mrs. Monk. Dana broke in.

"Sergeant Jones is taking me out for a hamburger."

"But I love your momma's cooking."

Dana gave me that look, the one that always told me to keep my mouth shut.

"Thanks for the offer, Mrs. Monk. Maybe tomorrow." She smiled as Dana and I headed out the kitchen door.

At first I didn't know how to read Dana, but soon she began laughing and warming up to me. It was like no bad blood between us. Thus an old love relationship began to relight and I began seeing Dana every day.

Christmas was just a couple weeks away. One morning my sister, Sandra, approached me.

"So, what are you getting Dana for Christmas?"

"Oh, I don't know; some clothes, maybe, or a necklace?"

"How about a ring?"

"A ring? You mean like a birthstone ring?"

"No, silly! I mean like an engagement ring."

"A what?" Sandra smiled as if she knew a little something.

"Okay, what's going on?"

"Oh nothing. Dana and I were just talking yesterday and I think she's expecting something serious from you this Christmas."

That got me to thinking seriously. Yes, before I left for the Air Force, we had discussed marriage. But I turned away and pursued the military. Dana then dropped me like a hot potato. I hadn't thought much about it since I was to be in for only a month. I'd have to give this some more thought...with my buddy Larry. Larry was in on leave as well, so I called him.

"Larry, me and you gotta talk tonight!"

"I'm with Kathy right now, but I'll tell you what. You stay put and we'll swing by there in about an hour."

Well, that was better than making this decision on my own. While waiting, Sandra told me that she thought Dana had settled down while I was gone. I found out that she and Dana had many phone conversations while I was away.

"I really don't think she dated anyone while you were away, Johnnie. We talked nearly every weekend and all she wanted to talk about was how you were doing in the military."

That made me feel better. Dana was the head majorette this, her senior year. She was beautiful and very popular. To wait for me sounded like she was serious to restore our relationship.

Larry and Kathy arrived about that time.

"Johnnie!"

"What'dya say Larry! Hi Kathy. You still hanging around this bum?"

"Got no choice now," she said, as she flashed her left hand.

"What? What is this?"

"Ah, Johnnie, she said I had to marry her or she was going to tell my parents about some things I did in 'Nam; I had no choice!"

Larry laughed as Kathy took a swing at him with her fist.

"Johnnie, you know better than that," she responded.

"So when is this going to happen? Before you go back?"

"No way!" they said together.

"I'll be out in less than a year," said Larry. "We'll set a date then. So how about you? Do you want to make this a double wedding?"

Kathy pinched his side.

"Ouch! That hurt."

"Well, that's why I wanted to talk to you. What do you think I should do?"

I recognized Kathy's smile.

"Okay Kathy, I just saw that same smile from my sister about an hour ago. Have you and Dana been talking?"

"Oh, a little bit."

"And...?"

"Well, I think it's time for you and Larry to settle down. You know, that pool hall will never fix your dinner and never wash your clothes."

"But I love shooting pool," said Larry.

"Then get you a basement with a pool table!" said Kathy.

"I don't know; I mean, I had thought about it, but I'm not sure I'm ready. I'm not even sure I can afford to take her to Hawaii."

"Hawaii? Man she can stay with Larry; I'll go with you to Hawaii!"

Larry pushed her away. "Go. See if I care."

"Come on guys, let's get serious here. I need your counsel."

Kathy spoke first: "Johnnie, you and Dana have been dating for four years."

"On and off," I interrupted.

"Mostly on," said responded. "She doesn't want anyone else but you and you've not really known anyone else but her, right?"

"Well, yes, but she's hinting at an engagement ring for Christmas. That's less than two weeks away!"

"Sounds like an easy gift for Christmas to me," said Larry. "Now you don't have to worry what to get her." Kathy pinched him again. "Ouch!"

"Johnnie, she is so sorry for becoming silent when you went into the military. Trust me, I think she really loves you and wants you two to be together again."

"There's a Christmas sale going on at Ben David's Jewelers," piped Larry. I'm telling you, Johnnie, now's the time."

Larry was all smiles. He and Kathy visited a few more minutes and then left.

I needed some think time. Dana was at school and I was waiting to take my mom and dad to work so that I could have the car to go see her. I dropped Mom and Dad off at the mill gate and headed down West Main toward Ben David's. It was less than a mile down the road. I had some extra money due to my military savings, so I went into the jewelry store to get some prices.

A gentleman showed me all sorts of engagement rings. And the prices?

"Whew, y'all must think this stuff is gold!"

He looked at me rather puzzled. "It is gold, sir. Look right here: 14-caret."

"Yeah, but don't you have, like, some cheap gold?"

"Well, there is one here that is 10-caret gold with a third-caret diamond. The diamond has a speck of carbon in it that no one would detect, except under a magnifying glass. It's a fine ring, plus don't forget that we offer trade-ups on any ring you buy from us."

"What's that mean?"

"It means that if she doesn't like the ring or you wish to give her a larger one down the road, we will give you a full-price credit for this ring, applied to another. It's a real bargain, sir."

Bargain; now I liked that word.

"Can you hold this ring for me?"

"Well, I'll have to ask Mister David. Wait here please."

The salesman went into the rear of the store, behind some curtains. A few minutes later another man came out.

"Hi; I'm Ben David."

"Hi; I'm Johnnie Jones. Sorry, if I've interrupted you."

"Oh no, no. James, here, says you want to put a hold on this diamond?"

"Yes sir; you see, I'm in on military leave and I'm not even sure my girl wants to even marry me."

"You're on active duty?"

"Yes sir." I produced my military I.D. card.

"Well that changes everything. With a small deposit, you can take this ring with you for twenty-four hours; How's that?"

"Forty-eight would be better." I smiled.

Mr. David laughed. "Okay, forty-eight hours, Mister Jones; or should I call you Sergeant Jones?"

"That's close enough."

"James, write up a ticket for Sergeant Jones. Thank you, sir, and good luck with your proposal."

That didn't seem so difficult. Now what do I do? I guess I need to go to Dana's house. I did.

Will You Marry Me?

Dana wasn't home. She and her mom had gone to the store. Her dad, Lewis, was there with the boys.

"Come on and sit awhile with me and the boys," said Mr. Monk.

Mr. Monk had mood swings, but most of the time, he was a fun and rambunctious dad with the boys. He loved to wrestle with them. Sometimes he'd let all three of the boys pinned him down, making them think they had him. Then he'd roll over on them, knocking them every which way but loose.

Mr. Monk didn't like to wait for anything. I remember each Christmas Eve, he would rush the boys off to bed, then bring out their presents, put anything together that needed assembling, run into their room and then bring them out to the Christmas tree. It usually took an hour at the most.

"Wake up boys! Santa has already come! Look! Look what's he's brought!"

The boys were awakened from their sleep for immediate enjoyment of Santa's quick pass. I'd never seen such a quick response from Santa, but it was definitely exciting.

"You want a beer?" asked Mr. Monk. I had never drank in front of Dana's parents and was not about to begin.

"No thank you, sir."

"How long are you in town for?"

"Oh, 'til January first, then it's off to Hawaii."

"Hawaii! Boy that sounds nice. How'd you get that?"

"Trust me, it wasn't my first choice. I wanted to go to 'Nam but I don't have the experience…yet."

Mr. Monk smiled. This was probably the first real conversation we had had since I knew him. Dana was always protective of my time at her house.

"Well let me tell you, it's no fun being shot at," he said. "You will probably enjoy yourself more in Hawaii and you'll come home in one piece." About that time, Dana and Mrs. Monk drove up. Mr. Monk got one more line in: "I'm proud to know you joined the military and I want to wish you the best of luck."

"Thank you, sir, and please…" as I lowered my voice; "…please don't tell Dana I joined. Tell her I was drafted."

He nodded approval as Dana approached.

"Hello Sergeant Jones," she said. "What are you doing here so early?"

"Early? It's never too early when it comes to seeing you."

"I think I'd better go," said Mr. Monk. He and the boys ran off to the back of the house.

"Lewis, help me with the groceries, please?" said Mrs. Monk.

"Can we go for a drive?" I asked Dana.

She looked at me curiously. My passive nature never was this aggressive around her.

"Well, sounds as if the military has done something to you."

"What'dya mean? I just want to talk."

"About what?"

"About what? I can't tell you here. We gotta go somewhere else."

"Mom! Dad! Sergeant Jones and I have to go somewhere. We'll be back."

"For supper?" Mrs. Monk asked, off in another room.

"Yes," I said to Dana.

"Maybe; we'll be back later Mom."

My nervousness was showing. Dana was eyeing me and a little quieter than usual. We drove down a small road off Westover Drive and pulled off the road near one of Dana's friends house, a place we had parked at before.

"Okay Sergeant Jones, what is this all about? It's a little early for smooching, don't you think?"

"Hey, I'm trying to get serious with you."

"Well, I'm first. I have a confession to make. I'm in love with another man."

"What!?"

"Yes. There's someone else I've fallen in love with."

I looked at her, but could not read her face. She was serious.

"I don't understand. Why haven't you told me? Who is he?"

"I have a picture of him. I think you know him."

I got a little anxious as she pulled a small pocket purse out. She fumbled through a few pictures before placing one in my hand face down.

"Here's what he looks like."

I turned the picture over. It was my latest military picture, in my dress blues.

She smiled and we kissed.

"You're crazy, girl."

"And you have changed, Johnnie, for the better I might add."

"Dana, I need to apologize to you."

"About what?"

"Well, remember when I joined the Air Force?"

"You mean drafted?" she interrupted.

"Well, I didn't really get drafted. I joined."

I flinched inside, awaiting a mild eruption. But she smiled again.

"I know. You forget my uncle is in the Air Force. He told me you don't get drafted into the Air Force anymore, Sergeant Jones."

"I'm so sorry I lied. I...I just wasn't ready for marriage. I had to get some space between us in order for me to figure things out."

"Space? Texas, Illinois, and now Hawaii? How much space do you need?"

"None anymore Dana. I don't want to live the rest of my life apart from you. Dana, I'm asking you to marry me."

There, I did it. Finally, it was me who initiated this decision. All I needed now was for her response. She began crying. Immediately I flashed back to the results of my very first love letter and how it had made Mandy cry. I vowed never to let this happen again, yet here I was with another love that was crying.

"I'm sorry Dana, I'm so sorry. This was too quick. I shouldn't have done this to you. I..." She put her hand over my mouth, slid over into the middle of the car seat, and began kissing me—we're talking serious kissing here. My ears must have risen a quarter inch. We finally stopped.

"YES, I'll marry you," she said. "On one condition."

"What's that?"

"No tours to Vietnam."

"What!?"

"You heard me: no tours to Vietnam. I don't want my man being shot at."

"But what about Larry?"

"You're not marrying Larry, you're marrying me."

She definitely had a point there. I smiled.

"You drive a hard bargain, but okay."

"So, what do we do now?" she asked.

"I'm taking you to my house to tell Momma."

We arrived in less than fifteen minutes. Mom and Sandra were home. It was obvious something was happening.

"Hi Dana," said Sandra. "What's up with you two?"
"Oh nothing; Johnnie just asked me to marry him, that's all."
Sandra screamed out and hugged her.
"I knew it! I just knew he was going to marry you!"
Momma stuck her head into the living room from the kitchen. "You two will make a fine couple. I'm so proud for you both."
"So Johnnie, I don't see a ring on her finger," Sandra piped in.
"Oh he just asked me about fifteen minutes ago. We haven't had time to even think about that."

As Dana began that reply, I slipped my hand into my pocket unnoticed, then lowered myself in front of her on one knee. I spoke as I began opening the small case.

"Dana Monk, will you marry me?" She looked at the sparkling diamond against the black velvet and screamed. Sandra screamed with her.

"What is this? You…you got me a ring already?"

"Yeah, I figured you might like this one; or, we can take it back and get another."

She snatched it out of my hand before I could bat an eye. "Let me see that thing! Ohhh no Johnnie, we can't afford this…it's, it's so big!"

I helped slip it on her finger. "It's paid for honey, compliments of eight long months in the Air Force."

After that proposal, Dana never took the ring off and hardly let go of me. We spent most of the holidays together, spreading the news and making wedding plans. I would leave for Hawaii on January 1st. As soon as possible, I would begin the process of finding us a place to live and then return in June for the wedding and for my bride.

On January 1st, Larry and Kathy drove Dana and me to the Greensboro, North Carolina regional airport. It had snowed about three inches the night before, making my farewell trip a beautiful ending of a momentous month: December, 1970.

"I'm going to miss you," said Dana. "It's going to be so lonely without you."

"Please write me often," I responded.

"Oh every day, as soon as I get your address."

"I'll get that taken care of as soon as possible. Plus, I'll start working on a return schedule for my return. Don't plan a big wedding, okay?"

"I bet we can have it at my church on Westover; is that okay?"

"Sure. Let me know if I need to send you some money for the planning."

"Oh don't worry about that. My mom and dad will take care of everything."

The airplane was a few minutes late, due to the weather. Not late enough, as far as I was concerned. I really didn't want to leave, now that I had made this big decision in my life. But the time came to board the flight to Atlanta for a non-stop to L.A., and then to Hawaii. We embraced, kissed, and I was gone. As the plane taxied down the ramp, I saw Larry, Kathy, and Dana on the observation deck waving at the plane. It was about 10:30 a.m., January 1st, 1971.

1971 – Hickam AFB, Honolulu, Hawaii

Flying was no big deal for me now. Every flight was basically paid for, so I just sat back and enjoyed the trip. I arrived in Honolulu about midnight. The night air had a sweet perfumed smell to it. Off at a distance, a red fog hung over the city.

"What's that red stuff in the air?" I asked an airplane crewmember. "Oh that's the remnants of the New Year's Day fireworks," he said. "It's incredible what they do here on New Year's Day. If you're here next year, be sure to go to Diamond Head Crater for the free rock concert inside the crater. Sixty thousand folks were there today."

"Did you say sixty thousand?"

"Yep. And most the women are in bikinis. It's a single man's paradise! You're not married, are you?"

"Not yet."

"You're in for the time of your life."

I took a shuttle bus over to a temporary dorm, designed for new arrivals, and slept until about noon the next day. As soon as I was able, I walked out toward the street. The sweet smell was still in the air, but now the air was clear of the red fog. A brisk and constant wind reminded me that I was no longer in Virginia. The first view down the street was breathtaking. It seemed right at the end of the street, tall and rugged mountains jutted high into the skyline. I would discover later that these mountains were actually about 25 miles away, but the clear air and bright sunshine made the peaks appear just a stone's throw away.

I had an address and phone number for my dormitory. Once repacked, I called for confirmation and shuttle bus locations. The trip across the base was beautiful. There were palm trees everywhere; and flowers! Hickam Air Force Base did indeed look like a paradise. What a difference from my first eight months. Maybe there was a God after all.

I checked into the dorm. My room would be on the second floor. The room already had two others in it. The dorm had a central bathroom—called a latrine—on each floor. Each room had a double set of bunk beds, a set of metal lockers, and one desk. That was all the room could handle. There were two men asleep in both lower bunks. It was Saturday morning, so nothing unusual. I chose a top bunk and opened the only unlocked locker. It was full of magazine centerfolds. In fact, centerfolds were the only pictures in the room. Acid rock was playing on the radio. I figured these guys must have had a long night. I started arranging a few things in, what I considered my space. I sat at the desk and began writing a few notes on some post cards. My habitual throat clearing finally woke one of the guys.

"Well lookie here, we gotta a new man in the room," he said, while rubbing his eyes. "Gotta smoke?"

"Not yet. I haven't had a chance to go to the exchange." In fact, I hadn't smoked for over a month. I didn't smoke around my family or around Dana…well, maybe a few times around her. She didn't like cigarettes.

"That's okay. Look in that shirt pocket on the chair."

"There's no shirt here."

He sat up and started looking around.

"Hmm, I know I had one on last night."

"Hey Jeff, wake up man! Jeff. Jeff! I need a smoke."

"By the way, I'm Johnnie Jones. Most folks call me Jonesie."

"I'm Hank and that's Jeff. HEY JEFF!" Hank screamed.

"Leave me the [bleep] alone," Jeff groaned under the covers.

Hank stood up and began searching for his shirt. My previous observation of the room knew the outcome of his investigation.

"Where's my shirt?"

"Maybe it's still in your car?"

"I'll check." He headed for the door and began opening it.

"Uh, don't you think you need some pants on?" I asked.

"Yeah, a good idea."

While Hank went downstairs, Jeff began peeping through the covers.

"Who are you?"

"I'm your new roommate, Johnnie Jones. You can call me Jonesie."

"Where's Hank heading for?"

"I think he's going to his car to find his shirt. He's looking for a smoke."

Hank burst back into the room, using the typical military language.

"[Bleep]! We musta had some party last night, Jeff. (Hank had a shirt in his hand and was smoking a cigarette.) My car windows were down and both doors were loose. But nobody touched my smokes," he said, smiling.

Jeff began creeping his way out of the covers, just enough to create a wrap around him. He started laughing.

"Yeah, that Lisa was some hot potato. Whew! I don't know what she was packing, but a few draws and I was chasing purple-haired women!"

They were laughing and continued describing to me a drug party of some sorts.

"What time is it?" Hank asked me.

"About noon."

"Whew, hurry up Jeff. We gotta go to the beach. It's Friday!"

"Don't you guys work?"

"Here, this base is a 24/7; Thursday and Friday are our weekends."

They headed toward the latrine to get cleaned up. My body was still about twelve hours out of sync, due to the flight. I thought about lunch, but decided to crawl up onto my bunk. I lay there thinking about what to do for the weekend. I wasn't sure if I had anyone in charge of me at my new assignment. Anyhow, it was Friday and I wasn't expected at my shop until sometime on Monday. I fell asleep.

Waikiki Beach!

When I awoke, Hank and Jeff were changing into their swim gear. It was about 2:00 p.m.

"We're headed for Waikiki; want to come along?"

"Nah, I still need to do a little unpacking and some laundry. Maybe next time."

A portion of Waikiki Beach from Magic Island, 1972.

"Listen man, it's Friday and it's your first weekend in Hawaii, and you're going to do laundry?" asked Jeff.

"Well, I haven't any clothes, other than these jeans and shirt."

"This is Hawaii. People wear everything imaginable here, especially at Waikiki. You'll do just fine."

"Yeah, come on and go with us. We'll drop you off by the beach and you can walk the streets," said Hank. "You've got to see this place."

"Okay, I'm in."

They decided to drive a long route by the ocean, showing me different places I could visit. We drove through Honolulu and down Hotel Street. Women were everywhere, talking to men on the street corners. One woman pulled her dress up, showing a man her thighs. I knew I wasn't in Danville, Virginia anymore.

"This is a serious street here, Jonesie," said Hank. "Don't go it alone and you better have some cash if you want some of these girls."

"That's why we do the beach," said Jeff. "The colleges around the world party at Waikiki."

"And it's winter break time," said Hank. We turned a corner and began passing a giant shopping center. Up ahead were rows and rows of hotels and tourist shops.

"Welcome to Waikiki," said Jeff. "Where do you want off?"

"Oh here will do just fine."

Hank pulled over and I bailed out.

"Which way back to the base?"

"Oh just ask any cabbie. He'll point you in the right direction."

Immediately, Hank spun out into the street, blowing his horn as he disappeared into the sea of cars and motorcycles. I looked around. There was a sea of people walking up and down the sidewalks on both sides of the street. I became one more fish in the sea.

My country naiveté did not allow me to go into hotel lobbies. I was afraid it might cost me money to look inside. I visited one little shop and bought some macadamia nuts. I made a mental note that I still had about $20 dollars on me. Waikiki was wall-to-wall shops and hotels. There were lots of entertainment shows, but I was just looking. A couple of times I wandered out onto the beach. I was amazed at its beauty, but equally amazed at the water pollution signs posted on the beach. Waikiki Beach polluted? Yep.

About 5:00 p.m., I became hungry. I stopped at a sidewalk concession stand and bought a hotdog, chips, and a drink. $3.95: Wow! Things were high! (1971 prices) I had already noticed gasoline prices were $0.599. It was something like, $0.369 in Virginia.

After eating, I decided to head back for the base. I had found a free map of the area, so I knew which way Honolulu was from Waikiki. I headed for the base. I walked about an hour before noticing something familiar. Up ahead was Hotel Street. There were a lot of questionable dinner theaters up ahead as well. I stopped at a hotel next to me. A cab was parked near the lobby. As I walked up to it, a cabbie came running out the hotel.

"Yes sir, you want a cab?"

"I'm not sure. I'm heading for Hickam Air Force Base. Can you tell me if I'm going in the right direction?"

"Sure. You continue in that direction and you will see a road sign saying 'Hickam, 6 miles'."

"Six miles!?"

"Yes sir. Can I drive you to Hickam?"

"How much will it cost me?"

"Oh, about $15 dollars, give or take a buck."

"That's about all I have. Okay."

This was my very first cab ride. I rode up front and watched the meter. It started at $1.50 and began clicking away as we drove. I didn't realize Hickam was that far away. As the cab entered the base checkpoint, $14.50 was registered on the meter. There was still about a mile left.

"You'd better pull over, because I don't think I have the money to get me to my dorm."

"Okay, sir." As he pulled over, the meter clicked $14.75. "Is this okay?"

"Yes, this will be just fine, thanks." I gave him fifteen dollars, expecting some change.

"Oh thank you sir; thank you very much." With those words, he pulled away and headed down the road, fifteen dollars and all. And to add insult to injury, he turned left at the road I was walking to, probably heading for the NCO Club right next to my dorm. Oh well, live and learn. Fortunately, my meals were free on base and there were free washers and dryers in the dorm. I only had to find some detergent.

First Impression is a …?

Saturday was uneventful, other than waking up to an empty room. I got up, ate breakfast, did my laundry, and read the newspaper in the lounge. There was some ping-pong and pool tables around that allowed me to meet some guys. There were a few guys who came in after lunch who spent a lot of time laughing and goofing off. I noticed one of them lived across the hall from me. He and I had met in the latrine yesterday. He didn't have much to say, but seemed to always smile.

Hank and Jeff came in right after supper.

"So how was the surf?" I asked.

"The surf? We never touched the water," said Jeff. "But those college girls' hotel room had a beautiful view. What were their names, Hank?"

"Beats me; one was blonde and the other brunette." They laughed and began talking about their partying. I left the room, probably unnoticed. I was engaged now and I had to stay away from temptation. I did not want to mess things up between Dana and me.

Monday came and it seemed as if every man in the dorm was vying for a latrine mirror to shave in front of. I got in line and waited. It was interesting to watch how men shaved. Most just went from top to bottom. There were several who shaved, what I considered against the grain, from the bottom of the neck area to the top, stopping at the sideburns. That might be something to try on a weekend morning, but not today; not on my first day at the shop.

My travel orders had a phone number for me to call on arrival. It was my squadron's admin office. The rooms had no phones in them, so I went downstairs to the lounge. I called and requested to speak to the First Shirt.

"This is Sergeant Phillips."

"Hi; this is Airman Johnnie R. Jones. I'm calling to announce my arrival on base."

"Oh, hello Airman Jones. I've been expecting your call. How was your trip?"

"Long." He responded with a chuckle.

"I know how you feel. Listen, I know you're probably anxious to get into your new room. I'll try to have someone over at the temp dorm to pick you up in 30 minutes."

"I've already checked into my dorm, sir."

"You have? That's even better! I'll check on your immediate supervisor, Sergeant Fidoe, and see if he can come by to see you. Hang around the lounge there and I'll call you back."

Sergeant Fidoe? An interesting name, I thought. I sat down and began reading a local newspaper. It wasn't long until the phone rang.

"Got a call for Airman Jones."

"That's me. Hello?"

"Airman Jones, Sergeant Phillips; Sergeant Fidoe will stop by your room at approximately 1600 hours (4:00 p.m., civilian time). He'll be heading for home so don't expect a lot of time with him today. In the meantime, if you don't mind, take the shuttle bus over to the post office and show them your orders. They will assign you an APO box number. After that, you can walk three blocks toward the flight line, hang a right, and you'll see our admin office attached to a large hangar. If I'm not in, they'll know you are coming and begin processing your paperwork."

"Thanks. I'll get right on it."

The day proceeded with a bit of nervousness. Would Sergeant Fidoe be like a T.I. or would he be normal? I remembered at that moment, Sergeant Cruz's statement: *"Listen to me Jones; put in for Hawaii and enjoy the good life of the Air Force. 'Nam is hell; Hawaii is heaven."* Maybe Fidoe would be okay.

About 3:45 p.m., my room door received a knock. When I opened it, I was taken aback. There stood a small, frail-looking man in the grungiest set of military fatigues I had ever seen. His hair was blown into at least three separate directions and he had black grease on his face and hands.

"Airman Jones?"

"Yes sir!" I snapped.

"Don't sir me, please. I'm no different than you." Inwardly, I begged to differ because I could never be that filthy looking, not in uniform. "Come with me."

We headed down to the parking lot and got into a car that had so many different body parts, I hardly recognized it as an old Ford. I got into the passenger side.

"Watch the floor; there's holes in it."

That was an understatement. Most of the floor was missing. I could see the ground underneath the car. When the engine started, it belched out a long stream of blue smoke.

"Where we headed?" I asked.

"We're getting off this god-forsaken base. I've been here for eight [bleeping] hours and I need a drink."

Fidoe began to introduce himself. He was from upstate New York, married, and had one child, a girl. He had reenlisted once and was in his sixth year. He was in his second year at Hickam.

Off base, he pulled into a beverage store and bought two six-packs of Primo Beer, a local Hawaiian beer. Once in the car, he popped open a beer.

"Here, have a beer."

"Oh that's okay, I'll wait." He stared at me.

"There are only two reasons a man doesn't drink a free beer. He's either a [bleep] or a religious fanatic. Are you either?" Well I wasn't a female and my religion wasn't fanatical, so I took the beer. He immediately popped open another can and began drinking it as we pulled onto the road.

"Where're we headed?"

"Home. You're going to eat supper with me. Any problem with a free, home-cooked meal?"

"Nope. Sounds great." I couldn't help but wonder inside if it was going to actually be great.

The main roads off base were full of vehicles. I had never seen so many cars and trucks on one road. And they all seemed to be creeping along the road. Fidoe let out a few curse words as he maneuvered through a few lanes to turn off the main trail.

"All the military idiots travel this way. I've got a shortcut."

Fidoe drove us through some back roads. His driving was a great incentive to drink another beer. When he finished a beer, he would drop the empty through the hole in the floor. He talked incessantly about how bad this place was. After about an hour and several beers, I began to loosen a bit.

"So where do you live?"

"Near Waimea Bay. There are some old Navy Quonset huts that have been converted into houses. They look like [bleep], but the price is right."

It took us about an hour and a half to get to his place. I had never seen a Quonset hut. It looked like a half-round metal drainage horn with windows cut into it. Of course we pulled into the front of the most cluttered one. Engine motors and car parts served as yard decorations.

"Come on in and meet the family."

A clean, sweet-smiling, and equally frail-looking woman greeted me. She had that "Twiggy" model look.

"Hello," I said. "I'm Airman Jones."

"He's the trainee they stuck me with," said Fidoe with sort of a smile. "I told him you'd fix us some food."

"Hi, Airman Jones. Do you have a first name?"

"Johnnie, it's Johnnie Jones."

"Johnnie, I'm Betty."

"Does Fidoe here have a first name?"

"Yeah I do, but I can't say it in mixed company."

"It's John," said Betty. "And that's Charlene playing in the next room."

Betty was very polite and John was very blunt, perhaps even rude. He spent about an hour telling me all the ropes and rules of working on base. His descriptions were nothing like I imagined the military workforce. Betty continued preparing the meal as we talked. I think John must have drunk six beers. He continued to try and get me to drink more, but after a couple, I began to wonder who would be able to drive me back to the base tonight.

The meal was great, plus the local fruit, mango, was delicious. We finished around 8:00 p.m.

"Well, I guess I'd better get back to the base, don't you think John?"

"Base? Tonight? I thought I told you that you were staying the night."

"No, I don't recall that conversation. I didn't bring any clothes."

"That's okay; you can wear a pair of my shorts and I'll drop you off your barracks first thing."

Stuck, I began to feel my trainer was not someone who I was going to enjoy being around. His wife and child were clean, but John didn't impress me. I really had no choice but to stay the night. I slept on the couch.

The next morning, John shook me. It was 4:45 a.m.

"Time to get moving, Jonesie."

Ten minutes later and we were on the road. We stopped at a store near his place and got some coffee and a sweet roll for breakfast.

"Our shift will be 7:00 a.m. 'til 4:00 p.m. We have three shifts. We're the 76th Air Rescue and Recovery Squadron. We'll train you on HC-130s. They're modified C-130s. You'll notice two things about them: they have a bumble bee stripe around the rear fuselage and two metal prongs attached to the nose."

"How many electricians do we have?"

"Right now, there's me, you, and two others on days, three others on swings, and two overnight guys."

"That doesn't sound like many for such a large base."

"Well you don't have but six planes to work on and usually two of them are never air-ready. We aren't the only electricians on base."

"Oh. Sorry, I'm new at this. So, do you like training guys?"

"You kidding? You're my first. I didn't ask for this, but one of the other day electricians is also the supervisor over all the other electricians as well. It was either me training you or I had to change shifts."

Things got quiet after that. Fidoe dropped me off at my dorm and suggested I check in with the First Shirt as soon as possible. I walked upstairs to my room, wondering how all this would play out.

First Day on the Job

The First Shirt took me over to the shop where I would be working. The shop was attached to a large aircraft hangar. Inside the shop, there were about twelve men sitting around a large table. Some were filling out work-order forms, but most were just shooting the breeze. There were all types of sergeants sitting there: three-, four-, and five-stripes on their fatigues. I only had one stripe. Sergeant Phillips introduced me to most of them, but I could never remember all the names. Fortunately everyone's last name was sewed onto his fatigue.

"Sergeant Miller is your supervisor, but he must be out on a work order," said Phillips.

"Yeah, he and Fidoe got called out onto a waiting plane," said one of the others. "They shouldn't be long."

"Fidoe will be your trainer, but Miller will be responsible to sign off on all your work orders," said Phillips. "Just sit here until they come in from the flight line. These guys will fill you in on all the shop details. Call me if you have any questions…by the way, when did you say you joined?"

"April seventh, sir."

"And just one stripe?"

"Well, it's a long story, but there was a delay in getting it."

Phillips seemed to be thinking hard about my stripe. "I'll be in touch, Airman Jones." Then he left.

Tech-Sergeant Jackson was the first to talk to me.

"Airman Jones, do you have a nickname? We don't use the 'airman,' 'sergeant' stuff."

"Well, most folks in the military have been calling me, 'Jonesie.'"

"Then 'Jonesie' it is. We have another Jones on swing shift, but we call him by his first name, 'Mike.' You'll soon discover that everyone usually calls each other by their last names since that is the one sewed on your uniform. It's easier that way."

In front of Apollo 15 space capsule on display in a typical aircraft hangar, Hickam AFB, August 1971. BELOW: Maintenance shops were located inside aircraft hangars.

"Yeah, I think I'm getting the hang of it."

"Where're you from, Jonesie?"

"Danville, Virginia; and you?"

"Near Indianapolis, Indiana."

"Yeah? I changed buses there when I left tech school."

"Oh really? How'd you like it?"

"Oh, I got there after dark and I left around midnight. Sorry. I stepped outside for a little fresh air, but never left the bus station. It was kind of cold outside."

"I'd probably do the same thing in a strange town. So you're an electrician?"

"Yep; and you?"

"I'm a radio/radar technician. You'll find radio/radar and electricians in this shop. All our systems intertwine so much that, many times, we go out together when a problem exists."

The shop had a number of machines and gauges on several benches. They were unlike those in my tech school. I was studying some of the equipment when the flight line door burst open. It was Fidoe and two others. One of the others had three stripes (a buck sergeant) and the other man had six stripes (a master sergeant).

"That [bleeping] pilot needs to turn his bars in," said Fidoe, sitting down immediately and lighting a cigarette. "There wasn't a [bleep] thing wrong with that [bleep] plane."

Fidoe hardly talked without a slew of curse words, except in front of his daughter. Master Sergeant Miller was the next to speak.

"Fidoe, it's not ours to question; it's ours to check out the problems."

"These guys are always trying to find something wrong with their [bleep] planes in Hawaii, just so they can have a little more R&R on the beach."

Jackson walked over to Fidoe and muttered something to him.

"Oh yeah, Miller, here's Airman Jones. He's our new guy."

Miller smiled and reached to shake my hand.

"Hi, I'm Jack Miller. Glad to have you on board."

"I'm Airman Jones, sir, and glad to be here."

"We're calling him 'Jonesie,' Jack," piped in Jackson.

A fun moment with Jack Miller, Radio & Electric Shop, 76th ARRS, Hickam AFB.

"Have you met the other guys, yet?" asked Miller.

"About a dozen of them. I've been over here studying some of this equipment."

"Oh that's some radio/radar testing equipment. It's not for us electricians."

"Yeah, you 'spark-chasers' don't wanna be [bleeping] with our stuff," said the arriving buck sergeant.

"That's Sergeant Goeken," said Miller. "He's a radio man and always seems to need a haircut."

"How'ya doing Jonesie; I'm so glad you and Day are here now. That means I don't have to clean the [bleeping] latrines anymore."

"Day is another new electrician on swings," said Miller.

"Yeah, we got two new [bleeping] rookies to train," said Fidoe. "What'd we do to deserve this?"

"I requested them Fidoe, so get used to it," said Miller.

"Watch him, Jonesie," said Fidoe. "He's a former T.I. He loves to 'train' guys."

I looked at Miller, but saw no semblance of the T.I.s I had encountered.

"Pay no attention to him, Johnnie," said Miller. "He's full of baloney, sometimes, but a good electrician. Learn his skills, but stay away from his mannerisms and especially his mouth."

Miller called me by my first name. I was impressed. He seemed to be different, someone who really cared about the people for whom he had responsibility. He smiled occasionally and he hadn't said one curse word in the exchange.

"Fidoe, show Johnnie how a work order is filled out."

Fidoe rolled his eyes and then motioned for me to join him. After a few instructions, he asked: "Got any questions?"

"Yeah; is Day undergoing training, like me?"

"Oh, he's a Filipino that arrived about three [bleep] weeks ago. He's a First Class Airman (two stripes). We should meet him during debriefing at shift change. He claims to speak English, but I can't understand half of what he says."

I knew Fidoe was from New York, so I had to ask him: "How's my English?"

"Oh about two-thirds understandable." I laughed and he smiled.

The shop had two group supervisors: one for the electricians and one for the radio/radar men. Whoever was the highest-ranking man got the position. Sergeant Miller was ours and Sergeant Elmore beat out Jackson by about 30 days. Then there was a squadron supervisor, a Senior Master Sergeant Collingsworth. He was the only one with a cubicle-type office. He wasn't in the shop at the time.

Miller sent Fidoe and me to get my tools requisitioned. Then we were assigned a work order for one of our planes in a hangar for scheduled maintenance. Fidoe began showing me the basic things required for an electrician to do on our planes. Things like safety wiring all bolts on anything that had to do with the electrical systems. There were large books on each aircraft that were called Technical Orders. Every piece of equipment and every wire had a diagram, number, and location. Bolts had to be torqued and systems had to be tested. Also, every item in your tool bag had to be logged in to ensure nothing was left behind. It was a tedious but necessary duty for the sake of safety.

About 3:30, we headed back into the office.

HC-130H aircraft. Our five had a yellow bumblebee stripe near its tail for international designation.

At four, I went to the exchange to purchase some stationery and stamps. I began writing my new address on post cards to my mom, Dana, and Larry.

My first week as an official aircraft electrician was exciting. Learning the systems, sitting in the cockpits, as well as testing engine generators at 100 percent throttle on the ground, were invigorating. As time progressed, several men became more interested in my development. Of course there were Fidoe and Miller; but Day and I had a lot in common as we were both learning the ropes of an aircraft electrician. Also, there was Sergeant Howard, a radio/radar technician, who seemed to be trying to get Fidoe to clean up his appearance. Howard, a Native American, was a beer-drinking buddy of Fidoe's.

"Hey, Jonesie; how about I pick you up tomorrow and we'll go visit Fidoe?" asked Howard. Tomorrow was a Saturday.

"Sure. What time?"

"I'll be by your dorm at 10:00 a.m."

This would be my third weekend in Hawaii as I was completing my second week of work. Each day, I hurried to the post office to see if a letter from home or Dana had arrived. Mail must be slow to Hawaii, I thought. Today was Friday, ten days since I had mailed my address to everyone. I checked my box and, again, it was empty.

Sergeant Howard was punctual in his arrival. His Hawaiian shirt really made him stand out.

"Wow, Howard, I'm going to need my shades just to look at you."

He smiled and took a peek at my room.

"You need to keep this room in top condition at all times, Jonesie. You know the Base Commander may still call for dorm inspections, don't you?"

I looked around and all I saw was my unmade bed. Hank and Jeff were not in, which meant most of the room mess was theirs.

"Let me make my bed. The rest of this mess belongs to my roommates."

Howard looked at the room and then at me. "I'll wait downstairs in my car."

Howard wanted to make sure I knew all the military protocol. He would drill me on various situations, wanting the proper responses. He was really driven to see that military personnel acted according to the rules.

We picked up Fidoe at his house and ran down to the local grocery store to by some chicken breasts for the grill and plenty of Primo. While there, we ran into a Native Hawaiian who gave us an enormous history lesson about how the Hawaiians basically gave their islands to the Americans. Yet he showed no animosity; he only laughed.

"That's why we're such a happy and friendly folk. We'll give you the shirts off our backs. Shaka, bruddah," he said, sticking out his thumb and little finger as he wiggled his wrist.

"What was that?" I asked after we got into Howard's car.

That's a native symbol and phrase for friendship," said Howard. "You're okay around guys like him, but watch those who may call you a 'houlie.' That's like a bad slang for those of us from the mainland. And don't call the mainland the 'states.' Hawaii is a state also."

"Yeah, you should have seen their faces when I asked for some [bleeping] Tabasco," said Fidoe. "They acted like I was from another [bleeping] planet."

"John, you need to stop cursing," said Howard. "You have a child now and she doesn't need to hear this kind of language."

"I don't curse in front of her, you know that. Hey Jonesie, did I say a bad word in front of her the other day?"

"Can't remember; you got us both so drunk, I didn't know what I was saying half the time."

"You're [bleeping] with me. Howard, he's fuller of [bleep] than a Christmas turkey."

I laughed, but it wasn't easy getting Howard to relax. We spent the rest of the day shooting the breeze and drinking beer. After supper, we headed back for the base. Howard was more talkative once we left Fidoe.

"Jonesie, Fidoe is a bright man, but he just doesn't see his mannerisms as a problem. He has no respect for his uniform and, therefore, for himself. Learn from him—both what to become and what not to become."

"If he is that bad, why is Betty here with him?" Howard hesitated. "That's none of my business. I know I wouldn't put a woman in that kind of living conditions."

"Howard, I'm engaged to marry my high school sweetheart this summer. Will you help me find a place for us to live in?"

"There are lots of apartments just off base and in Honolulu. Check the paper as you near the time. If I hear of something, I'll let you know."

Sunday was another sleep-in and laundry day. I thought about calling home collect, but was afraid of the cost. I was getting anxious to hear from home and from Dana.

Monday was a non-eventful day. When I ended my shift, I walked over to the post office. Again, there were no letters. There was, however, a handwritten blank card with my p. o. number on it. I threw it in the trash and headed for my dorm. On Tuesday, again there was no mail, but another handwritten card with my p. o. number on it. This time, I went to the window. It closed at 4:00 p.m.

Wednesday, during lunch, I headed for the post office. I checked my box again and, again, no mail and no card this time. I went to the window with yesterday's card.

"Sir, I found this card in my box. What does it mean?"

"What's the number on it?"

"1098."

He walked away, returning with a large bundle of mail. "If your mail won't fit in the box, we'll leave this card in it. Just come to the window and we'll give it to you."

"Thank you, sir. Thank you!"

I grabbed the bundle and soon discovered about a dozen letters from Dana, as well as letters from home and friends. I ran out to a picnic table nearby and began opening letters from Dana. I began to realize that she had begun writing me a daily letter since the day I left her. As the dates progressed, she was getting anxious to hear from me. I had written a couple times to her, but had said I would wait to hear from her before I'd write again. That was about five days ago. I knew I had a job to do this evening.

Throughout the rest of January and February, Dana and I pursued our plans of marriage in June. She would be graduated by then. She was our school's head majorette this year, something I was proud of for her. I remember the many hours of practice she did in front of me in her front yard. She even tried to teach me how to twirl a baton. I stopped trying after the incident when it slipped from my hand and put a knot on her leg.

It was mid-March now. I was improving in my electrical competence. Fidoe was getting further away from me as I repaired airplanes. Miller still had to sign off on my work orders, but he rarely had to make any corrections. Sometimes I would twist the safety wire incorrectly, but I was getting better. Miller had assigned me to a Technical Order reading and interpretation class. That went well. I was also getting information about an electronics school in Cleveland, Ohio, that would allow me, through correspondence, to get a journeyman's degree in electronics. The computer field was very attractive as well as television and radio repairs.

I made my usual trek to the post office, after work. Now that Dana's letters had caught up to the current date, I received at least one every day. Today, however, there was none. It must have gotten misplaced in the mail, I thought. The next day, there was none; then the next and the next. I checked at the postal window during lunch the following day.

"Sorry, we have no mail set aside for that box number."

I wrote to Dana. I told her what had happened and asked her if everything was okay. In fact, I began writing her daily for about a week. Maybe, perhaps, this would stimulate a greater response. Still, no letters. I didn't know what, exactly, to do. I decided to call home.

"Collect call from an Airman Johnnie Jones," stated the operator. "Will you accept the charges?"

"Yes ma'am," said Sandra, my sister.

"Go ahead, sir."

"Thank you, ma'am. Sandra, it's me, Johnnie."

"Hey Johnnie! So good to hear your voice. How are you?"

"I'm great; and everyone at home?"

"Okay, I guess. Mom's feeling better. She had another disk problem in her back. I don't think she'll ever get to work again in the cotton mill."

"And Dad, Joe, Gary?"

"They're all fine. Joe's moved to an apartment off Main Street and Gary's somewhere out there with you in the Pacific Ocean."

"Hold on a second...yeah, I see him. His ship just went by. 'Hey Gary! How's it going?' Gary said to tell you everything's okay."

"Oh Johnnie. You're still a nut!"

"I haven't heard from Dana for weeks now. Do you know what's going on?"

"Johnnie, I don't know what's gotten into her. She was calling me nearly every day until about the first part of March. Then she stopped. I called her a few times, but she was never able to take my call. I heard something, and I hate to tell you this. I've heard she is dating another guy, Johnnie. Do you know about any of this?"

"No; not even a hint that something was wrong. I don't understand. I thought we were engaged."

"I don't understand it either. I think maybe she got a little too popular during football season. She was always leading the whole band and her name and picture has been everywhere at school."

"I'll try to get her to write me and see if she'll explain herself. In the meantime, see if you can talk to her for me, please?"

"Okay, I will. Now here's your momma before she yanks this cord around my neck. Bye; I love you."

"Bye, Sandra."

I spoke with my mom for a while, promising her I would send money home to pay for the phone call. We didn't discuss Dana much, other than to tell her we were planning the wedding for mid-June.

Wedding? That word didn't seem to have the same sound as it did before this silence from Dana. Would there even be a wedding in June? What do I do now? I already had my two weeks leave approved. I was on an on-base housing list that Sergeant Miller told me about. Howard and I were constantly following the renting trends at various apartment complexes. There was nothing left for me to do except plan on returning to Virginia in June.

I continued writing to Dana, begging for a response. I contemplated making a collect to her, but was afraid it might agitate the problem further between Dana and her parents. I wrote her one final letter in May, saying that I would be home in a month and that I would see her. I never told her that the wedding was off. Somehow, I wanted that possibility to remain, even though she was not writing to me anymore.

When June arrived, I was officially promoted as a 5-level electrician. That meant that I could now sign off my own work orders without Fidoe looking over my shoulder and without Miller's signature. I was also a First Class

Airman with a second stripe on my sleeve. This made me feel more confident in my abilities. Miller and Howard both instilled in me a drive to excellence in my work. Fidoe was glad to get a "normal life" back. He thought all the hoopla and pageantry over the promotion was a bunch of [bleep]. But, I could sense he was proud to have been a part of that "[bleep]."

But going home was a journey of mixed emotions. What was to happen? Would Dana even see me? What changed her?

1971 – Wedding Bells?

I booked a flight on a C-135. It had a bunch of webbed seats along the fuselage, with cargo in the middle. The flight was free and was headed all the way to North Carolina. I would get a bus ride from the base there to Danville. I bought a boxed lunch for the trip and got on the plane in the middle of the night. The trip board said only that we would arrive in North Carolina the next evening. We would be flying about eleven hours against the clock this time. I wore only my khakis uniform, since the weather seemed to be okay from the reports I received about North Carolina and Virginia. What wasn't told us, however, was that we would make two additional stops: one in North Dakota and one in Upper Michigan.

When we stopped in North Dakota, it was cold and raining. We had to deplane for refueling. I nearly froze, but was glad to get some coffee inside the terminal. Once thawed, we were put back into the now cold plane.

In Upper Michigan, we landed again. This time, it wasn't raining, but there was snow all on the ground. We did not have to get off this time, but a large pallet had to be unloaded from the front side. Again, many of us froze.

On to North Carolina. Finally, the plane heated up and the bad weather was soon forgotten. From the base, one of the passengers drove me to the bus terminal in Goldsboro. I was fortunate to get an evening bus headed to Durham where I could transfer to a Danville-bound bus. Total cost, excluding the boxed meal and coffee: $7.50, from Honolulu to Danville. What a price!

I arrived in Danville about midnight. Dad got off work about then and came to the bus terminal. We hugged and talked a bit. He, being an ex-Navy man, wanted to trade stories about basic training, tech school, and of his adventures on the seas during WW II. I think he was happy to see me. I was glad to be home on familiar ground. Mom, Sandra, and Ricky had all stayed up to await my arrival. Mom had cooked up some homemade fudge and hot chocolate. School was out, so no one, except Dad, was anxious to get into bed. I suppose it was about 3:00 a.m. when we all went to bed.

The next day, I slept until about noon. Everyone else was up. I could hear the T.V. downstairs. Mom cooked me up some sausage, eggs, and pancakes.

I began passing out some small gifts from Hawaii to everyone. I knew Dad would plan on leaving for the mill around 2:30.

"Dad, can I take you to work? I'll pick you up afterwards."

"Sure son."

This would be the day I would go and see Dana. This would be the day when questions would be answered.

I arrived at Dana's about 4:15 p.m. Mrs. Monk was there with her usual bright smile.

"Well hello, Sergeant Jones," she said, reaching out for a hug. "It's so good to see you again. My, my; you look so grown up now."

"Thank you, Mrs. Monk. I feel like I've grown a bit this past six months. And you?"

"Well, I've got to tell you some good news before Dana takes you away from me: I'm pregnant."

"You're what? I can't believe it! Congratulations!"

"Thank you, thank you. And I feel great."

"That's great. When is it due?"

"October."

"Oh, I wish I could be here then."

"Well thank you. I know your thoughts and prayers will be here."

"Yes, they will. Now I need to see Miss Dana."

"Oh, that person. Well I think she's hiding again in her room, but I'll go fetch her. Johnnie, she's not been herself for months. I really don't understand what's happened. Maybe you can figure her out."

"If it can be figured, I intend to do it."

Mrs. Monk knew me well enough to trust my ability to maintain control during this encounter. I think she wanted answers just as the rest of us. I got back into my dad's car for little privacy.

After a few minutes, Dana slowly walked out of the kitchen door onto the carport. She motioned for me to come sit with her. I motioned for her to come sit with me. She started her approach to the passenger's side of the car. As she walked, I noticed a large school ring hanging around her neck. She came to the window.

"Won't you get out so we can sit in the shade?"

"No Dana, I need you to get in and sit with me." She did. "Nice ring you got there. Who's the lucky guy?"

"You don't know him, Johnnie. I met him at a dance after a ball game."

"So what happened?" I looked into her eyes and saw something I had never seen before. It was like previewing a video recording of a past event. I couldn't believe it.

"I can't tell you."

I turned away from her and stared straight ahead. "You already have, Dana." The silence was but for a few seconds as tears welded up into my eyes.

"Why, Dana? Why couldn't you wait?" She started crying.
"I'm so sorry, Johnnie, oh I'm so sorry. Please forgive me."
She reached for my hand. I grabbed hers instead.
"Where is it?" Her ring finger was empty.
"It's right here in my pocket. Oh Johnnie, please listen. I've thought this all over and I want to go back with you. I want to marry you, Johnnie; I want to be with you, not him."

As she said that, she grabbed her—his—ring, tore it from her neck and threw it out the window. She reached into her pocket and pulled out the engagement ring.

"This is the ring I want to wear again." She handed it to me. "But you'll have to be the one to place it back onto my finger."

I took the ring and began to turn it into the late-afternoon sun. It no longer matched the eyes of the one to whom it was meant. I looked at her awaiting finger. With the ring in my left hand, I gently took her left hand with my right hand and closed her fingers into a fist inside mine.

"Not now, Dana. Not this time. What if I have to leave you for some temporary duty? Could I trust you?"

"Yes, yes," she said, crying. "You can trust me, Johnnie. I swear."

"I'm sorry. I can't do this now. I'll need some time. The wedding is off, Dana."

She immediately got out of the car and ran inside her house. I wanted to leave in a huff, but I didn't. I sat there for a moment, thinking it all over again. About that time, Mrs. Monk came out the door, still smiling, but with a note of seriousness. She walked up to the car.

"Johnnie, regardless of how she treats you, you are always welcomed at my house."

"Thank you, Mrs. Monk. I hope to see you again someday."

"Oh, you will. Come by and see my new baby the next time you're in town." With that, she squeezed my hand, turned, and walked away. I started the car, backed out the driveway, and slowly drove away, heading for Riverside Drive.

A 'Monkey Wrench' in Life

The return trip to Hawaii cost a little more. I flew S.A.M. (Space Available – Military), which was better than half-price. While flying, I was offered complimentary champagne. This time I partook. I was mentally drained from the Dana trauma and had no real future planned. What do I do with my life now? What will become of me? I thought about Fidoe, Miller, and Howard. Who would I turn to for guidance? They all knew I was to bring back a bride. Only Howard knew there was trouble in the relationship.

The next few weeks found me floundering in my commitment to excellence. I didn't care what I did or said. My drinking, smoking, and cursing increased. Even Fidoe made a comment about my mouth. I just didn't care what anyone thought about me anymore.

One day, Senior Master Sergeant Hollingsworth called for a shop meeting. He gave a report on a quality control inspection, stating that there were more write-ups this time than in the past six inspections.

"I'm disappointed in this report," he said. And I expect this to change the next time. I have authorized a surprise inspection of this whole squadron. I want every room cleaned from top to bottom. Every aircraft will be readied for a full inspection. Each supervisor will be in charge of this order. You're dismissed...except Fidoe, Goeken, and J. Jones. I want you guys in my office."

This was not good. I knew what the others might be in trouble for, but I was clueless. Sure enough, Fidoe was reprimanded for his sloppy appearance and filthy fatigues. Goeken was ordered to get a haircut and to keep it under his hat whenever he was outside. I was next.

"Jones, sit down. Up until this inspection, you have been given exemplary marks from Q.C. Several weeks ago, our top Q.C. inspector, complimented me about you. I just recently recommended you for the Base Airman of the Year Award. Now listen to this. You were cited for three minor and two major write-ups on this last inspection. Had they not been discovered, you could have jeopardized the next mission of this aircraft.

"What am I to do? I cannot recommend you under this condition. I'm changing my recommendation to Airman First Class Shipman. He's not as high up on the Q.C list as you were before this inspection, but now he's the best I got. Jones, I don't know what's happened to you. Miller says you had a problem at home. Those things happen, but you cannot allow your personal life to affect your job performance. Many Air Force personnel stake their lives on your quality of work. Basic training is designed to weed out the weak minded. You received high marks by your T.I. and I believe you have what it takes to be the best electrician ever. But you must focus on your duties and responsibilities here and today. Is that understood?"

"Yes sir."

"Now get out there and don't ever let me have to call you into my office for a reprimand again."

Things were quiet in the whole shop. Cubicles have thin walls and I was visibly shaken. I didn't know what to expect from Sergeant Miller, but there he was with a work order in his hand.

"Johnnie, I have a plane trying to take off. They have a fire warning light flashing. They think it's a faulty bulb. You and Fidoe get out there and check it out."

I grabbed the work order and my tool bag. Fidoe was already on Hotel Four (code name for our shuttle trucks). He was sitting there with a lit cigarette.

"Ready to go?" he asked.

"Let's do it," I responded.

"Ready, driver."

"Hotel Control, this is Hotel Four. I have two electricians in route to Aircraft Zero-Nine-Eight-One on Taxiway One-Niner, over?"

"Copy that, Hotel Four. Stop at row fifty-two, until clearance granted for taxiway, over?"

"Ten-Four."

"Cigarettes out and tool bags fully zipped guys," said the driver. "We're entering a hot zone."

A 50/50 Chance at Religion #2

Miller knew the best thing for me was to put me right back into the battle. It got my mind back into the real world. That day was one that I would never forget. It brought me back to the realization that what I was doing was important. Hollingsworth would never reprimand me again, and at the end of that year, I did receive recognition for our squadron's Airman of the Year Award.

On Friday of that week, Miller came to me.

"Johnnie, my wife and family are going to a get together at our church tomorrow with a group of youth. There'll be a lot of food and fun. I'd like to invite you to go with us."

"Oh, okay. Sounds good."

"Okay, here's my address; it's down by the tower. Be there by 9 a.m."

Wow, I thought; a master sergeant inviting me to his house? Earlier this week, I was being reprimanded; now I'm running with the big dogs!

By now, I had purchased a bicycle. I rode it over to Miller's house for the church outing. Sgt. Miller was married to Dahlia. They had two daughters, Sherry and Jackie. Sherry was about eleven years old and Jackie, about eight years old. All three were very pleasant to be around. Jack introduced me to the family and then we headed off base, east toward Honolulu. In fact, we got on Interstate H-1 and drove around Honolulu, about a 25-30 minute drive.

We arrived at a church called, Waialae Baptist Church on 21st Street, on the backside of Diamond Head Crater. There were about a dozen cars and about 30 youth and adults on the parking lot. Again, I got introduced to a bunch of people. The youth director was Wayne Meeds.

"Okay everyone," said Meeds. "Gather around for instructions."

I thought this was an interesting way to start a party. I thought we were going to the beach.

"I'm giving each driver two envelopes," Meeds continued. "You must fill your car with youth and then follow the instructions that will lead you to your next envelope. That envelope will lead you to your next rendezvous point."

"What's the second envelop for?" someone asked.

"In case you get lost, it's your emergency address. But you must turn it in at our destination, and it must be sealed in order to be a winner. There will be prizes for first and second place. This is a race, but it is based on you driving the speed limit and your actual mileage. It's 10 a.m. and you should be there by 1:00 p.m. Any questions? (There were none.) Okay, let's pray and let's load up."

Dahlia and Sherry got in another car with a friend, while Jackie and I stayed with Jack. Two additional youth jumped in the car with us. Each car was separated by ten minutes. I was thinking this should be easy as long as we had someone who knew street names. Also, I noticed a convenience store near the church. We could purchase a map. But that was not how the instructions were designed. Since I was riding shotgun, I became the navigator. I opened the instructions as we approached the parking lot exit. I couldn't believe my eyes!

"Jack, the instructions say, 'Turn left out of the church's back parking lot and stop at the intersection. Turn right and proceed three tenths of a mile and turn left.'"

"What?" asked Jack. "Is that all it says?"

"Yep, that's it."

"Jackie, you sit here by me and watch the numbers on the odometer."

Wow! This was going to be one interesting road trip. But it was very creative. We began traveling through various housing developments until arriving at a small shopping center.

"What next?" asked one of the youth.

"Well, all it says is to go to people at this location and say, 'I'm a little tea kettle, short and stout; here's my handle and here's my spout,'" I said. "And it says you must use your hands to animate what you're saying."

As I finished my explanation, we saw another of our "race" cars pull out the center's parking lot. They were screaming at us and waving another envelope.

"Okay guys," said Jack. "Look for someone you might know and do your thing."

We all piled out of the car, running toward the shopping center's walkway, the two youth stopping in front of several strangers, doing their little stint. Some were laughing; others smiled and walked away. After about six tries, one of the youth saw someone familiar.

"There he is," she screamed. She ran to him as he tried to act surprised. But after the little saying, he finally smiled and handed over the envelope. We ran to the car and took off again. After a few short turns, the instructions read to travel twenty-some miles.

"This takes us around Pearl Harbor," said Jack.

It did indeed. In fact, we drove through a pineapple farm, per instructions, to the Schofield Barracks area, near the center of Oahu.

"It says, 'Turn left here and drive two tenths of a mile'," I said. We were in a pineapple field.

"Look around the pineapples," said Jack. We all began walking the rows. Finally Jackie screamed.

"Here it is!" she cried, and grabbed the envelope that was partially hidden in the dirt. We opened the envelope and found two more envelopes. One was for a route with a military pass and one was for a non-military vehicle.

"Let's go," said Jack, and off we headed for Schofield Barracks. This old army base was near a pass that was made famous by the Japanese who flew through it just prior to bombing Pearl Harbor. Our instructions were taking us through the pass. This was a breath-taking view of the shoreline of the Oahu Island. The mountains formed a horseshoe around a deep valley below. There were a few waterfalls pouring off the sides of the mountains. I was seeing a beauty like no other place I had ever seen.

As we neared the bottom, things began to look normal again. In fact, it looked a little bit familiar."

"Jack, Fidoe lives over here," I said. "I remember this road."

"Oh yeah? Well, tell us where to go next."

This was great, as I was the only one—the new kid on the block—that was familiar with the area. The instructions took us through a few back roads, but we eventually ended up at Waimea Bay Beach Park. It was 12:45 when we arrived. There were a few people playing volleyball and others were in the water. A grill was cooking up some burgers and wieners. I think we came in third place because our travel time was a bit short.

The whole afternoon was a blast. I could not recall ever having this much fun at a church function. The only church functions I had ever been to were Vacation Bible School and an occasional 'dinner-on-the-grounds.' At these dinners, the men would gather around a radio to listen to the stock car races, while the women-folk just sat around the tables to visit. We children usually played 'tag' around the trees by the church.

But this was definitely different. As the evening sun began to skirt behind the mountains, some girls pulled out a guitar and began singing contemporary Christian songs. Others joined in. I sat and listened because I had never heard of Christian songs outside of a hymn at church. But these songs had a more appealing sound to them; more folk-music style. I laid my head on the grass and enjoyed a calming effect of the music.

After about an hour, a young man stood up and began to give a testimony of how he became a Christian. Several others did likewise. I suppose I should not have been, but I was truly surprised how these young men and women spoke of their new life as a Christian. These folks were different: happy, peaceful, and fun all wrapped together.

As we traveled back to the base, Dahlia and the girls (mostly the girls) were asking me a thousand questions about my life and me. I opened up some, but wasn't ready to bring up my current stressful situation back in Danville. I was still in a withdrawn type of mood. Then Dahlia spoke up.

The Miller's: Sheryl, Dahlia, Jack, & Jackie

"John," she said. "We'd like to have you visit our church with us tomorrow morning, and then come have lunch with us."

"Well, I'd like to, but I have to do laundry tomorrow and I have several loads."

"He could bring them over and we could help him do his laundry," said Jackie. I was a bit embarrassed.

"Oh you don't want to see my dirty underwear," I replied, pinching my nose. They laughed. "Besides that, they won't fit on my bike."

"We could stop by the barracks, after church, and John could get his laundry and put them in the trunk," offered Sherry.

"Yeah!" said Jackie.

Jack piped in: "It's up to John, girls. He may have other plans tomorrow."

I thought for a moment. Yeah, I do have to do my laundry and I still wanted to smoke a cigarette and maybe go drink a beer somewhere. But, man, today sure was fun and it got my mind off of Danville and Dana.

"Okay," I said. "You've got a deal, as long as you don't laugh at my smelly underwear." That one statement seemed to make four people in the car satisfied. And, once again, I was fulfilling my childhood promise to make people happy.

Church, two days in a row, was a new experience for me. Here I am, in "Paradise," with access to the world famous Waikiki Beach and I'm dressed to go to church. Something just didn't seem right, but at least I was making some folks happy. Some of the early-riser guys in the dorm lounge looked me over as they passed by. They were dressed for the beach or the gym. The Miller's finally arrived and we headed for Waialae Baptist Church. This time the girls were a little more subdued and dressed up a bit. Jack was the most casual.

"Well, did you enjoy the car race yesterday?" he asked.

"Yeah, sure did. I really liked driving across the island and seeing all the different places. And that mountain pass was awesome!"

"What did you think about the speaker?" asked Dahlia.

"Oh, he was okay. I really found everyone's talk about being a Christian was interesting."

"Are you a Christian?"

"Yes ma'am. I went forward in our Baptist church when I was about six or seven. I'm a member of Mt. Hermon Baptist Church in Danville, Virginia."

"That's great," piped in Jackie. "Why is it called, Mt. Hermon?"

"I don't know; maybe some guy named Hermon lives nearby on a mountain. We have lots of mountains in Virginia."

"I bet it's named after the Bible 'Mt. Hermon' instead," replied Sherry.

"Oh really? I didn't know there was a Mt. Hermon in the Bible."

"Do you have a Bible?" asked Dahlia.

"Yeah, I have a New Testament back home and our family has a large Family Bible on the coffee table."

"You don't have a Bible with you here in Hawaii?" queried Jackie.

"Nah. I only came with my duffle bag…not enough room for books."

Things got quiet after that. We arrived at the church at 9:00 a.m., which is a little earlier than I remember going when I was younger. Jack parked in the rear and we got out of the car. Before I hardly got out of the car, a number of youth were greeting me and hugging me. Again, this was unlike anything I recalled occurring at my previous church experiences. I was taught that you went to church for a serious meeting with God. Church was the only place where I had to control my dry humor.

The dress code of the youth was extremely different also. Some of the girls wore shorts and 'flip-flop' sandals. One guy had sandals, jeans, and a tank top for a shirt. Most clothing was very flowery and bright.

"Have fun, John, and we'll see you in church later on," said Dahlia. At that point, the Miller family left me with all these happy young people. They took me to a classroom, where two college-aged women were leading. One had a guitar. I remembered them from the previous day, as they were a part of the singing service on the beach. We—they—sang some songs, and then had a Bible lesson. It was cool.

The church seated about 500 people. There was no air conditioning, but both sides of the sanctuary had clear-glass Venetian-styled windows that were twisted open for a constant breeze, called the Trade Winds. There were no screens, so an occasional bee or a bird flew into the area. The wind, however, usually kept flying intruders from entering in.

Wayne Meeds was at the piano playing some type of jazz music. Actually, it was jazzy hymn music, but I didn't know that at the time. A choir came in as I made my way to sit by Jack. Sherrie and Jackie were seated with him, but no Dahlia. Then I saw her in the choir. The momentum of the service picked up a bit when the choir entered, and Wayne was leading the song service from the piano. This reminded me a little of Randy Holley's church, a Pentecostal church in Dry Fork. But this was a Baptist church, only jazzy.

"We'll be 'on air' in a moment," stated Jackie.

"What does that mean?" I asked.

She pointed to the wall behind us. I looked and observed a sign stating, 'on air,' methodically flashing on and off. Then it stopped flashing and remained lit.

"Now we're 'on air,' said Jackie.

"Okay, so what does that mean?"

"Just listen to Brother Bill."

At that moment the pastor, Bill Smith, welcomed everyone to the morning worship service. Plus he welcomed those who were joining our service, on the air, over KAIM radio. At that point, Jackie punched my ribs and smiled.

I looked at her momentarily and stated, "We don't have radio in Danville, yet."

She looked at me with a shocked and serious face. "Really?"

I looked back. "No, but I just wanted to trick you." She poked me again.

The singing was very upbeat, very contemporary.

The pastor preached for about 30 minutes, and then offered an invitation to make a decision while a song was being sung. I remembered this portion of the hour as very similar to my early days at Mt. Hermon Baptist Church. During the invitation, I noticed the 'on air' light had turned off. Great! I was getting hungry.

Some youth had walked to the front to speak with the pastor. When the song was ended, Brother Bill had us sit down. Next thing I heard was for all visitors to please stand and tell everyone where they were from. Jackie punched me again.

"No," I said.

"Yes," she responded.

"I don't want to; this is my first time here."

"That's why they call you a 'visitor'."

I didn't stand. As each visitor introduced themselves, a beaded lei was placed over their neck by a member of the opposite sex with a kiss on the cheek and an 'Aloha' greeting. About fifteen visitors stood. The Sunday School teachers from my class were passing out the leis, but I still was not ready to be singled out. One of the youth who had gone to Brother Bill during the invitation, whispered in his ear.

"Welcome, guests, to our services," said Bill. "God bless you for coming. I've been informed that a Johnnie Jones from Virginia is with us also. Where are you, Johnnie?"

I looked at Jackie as she gave me an *"It's not my fault!"* return look. *"Well,"* I thought. *"At least I'll get a kiss from one of those pretty teachers."* But that wasn't about to happen either. As I stood, one of the youth from Bill's side came running down the aisle with a lei. She wasn't ugly or anything, but let's just say she wasn't my type. After the kiss, Jackie snickered.

The service ended, but we still did not leave immediately. Again, all this joy and fun surrounding the church was unlike anything I had ever experienced in Virginia. Jack was talking to a few young people while Dahlia disappeared with the choir. Young people were introducing themselves to me, left and right. I smiled courteously.

The service ended around 12:15 p.m. We finally got into the car about 12:45 p.m.

"Well, did you like church?" asked Dahlia.

"Well, it was okay," I responded. "A little long for me to be in church clothes."

"Church clothes? What's that?" asked Jackie.

"You know, the kind that's tighter than your regular clothes."

"Why don't you buy some looser ones?"

"Because you're supposed to be uptight at church."

Jack and Dahlia laughed, as Sherry remained quiet, and Jackie continued to evaluate whether I was telling the truth or trying to trick her again.

Jack dropped me off by the dorm and waited while I went upstairs to change clothes and to get my laundry. I managed to get a draw or two off a cigarette before going back to the car.

"You smoke," announced Jackie.

"No I don't."

"Yes you do; I can smell it on you."

"Jackie, hush," said Dahlia.

Jack knew that I smoked, so I knew I had to come clean with my lie. "What if I do smoke? You want a draw off my cig?"

"No way! Those things are nasty."

"Well good. I guess that means you won't be stealing any of my cigarettes."

"John, do you know that you double the risk of cancer when you smoke?" asked Sherry. She was the serious one. I could get a laugh out of Jackie easily, but with Sherry, a slight smile was about the best I could muster.

"What's cancer?" I responded.

Sherry smiled while Jackie, once again, fell into my trick and began telling me about cancer.

At the Miller's home, I enjoyed a great meal and had plenty of help washing clothes. Jack had a volleyball net strung between two palm trees in his back yard, so we played a while. It was a fun afternoon. About 5:00 p.m., Dahlia made another announcement.

"Girls, it's time to get ready for church. Come in and clean up before we leave."

Church, again? Now this was a strange thing indeed. We had just left that place about 4 hours ago.

"John, would you like to go with me and the girls? Jack's not going."

"Oh no, I couldn't go again. I, I have to straighten my room and fold my laundry. Maybe next time."

"Okay." With that, she turned away and went back inside the house. Then she reappeared with all my clothes, folded military style, and placed them into the trunk.

"We can drop you off at the dorm while leaving."

I jumped into the back seat and off we went.

The week began with a different attitude from me. I was returning to my previous funny and confident self again. Jack was his usual self as well. It was Fidoe and Howard that kept trying to pick my brain.

"Jonesie, Fidoe and I are going to do some serious grilling this Saturday," said Howard. "I'll pick you up at the dorm around 9:00."

"Sure; sounds great!" That was Howard's way of inviting folks to be with him. He was a good man and was always trying to help the underdog. Every time I rode with him, he would announce a new military law or procedure and then drill me on whether I understood and practiced it.

That Saturday was quite different from the last. Fidoe, Howard, and I sat around the open grill and drank beer while trying to solve all the problems of the military life. Betty stayed inside with the baby. Fidoe cursed about everything. Howard always countered with the positive side. Sometimes I thought, perhaps, they would become angry at each other and fight. But Howard knew how to divert the subject to a different point. He was also about twice the size of Fidoe.

"So why didn't you get married?" Howard asked.

"It wasn't going to work out. She cheated on me while I was down here."

"Maybe, she wasn't ready to travel 5,000 miles from home."

"Maybe; but she could have just said so."

"I bet she was under a lot of pressure at school and just needed a shoulder to lean on."

Once again, Howard was defending the underdog.

"She did more than just leaning on a shoulder, Howard. Plus she lied about it."

"Didn't I hear you say you lied to her about being drafted?"

"That's different."

"How's that? A lie is a lie."

"What am I supposed to do? Just let bygones be bygones? How could I trust her?"

"Trust takes time, Jonesie. If you had responded to her with a possible second chance, you probably would have married a woman who would follow you anywhere."

I paused briefly to absorb that counter-thought.

"Well, it's too late now. I broke it off, and off for good."

Howard laughed. "Jonesie, you've got a lot to learn about real love. She'll be writing you soon." With that, we went on to other subjects.

Howard dropped me off at the dorm around midnight. There was a note for me on the message board from Jack. He would drive by the dorm in the morning, same time, if I wanted to go to church again. *"Oh boy,"* I thought. *"Not again."*

I headed down to the recreation room and shot some pool with a few of the guys. One particular guy was very muscular and had tattoos all up and down his arms. He was a Buck Sergeant (three stripes); Frank was his name. Airman Day was there also. Somehow or another, we three decided to go to Honolulu tomorrow. Frank had a car and wanted to show us where he got his tattoos.

I went to my room about 1:30 a.m. and lay down in my bed to think over the day and how different Hawaii was from Virginia. The next thing I remember, my roommates were bursting into the room, screaming and laughing.

"Hey, guys; it's late and I'm trying to get some sleep."

"You [bleep] right, it's late; and if you don't hurry, you're going to miss lunch at the mess hall."

I was silent for a moment before his statement registered. "Lunch?" I rose up and looked at my watch. 12:15 p.m. Oh [bleep]! Well, that's okay; I had missed the Miller's and I was sure Frank and day hadn't made an early appearance as well.

It was around 2:00 p.m. when the three of us gathered and headed off for Honolulu. Frank was a talker and was curly-haired robust type of guy. He wore a tank top that clearly outlined his mountain-range looking chest. He had additional tattoos on his chest and back.

"Some of these tattoos would not be allowed on me if I got caught on base without a shirt on," he said.

He and Day chattered a lot while I sat and listened, observing the scenery. It wasn't long before I began to recognize the area: Hotel Street!

"Hey, my roommates warned me about coming into this area."

"Some of it is harmless, but you're with me...you'll be okay." We stopped on a side street and Frank led the way, passing by numerous apartment-looking entryways with interesting looking men and women standing up against a wall or sitting on small chairs. We finally stopped at a small entryway; it was a small room with three walls full of tattoo patterns. The man behind the counter recognized Frank.

"Aloha, my friend. Have you returned for that special engraving for the thighs?"

"Nah," said Frank. "I still need some time to think on that one." Then he pointed to Day and me. "But these young men need something manly, don't you think?"

He smiled as he seemed to scan over Day's and my body. "Oh I think something small on the upper arm would be a great start. And your name is?"

"Jones, Johnnie Jones."

"Yes, Sergeant Jones. Please have a seat right over here and I will show you a typical size for a small arm tattoo."

I stared at the tattoo engraver as he motioned for me to take a chair. Frank wanted to "introduce" Day and me to the world of body art. Both he and the engraver were standing before me covered with sculptures of women, insignias, dragons, and snakes, proving that one's body can survive the multiple stitching of a dye-cast needle. I hesitated.

"Look here at this baby," said Frank, while rolling up his left sleeve, flexing his bicep. He revealed a beautiful sculpture of Diamond Head Crater, located just a mile or two from where we stood. I'm thinking, *"Here I am at a tattoo parlor on Hotel Street in Honolulu, Hawaii, a street with numerous "off limits" facilities for military personnel, and I'm about to get a permanent tattoo?"*

"Jonesie, the women love this one," said Frank, as he showed off his eagle and flag insignia on his other arm.

"Do you have one with a heart that says 'Mother' on it?" I asked, remembering my dad's tattoo. Frank rolled his eyes.

"Oh that's an old one," the engraver responded. "I haven't done that in a long time. Let me look in my art books and see. While I'm looking, perhaps you guys would like to watch a movie?" With that question, he immediately stepped over to a curtained entryway and revealed a small theater as the back portion of his parlor, seating for about twenty-five or so. A few heads were silhouetted in the seats. From a distance I could see an adult movie projected onto a screen.

"I think we'll pass on that for now," said Frank. "I've got bigger plans for us tonight!"

"Bigger plans?" I thought. *"Surely with none of these creatures on Hotel Street!"*

"Yeah, I'm not ready for a tattoo decision at this time."

"Me too!" stated Day, in his Filipino dialect.

Frank looked at us in disgust. "Fellows, if you're going to be men in the military, you've got to start handling yourselves as men."

"I was wanting something less painful," said Day. "Like a movie!"

"Yeah," I quipped in. "Don't they have regular theaters down here?"

Frank looked at his watch. "I think if we hurry, there's a live show just up ahead around the corner. They always have something good."

Day and I had to step up the pace as Frank moved in large strides down the street. We arrived at a restaurant-looking facility with a large overhang over the sidewalk. There were two lines formed at a ticket booth. Frank looked relieved as he saw the lines.

Oh good; this means the show hasn't started. I looked at Day and he shrugged his shoulders, as if to say, *"This looks safe, don't you think, Jonesie?"*

I responded with a *"Yeah, this'll be okay"* nod.

Frank bought our tickets and we paid him. "Just follow me guys; I know where the best seats are." We sat near an aisle at a table. I waitress came by and took our drink orders. When she left, I looked at my ticket stub to discover the name of the place: "The Forbidden City." I recalled seeing this name before. I leaned over to Frank.

"Isn't this an "off limits" restaurant?"

He smiled. "You look civilian enough. Don't worry about it. Just enjoy your drinks and the show."

I looked at Day. He seemed to be okay. So we sat back, with Frank, and watched one of the most interesting "live" adult shows imaginable. After that, I reminded myself that I was no longer in Virginia and that I had to be more responsible with who made my decisions for me.

A 50/50 Chance at Religion #3

I had Monday off, so I just hung out at the base. For lunch, I walked over to the concession stand in front of the exchange. I was thinking and walking, when I noticed a red-haired guy ahead, walking slowly with a base map.

"What'cha looking for?" I asked.

"Oh, the base exchange. I'm here on TDY and can't seem to figure east from west."

"Follow me; that's where I'm headed. I'm Johnnie Jones."

"Hi, I'm David Hiler."

"Where's home, David?"

"Ohio."

"Another Ohian? Man, it seems every time I turn around there's another person from Ohio. What's going on in that state?"

He grinned. "We prefer to call ourselves, 'Buckeyes.' And there's really nothing wrong with Ohio, just a lot of folks live there."

"Tell me; my whole basic training flight was from Youngstown and, now, I have a friend here with a family from Ohio."

"You know how to keep good company then."

"I guess you're right. Listen, before you go inside, I'm hungry; so if you want to remain my 'good company,' how about I buy you lunch and a beer?"

"Lunch is fine, but I'll have a Coke instead."

"That's fine with me."

I ordered the island-famous teriyaki burger with fries. David and I sat awhile, talking about the military. Then he shifted the conversation.

"What do you know about Jesus Christ?"

"What do you mean?" I asked, thinking I deserved this since I missed church yesterday.

"Have you ever asked Jesus Christ to come into your life to become your personal Savior?"

"I'm a Baptist; does that count?"

"Well, being a Baptist is okay for a religious connection to a church; but I'm asking you if you have ever received Christ into your life?"

"I don't know what you're talking about."

From that point, David explained the difference between being a Baptist and having a personal relationship with Jesus. Although he had no Bible, he was able to quote Scripture from memory like I'd never heard before. He was very convincing, but I wasn't ready for his "invitation."

"You know you can receive Christ right here and right now, if you mean it from your heart," he said.

"I need some time to think about it."

"I understand. It is the most important decision you'll ever make."

"I thought that was when I told my girlfriend to go fly a kite." I was trying to lighten up the conversation, but it didn't work.

"Listen, I want to give you this small booklet. Read it this afternoon and then meet me at the mess hall for supper, my treat," he said, smiling.

"Yeah, you know my meals are free there. Okay."

I headed back to the dorm thinking about the religious side of life. I had a great respect for Jesus Christ and considered myself a good Christian. I didn't hurt people and I worked hard on my job. Plus, I was recognized as an outstanding airman. What else could Jesus want from me?

The small booklet given me by David spoke of a personal relationship with Christ. It was that 'personal relationship' thing that I did not understand. What does it mean to get personal with Jesus? Do I talk to Him more often? Do I go to church twice on Sundays? The booklet mentioned at its end that to receive Jesus, you should pray a prayer asking Him to come into your life. After I locked my room door, I got on my knees and started to pray. I remember praying something like this: *"God, I'm not sure what this booklet or what David means. If I'm not a real Christian, please help me to know that. Amen."*

While walking to the mess hall, I wondered if David would find the place. At a distance, however, I saw his glowing red hair at a bench out in front. When he saw me, he stood up and grinned.

"Man, I need sunglasses just to see you," I said.

"Yeah, red hair and sunshine makes me glow on the outside, but Jesus makes me glow on the inside. Speaking of Him, did you read the tract?"

"Tract?"

"Yeah, the small booklet I gave you; it's called a tract."

"Yeah, I read it and got on my knees and prayed."

"So did you ask Jesus to come into your life?"

"Yep; sure did," I replied (but I lied).

"Praise the Lord!" he shouted. "Do you know the angels in heaven are rejoicing over your decision right now?"

"Really? I don't hear anything."

"Oh, but the Bible says that they did the moment you asked Christ into your life."

"Oh boy," I thought. *"I'm not only a liar, but now I have a bunch of angels upset with me."* This really disturbed me, but David was so happy that I dared not tell him that I was lying to him. I continued to act out the lie.

"How come you know so much about the Bible?"

He pulled out a 5x7 envelope and began revealing its contents.

"I have some Bible study materials that I want to leave with you. They are written for new believers from an organization called the Navigators. If you will read and study their material, it will get you started in your Christian walk. I will also contact them to see if they have a group of Navigators here on base. Usually every base has a group of Navigators that meet for Bible study. Let me have your dorm address and your mailing address."

I obliged to his every request, but deep inside I wanted to leave him. We ate supper together, and then parted ways. His plane was leaving early the next day for Guam. From there, he would have a short return layover, and then fly back to the mainland. I returned to my dorm and put the envelope in my locker. Out of sight, out of mind.

Tuesday was different. My feelings were out of balance. I couldn't shake what seemed like a dark cloud hovering over me wherever I went. Jack was cordial in his greeting.

"Hello, Johnnie. Missed you Sunday."

"Yeah, sorry. I didn't get back from Fidoe's until about midnight; then shot some pool. I fell asleep before I set my alarm. Man, I even missed lunch at the mess hall."

"Oh really? You also missed Pat Boone at church."

"Pat Boone? Isn't he a singer on the radio?"

"Yeah, but he's also a Christian. He and his daughter, Debbie, sang a special. It was good."

"Maybe next week?"

"Sure. Dolly (that's Jack's name for his wife) said to invite you over for supper this week. Any night better than the other?"

"Oh I don't know. How about Wednesday?"

"Well, she goes to church on Wednesdays. How about tonight?"

"Tonight? Sure. Sounds fine to me."

Jack was a nice man and he was very dedicated to his job. He was very meticulous about everything he did and touched. He kept a small writing pad in his shirt pocket and would take notes on just about everything he did. But Jack wasn't like David or Dahlia. Religion had its place, but he didn't seem dominated by it like they were. I began to admire Jack's dedication to his work and hoped I would become as conscientious about my work on airplanes.

Later, I received a letter from Dana. In it, she apologized for doing me wrong and hoped I would forgive her. Normally, I would write to her immediately; but I was headed for the Miller's that night, so I threw her letter into my locker. Maybe I would write to her later on.

The Millers were a happy family and I enjoyed their company. For several weeks, I was invited more and more to their house for meals. Finally Dahlia explained the reason for the increased invitations.

"John, Jack and I know how hard it is for you to be so far away from home, so we want you to feel welcome to come over here anytime, any day. You can come unannounced and if it's mealtime, you can eat what we eat."

"Did you say, 'every day'? I asked with a smile.

"Sure; and bring your laundry. You can wash your clothes over here. I also have an ironing board and Jack has a shoe polish box."

"Does this mean I have a big brother?" asked Jackie.

"Sure," I responded. "But I'm no pushover." With that statement I gave her a headlock and scrubbed the top of her head with my knuckles.

"Ouch! Quit it, Johnnie!"

I decided to go back to church the following Sunday with the Millers. As expected, everyone greeted me with a huge smile and stated how glad they were to see me again. After Sunday School, Carol and Trisha, the two ladies who led my class, approached me and invited me to join them and some others for a lunch after church.

"Thanks, but I'd better stay with the Millers. I'm their guest."

"Oh I wouldn't be surprised to see them at this gathering also," said Trisha.

Before church started, I found Jack at his usual pew spot.

"Hey Jack, Carol and Trisha invited us to join them for lunch at the Yum Yum Tree restaurant."

"Oh yeah? Let's see if Dolly has a lunch started at home."

The service ended with Brother Bill extending an 'invitation' to come to Jesus. I was beginning to feel better at the church, except an inner urge to deal with my previous lie to David Hiler kept creeping in my consciousness. But no one had any knowledge of it or of David.

Dahlia had no plans for lunch, so about twenty of us headed down 21st Street to the Yum Yum Tree. They had awesome burgers and fries, but their specialty was their pies. They lived up to their name: yum-yum! A favorite seemed to be hot apple pie with a slice of melted cheese on top. It sounded a bit strange, but it was delicious.

Monday in the shop, I received a phone call.

"Johnnie," said Jack. "You have a call on the Ops line from a Sergeant Hiler."

"Ops line? What's that?"

"He must be on an airplane or flight line vehicle. It's a two-way radiophone. You can take it at Sgt. Hollingsworth's desk."

David was on his airplane. It was being refueled and he wasn't allowed to leave.

"Listen, brother, I just wanted to say that I've been praying for you and trust you are growing in the Lord."

"Well I've been to church a lot."

"Yeah, you told me that before you were saved. Johnnie, church is a great place to learn about Jesus and Christianity, but you will not grow in your relationship with Jesus until you make it a daily priority to talk to Him and let His word talk to you."

"Every day? I'm not sure what to say every day. Doesn't He remember what I said yesterday?"

David laughed. "Yes, just like your girlfriend."

"Oh, okay; now I get it."

"Listen, I've got to go, but I'll be in touch. See ya, brother."

"You bet, brother. Bye."

I hung up the phone. Jack was in the next room, but the Ops line required I speak up and speak plainly.

"So, do you have a stepbrother?"

"Oh, no, that was a friend I met here a few weeks ago. He's on TDY and is headed back for the mainline."

"So why did you call him 'brother'?"

"You know, he's a Christian and I think he calls all Christians that same name."

"So you are a Christian?"

Jack's question weighed in heavy. Would I lie to Jack like I did to David?

"I don't know, Jack. I mean, I think so. I'm a member of a Baptist church back in Virginia, but this David guy wouldn't get off my back about having a personal relationship with Jesus and saying some prayer from a booklet."

"Some people are very fanatical about Christianity. I believe there's a place for recognizing God, but I don't think He intended to control our every move."

"Yeah that's how I've always believed it. I believe in Jesus and the Bible, but I don't think He wants me to forget about everything else that life has to offer. God made the world and I'm going to enjoy it."

Jack nodded his head in approval and we went about our business. I don't recall having another discussion with Jack about religion. But it was a different story with Dahlia.

"John, would you like to sing in the church choir?" asked Dahlia.

"Me? I don't think I can even spell the word: k-u-a-i-r, choir." When it came to religion, Dahlia was not easily distracted.

"We practice on Wednesdays after Bill gives a Bible study. Why don't you give it a try?"

Singing Flashback: 1961

Singing...I remember my first ever solo was when I was in the fifth grade, trying to impress Mandy. I was hanging out with a friend in the sixth grade, Steve Lynch. Steve sang a lot of spiritual songs in our class during the opening class devotional. Mrs. Mitchell always praised him for his great voice. I wanted that praise as well, especially in front of Mandy. I announced to Mrs. Mitchell that I wanted to sing the next morning.

"What? Oh Johnnie, dear boy, I didn't know you could sing. That will be so special. Tell me, what will you sing?"

"Oh, it'll be a song I learned in Sunday School."

The problem was that I didn't learn any songs in Sunday School. As soon as I got home that day, I ran up to Ronnie's house.

"Ronnie! You gotta help me sing a song!"

He laughed. "You've never heard me sing, Johnnie, and that's the way it'll always be."

"But you go to church all the time. Surely you know something."

"Well, I've heard some Negroes down at the revival tent sing a little chorus. It goes something like this: 'Not my brother nor my sister, but it's me, oh Lord, standing in the need of prayer. Not the preacher nor the deacon, but it's me, oh Lord, standing in the need of prayer. It's me, it's me, oh Lord, standing in the need of prayer; it's me, it's me, oh Lord, standing in the need of prayer.' Try that one, and you can add anybody's name as you go along."

With a little tone help from my brother, Gary, I practiced all evening. The next morning, I was as nervous as a long-tail cat in a room full of rocking chairs. To everyone's shock, Mrs. Mitchell announced I was singing this morning. I stood up and walked forward, tripping on a desk leg. There were a few snickers, but I managed to stand in front of everyone. I began the song, in tune, but it didn't take me long to get all the people in the song all mixed up.

"Not my momma, not the teacher, but it's me, oh Lord, standing in the need of prayer..."

Well, I did it. Steve and Mrs. Mitchell were proud of me, but I think that's about as far as it went. That would become the beginning and the end of my singing career in school.

Moment of Truth

I went to Wednesday night church for the first time in my life. I dressed up a bit but noticed Dahlia and the girls didn't.

"Sorry, John. It's very casual on Wednesday nights."

"That's okay. Maybe I'll meet a movie star and get asked out for a date."

The girls laughed.

Bill was a fine preacher. He seemed so connected with everyone and everything. He always dressed as if he had just left a men's store. Not only did he preach live on the radio every Sunday morning, but he also had a 30-minute television show each week, called, The Good Life. I was beginning to enjoy his lessons.

Choir was interesting. I decided to hang out with the bass section because their lines were on the bottom, which made it easier for me to follow. I think I did okay. At least I was asked to return for practice the following week.

Several weeks passed. It was now August 1971. I was singing in the choir that morning. I remember not feeling comfortable during Bill's message. It was a message about living a lie and how it would eat you up on the inside like a cancer. It reminded me of the lies of my life and how I was hiding them. At the end of the message, there was an invitation song that would allow a person to come to Bill and accept Jesus or to do some other thing or two. I recall feeling an urge to do something, but I resisted. I was a choir member now, so I couldn't go down to the front. The service ended with a few folks making some kind of "decision."

Going home, everyone seemed so talkative except Dahlia and me. Occasionally she would smile and get in the conversation, but when she looked at me, it was as if she was reading my mind. I felt that she knew every lie I had ever told. But how could she? That day was long at the Miller's. For the first time since being around them, I wanted to leave. I thought about faking an upset stomach. *"Another lie?"* I kept condemning myself with every thought. It was like my mind was under some kind of truth serum. Every bad or negative thought was being countered by a truthful thought. No, I was not going to lie.

Near evening, Dahlia told the girls to get ready for church. I had other plans.

"I think I'm staying here with Jack tonight."

"Oh really?" asked Dahlia. I was hoping you would go with us to the Yum Yum Tree after church, my treat."

I felt like I was being set up, but that offer was more than I could refuse because I loved that hot apple pie with melted cheese on top.

"Count me in!" And off we went to church.

The song service went well. I really enjoyed the contemporary songs and Meeds was a comic, like me, full of one-liners. It was relaxing.

Bill got up and preached. His message was on the uncertainty of life and how that you could not determine how long you would live. Once again, the urge came in me to do something. *"What is going on with me?"* I wondered. Bill began giving some statistical reports on how many deaths occurred each year on H-1.

"This could be your last opportunity to give your life to Christ," he said.

Once again the urge increased. I fought it though. I argued within myself: *"Yeah, it's easy for Bill to talk about the dangers of H-1 because he doesn't even have to drive on it to get home. It's guys like me and the Miller's that have to spend twenty-to-thirty minutes driving that silly road every time we come to church. He's got a lot of nerve warning us about dying on H-1 and the uncertainty of life."*

That conversation made me feel better. I successfully countered the urge to do something. The invitation was given and, although I grasped the pew back in front of me, I did not go to the front. The song ended and the service was over.

After the dismissal prayer, Bill walked to the foyer to greet folks. I hung out at the front with Dahlia and a few youth. We were laughing and joking a bit, when a loud scream rang through the auditorium. It came from the foyer. About fifty people were still in the church, so it was impossible for us to get near the foyer. Then the word began to filter back into the auditorium.

"Bill's had a heart attack," said Wayne. "Everybody, please come back to the front and let's pray for him. There's an ambulance on the way."

Bill was lying on the foyer floor with several people helping him feel as comfortable as possible. People began praying and crying at the front. I was in the second pew from the front, trying to pray as well. But here came that urge again. And this time there seemed to be a stronger voice than mine to accompany the urge.

"Johnnie, remember that excuse you used tonight to keep you from committing yourself to Me? You said Bill was not qualified to talk about the uncertainty of life. Well, not only did he tell you, but tonight he has shown you that life is indeed uncertain. You have no excuse."

"But what am I supposed to do?" I asked the voice within.

"Do just as you were told. You must ask forgiveness of your sins and you must invite Me into your life to take charge of your life."

"But how can I trust myself to believe in You?"

"You make the commitment and I'll do the rest."

"Okay. Jesus, I really, really mean this. I'm so sorry you had to hurt Bill to get my attention. I ask you to forgive me of my sins and to come into my life. Please do so and please take charge over me right now. I pray in Jesus' name, amen."

The prayers for Bill were still ongoing, but there was a peace in my heart that actually made me smile. Fortunately everyone else had their eyes closed as they were praying. We finished the prayer time after the emergency crew had left with Bill. Dahlia gathered the girls and we left for home. No Yum Yum Tree tonight. But that was the furthest thing from my mind. I had a deep, deep burden lifted off me.

We were driving down H-1 when Dahlia turned to me.

"John, I really feel led to ask you about your salvation. I've felt this all day, but after tonight, I just have to ask you if you really know that you are saved?"

"Dahlia, while the prayers were being made for Bill tonight, I asked Jesus to come into my life."

I noticed tears dropping off her cheek as she continued to drive. The girls in the back seat were delighted.

"That's wonderful, John! Oh, why didn't you say something earlier?"

"Well there was a lot going on back there and I didn't want to distract from that need."

"You know, I really felt you were going through a struggle today and I asked the Lord for strength to share Christ with you."

"You don't know the half of it. I fought the urge to go to the front during the invitation song both this morning and this evening. Oh I hope Bill survives this so that I can tell him."

"I'll try to check on him tomorrow, John. Come by the house after work."

The rest of the ride to the base was one of reflection. How many times had I wanted to make a commitment to Christ, but only pretended or made some silly excuse for not doing so? And why was Bill's life put on the line? Was it just to get my attention? Would God put someone to death just to save me? That's when I remembered the cross of Jesus. Jesus died for me, me personally. Someone has already died to save me. God put Jesus to death for my sins because my sins were against Him...wow! That's what Bill meant when he said that Jesus died in my place. I thought about this for a moment; then I thought about tonight's ordeal.

"Lord," I prayed to myself. *"I'm yours now, and I thank You for dying for me. Bill doesn't have to die for me also, does he? Please save his life so that I can tell him what happened. Amen."*

1973 A.D. – A New Creation

Monday at the shop was different. Everyone seemed to be brighter than usual. I couldn't help but smile a lot. Several guys gave me some stares. One guy, who was known for his singing in the base talent show, interrogated me.

"So what's all the smiling for, Jonesie?"

"Well, I became a real Christian last night."

"You did!?"

"Yep."

"Well I'll be [bleep]! You know, I sang 'How Great Thou Art' at the base talent show last year and came in first place."

"Really?"

"Yes sir. Those judges really like that religious stuff."

"So you're a 'real Christian'?" the other guy, Sergeant Mallory, asked me.

"What does that mean?"

"Well, I'm not sure. I became a Baptist when I was about six years old, but for weeks now I've been feeling a need to receive Jesus Christ into my life as a personal Savior in a new spiritual relationship."

The talent-show guy, Sergeant Hill, began walking away.

"Have you ever read the Bible all the way through?" he asked.

"No I haven't," I responded.

"Well don't bother, because the hero dies about two-thirds of the way through the book."

With that statement, he left the shop. Sgt. Mallory stared toward Hill's exiting door.

"Don't let him get to you, Jonesie. He may sing a spiritual song, but he's far from being spiritual. By the way, I have a niece who is flying in from the mainland for a week's stay. She's just finished high school. Would you like to come over to my place for a meal? I'd like to introduce her to you."

"Well, I really have to be in church this Sunday, because I need to announce my decision to become a Christian during that last song of the service."

"Sure. Let's plan on Saturday afternoon, say, around 5:00 p.m.?"

"Okay. That sounds good."

Jack wasn't in the shop until about mid-afternoon. He caught up with me in an inspection hangar.

"Hey Jack!"

"Hello Johnnie. How's the inspection going?"

"Fine, just some minor stuff. Did Dahlia tell you about Bill last night?"

"Yeah; I bet that was a shock. I think she said she would try to visit him today, if she could find him."

"So you haven't heard from her?"

"No, I've been in a meeting all day...management stuff. You would not believe all the reductions they're trying to do in MAC [short for: Military Airlift Command]. They're talking of merging our squadron with the 619th MASS [Military Airlift Support Squadron]."

"What does that mean, Jack?"

"Well, it usually requires some shifting of personnel when you merge two squadrons. I don't know the outcome yet—Collingsworth may know something more."

"Did Dahlia mention my commitment to Christ to you?"

"Yeah, she said you became a Christian last night." He smiled. "Congratulations."

"Thanks."

"I'm a Christian also, but I'm just not into attending church every time the doors are opened. I'm not against that, if that's how you want to spend your time, but I need some time alone—time to think through my responsibilities as a supervisor."

"Sure, Jack, I understand. Speaking of which, would you sign off my inspection completions before you go?"

At shift change, we had to stay over for a briefing from Sgt. Collingsworth. He came into the room with a few papers in his hand.

"Guys, I've been notified by the base commander that the Air Force is downsizing. I can't give you the details just yet, but plans are underway to combine the 76th Air Rescue & Recovery Squadron with the 619th Military Airlift Support Squadron. (There were a number of groans and cursing.) Most of us will remain in the merger, but some of you will be reassigned to a new squadron. As soon as I get the details, I'll pass them on to the shop supervisors and they will entertain your selection requests."

"Does that mean that some of us can leave this island?" asked Goeken.

"There may be some transfers off the island, but most will stay here. Any other questions? That'll be all; you're dismissed."

The military didn't make a lot of sense to me. It seemed that those who were committed beyond the first stint understood and accepted erratic changes all the time. I knew that Jack was a bit bothered by his earlier meeting, but I had too much of my new life on my mind to be concerned about military changes just now. As soon as I could, I hopped on my bicycle and rode over to the Miller's.

"Dahlia! Did you see him? Did you see Bill? Is he okay?"

She laughed.

"Whoa, John. Yes, he's going to be fine. He had muscle spasms around his heart. It wasn't a heart attack."

"Well that's great, isn't it?"

"Well, the doctor told him he needed to slow down a bit and rest more, but he'll be just fine."

"Did you tell him about me?"

"Yes, and he said, with some pain, 'Oh that's wonderful!' I only visited briefly because of his orders for rest."

"He's going to be fine" were the sweetest words I ever heard. My happiness from my commitment could hardly be contained. Yesterday (Sunday), August 8, 1971, I gave my life to Jesus Christ. And now, in less than twenty-four hours, it seemed as if my whole life had a new direction—a new priority. Today's military events seemed secondary to Bill's well being. Two months ago, I had signed a contract to begin journeyman certification training, by correspondence, in radio, television, and electronics with Cleveland Electronics Institute. Now, even a career in electronics seemed a distant third in my life's priorities.

The week passed fast. Overnight, it seemed as if everyone became a religious specialist, trying to tell me what to believe and what to do. Everyone, that is, except Fidoe and Howard. They just kept a distance from me and my newfound faith. Finally, Friday came.

"Don't forget our supper tomorrow, Jonesie," said Sgt. Mallory. "I'll be at your dorm at 4:30."

"Okay, I'll be ready." Really, I did not have an interest in going. Another girl in my life right now was not what I wanted.

Saturday came and so did Mallory. He was right on schedule and alone. Good.

"Mike, I appreciate your interest in me and this chance to meet your niece, but please remember that a lot is going on in my life right now. Don't be upset with me if I don't warm up to her, okay?"

"Oh Johnnie, that's no problem. I just didn't want her to feel alone, you know, three adults and one child?"

Good. I felt better knowing that he wasn't trying to be a matchmaker. The evening meal went well. Stacy, his niece, was very attractive and was excited about being in Hawaii. We four adults played Monopoly, and then Mike and his wife disappeared to put their son to bed. Stacy and I remained on the couch. She moved over into the middle to sit closer to me. I moved further into the corner. *"Oh Lord,"* I prayed. *"What am I supposed to say?"*

"Tell her about Me," was the response. And so I did. I began telling her about my commitment to Christ this past week and how much peace I sensed inside of me. The more I shared the closer I got to her. The closer I got to her, the more she began to scoot to the other side of the couch. It worked!

Soon, she excused herself and went down the hallway. A few minutes later Mike showed up.

"I'm sorry, Johnnie, but Stacy says she's not feeling well. I think she went to lie down. I'll drive you back to the dorm."

"That's okay." Actually, it was great. I got out of a situation that I did not feel comfortable in. Plus, I was pumped about tomorrow morning—Sunday!

Word traveled fast that I was a Christian. I could not make Bible study last Wednesday because Dahlia had some school responsibility with the girls. But when I arrived at church, several of the girls ran to me and gave me hugs. There was Bev Ashbaker, Lacy and Twyla Harmatsu, and Dennis and Denise Cook (twins)—all about my age.

I could not keep up with who said what, but there was an obvious juggling to sit by me. This, I was not prepared for. I wanted to see Bill, but the Harmatsu sisters were not about to let that happen. Bev and Denise sensed the overcrowding and bowed out. Lacy and Twyla were short with oriental features. Lacy was the girl that had put the lei on me at my first service. After Sunday School, she and Twyla escorted me to the main service and had me sit with them.

50/50 CHANCE TO LIVE   126

Finally, there came Bill. I wanted to approach him, but it seemed that everyone wanted to hug him. Plus, if I moved, Lacy and Twyla moved with me. I sat there and watched him pass by. He looked over, managed a wink, and then headed up to the platform. Meeds had already begun the music and the "on air" light was flashing. Jackie peered back at me from our usual spot. I rolled my eyes to both sides of me and shrugged my shoulders at her.

Bill preached a lower-keyed message, apologizing for his lack of energy, due to some new medication and doctors' orders. When invitation time came, I jumped out of the clasp of the girls and headed towards the front to grasp Bill. We hugged and we cried.

Bill Smith & me at Waialae Baptist Church

"Bill, I'm so happy I didn't kill you—I mean I'm so glad God didn't hurt you too much."

He laughed, showing some signs of weakness, but rejoicing in the moment.

"Oh Johnnie, I'd do it again, if that's what it would take to get a person saved."

Bill announced my salvation decision and everyone gave me a hearty "Amen!" After the service, nearly everyone came to me to welcome me into the Christian family. Lacy and Twyla came and stood beside me.

In the car, Jackie could hardly wait to speak to me.

"So did the claws hurt you?"

"What? Oh, you mean Lacy and Twyla. Yeah, what's with them anyhow?"

"Oh they fall in love with every new man that pays any attention to them."

"That's enough, Jackie," said Dahlia.

"Well it's true, Mom," piped in Sherry. "I can't believe how rude they are."

"They just want to be friends," replied Dahlia.

"Maybe," I responded. "One of them gave me a small piece of paper…let's see if I can find it. Yeah, here it is."

Sherry and Jackie's eyes lit up as I pulled a piece of paper out of my pocket.

"It says…"

"Yeah?" asked Jackie.

"Well it doesn't say anything. It just has two numbers on it: a 5 and a 5 ½. I think it must be their ring sizes."

Dahlia and Jack laughed as Jackie jerked the paper out of my hands.

"It's a receipt," Jackie said. "There are no ring sizes on there."

Jackie and I started pushing each other in the back seat.

"Will you guys knock it off!?" screamed Sherry.

Fortunately for me, Lacy and Twyla rarely attended the evening service. Bev and Denise came and sat by me this time. They were best friends and totally enjoyed each other's company. Dennis was also a pleasure being around. He and Denise had an older sister about my age. Bev's dad was a retired Marine. He and Bev's mother ran a small business in Honolulu. Bev was very comical. I liked her, but it wasn't easy getting a serious word out of her. She was a hard read, if you know what I mean.

Roller Coaster Christianity

My Christian life progressed with ups and downs. I was baptized at Waialae on September 5, 1971. I attended church as often as Dahlia drove and as often as my job would allow. The merge of the squadrons took place and I was put on a rotating shift, plus I had to work many Sundays. The rotating shifts meant that I would have to work the day shift for three months, and then go to evenings for three months, and then to the overnight shift for three months. It was rough on the body system, but it was typical military procedure. I purchased a small transistor radio to place in my tool bag so that I could listen to our church worship service, if the jet engines weren't fired up.

Another significant thing that occurred during this time is that I began writing to Dana. I told her that maybe I had been a little too harsh with her and that I was sorry. She wrote back that she was so sorry for doing me wrong and perhaps we could still work things out. I responded that perhaps so, but she needed to understand that I had given my life to Jesus Christ now and that He would have to play a significant part in our future relationship. She quizzed me a bit on what that meant, so I wrote to her in detail about how to have a personal relationship with Jesus.

Dana wrote one final letter to me in October. She was upset about my last detailed letter and responded that I had ruined our future plans. "I don't need a preacher for a husband and I don't plan to marry one. So long, Reverend Jones, and don't write to me ever again." I didn't and she never wrote to me again.

The USO Club Show, with Bob Hope was coming to Hawaii. Our First Shirt selected me to be a member of the host committee that would be right up in front. I sat on the front row, right in the middle, by the cue card guy. I marveled at how much Bob Hope read off these cards. I always thought he

TOP: Bob Hope, USO Tour
BOTTOM: Jim Nabors

had everything memorized. The Debonair Dancers were there. There were about twenty of them on stage. Then, there was Jim Nabors. He joked a lot, but he also sang some beautiful songs. Again, I was taken aback by his talent. All I knew of him was that he was Gomer Pyle on television.

After the show, the host committee was to go to a meeting hall to eat with the USO travelers. This was a delight, because I got to speak with Nabors and I got his autograph on my nametag. But the shocker of it all was when the Debonair Dancers began filing in with their table escorts. Right in the midst of a group of these beautiful dancers stood Bill Smith, my pastor. I couldn't believe it!

As soon as his table was seated, I walked right over to him.

"Johnnie Jones! What on earth are you doing here?"

"Me? Look at you! What are you doing here with all these girls? Does Ruth know about this?"

We both laughed.

"Oh the mayor asked that I make sure these girls were protected from you girl-starved military men."

"Oh, so that's what it is."

He introduced me to the girls. I then returned to my table to eat. The guys at my table could not believe my aggression toward the girls.

"Airman Jones, what got into you?" one of them asked. "Did you get a name? Did you get a promise for a dance?"

That hadn't occurred to me. Dance? That's what this place was set up for. After lunch, we were supposed to dance with the girls. Mind you, I was a new Christian; plus I was a lousy dancer. I had only danced once before...while sober, that is. Dana had made me dance at her best friend's birthday party in Ballou Park. And to top this off, my pastor was sitting two tables away from me.

The meal went quick. Then the music cranked up. Jim Nabors grabbed one of the girls and began dancing like there was no tomorrow. Other guys began filtering onto the dance floor seeking out dance partners. I sat in my chair for a while. I looked over at Bill and he was speaking to one of the girls seated with him. He was pointing in my direction. She came right over and looked me straight into my eyes.

"Would anyone care to dance with me?"

I looked over at Bill. He was having a blast waiting to see what I was going to do. I shook my head, no, to which she turned to the guys around me. They took her up on it and started dancing. Bill was laughing and raising his hands as if to say, "Hey, I gave you a chance of a lifetime to dance with a celebrity, and you blew it."

I can remember many incidents that involved my spiritual growth. Most were favorable, but some carried me into some deep soul searching for the truth of a "personal relationship" with Christ. Allow me to share some of the favorable moments.

Tom See was a deacon at Waialae and became my Sunday School teacher. Also, I was placed on the Sunday School teachers roll as a substitute for the elementary-aged boys classes. Dennis Cook was the regular teacher. Dennis had joined the Army Reserves, so once a month he would be gone. My first call to teach 4th grade boys came. Pastor Bill's twin sons were in this class, but I didn't know that at the time.

The Bible lesson was on Daniel and the lion's den. I studied the lesson from Thursday to Saturday. I felt I was ready to describe the whole incident and to teach about trust and faith in God. When I arrived in the classroom on Sunday, I began to observe that the boys who were there had these new miniature cars, called Hot Wheels. They had taken several chairs with desks attached and had created a ramp. There was also a board with racing lanes marked down it. Each lane had a car with a string running through the base of the car to keep it on track and in the correct lane. Each lane had a boy's name at the beginning and was marked according to the number of Sundays in a quarter. A quarter-mile racetrack, I thought. How clever.

Finally, it was time to start the class. I introduced myself as their substitute teacher.

"We know who you are," said one of the twins. "You're the new guy that all the girls like."

I couldn't deny that, but I wanted to get into the lesson.

"Okay boys, our Bible lesson is on Daniel and the lion's den. Do any of you know where that story is found?" Wrong question.

"Sure," said the other twin (I think it was the other one). At that prompting, the boys began to tell me more about Daniel and the lion's den than I was prepared to teach. I mean, in five minutes, they explained more about Daniel than I knew. They also began telling me the names of the mean people who put Daniel in the den, and they told me the names of at least four lions. I didn't know the lions had names. [They actually didn't, but I was still wet behind the ears in my Bible knowledge.]

"What else are you going to teach us?" asked one of the twins.

"Well, I don't know; let me think."

I tried to think of another Bible story that related to Daniel, but nothing clicked.

"Have you ever heard of Ronnie Sox?"

"No," they responded."

"Well, back in Rockingham, North Carolina, there is a quarter-mile drag strip—just like your board here—that people come from all areas just to drag race with Ronnie. But Ronnie was unbeatable!"

"Really?"

Now I had all their attention.

"Yep, and I got to meet Ronnie one Sunday afternoon. And you know what I found out about Ronnie? He practiced and practiced racing his car so much that you couldn't even hear the gears change when he shifted. And after every practice run, he would pull his Plymouth Hemi right over to a shade tree, raise the hood, and replace the spark plugs. He pitched those hot plugs to the crowd and I got one of them."

"Wow! You really got to go see drag racing on a Sunday?"

That day, the boys' 4th grade Sunday School class was late dismissing as we raced each boys car down the desk track. I'm not sure the story had a biblical lesson, but Dennis saw me that evening at church and commented how much the boys enjoyed me teaching.

I left Dennis's comment alone, but I knew that I needed some serious training in Bible knowledge. It was this acknowledgement that drove into studying the Bible systematically. I also found that radio station, KAIM, had a number of Bible teaching shows throughout the day. I listened to many programs each week, soaking in every word like water on a dry sponge.

Jack was reassigned on base to another squadron. He struggled with the leadership at his new post, but managed to improve the performance of his new shop. He also attracted other young airmen who also seemed to find their way to the Miller's house and eventually to church. I eventually ditched my bicycle for a motorcycle. After forty-five days of dangerous maneuvers around moving vehicles, I sold my motorcycle and bought a '65 Ford Fairlane. It had a leaking master brake cylinder, but I knew that if I pumped the brakes it would stop.

Bev and her family lived atop a high slope behind Diamond Head Crater. Its winding road was a joy to drive. It also had a street that went straight down the slope, stopping at every intersection of the winding road. One day, I was helping Bev do some painting at her house. She mentioned going somewhere to get us some lunch.

"Take my car, it's already out on the street."

"Are you sure? I'm just going down to the bottom of the hill to get some sandwich fixings."

"Yeah, take it. But the brakes are weak, so pump them and they'll build up."

She left in my car. About thirty minutes later, she returned, visibly shaken.

"What's wrong?"

"Your car! I nearly wrecked it! The brakes wouldn't stop at the stop sign. I ran through two stop signs before I could stop the thing, using the emergency brakes."

"I told you to pump the brakes."

"I did, but it didn't work!"

"You have to keep pumping them rapidly and they will build up."

"You didn't say anything about pumping them rapidly."

I found out then that non-mechanically inclined people needed more specific instructions on how to stop a car, should the master cylinder be weak. Bev thought she was about to die going straight down the slope. I apologized when I saw she had been crying.

Bev and I began dating. It was one of those "on-and-off" types of relationship. I liked her and she liked me, but our personalities were too much alike. She joked and clowned a lot and so did I. She was a bit passive, but I was probably more passive. That really frustrated her.

But my spiritual growth was running smoothly. Within a year I began substituting, not only for Dennis, but also for the single men's class—my class! Our teacher, Tom See, was in the National Guard. He asked me to fill in for him as well. I obliged, but teaching my peers was more difficult. I studied more and more. I visited a Baptist Book Store in Honolulu where I purchased a series of books on the history of the Bible. Each book offered me credit toward some type of Bible reading certificate. After about six months of periodic teaching, Tom came to me.

"Johnnie, I hear good reports of your teaching. The guys really like your style. I will be gone for about a month, so I want you to take over my class permanently."

"But Tom, this is your class. I'll give it back when you return."

"No, Johnnie; I sense God is using you in there. The attendance has grown since you started teaching regularly."

"Well that's because I'm filling up my car with airmen."

"It doesn't matter. What matters is that you allow God to use you in teaching His Word. Now I've already informed Brother Al about the change." Al Chong was the Minister of Education.

That was the beginning of my weekly Sunday morning teaching; then came the Sunday evening 'Training Union' hour with the teenagers. Wayne Meeds was in charge of that. I came in early one night to find him writing a list of personal sins he had committed recently.

"What are you doing, Wayne?"

"I have to write out every sin I've done so that I don't forget to confess any of them."

"What? Wayne, you don't have to do that. Look at this verse, First John 1:9. What does it say?"

"Well, 'If we confess our sins, He is faithful and just to forgive us our sins and to cleanse us from all unrighteousness.'"

"Okay, doesn't that last phrase pick up any stray sins out there?"

"Well, maybe."

"No 'maybe' about it, Wayne."

"You know, I've never seen it that way…wow!"

By this time, about six youth had arrived and were gathered around us.

"Really, Johnnie, does that verse say that?" asked a youth.

"Why don't we all sit down and read that verse in its context."

From that Sunday on, Wayne asked me to come in and teach the youth Training Union. So, in about a year-and-a-half's time, I was teaching two classes at church, singing in the choir, and leading in a beach evangelism strategy on Waikiki Beach. Plus, Jack was always instigating a volleyball game or two after Sunday evening church.

Al Chong came to me one day and handed me a church key.

"Johnnie, I'm tired of seeing you here, sitting on the curb, waiting to get into the building. If you beat me to it, unlock the main doors."

"Oh, okay; thank you, Al. You bet! And I'll be careful who comes in."

Downstairs, there was a ping-pong table. I bought some paddles and balls and started to challenge the youth to meet me early for a little ping-pong. I had played ping-pong at Lackland and thought I was pretty good. But these Hawaiians were ping-pong players. Most all of them held their paddle downward, with the handle part sticking up through their hand. I'd never seen ping-pong played with such fury.

Once I formulated a table tennis tournament—couldn't call it 'ping-pong' anymore—for the youth. Dozens of youth began showing up for the tournament. Al went out and bought several more tables. Of course, I required every entrant to attend church in order to qualify for a placement in the tournaments.

Alongside of that, I began forming volleyball tournaments. Jack basically had volleyball going, but we began to form teams for competition purposes. It wasn't long before I was appointed recreation chairman of the church. All this led to an increase in church attendance, especially on Sunday nights.

A 'Call' Into Ministry?

In the spring of '73, a man and his son joined our church. B.J. Sams was his name, and his son's name was Billy James, Jr. B.J. was a news anchorman just hired by a Honolulu television station. Although he was a few years ahead of us, we took him into our group of college/career types. B.J. was very outgoing and Billy James was always with him.

I bring B.J. into my story because he is tied to the next major event in my spiritual life. It began on Good Friday, at the base. I had been given a work order for a minor job on a C-5A. As I traveled to the aircraft, the driver and I noticed black smoke boiling up at a warehouse near the end of the Honolulu runway. About the same time, we had to pull over for our Air Force fire trucks. They were responding to the fire.

"What's going on?" I asked the driver.

"Don't know; must be a plane down or something."

Sunday was Easter Sunday. Our church participated with numerous churches in a sunrise service. It was Bill's turn to preach this year. The singing went well, but when Bill got up to preach, he was not his usual upbeat self.

"Folks, I have to tell you of a tragic event that has occurred in our fellowship this week. One of our newest members, Mister B. J. Sams, and his son, Billy James, were involved in a plane crash Friday morning. Another T.V. anchorman invited them up for a scenic flight around the island. As they took off at Honolulu airport, the engine shut down. They tried to turn the plane around immediately, but it clipped a warehouse near the end of the runway.

"B. J. and the pilot were able to get out of the burning plane, but little Billy James was pinned in the rear seat. His dad tried frantically to get him out, but the flames became too intense for the rescue. I'm sorry to have to inform you that he burned alive in this horrible, horrible accident. B.J. is in the hospital with multiple burn wounds on both hands and arms and in other areas. This morning, I'd like to ask that, instead of a traditional message, we join together to pray for B. J. and for his future."

I was stunned. I saw the plumage of that burning plane, never realizing that several of my friends were involved. That Sunday morning service was as subdued as the previous sunrise service. The message of the death, burial, and resurrection of Jesus Christ took on a personal pain for most of our congregation.

After the service, I was invited to join the Miller's at a traditional festive meal at the Murray's house on the side of Diamond Head Crater. It was always a treat to go to Timmie and Cissie's house because they loved company and loved to share their home with their church family. Their home was beautiful with a back yard that you could get lost in. It had a beautiful layout around the plants, trees, and water gardens. I always imagined this was what heaven would look like.

While everyone was still a bit subdued, most were trying to cope and enjoy the fellowship. I, however, could not shake off the events of the morning. For some reason, I had a burden inside that reminded me of the time when I was resisting the urge inside me to become a genuine Christian. While the food line assembled, I asked to be excused. As I headed for the water gardens, Cissie asked me what was wrong.

"I don't know, Cissie. My stomach is a bit unsettled at the moment. I'm going outside to sit for awhile and I'll be back."

She yielded and I walked out into the back yard alone. I sat on a bench in a secluded area and began to talk to God about today's events.

"God, why am I upset over this? What's wrong with me?"

God spoke to my heart: *"Johnnie, you know Billy James was a young boy."*

"Yeah, I know. Why did he have to die like that? I mean, God, I was just watching him shoot hoops at the church basketball game the other night."

"Was he one of mine?"

"What?"
"Was he saved?"
"I don't know. Why are you asking me?"
"Could you have asked him about being a Christian while he was still alive?"

I looked around to make sure no one was listening to me talk to God.

"Well, yes...I guess so, but was I supposed to talk to him?"
"That's not the point, Johnnie. There are hundreds and thousands of little Billy James's out there that need to hear about salvation. What I'm asking you is if you'll become a person that I can use to tell people about the good news of salvation?"

"I don't know, God. You know my passive personality; I'm not a public speaker and, if you were there, you'll remember I barely graduated from high school."

"I was there, Johnnie, and I know everything about you. What I'm asking you today is this: Will you allow Me to be used through you to tell others about Me?"

I do not remember all the conversation, only that I volleyed a few more objections as to why God couldn't possibly use me in ministry. The conversation became quiet. I thought of my last two-and-a-half years as a Christian. I thought of all the people I had begun teaching the Bible to at church. I thought of all the college kids on school break that I witnessed to on the sands of Waikiki Beach. I thought of the time I was used as a telephone counselor at the television studio after some of Bill's T.V. messages. I began to tremble.

"Oh God, I know that I cannot do anything of spiritual value to anyone else, unless you do it through me. You know who I am and you know what is in me. If you want me to become a minister, you will have to do it all. You'll have to send me back to school and pay for it, but I will do whatever you want me to do with my life. I am yours and you have changed me. I give to you all that I am."

When I said that, I felt such a swelling inside me that I thought I was going to either choke or vomit. I did neither as the welling up inside me subsided, but I did cry. I stood up, wiped my tears, and began to sing to myself a song that said, "I surrender all, all to Jesus I surrender, I surrender all." After a few moments, the burden was lifted and I got hungry. So I headed back inside to eat.

That evening at the end of the church service, I went to the front during the invitation song and told Bill of my new commitment to give my life to God in a full-time ministry. We hugged and we prayed. Bill shared with the others of my commitment to surrender to the ministry. It was Easter Sunday of 1973.

'Aloha' Also Means 'Goodbye'

My time in Hawaii was coming to an end in August. The Air Force was still trying to downsize. The First Shirt came to me with an offer.

"Johnnie, how do you like Hawaii?"

"Oh, I love it, sir!"

"You know, I've noticed that about you. You seem to be the happiest guy in the shop. Listen, what if I told you that I can get you an early out from the Air Force right here in Hawaii?"

"Really? I'm supposed to stay in until next April."

"That's what I'm saying. I can arrange for your early release right here in Hawaii, as long as you check in for a weekend stint once a month for two years, doing what you've always done."

"The reserves."

He smiled. "That's right. What do you think?"

"Let me pray about it."

"Somehow, I thought you would say that. Take a few days to think it over—I mean, pray about it—then come by my office Monday."

I was excited. Living in Hawaii was a dream in the back of my head for several years. But it was expensive to live in Hawaii. I recalled a recent letter from Jr. Gunn telling me about the gasoline crisis going on and how that regular gas was at an all time high of 89 cents a gallon. I smiled as I looked at our Hawaii prices, which currently were $1.39 a gallon. But how could I live in Hawaii? And what about my commitment to become a minister? I needed to pray, and pray I did.

Numerous things were happening in my life at this time. I was to sing a solo part in our choir's summer special this weekend. My voice apparently was improving, because after the song service, Bill came up to me and commented.

"Johnnie, that was great. I didn't realize you had such a good voice. Maybe God is going to use you as a music minister."

I smiled. "I'm not sure Bill, but I need to ask you a question: Is there a place on the island where I can get an education for the ministry?"

"No, not to my knowledge. But I know a place in South Carolina that I'd like to recommend you to. North Greenville Junior College will get you started and is a great place for your training. I went there."

"You did?" That was interesting, because my hometown, Danville, Virginia was only a few hours from Greenville.

I sat there during the fellowship thinking this in my mind. *"God, is this what I'm supposed to do?"* I had barely gotten the words out of my heart when one of our deacons approached me: Mister Burrows. Now he was a giant of a man in my opinion. He was a commercial construction boss. He had a beautiful home with an additional guesthouse adjoining it through another beautiful garden. He also had two charming daughters, a couple years younger than I.

"Johnnie, I understand you will be leaving us soon."

"Yes sir, Mister Burrows, I'm due to ship out in late August." He embraced me and spoke to me in a broken voice.

"I don't want you to leave us, Johnnie. You have been a blessing to our church and our youth program has never been better. I want to make you an offer to stay."

This was an interesting statement, since no one knew of my early-out option. He continued: "I build commercial high rises, Johnnie, and I need someone to learn the air conditioning sales trade that goes along with my construction deals. I want you to be in charge of that division and I will start you at twenty-four thousand a year, plus give you my guest house to live in until you find a suitable place to purchase."

Twenty-four thousand?! Plus a house?! I was earning about eighty-five hundred dollars in the military, plus benefits. I could not believe what I was hearing. But then I could not believe what I began saying to Mister Burrows.

"Mister Burrows, thank you for the job offer. I appreciate you and your confidence in me, but I firmly believe I heard from God that I must enter into the ministry. In order to follow my heart, I must return to the mainland and pursue an education that will allow me to serve God."

He burst into tears and embraced me again. "Do what God leads you to do; but if you have any doubts about it, please call me."

"I will." With that we embraced and then shook hands. Both daughters were standing there by his side. I turned away from what was surely a secure offer for me to live—and live well!—in Hawaii. I must admit, I thought this idea over and over for the next few months, even after I had left Hawaii.

"So what was it with Mister Burrows?" Dahlia asked while we were traveling home that Sunday evening.

"Oh, he made me a job offer in an attempt to keep me here in Hawaii."

"And?"

"I told him, no."

She smiled. "John, if God's calling you into ministry, you will become distracted by many worldly offers. Always search your heart in these matters and remember that money does not impress God." She was right, as usual.

Monday came and I finally was able to scoot over to the First Shirt's office. I told him I didn't want the early-out offer and wanted to be transferred back to the East Coast, as close to South Carolina as possible. He filled out some paper work and sent me to the base admin office.

"Sergeant Jones, you know the process," said the personnel sergeant. "Give me three location areas you want and I will put these into the computer to see if your position matches the location."

I chose Charleston AFB, SC, a base in Florida, and the East Coast region. He entered them quickly and did not allow me to review the selections. I was a bit nervous as he began the process right then and there.

"Don't I need to come back another day?"

"Nope; not anymore. We're connected directly to the main computer now. So let's just sit back a few minutes, enjoy a smoke, and your orders should print out within minutes."

I declined a cigarette as we waited. Soon the printer was reacting to a command.

"There, I bet this is your orders now."

They were. He tore the wide green and white striped paper off and began to study it.

"Did you say 'Carswell AFB' as your first choice?"

"Charleston...Charleston AFB, South Carolina."

He kept studying the printout. "Well, it says you have been reassigned to Carswell AFB."

"Carswell? Is that on the East Coast?"

"Carswell AFB is located in Fort Worth, Texas. You are instructed to report to your shop supervisor on October 1st."

"Whoa, wait a minute! I didn't request Texas; I said East Coast!"

"Sorry, but these are your new orders, Sergeant Jones."

"Can I dispute them?"

"You can, but no one's ever gotten them changed, unless you can convince a military board that this reassignment is a family hardship."

"Fort Worth, Texas? Why Lord?" I asked Him, as I left the building. *"What could possibly be in Texas for me?"* Silence from Him.

I knew no Christians in Texas, except our summer youth and music interns at the church, Jimmy and Cindy Plummer. This caused me to question my decision not to stay in Hawaii. I called Bill and set up an appointment to visit with him. Bill and I met before church on the following Wednesday evening, before church.

"Bill, I don't understand why I'm going back to Texas."

"I don't either, Johnnie, but you have to trust God in this matter. He sees the bigger picture, so trust Him."

"But I don't want to go to Texas. I don't know anyone in Texas who can help me."

"Have you spoken with Jimmy and Cindy?"

"Not yet."

"See them after church tonight; maybe they'll have something to add to this situation."

Jimmy and Cindy, a bubbly couple, were full of enthusiasm and love for God. They came to Waialae in early June and were scheduled to leave in mid-August. They had been offered our youth and music position at the church because of Wayne's departure, but they declined it because both were close to completing their degrees in colleges in Denton, Texas. Maybe they could help me.

"Carswell? Sure we know where Carswell is," said Jimmy. "It's on the west side of Fort Worth."

"But what is Fort Worth? Does it have a college for ministers?"

"Not exactly; but it does have a seminary for ministers after college," replied Cindy.

"What's a seminary?"

"Oh boy," said Jimmy. "You really do need some help. I tell you what, here's our school residence address in Denton. When you head for Fort Worth, drive over to Denton first and stay the night with us. Our pastor near Denton is resigning and transferring to another church somewhere in Fort Worth. We'll get in touch with him and see if he can help you."

Time was running out for me in Hawaii. I had to sell a car, eat a dozen meals with church friends, and prepare for my transfer. Bev and I were trying to figure if we were serious about each other. We met one day at her house.

"I want to take you somewhere special," she said. So we drove through some residential areas on the Leeward side of Diamond Head. We finally ended on a dead end road, full of houses near the beach.

"Come with me." She took me by the hand as we walked through a narrow path between two houses. We came out onto a beautiful portion of the beach. There were rock formations coming out of the water and a coral reef about fifty yards out where the waves crashed onto. As we walked further, I noticed the rocks were getting closer to land. At one spot, the rocks came all the way in to the sand on the beach. It was a narrow trail that led all the way out to the coral reef.

"Follow me." So I did, and we carefully walked out to the coral reef, with Diamond Head jutting out into the crystal blue Hawaiian shoreline as a backdrop.

"I've never shown this place to anyone else," said Bev. "When I need to get alone for answers, I always come here. It's like me and God all alone."

"It's beautiful, Bev; but what does this mean?" She turned to face me.

"Johnnie, I feel called of God to stay in Hawaii. All the years I've been here, God has spoken to me right here. I don't think I could ever leave this place. The man I marry will have to agree to stay here and live here."

"I understand. I know we have expressed our love for each other, but you know that I must go back to school on the mainland if I am to become a minister."

"I know that, but I had to try and make you understand why I cannot go. This is my place; this is my home." With that statement, she turned away from me and faced the waves breaking on the reef. I stood there for a moment, turned, and then walked back to the shoreline alone.

After about thirty minutes, Bev came back to the shore and we returned to her house. She was crying when I dropped her off at the house. We hugged and kissed, and then she walked away. I knew that I had to leave, but breaking off my close relationships were heart wrenching. It has never been in my nature to disappoint people, so this was killing me.

My next difficulty would be in leaving the Millers. They had become family to me for nearly three years. They had helped me through several sprained ankles and numerous relationships at the church. Dahlia was like a spiritual mom to me. She challenged me to study God's Word and to seek Him thoroughly in all decisions. Jack taught me to remain focused on my work, to do my best, and to uphold the truth in all situations. The girls and I loved each other as brother and sisters.

I was scheduled to leave from Honolulu International Airport about mid-morning on a Tuesday. The Millers were to drive me over to the airport. I said my goodbyes at church on Sunday night, so I was expecting just the Millers at the airport.

Me, Dahlia, Sheryl, & Jackie

The girls sewed a couple of flower leis for me to wear on my departure. As we neared the departing gate, however, I began to see some familiar faces. There were about twenty church friends waiting for me, including Bill.

"You didn't think you were going to get away without some noise, did you?" he asked.

That's when everyone began placing leis around my neck, kissing my cheek, and saying, "Aloha." I was deeply moved by the attention. People were crying and hugging me. My neck could hardly move with all the leis on it. Bill gave a brief speech and then we all held hands in prayer. The whole gate personnel began applauding. I looked at the Millers and then I looked at them all.

Bill & me with Jack in the background

"I love you all. You have shown me a life I never knew could exist. I never knew Jesus Christ could make such a difference in bonding strangers together in like-minded faith. I will miss you all."

The hugging began again as the plane was loading. I was the last to get on. A gate attendant wrestled me away from everyone. I heard shouts of

"Aloha" until I was practically on board the airplane. The attendant came to my seat with two trashcan liners.

"Sergeant Jones, I've never seen so many leis on one neck. Let's put them in these bags and store them until you get to your destination."

The leis made the plane smell like Hawaii and no one complained. In fact, these flower necklaces ended up hanging all around my dad's rock shop in Virginia during my entire leave time. Hawaii had almost captured my heart and my life. It was only my love for Jesus Christ and to discover His will for my life that was stronger.

Danville, Virginia

TOP: My dad and his dad, Willie A. Jones;
BOTTOM: Our family with Joe's two boys, Chris & Eric, August, 1973.

My mom, dad, sister, and brother moved into a basement house on Highway 58, west of Danville. My buddy, Ricky Payne, married and needed his dad's rent house, the house we had lived in. Dad had always wanted a rock shop, so he developed a partnership with a Mr. Ed Bryant and converted a former restaurant/beer joint into a nice shop. It had a large kitchen with a bar. Dad and Mr. Bryant set up numerous tables with all types of odds and ends, as well as Dad's prized rocks—gem stones were their proper names now. My family lived in the basement of the shop.

When they first opened the shop, several salesmen stopped to see if anyone was cooking lunch for business. So my mom began cooking for a number of folks at lunchtime. Neither my dad nor mom had retail business experience, so they did not make any profit off their sales. Both had quit working at the cotton mill due to health reasons.

My sister, Sandra, was dating Donnie Taylor at the time. My brother, Ricky, was in high school. I had nothing much to do for thirty days. I wasn't interested in seeing Dana; and my friend, Larry, was now married to Kathy. He was working for the Goodyear plant in Danville.

I decided to drive around and visit some of my old work places. I stopped by J. C. Penney's; the Auto Center had some new personnel, but Randy and Ronnie were still salesmen there. My boss, Fred, had left, as well as Shorty. Penney's was getting out of the gasoline business, so Shorty hired on at another gasoline station on South Main.

I found Junior Gunn working at Danville's Oldsmobile dealership as a mechanic. He helped me purchase a '67 Cutlass Supreme. Other than being a 4-door, it was a nice ride. It would be my vehicle in which to travel to Texas.

I ventured over to visit Mrs. Monk one day. She had her new baby girl now, named Moriah. She was cute and seemed to keep Mrs. Monk occupied. Dana was at work at the time I visited. I didn't seem to fit anywhere anymore, so I hung out at the rock shop with my family.

One project I tackled was to paint over Dad's hand-written sign out front by Highway 58. I measured my lines and used masking tape to stencil his lettering: Wallace's Rock Shop. It looked so much better.

One day, while hanging out at Penney's, Ronnie asked to speak to me in private.

"Johnnie, I'm having problems with my wife. Could you come over to the house, Saturday, to talk?" I could tell he was visibly shaken.

"Sure, Ronnie. I'll be there around ten."

When I first started to work at Penney's, Ronnie was the coolest guy there. He had a sharp-looking Mustang, with all the latest gadgets. He was smart as a whip when it came to automobiles, and helped me purchase the best eight-track player for my '64 Fairlane.

Saturday came. Ronnie was home, waiting for me. We had our usual exchange of greetings and then he got right down to business.

"Johnnie, things have really changed in my life since you left. You know I was a hell-raiser and was in charge of my life. Well, I gave my life to Christ, just like you have, and started going to church regularly. At first, Joann was really excited about the change. Just recently, the church asked me to consider becoming a deacon."

"Really? You, a deacon?" We laughed together momentarily.

"I know you can hardly believe it, but it's true. I told Joann, thinking she would be delighted. But she didn't like the idea. She felt church was beginning to crowd her out of my life. I disagree, but now, lately, she has been staying out at nights with some of her girlfriends."

Tears began to form in his eyes. "Johnnie, six months ago, I would have kicked her [bleep] out the front door if she had stayed out all night without me. But now it's different. I don't want to lose her. We have a son and I love them both."

"Why is she reacting like this?"

"To be honest, I don't blame her," he responded. "I treated her like dirt for so many years. I controlled her every move. Now it's payback time."

"Well, Ronnie, I know what you are going through. You remember Dana, the gal I was talking about marrying?"

"Yeah, she was a beaut."

"Yeah, well when I got saved, everything turned around for us. She didn't want to marry a preacher."

"So what happened?"

"We split. She's out there somewhere and I'm sitting here with you." We chuckled a bit. "Ronnie, if your commitment to Christ is real, you just need to back off the deacon thing and concentrate on your wife and child. She needs to see that she is more important to you than any church position. God established the home before He established the church. You just focus on praying for your family and doing everything you can to get her on the same page with you."

We prayed together and I left. Ronnie's situation made me realize how different Christ changes a life. I marveled at my own new role among those who knew me.

The time came for me to focus my attention toward Fort Worth, Texas. Junior put my Olds through a diagnostic test to ensure its performance.

"Johnnie, this thing will cruise at 80, easily, so watch yourself. Make sure you go by and see Dad before leaving. He talks about you all the time."

"You bet. Thanks, Junior, and I'll see you in the spring, when I get out."

"When's that?"

"April 7th, 1974!"

At Gunn's West Main Shell

"What are you planning to do then?"

"My pastor wants me to attend a junior college in South Carolina. I'm going to look into it in a month or so. I'm going to pursue a ministry."

"A preacher?"

"I don't know, Junior. I may just teach or sing. I'm not sure I can speak in front of folks."

"You just turn that part over to the Lord, Johnnie. He'll give you words to say."

I was reluctant to agree. "Turning it over to the Lord" was still a new thing for me. For now, I just wanted to start preparing for an education in ministry.

Carswell AFB, Fort Worth, Texas

It was now mid-September, 1973. My bags were packed and I said my goodbyes. My mom cautioned me about taking it easy and to get out and walk around the car about every hour. I recorded my mileage and headed out of town. I traveled to Nashville the first day. The next day, I made it to Texarkana, Texas around 4:00 p.m. According to my records, I had driven exactly 1,200 miles when I crossed the Texas state line. I smiled as I realized what a difference a few years had made in my life.

My map informed me that to get to Denton, I had to go east on US 380 in Greenville. Once past Greenville, the highway became a two-laner. As I approached vehicles ahead of me, most of them would scoot over onto the paved shoulder. I wasn't sure what this meant, so I would slow down. Finally, several of the shouldered vehicles would motion for me to pass them. I obliged, passing them slowly. I had seen several signs that said to "drive friendly," so I figured that was why folks moved over.

I arrived in Denton near dusk. I pulled out Jimmy and Cindy's instructions for finding their apartment. When I arrived, there was a note on their screen door with my name on it. "Johnnie," it read. "We have moved out in the country. Go west on 380 out of Denton and..." The instructions were pretty thorough, so I was out on a gravel road in no time, heading for Ponder, Texas. One thing peculiar to the drive was the numerous tarantulas that crept slowly across the road ahead of me. I couldn't tell if I were hitting them or if they were jumping on my rear bumper, planning for a takeover down the road a bit. I finally arrived at an old farmhouse.

"Hello Johnnie!" said Cindy, as she ran out the door to hug me. Jim followed with a big grin.

"So you found us," he said. "How was the trip?"

"Long but great! Just glad to see a familiar face way out here in Texas."

We settled down around the kitchen table to get caught up on all the happenings. They were house-sitting for a man they knew who was out traveling around the world for at least a school semester. We talked about school, Hawaii, and our mutual friends. I retired early because of the traveling.

The next morning, when I awoke, Cindy had left for school. Jim decided to stay with me for the day. We talked about everything. Finally, it was lunchtime. Jim wanted to take me into Denton for some Mexican food. I was wondering why he wanted to eat somewhere so fancy for lunch. But the "fancy" description changed when he turned into a business strip center along the road. The placed looked like a made over laundry mat.

"This is a restaurant?"

"Oh yeah! They serve the best Mexican food in town, and it's cheap."

"Oh, okay. Sorry Jim, we have no Mexican restaurants in Virginia and the La Poloma was the only Mexican restaurant I knew of in Honolulu."

"Well you're in Texas now. There's a Mexican restaurant on every street corner down here."

A bowl of Mexican chips and sauce were placed on our table as we prepared to order. Jim helped me order and encouraged me to eat the chips.

"Shouldn't we wait and eat the chips with our meal?"

"Oh no, Johnnie. You just keep eating them and they'll keep bringing them out."

"Doesn't that cost more?"

"Nope. The chips come with the meal, no charge."

"Wow; so this is Texas. Things are bigger in Texas."

Jim polished off two bowls of chips while I sort of nibbled on them. When the enchiladas were served, there were beans and rice as well as chili smothered over the enchiladas. I could only eat half of what was poured into my plate. We finally left.

"Whew, Jim, that was a lot of food for two-fifty."

"Yeah, that's why I go there. Now for supper…"

"Don't even bring it up," I interrupted him.

"Tonight's going to be a Hawaiian luau at the Linam's ranch."

"What?"

"Yep. You'll love it. Ron and Georgia Linam are close friends of Bill Smith. Ron's a dentist in Dallas, but lives just down the road from our farmhouse. When I told him you were coming in this week, he said to call him and they would host us for a Hawaiian meal."

The Linam's were close friends of Bill. Their ranch house even had a special bedroom designed for Bill. They had a tennis court and a nice pool with a cooking area. The Linam's would become instrumental in my college decision later on.

The Plummer's former pastor was David George. He pastored First Baptist Church of Krum, just north of Ponder. David was now the pastor of Tarrant Road Baptist Church on East Berry Street in Fort Worth. He would be the person for me to visit with when I got settled in at Carswell Air Force Base.

My entry into Carswell was uneventful. I presented my papers and was assigned a dorm room. I arrived at my shop the next day, which was October 1st, 1973. The electrical shop supervisor, Master Sergeant Ramsey, studied my orders.

"So, Sergeant Jones, your papers indicate you were trained on C-130s. Is that all you worked on?"

"No sir. I also repaired C-141s, C-5As, the Super Jolly Green Giant Helicopters, and assisted on a few fighters."

"No C-135s or B-52 bombers?"

"No sir, not a one." He threw my orders down on the desk, swearing.

"Why in [bleep] would they send you here for six remaining months when I have to have someone sit with you on every repair? Our systems are totally foreign to everything you've ever worked on."

"I'm sorry, sir. I questioned the transfer but was told I could not challenge them unless I could prove this would be a family hardship."

"Well I can't use you until you've been qualified for KC-135s and B-52 bombers. This is a SAC (Strategic Air Command) base. Those idiots in admin should have known you would be useless to me here for six months. Go back to your dorm and report back to me at 1400 hours. I'm going to make a few phone calls."

Well, so much for a first impression. I walked back to my dorm. The game room had about eight men there, shooting pool. Some were drinking from a wine bottle. Wine, beer, and cigarettes seemed to be the military thing to do when you're off duty. I went to my room and lay there on my bed, thinking.

At 1300 hours (1:00 p.m.) I went to the mess hall, and arrived at my shop at 1400 hours. Sergeant Ramsey was there, along with three additional sergeants. I stood near the area so that he might see me.

"Come here, Sergeant Jones. This is Sergeant Thompson, from QC (Quality Control), Sergeant Baker, and Sergeant Adams, both electrical shift supervisors. We've been trying to figure how in [bleep] to use you. Sergeant Thompson says you cannot perform any maintenance without supervision, but I think we're going to get a special release from headquarters to allow you to work by yourself as long as someone else signs off on your work orders. If this is approved, you'll have some semblance of a job to perform here and might actually be of some help. In the meantime, I want you to stay in the shop, on day shift, and find something to do. Look around; you may see an area that needs cleaning or straightening up. Just stay busy."

"Yes sir."

I found a supply closet, with all sorts of cleaning materials, and began straightening it up. After that, it was sweeping, mopping, and buffing the floors.

To start, I had Saturdays and Sundays off. This would allow me the opportunity to try and find Tarrant Road Baptist Church. Originally, my plan was to find the closest Baptist church to the base, but now I had a reason to search for David George. To my dismay, however, Tarrant Road was on the east side of Fort Worth. So much for "close." I purchased a city map and headed for the church early Sunday morning. I wanted to get there before 9:00 a.m., just in case they started as early as Waialae. They didn't.

When I arrived, there were no cars in the parking lot. I got out and examined the area. The church was located in an older part of Fort Worth on East Berry Street. Although the church complex was large, it looked to have been built many years ago.

As I was walking on the backside, a man came from a house on the west side of the complex. He headed in my direction.

"May I help you?" he asked.

"Oh, no, I'm just waiting for the church to open."

"Well come with me. I'm David George, the pastor here."

"Hi; my name is Johnnie Jones. Jimmy and Cindy Plummer sent me here."

"Well I'll be. Really? How are they doing?"

"Fine. They're staying in a farmhouse out near the Linam's."

"So, are you a student from North Texas State?"

"No, I was just recently stationed at the Carswell Air Force Base. I met Jimmy and Cindy this summer at our church in Hawaii. They suggested I come visit your church first. So here I am."

David had me tag along with him as we unlocked several doors. Jimmy and Cindy had been his music leaders at Krum and the Linam's were members there as well. David had met Bill Smith once, but was not well acquainted with him. David was a student at Southwestern Baptist Theological Seminary. He was married to Brenda and they had a little daughter. David was tall and slender and looked more like a college basketball player than a pastor.

The folks at Tarrant Road were real down-to-earth people. They showed great enthusiasm for the Lord and for their church. David's preaching was not as structured as Bill's, but was very thorough in its content. Bill used planned illustrations, whereas David's illustrations seemed to be randomly selected and spontaneous. I liked David's style. It only took a few weeks for me to join Tarrant Road.

The College and Career class seemed to be very active. I was immediately drawn to the piano player who was a single woman my age. Her mother was the church secretary and was very nice to me. There was another guy in my class, Bobby, who was the church's part time custodian. He had been previously messed up with drugs, but was going through an extensive rehab program. You could tell by his speech that the drugs had an effect on his mind. I remember one night at church when he played a guitar and sang, "Why Me, Lord?" It was a real touching and emotional testimony.

I believe it may have been the next week that I had a weekday off from duty. So I drove over to the church, planning to visit the secretary and perhaps David. As I was approaching the church, however, there were cars all around the buildings and a couple of funeral cars. I drove on past and turned around. Coming by again, I noticed several of the college/career girls go into the church. I was tempted to stop, but was not properly dressed. So I headed back for my dorm.

Sunday came and I made my way back to church. I was informed then that Bobby had taken his life this week and it was his funeral that I happened upon. I was saddened by the loss. Trey George, David's younger brother, apologized to me for not calling me.

"Man, Johnnie, I'm so sorry you didn't know about it. I tried to call everyone in our class, but just forgot you."

"Don't worry about it, Trey. I understand. You can't remember everyone."

The reason for Bobby's death was a bit sketchy, so I went over to visit the church secretary later that week. When I saw her, she had a black eye and a few bruises. It turns out that Bobby had come into the church for cleanup, locked the door behind him and tried to rape her. She was telling me this.

"He had me pinned to the floor, Johnnie. I just kept telling him no and kept asking Jesus to make him stop. Suddenly he did and bolted out the door. I called David and he ran over. Then we called the police. I couldn't tell which way he left, but within a few minutes the police received a call about a suicide at the corner pawnshop. Johnnie, he went straight down there, purchased a pistol, went out back, and shot himself in the head."

I couldn't believe something like this could happen in a church. I guess my country-raising naivety was trying to adjust to the city world. Bad things do indeed happen to good people.

I met with David a few days later. We talked about a number of things. One thing was an offer for me to become the part-time custodian. My military experience made me a pro at cleaning things. I accepted the offer and began immediately.

College in Texas?

Another thing we discussed was my college education. I had told David that I was planning to return to Virginia to attend the college Bill recommended in South Carolina.

"Have you considered a college here in Texas?" he asked.

"No. I don't know a single college to check on in Texas."

"Well, I received a letter from a student scout from Dallas Baptist College asking me for some recommendations. Would you be interested?"

"I don't know, David. I just don't have any connections down here."

"Let me call Ron Linam. I think he's still on the Board of Directors at DBC."

Ron Linam? Now that was an interesting connection. David called him while I was in his office. Everything sounded good as I listened in on the conversation. David hung up the phone.

"Ron wants you to go to the president's office at DBC as soon as possible. He's calling him right now."

It was my day off, so I headed east to Dallas Baptist College. Fortunately, DBC is on the southwest side of Dallas, so it wasn't that long of a drive over there. The college set atop a large hillside overlooking Mountain Creek Lake. I was impressed with its beautiful location. I drove atop the hill and parked my car. After several enquiries, I found the president's office. A secretary was in the first office.

"May I help you?" she asked.

"Hi. My name is Johnnie Jones. Ron Linam sent me here to visit with the president."

"Yes, Doctor Briggs is expecting you. Please have a seat."

She disappeared for only a moment, returning behind the president.

"Mister Jones, thank you for coming so quickly. I'm Doctor Briggs, please step into my office."

I obliged.

"Johnnie, I'm authorized to offer you a ministerial discount of $27 dollars per semester hour and it'll be locked in at that rate for as long as you remain a fulltime student without missing a regular semester. Also, as a recommendation from a board member, I'll give you an additional $200 dollar grant per consecutive semester."

"But I'm not sure this is where I should attend."

"Oh you'll love this place. We have the finest Bible teachers in the State of Texas. Let me call one of our student representatives over to show you the campus."

With that statement, he sat down and called. A few minutes later a man showed up in the office. Doctor Briggs introduced me.

"Andy, this is Johnnie Jones, a prospective ministerial student. Please show him around the campus and then take him over to registrar for all the paper work necessary for him to start in the spring semester. Johnnie, Thanks for coming. Andy will get you started and if you have any questions whatsoever, be sure to call me first." He shook my hand and we departed.

"Wow!" I replied as we left the building.

"Yeah, he's really excited about you coming here," replied Andy. "Tell me a little about yourself, Johnnie."

I gave him a brief of how I arrived at the college.

"So have you taken any college preadmission tests—SAT or ACT?"

"No. What are they for?"

He then began to inform me about college entrance exams.

"Let me check to see if there are any exams being given this Saturday." We went to his office. After a few checks through several stacks of paper, he pulled one out."

"They're giving the test this Saturday at TCJC, South Campus. Can you attend?"

"What's TCJC?"

"Tarrant County Junior College. It's right off the south loop around Fort Worth."

"I'll have to get permission to change days off, but it should be no problem."

"Okay, here's the paper work you'll need to fill out. Since the time is so short, I'll have to call and pull a few strings to get you in, but it should work. Call me Friday to confirm."

"But I'm not supposed to get out of the military until April."

"April? Goodness! I'll need to get a letter signed for you to get an early out."

"My First Shirt in Hawaii mentioned that."

"Yeah, it's a nationwide military reduction going on. Colleges have been notified of early options offered."

I couldn't believe all this was happening—and happening so quickly! Andy put together a few pieces of paper and then sent me over to the financial aids office. It was there I was getting a little concerned. I had no money and my checkbook was in Fort Worth.

A Mister Luceney was "interrogating" me.

"Mister Jones, Here are the financials for entering our college. A minimum of 12 semester hours is considered fulltime. At the rate of $27, that'll be $324, plus entrance fees equal approximately $450. You should also qualify for the G.I. Bill and you have a $200 grant per semester. Do you have any other hardships or disabilities?"

"Not to my knowledge, except my cut hand."

"A cut hand? Let me see that." I showed him my six-inch scar. "Wow! Did you try to kill yourself?"

I laughed as I described my watermelon incident. Mr. Luceney was listening with one ear and running his fingers through a Rolodex at the same time. He picked up the phone to make a call.

"Hello, this is Larry Luceney, from the Dallas Baptist College. I have a student with a slight handicap that I need to have evaluated for a state rehabilitation scholarship. Okay. Okay. Let me ask. Can you go to a doctor's office around four today?"

"I guess. Where?" He waved at me.

"Yes, he'll be there at 4:15. Thank you. Okay, you live in Fort Worth, right?"

"Right."

"There's a Doctor Rylie on South James Street. Here's the address and he's expecting you at 4:15. If approved, you may qualify for up to half of your tuition for two to four years. Johnnie, if I calculated this right, you'll be getting paid by the college to attend. Congratulations!"

I managed a smile, but all this information was mind-boggling. I wasn't even sure I wanted to go to DBC. I left the campus around 3 p.m. and headed back for Fort Worth. I used my local map to find the doctor's office. I was a bit early, but there wasn't enough time to go back to Carswell. The doctor evaluated my hand. He was impressed with the story and seemed to enjoy the confused nerve endings in my fingers.

"I'm going to recommend you to the rehab board for scholarship, but they may require a second opinion. Good luck."

"Thanks, Doc."

The next day was Wednesday. It was still October of 1973. I spoke with my supervisor about Saturday's schedule change.

"It should be no problem, Jones. I'll expect you in for swings that day, understood?"

"Thanks. I'll check in as soon as possible."

As soon as I could, I ran over to the admin's office to turn in my early-out request for college. The sergeant looked at the papers and shook his head.

"This request is too late for a January early-out, Sergeant Jones. When did you say your classes started?"

"January 7th, sir."

"I don't know. I'll submit them, but don't make any financial commitments until you hear back from me."

"Sir, I understand that you can now get immediate responses through the computer."

"Jones, who told you that? That's classified information."

"Oh, no sir. It's been downgraded now. That's what they told me in Hawaii."

"Hawaii? You came from Hawaii?"

"Yes sir."

"I've always wanted to be stationed there. How'd you like it over there?"

"Great. It was an awesome three years."

"Man, some guys get all the luck. Let's see how your luck holds. Stay here while I check on this computer stuff."

Decisions, decisions, decisions. I was making decisions in this two-day period that would shape my entire future. I couldn't help but feel a bit uneasy, but I prayed to myself for God to please don't let me do the wrong thing. The sergeant returned after about ten minutes.

"Well, Sergeant Jones, congratulations, you have been approved for an early release date of January 7th, 1974."

"But I need a few days to move and…"

"Wait a minute, I haven't finished. You have accumulated twenty-nine days of leave time and twenty days for not being sick. This means you have forty-nine days to play with."

"Wow, that means I could be out in a couple weeks?"

"Well, maybe. But may I suggest you allow a bunch to be given you as a part of your exit pay?"

"Really, I can do that?"

"Yep, any and all of it. Give it some thought and return in a few days with a release date and a destination address. I need those two bits of information."

My mind began churning. I needed money for rent and I know my custodian job will not be enough to get me started. I decided to work through Christmas and finish my active duty on January 6th. That would give me about thirty-five days of extra pay which would allow me enough money to put down as a deposit on an apartment or something. The next day, I informed my supervisor.

"What?! Early out? January 7th? [Bleep], Jones, you just got here!"

"Blame it on the military, sir. They're trying to downsize, you know."

"Yeah, yeah, yeah. Don't remind me. So let's look at your schedule. I want you to work through the holidays so the other guys can at least have some time off with their families. You'll be on call both weekends. Any questions?"

"No sir."

"Okay. Now catch the next truck out and help the electricians on plane 641. It's past due for a takeoff."

Now I was pumped. I couldn't believe I was actually that short of time as a regular. I went out to the truck pick-up area. About six men were there waiting. I began joking about me being the "shortest." I turned around about the same time a colonel walked by us. Quickly, I greeted him with a salute. The rest of the guys turned away as if they didn't see him. It was unusual to have commissioned officers walking in this area. He continued walking toward the parking lot. Some of the guys began laughing about my response, but it was the right thing to do. About that time, a truck horn tooted. The truck was parked about thirty yards away, opposite the direction of the colonel's destination. The driver motioned for me to come to the truck. I thought it was my shuttle out to the flight line.

"Sergeant Jones, did you see that commissioned officer walk past you?" said the driver, a Tech Sergeant.

"Yes sir, and I saluted him as soon as I recognized him."

"Your job, Sergeant Jones, is to call all those guys to attention, then salute him. It's military protocol for the ranking officer to call all the rest of a group to attention when a commissioned officer enters an area. If you ignore your duties again, I'll report you to your ranking supervisor. Do you understand?"

"Yes sir," I said, as I snapped to attention.

The sergeant studied me for a moment then told me to go on about my business. I walked away, wondering why the sergeant did that. I guess this wasn't going to be a good day for any of us, because while I was preoccupied with my early release, I wasn't aware of a potential crisis halfway around the world that would affect me after supper.

After supper, I walked back to my dorm and lay my head down on my pillow to spend a few moments working through all the things I would have to do in the month to prepare me for dismissal from the air force. I barely got horizontal when there were shouts coming from down the hallway.

"All personnel report back to duty. We're under a red alert. All personnel report back to duty. We're under red alert."

"What does 'red alert' mean?" I asked the guy in the next room.

"[Bleep] SAC's way of screwing your evening. They pull this [bleep] alert stuff all the time just to see if we're ready."

"Ready for what?"

"For deployment to some war zone or in case of an attack on our borders."

"So what do I do?"

"You'd better throw all your belongings into your duffle bag and high tail it down to your place of duty. Leave all your civies and take the rest."

Great. I just finished eight hours and now I have to go back? I reluctantly and slowly began to empty my locker, folding my fatigues and other clothing into my bag. About that time my room door swung open with a bang.

"Sergeant, I suggest you get the lead out of your [bleep] and report for duty now!"

I immediately zipped my bag and walked out of my room, acting as if the man didn't exist. He went to the next room and the next, telling everyone to get out immediately. Outside, there were red flashing lights appearing throughout the base. The whole base was under the gun. This was something I had never experienced before. As I was walking along the sidewalk, a truck pulled up beside me.

"Where are you headed, sergeant?"

"Electrical shop, sir."

"Jump in."

At the shop, everyone was checking in with their supervisors, so I found mine.

"Sergeant Jones, welcome back."

"What's going on?"

"Find you a spot against the wall over there. We'll be briefed in a few minutes."

About thirty minutes later, our squadron supervisor showed up with a captain.

"ATTENTION!"

"At ease men," replied the captain. "Men, I regret to inform you that the President has put the U.S. military on 'ready alert' due to some Russian troop movement into Egypt. If this Russian buildup continues, you will be deployed over to Turkey for an indeterminate amount of time, and from there you may be shipped to other areas as needed. All our bombers and tankers are being prepared for immediate departure. This is what you are trained for, so let's do our duty. That is all."

I couldn't believe what I was hearing. Russians? Egypt? Turkey? Apparently the skirmish between the Israelis and Egyptians was escalating. But surely they won't send me; I'm too short.

"Sergeant Rawlings, sir?"

"Yes, what is it, Jones?"

"You know I'm getting out pretty soon, so they won't send me will they?"

"You are the property of the United States Air Force. You will do what they tell you and you will go where they send you. Is that understood?"

"Yes, sir," I said as I turned away. Once again, I wondered how anyone could stay in the military as a volunteer. Your whole life had to be under the whims of the military. I went to the wall and joined all the other complainers. We began to lie out on the floor, some starting card games, while others (like me) pulled their caps down over their faces for a nap. I tossed and turned on the concrete floor for hours. About midnight, my name was called. Immediately I jumped, thinking I could go back to the dorm.

"Jones, head out to bomber row. The electrician needs your help."

With the assignment on a different type work order, I headed downstairs. A truck was waiting for me.

"Sergeant Jones, you have your military I.D.?"

"Yes sir."

"Good. You're going to need it for this job."

As we headed out onto the flight line, there were military police everywhere. All the planes were sectioned off with an armed guard standing in front of each. When I arrived at my plane, I had to immediately show my i.d. Then I was allowed onto the plane. The crew chief met me at the front steps.

"Where is the electrician?" I screamed over the rotating engines.

"Follow the fuselage catwalk. You'll see him in the converter compartment on the left. And listen, be careful in there."

I had never been cautioned by a crew chief before, but as I entered the fuselage I knew why. There were four large bombs already mounted into the fuselage. The fuselage of a B-52 was narrow, but very long. The four bombs filled the entire area. *"Oh boy,"* I thought. *"One misstep and I'm history."* I literally had to crawl down the catwalk, keeping my tool pouch ahead of me. I found the electrician in the converter compartment.

"Jones, this converter blower casing is bent and won't secure itself. Help me hold it on the other side."

"Man, Q.C.'s going to love this."

"Ain't got time to order another. We'll just have to wire it shut the best we can."

B-52s were old airplanes, so it wasn't uncommon to see some bent up stuff. We tightened the casing as best as we could, then safety wired the thing so that it would not loosen in flight. We had to sign out at the plane as well, and then we headed back to the shop.

The night was long as everyone tried to get some rest. Some guys played cards. I slept on and off, thinking any moment I would be called to fly out to Turkey. This seemed so unreal.

The next thing I recall is being awakened by the early morning sunrays shining through the eastern window. Most of the guys were still laid out on the hard floor. I stood up, stretched a bit, and then walked over to a supervisor's desk.

"What do you want, Jones?"

"Sir, I'm hungry. Can I go to the mess hall?"

"We're still under red alert, Jones. Do you know what that means?"

"Yes sir. But my stomach is on 'red alert' also and I'm afraid it is going to start a war from within if I don't feed it."

He looked me over as I managed a grin and raised my eyebrows.

"Just a minute," he said as he grabbed a phone. "Mess hall, you guys open for business? Okay."

He hung up the phone. "Jones, I want you back in fifteen minutes, do you understand me?"

"Fifteen minutes? Sir, the mess hall is two blocks away. I need twenty-five."

"Twenty, and that's all. Either take it or leave it."

I bolted for the door.

"Where're you headed Jonesie?" asked a fellow electrician.

"Mess hall!"

"Mess hall? Hey wait for me!"

By the time we got to the stairway, six of us were bolting down the steps, never looking back. When we arrived at the mess hall, the workers were all seated and piddling around. Only a handful of people were eating. When they saw us, they ran to the food line as if we were the only ones they had seen for days. The workers fixed us a bodacious plate of eggs, bacon, sausage, and the famous S.O.S.

We wolfed down everything and headed for the door. As we were leaving, another group was entering. We arrived back at the shop about twenty minutes from the time of departure. The sergeant looked up at the clock as we entered. I nodded to him and he nodded back as if he were saying, "You did good, Jones."

About 9:00 a.m., our day supervisor called us all together. "Men, the alert has been cancelled. The Russians turned around their deployment. You may return to your normal schedule." With that statement, he departed.

"Okay guys, day shift will remain on duty. The rest of you may leave."

Ugh. That meant I had to stay for another shift.

AWOL...Happy Holidays?

My supervisor was not happy that I was getting an early out for college. I wanted off for Christmas and New Year's, but he wasn't budging.

"Jones, you are leaving for good on January 6th. I want you to work both holidays so others can have time off with their families."

"But can't I have some time off for my family?"

"I know your family is in Virginia, so that ain't happening."

"But I have a church family here in Fort Worth."

"That's different."

I disagreed.

"Tell you what," he continued. "I'll put you on standby for Christmas Day. You may not leave any further than fifteen minutes from the base and you must provide a telephone for wherever you go."

I accepted. Although Tarrant Road Baptist Church was a full twenty minutes drive, I didn't want to argue the point any further. On Christmas Day, I prepared for church. For dinner I was invited to eat at the Rowley's.

✦ 50/50 CHANCE TO LIVE ✦ 155

After church, I called the shop to see what was going on. It was dead, according to the man in charge. So I left church for dinner.

I had a great time and the meal was excellent. In fact, it was such a great day that I completely forgot to phone in. I remembered about mid-afternoon.

"Oops, I gotta go folks. I'm on standby today. Thanks so much for the meal. Everything was great." With that I left.

When I arrived at the dorm, there was a note on my room door. It instructed me to call the shop. I did immediately.

"This is Sergeant Jones."

"Jones, where have you been?"

"To church, sir."

"You missed a work order on a standby plane. We don't need you now, but you'll need to report to your supervisor first thing in the morning."

"Yes sir." I hung up the phone. *"Oh great,"* I thought. *"Now what?"*

I had only two weeks left of active duty and now I'm in trouble again. The night was long, but the morning found me waking up early and preparing myself for the scheduled meeting. I put on fresh fatigues and shined my shoes. As I entered the shop, the day supervisor was at his desk. I walked over to him and stood at parade rest squarely in front of his desk.

"Sir, I'm reporting as ordered."

"Jones, where were you yesterday? I thought I made myself clear to you to be on standby all day."

"Yes sir, you did. I went to church and got so caught up in the service that I forgot to call in."

"When they couldn't find you, they had to call on another guy who was to be off for Christmas. Jones, I know you are 'short' (a term for leaving soon), but you disobeyed my orders. I'm thinking of reporting you as AWOL (Absent Without Official Leave)."

"I apologize, sir. I didn't intend on being away from the phone that long. I did call once but simply forgot to check in later on. I'm not excusing myself and I did do wrong, but I ask you to please consider my four year record as being clean of misconduct."

"I don't know, Jones. You should think of others as well as yourself. You let your fellow comrades down yesterday and you should be punished for that."

"Sir, I agree and I accept the punishment you require. I only ask that you punish me by placing me on double duty or let me clean the latrines and the shop. I'll pull my normal shift and then work an additional shift for the rest of my active duty time."

He looked me over and then pulled some papers out of his top drawer. "This will be the last time I will warn you. If you do anything wrong in the next two weeks, I swear this incident will go into your permanent records."

"Yes sir. Thank you sir." I walked away carefully from him. Now I had to watch every step I took, praying that I would make it through the next two weeks without incident.

Several days later, as I was headed to a plane in the hangar for a routine inspection, a Q.C. man hollered at me.

"Sergeant Jones, from the electrical shop?"

"That's me."

"Come here for a minute, please." I obliged. He pulled out a previous work order. "Is this your signature?"

"Yes sir. During the red alert, I was called on to assist on a bomber."

"Yes, I'm aware of that. I had to write you guys up on that casing install. It was too bent to be serviceable. You guys should have R and R'd ('Remove and Replaced') the thing."

"Yes, sir. I know that. But the engines were turning and we were instructed to make ready the craft for immediate takeoff. Sir, if you noticed, we safety wired the thing securely. The whole converter and mounting carriage would have to be damaged for that thing to dislodge."

"I understand all that, but it was still repaired in violation of the proper procedure in accordance to the technical order."

"Sir, I'm sorry. The lead electrician and I made the decision to secure the casing so the aircraft could take off if needed. Sir, I have six more working days left on active duty. If you write me up on this, my record will be blemished for the rest of my career. Please, sir, please understand the situation we were placed in for that repair. There were four bombs loaded on that aircraft and the Russians were coming." I grinned at him, after that last statement.

His countenance changed and he laughed. "The Russians were coming?"

"Yep, that's what the pilot said as we departed from his craft."

"Was he made aware of your repair?"

"Yes sir. We explained the bent casing and how we had safety wired the thing. He said it sounded as if we had it secured, and we did, sir; trust me, it wasn't going to move."

"Oh I agree with that. You were a bit excessive on the safety wiring. Tell you what, Jones, I'll speak with the lead electrician and inform him to order a new casing. I'll not report you to your supervisor, since you're so 'short.'"

"Thank you, sir."

"By the way, what are you going to do when you get out?"

"I'm going to college to study for the ministry."

"A preacher?"

"Maybe. I don't know yet."

"Well, you're a good talker. I think you'll do just fine."

"Thanks." With that statement, I left him and returned to my work order. I felt as if God had intervened in that conversation, because my supervisor was looking for anything to happen that would persuade him to pull those papers out of his drawer and write me up.

I finished active duty without further incident. I had set up an agreement with my pastor, David George, to move into his parents' house in Bedford. Trey and another guy, Dickie Reed, were living in the house. There was another bedroom that I could rent. I had several weeks left before school started, so I booked a flight to Danville and back. Trey would pick me up from the airport when I returned.

The vacation was enjoyable, but my heart was turned toward getting prepared for college. I would be the first of the siblings to attempt a college degree. Joe was doing well at Dan River and Gary started working for the cotton mill as well.

In the Grips of Death #4

Although I had departed from Love Field in Dallas, my return flight sent me into the newly opened Dallas/Fort Worth International Airport. At the luggage area, I saw Trey. We loaded up and then headed for Poncho's Mexican Buffet in Richland Hills for supper. Trey was griping about his job and how they were messing with his hours. I didn't think much of it. We left the restaurant and headed over to the loop around Fort Worth. Trey headed south, merging onto the main lanes. He began speeding up and moved over to the left lane. When he did that, it seemed he was exceeding the speed limit. I thought to myself that he just needed to blow off a little steam. As we increased in speed, I noticed the cars in our lane ahead of us were coming up rather fast. *"Okay Trey,"* I thought to myself. *"It's time to let off the accelerator."* When it seemed he wasn't, I quickly looked over to him.

"Trey, slow down!"

What I saw in his face I'll never forget. His eyes were bulging and his mouth was tight and drooling. "Trey!" That very moment, he fell over into the middle of the front seat, jerking uncontrollably. I leaped over him grabbing the steering wheel. As I looked up we were about to hit the car ahead of us. I quickly jerked the car left into the median. We immediately passed the two cars in our lane in front of us. I maneuvered my leg over Trey's jerking body to apply the brakes, but his foot was wedged between the brake and the accelerator. We were probably traveling about 90 mph by now. I pushed the gearshift lever into neutral and began looking for the ignition key. It was somewhere on the dash. The engine was racing in rpm's as I finally managed to push Trey's foot from between the brake and the accelerator. I looked ahead and saw a bridge approaching as I slammed my foot onto the brake. Most of the car was in the median grass, but the right side was still on the pavement. I managed to slide the car to a stop, just a few feet from where the bridge railing began, about a hundred feet from the Trinity River bottom.

I put the car in park and turned off the engine. I got out of the car and ran around to the passenger side to help Trey. The car door was nearly in the left lane of oncoming traffic. Trey was still jerking a little but his seizure was subsiding, as I held his head on my knee. Some cars were honking their horn at us. As each passed me, I cried out for help. Finally, a convertible came by. The guys in it stopped.

"Please call for an ambulance. Something's happened to my friend."

"We'll go right up to the next exit and call for some help."

"Thanks."

Trey was now as limp as a wet noodle. Although he had some blood trickling out of his mouth, he was breathing normal. He finally opened his eyes, looked up at me, and then patted me on my head. He closed his eyes as if he was very tired. A few minutes later I heard a siren in the distance. The ambulance saw where the car was located and cordoned off the left lane. One of the EMS guys ran up to us.

"What's the problem here?"

"I don't know. He just started jerking and fell over into my lap."

"Was he driving?"

"Yes sir."

"[Bleep]!"

The other EMS came up. "What's his name?"

"Trey George."

"Hey, I know this guy. He has epileptic seizures."

"What's that?" I asked.

"You didn't know that he has seizures?"

"Nope."

"Trey! Hey, wake up man!" said one the guys. "Trey, you okay?" He opened up his eyes and spoke softly.

"Yeah, I'm okay. Where are we?"

"Out in the middle of the [bleep] freeway man," said the EMS. "You want us to take you in?"

Trey was not responding very well. He mumbled something.

"He's going to be out of it for a while. You want us to take him in?" They both looked at me.

"Hey, I don't have the slightest idea what he needs," I responded.

"Okay, let's take him to the emergency room. You can ride in the back with him."

"But what about the car?"

"Will it run?"

"Let me try." I started the engine and it fired right up. "Yeah, it's okay."

"Okay, do you know where the hospital is located?"

"No, I sure don't. I'm sort of new in town."

"Okay, just follow us."

They put Trey on a stretcher and placed him in the back of the ambulance. As they pulled forward I got in right behind them. We began to head southbound, signaling to get into the right lane. As Trey's car began to increase in speed, it started shaking as if it had a flat tire. I managed to stay with the ambulance, but the car was getting more and more difficult to steer. It also began to overheat.

The EMS exited at the next highway. I followed, seeing a gasoline station up ahead. I began to give them my high beams, on and off. They pulled into the station as I parked the car over on the side. I hollered something to an attendant at the station as he saw me jump into the ambulance.

"Something wrong with his car?"

"Man, it was shaking like it had a flat tire, and then it started to overheat."

"The tires looked okay when you parked it."

"Yeah, I know. I don't know what's wrong with it."

We proceeded to the emergency room. When we arrived, they took Trey on back while I phoned David's house. About twenty minutes later David arrived.

"Where is he?"

"They took him on back."

David went up to the desk and then proceeded to go back. He motioned for me to follow. Trey was sitting in a chair, putting his shoes on.

"They said I could go now."

"How do you feel?" asked David.

"Like [blccp]."

The three of us began walking out.

"Where's my car?" asked Trey.

"I had to dump it at a service station on the service road near 820. It was shaking too much to drive and it began to overheat."

"[Bleep]. I just put a new set of tires on that thing last week."

"I'm taking you guys home. We'll worry about your car tomorrow. Johnnie, didn't you know about Trey's seizures?"

"Nope. This is the first time I've heard anything about it."

Trey shut his eyes as we headed for Bedford. We put Trey in bed and closed his door.

"Where did this happen, Johnnie?"

"We were getting onto the loop heading southbound just before the river bottom. I got the car over into the median before we hit anyone. We stopped near the beginning of the bridge railings."

David looked at me. "That close?"

"I don't know, David. It was dark."

"I'll take a look at it."

With that statement, David left and I went to my bedroom.

The next morning, I ate breakfast. Trey got up and asked me to take him to his car. In the daylight, everything was a lot clearer. We pulled off onto the median where his car had slid. There was a black skid mark on the shoulder. We studied the area, looking for anything that may have fallen out of or off the car. We found nothing. The median ended about a hundred feet ahead of where the car had stopped. From there it went down into the river bottom, about thirty feet or so.

"Let's go find my car."

I took him up to the next exit and to the service station. His car was where I had left it. Trey started it up and pulled it over to the island, where we refilled his radiator. The tires were inflated and looked normal.

"I'm not too far from where I got the tires. I'll have them look it over."

"Okay. I'll be at the church, cleaning it. Call me if you need me." Trey left and I followed for a while. Then I took a left and headed for the church. David was there.

"Hi David."

"Hey, guy. Come in my office for a moment. I saw the skid marks. You guys were lucky. Another hundred feet and you would have landed in the Trinity bottom."

"Yeah, I know. Trey and I just left the place."

"Where's he now?"

"He's taking his car over to where he purchased his tires to see what's making it shake."

"You probably broke a tie rod or something. I'm surprised you could even drive it."

"David, what's wrong with Trey?" David began to tell me the story of Trey jumping out of trees and off the house when he was a young boy. Sometime or another, he fell and landed on his head. From that fall, it was determined that he must have injured something inside his skull, causing the seizures.

"He's not supposed to be driving at all. He's okay unless he gets upset or agitated about something. He's got medicine to take, but it makes him sluggish, so he doesn't take it. Johnnie, if you hadn't been there, he would probably be dead today."

I did my cleaning chores at the church and went home. Trey was there.

"Hey, Trey. How're you feeling?"

"Better. Say, if this ever happens again, you don't need to take me to the hospital. Just let me rest for a while and I'll be all right."

"Sure, you bet."

"Also, please don't ever try to put anything in my mouth. I won't swallow my tongue like everyone thinks."

"Sorry, Trey, I don't know what you're talking about."

"Oh, people think when someone has a seizure, they will swallow their tongue and choke on it. It's not true."

"Well you did have blood trickling out of your mouth."

"Yeah, I bit the edge of my lip."

"And your car?"

"Yeah. When you slid to a stop, you made a flat spot on both right tires. The bottom radiator pipe was loose also, causing the leak."

"I'm sorry about your car. I can pay you for the tires if you like."

"Oh no; they replaced them at cost. No big deal."

Trey settled down after that and we maintained our friendship. A few days later he came back to me and apologized for his sharp response toward me. I found out later that David had chewed on Trey quite a bit for not telling me about his epilepsy.

1974 – Dallas Baptist College, Dallas, Texas

I was only days away from my first trip to Dallas Baptist College. Registration was to be my first experience of the college life. I had no idea what to expect or what to do. All I knew was the time I was to show up for registration. I had already submitted my application for the G.I. Bill. I had to send in proof of my hours. I never heard from the Texas Rehab Office concerning a scholarship.

Registration was rough. I was asked which classes I would be signing up for. I honestly did not know.

"I thought you would tell me," I responded.

The lady looked at me and at my papers. "Have you a degree plan?"

"Religion major, ma'am."

"Okay, have you any credits at all?"

"No ma'am."

"Okay, so you need to select your basic courses from this list."

I did as instructed. I signed up for English, Math, Speech, an Introduction of the New Testament, and a History course, fifteen hours total. I was also informed about the chapel requirement each semester.

"Go to the financial aids office for payment of your classes," said the lady.

When I arrived there, I had to wait in line for about an hour. Finally it was my turn.

"Johnnie Ray Jones. Let's see what we have on you. Okay, you have the G.I. Bill, the ministerial discount, a presidential grant, and Texas Rehab scholarship. Looks like we may owe you a few dollars, Mister Jones. We'll process this and you'll get a final statement in the mail. Please make sure your address and phone number are correct."

Wow, I couldn't believe I was actually starting college. Plus, I didn't have to fork out any money I had saved up for this first day. Classes would begin the following Monday morning at 8:00 a.m. I was pumped!

Monday morning arrived with a lot of excitement. I arrived at DBC a little early. Freshmen had to park at the bottom of a large hill that led up to the main campus. My first class was Speech. I figured if I was going to preach, I had better learn how to speak better. I sat on a side row, near the back. As the other classmates began to find their way into the room, I began to notice my age difference from the others. They looked like they were just out of high school. In fact, they were! Finally, a guy my age walked in. He sat in the far back opposite corner from me. The class was nearly filled to capacity.

A Mister Jones was the professor. He came in, introduced himself, and gave out the syllabus and book requirements. After that, we were dismissed. My next class was in a large, modern learning center. I found the classroom and sat down at a round table. The guy, about my age, from Speech class also walked in. When he saw me, he smiled and walked over to me and sat down.

"I was hoping somebody my age would be in these classes. I'm Ed Ethridge."

We shook hands. "And I'm Johnnie Jones. Pleased to meet you, Ed."

"Were you in the military?" he asked.

"Does it show?"

"Well guys our age don't usually start these beginner classes unless we've been away for a while."

"Yeah, I just got out of the Air Force a couple weeks ago."

"Really? I was a crew chief for B-52 bombers. And you?"

"Aircraft electrician."

"Spark chaser!"

"You got it!"

"Did you work on B-52s?"

"Barely. I got to Carswell in October, but never was officially trained for them. Most of my days were with MAC in Hawaii."

"I was stationed at Carswell. Boy, I bet SAC really woke you up."

"Man, tell me! They were serious about the military. I got into more trouble these past three months than all my first three years put together."

Ed and I became immediate friends. We compared schedules and found we had four classes together. Ed was also a ministerial student. He had moved up from Corpus Christi, where he was working for an insurance company. He was married to Judy and had a little girl, Holly. They lived in Grand Prairie.

As the day wore on, we discovered the Student Union Building (SUB) had a snack bar with a coffee pot. This was a popular spot for eating lunch and skipping a class or two. Since I was new to this type of surrounding, I was reluctant to skip any classes. But it wasn't too many weeks before Ed had me joining him for coffee several times a day.

I commuted from Dallas to Fort Worth five days a week. I also continued to clean the church. Our church mailed out a weekly newsletter. Mrs. Rowley, the secretary, and I were talking one day about my school while she kept trying to fill in some spots on the newsletter.

"I can't think of anything else to put in this week's newsletter," she said. How about you, Johnnie? Do you want to write an article about something?"

"Well, I could say something through the eyes of maintenance. Maybe say something about the building?"

"You could, or you could write a religious article since you're studying to be in the ministry."

"What could I say?"

"I don't know, but go write me something right quick." With that statement, she handed me a blank sheet of paper and a pencil. I walked down the hallway to the custodial room and set at a desk. This began my writing "career." My articles were called, "Through the Eyes of Maintenance." They were well received by the church and everyone began to look forward to my writings.

My first semester in college was interesting, to say the least. I found out that each class syllabus contained a schedule for items due and for tests. I was used to teachers warning me of things to be done for each class, but not in college. When a paper was due, my fellow classmates turned in their papers. I walked up to the teacher at the end of the class.

"Doctor Trammell, is there something due today?" He smiled kindly.

"Oh, I'm sorry. Didn't you get a syllabus?"

"Yes, sir, but I didn't hear you say anything about the paper due."

"Well, normally, you read your syllabus and do all that it tells you to do."

"I'm sorry. This is my first semester in college and I know absolutely nothing about schedules."

"Tell you what," he said. "Turn in your paper by the end of the week and I'll only deduct five points from your grade."

When I arrived home that evening, I opened all my class syllabi's and began to chart all due dates for papers and exams. I realized then that college is nothing like high school. If I were going to pass my classes, I'd have to get busy with my course requirements.

I finally received a check from the G.I. Bill. It came to my house address. I took it to the Business Office the next day.

"I think this belongs to the college. It was mailed to me."

"Let me check your account," a lady said. "No, you're paid in full for the semester. This check is yours, plus I show that we owe you nearly two hundred dollars. It'll be mailed to your home address soon."

"Really?" I couldn't believe it. I had always been told that college was too expensive for most people to attend. You had to be very talented in order to get a scholarship or a grant for financial assistance at any college. Yet, here I was, a country boy from Virginia, attending a major college in Dallas.

I turned in my late paper to Dr. Trammell. He smiled and made a note of it being late.

"Doctor Trammell, is there someone on campus that can help me understand what courses I should take?"

"Well, you should have been assigned a counselor when you registered. What is your major?"

"Religion, sir."

"Oh, well that's one of my positions. I'm assigned a number of ministerial students each semester to help them along the way. I tell you what, can you follow me over to my office now and I'll help you find out who's your counselor."

We headed over to another building where the religion professors had their small offices. Dr. Trammell sat down, with his Dr. Pepper, and made a phone call.

"Oh I see. Thank you."

"Well, did you find out who my counselor is?"

He smiled. "Yes, it appears that I'm your counselor."

"You? I don't recall hearing of you or seeing your name on any papers."

"Well, perhaps it was overlooked. Why don't you check your schedule for tomorrow and let's try to meet and discuss your goals."

I did and we met the following day. It turned out that, as a religion major, Dr. Trammell's "Intro" class that I was taking was the only class I should not have signed up for. Religion majors were supposed to take the more advanced religion courses. It would, however, be allowed on my degree plan as an elective. I finished the semester with some Bs and Cs. That was encouraging, because I had no idea how I would do in college.

The summer also found me having to move. Dickie was having difficulty paying his part of the rent and utilities, so when Trey's job began to fluctuate, his dad decided to sell the house in Bedford. Through a church contact, I moved into a house with an elderly lady near the church. Mattie Doyle was her name. Mrs. Doyle's deceased husband's name was Johnny, so she always smiled when she called me by that name.

That summer found me working with Gunn and Briggs Construction in Fort Worth. The big boss man was a member of Tarrant Road and offered me a good salary for the college break. I was a helper for several men (a dad and his son) who installed metal studs and ceiling grids and tiles in businesses. It was a good job, except for the high walls we had to construct with sheet rock. Lifting those 4'x 8' sheets up onto a scaffold was extremely difficult. It was satisfying, however, to go to a steel frame, attached to a concrete slab, and leave it a few weeks later with walls and doors installed.

Somehow, I convinced my younger brother, Ricky, to ride a bus from Danville to Dallas and spend a week with me. We talked about going and watching the Dallas Cowboys play a preseason game. I think that was the clincher that got him to come. But when he came, I received a call from

Dahlia Miller that they were moving back from Hawaii. Jack was retiring and they planned to settle in Marion, Ohio, his hometown. Dahlia was from San Antonio though and they were there visiting her family before moving on to Ohio. I wanted to see them badly but Ricky and I would miss the Cowboys game if we drove to San Antonio.

"What do you think, Ricky?"

"Boy, I've never been to a professional football game before."

I knew he really had his heart set on going but my heart was equally set on seeing the Miller's. After talking to him about the sights in San Antonio and my only opportunity to see the Millers this year, he finally succumbed to my wishes.

We drove down early one morning and arrived at Dahlia's parents' house about 10:00 a.m., yet everyone was still in bed. I'd forgotten the Millers frequently stayed up late playing card games. It was such a delight to see them. We talked for a few hours, getting caught up with all the Hawaii news and news about my first college semester.

"Mr. Burrows found out which college you entered," said Dahlia.

"So?"

"Oh, don't be surprised to see one of his daughters attending this fall."

"Dana?"

"Yes, and he's so hopeful you will see her."

"Oh she's nice and all, but I'm not available at the moment. I've dated a couple girls this semester, one from my church and one from the college."

"John, I'm so excited for you. I just know the Lord will lead you into a great ministry, but be wise with whom you date. She also must be a woman called into ministry with you or you will regret it."

I met Dahlia's parents. They did not speak English, so Dahlia had to refresh her Spanish. After lunch, we piled into our cars and headed for the Alamo, the River Walk, the Hemisfair Plaza, and finally ended up at Breckenridge Park. Ricky seemed to enjoy himself, so it wasn't a complete wash for him. I was glad because I felt bad about his missing the football game.

We said our goodbyes and left the following day. I believe it was a Sunday because I can't remember Ricky going to church with me at Tarrant Road. He had to leave Dallas about 11:00 p.m. that night, so I gave him a brief tour of the DFW metroplex. Theresa, the girl from college I was dating, had invited us over for supper that evening. We went and enjoyed a good meal. When it came time to take Ricky back to the bus station, Theresa's dad allowed her to go with me. She knew Dallas much better than I, so I was glad to have someone with her knowledge around.

I gave Ricky ten dollars for his trip back to Virginia. Later on I discovered he had spent all his money by the time his bus arrived in Atlanta, Georgia. So when he got back to the rock shop in Danville, Mom said his first words were, "Fix me three hamburgers; I'm starving!" He survived and I think he was glad to have had the opportunity to visit Texas.

I still worked at the church as the custodian. I really enjoyed being at church nearly every day. The secretary, Mrs. Rowley, enjoyed my presence, especially after the Bobby ordeal. My weekly "Thru the Eyes of Maintenance" article was a real hit with many church members. It basically became a devotional writing. Brother David and I met occasionally and discussed the church and ministry. Tarrant Road was in a high transition area and the leaders of the church were discussing moving the church family to another location, possibly Arlington.

The fall semester (1974) was about to begin at DBC. I had a better experience signing up for classes. Ed Ethridge and I chose the same classes this time. I visited his home in Grand Prairie often, enjoying his company and Judy's fine cooking. Their daughter, Holly, was a preschooler and loved calling me a "cull" and a "mullet." I'd bounce her on my knee and play with her. Judy was also expecting another child.

Ed had been out of the military for about nine years. His story is that he knew God wanted him to become a preacher, but he ran from the "call." He had become a safety director and an insurance consultant for a company in Corpus Christi and was beginning to enjoy a successful career. But this "call" continued to gnaw at him and he finally surrendered to it. With only a prayer and a promise from God, he moved his family to Grand Prairie and enrolled at DBC. Why DBC? I think it was due to the fact that they had a reputable baseball team and Ed was interested in playing. His story is that he went to tryouts as a "walk on" and made the team. After a few practices though, he realized that he could not pursue a baseball career, go to school fulltime, hold a part-time job, and have a family life. So he dropped out of his baseball career.

My second semester included some sort of an advance English literature class. Miss Ricks was the professor. To say the least, she and the class lectures were different. She had us "traveling" into our sub-consciousness and relaxing. She also got permission for us to paint a classroom wall to express our feelings. Ed and I painted an area black with a red line running from top to bottom, and ending with a drop of blood above a cross, symbolizing a line of redemption through a darkened world.

The sub-conscious "traveling" became a regular affair in class. Ed and I both didn't like it, so he and I made occasional noises, like birds, to "help" the others travel. Miss Ricks didn't like the sound effects, but several others giggled. One such giggler was Diane Leroy. She sat ahead of us in the class. Although she never turned around, you could tell our sound effects were a pleasure to hear. I don't think she liked the travels as well.

Diane Leroy

I bring Diane Leroy into my story for an important reason. She was in my English class, my gym class, and my Greek class. Diane was a beginning freshman. Although there were girls a plenty at the college, Diane appeared different than all the rest. She had a very light complexion, didn't seem to wear makeup, and wore an occasional long gingham dress. She was always walking by herself between classes.

I was still dating Theresa from my first semester, was struggling with my relationship with her. She lived in East Dallas and going to see her was a major commitment of time…time, a commodity that was getting more and more precious to me. I talked to Ed about it.

"Ed, I'm breaking off my dating with Theresa. I just don't have the time for a relationship with a girl."

"I understand, Jonesie, but one of these days, you'll have to find time for a girl."

"I know that, but not now. If I'm going to survive this college stuff, I've got to focus on it more than I am. Plus, there's a ministry job board at the SUB that shows an opening in Forney, Texas."

"Well, I can understand your predicament."

"I'm going to stop dating her and explain that I'm just too busy right now. Then I'll just steer away from her and anyone else interested in me."

All this was occurring during September. I applied for the youth minister's position at First Baptist Church in Forney. I think it was my age that put me in front of the others for the position. FBC, Forney had never had a youth minister, so the process was very slow. Forney was about forty-five miles east of the college. In late September, Jerry Griffin, the pastor, invited me to come out and visit with the youth. I was so green behind the ears that all I planned to do was to give my personal testimony of how I became a Christian. A fellowship followed my speech.

October came with no call from Forney. Mid-term exams were in process. I used the mid-terms to space myself from Theresa. We dated a couple more times in October. It was about this time when I finally heard from Jerry Griffin again.

"I'm sorry, Johnnie, for not calling you sooner. We've been very busy and this youth ministry position is something new. I don't think you understood that we were expecting you to do something with the youth during your first visit, you know, like a game or something."

"Oh, I'm so sorry. This is new for me as well. Can I come back?"

"Yes. The committee liked your testimony and feel you will be a great mentor for the kids. Can you come again in a couple weeks?"

I accepted, of course, and felt that this was a positive move for me. I really needed the experience and worked very well with the youth at Waialae in Hawaii. I called Ed for help.

"Ed, I need a youth fellowship idea. Can you help me?" Ed was working in the youth department at his church in Grand Prairie. Chris Leibrum was the youth minister there.

"Sure thing, Johnnie. We're having a youth fellowship this Sunday evening. Why don't you come over and join us."

"Great!"

Mid-term exams were not a priority in my life at this time. I was trying to continue my job at Tarrant Road, plus I was still seeing Theresa a little, and now trying to fit a part-time ministry tryout in my life. My exam results were not good. Most were C's and D's, but one was an F. I failed my mid-term Greek exam. This was not good. I thought about dropping the class, but decided to first visit with my professor, Dr. Fred White. Dr. White was such a joy to be around. He was always telling stories of his younger days in Teneha, Texas. I went to his office.

"Dr. White, I need some counsel. I flunked my mid-term." He let out his customary chuckle.

"Well, I wouldn't fret too much over it. I remember when I struggled through a few classes of my own." He then proceeded to tell me another of his stories. I interrupted him.

"Dr. White, what can I do? I'm thinking of dropping the class." That statement brought him back to the present.

"My advice is for you to get with an A-student and let him help you understand the fundamentals of the Greek language."

"Do we have A students in my class?"

"Well, just let me take a look." He began flipping through his class planner book. "Yes, there are two students who made an A on the mid-term. One is Gary Dement and the other is Diane Leroy. Do you know either of them?"

"Not really. I don't recognize the Dement name, but I have several classes with Miss Leroy."

He chuckled again. "Well, I suggest you go to the next class and ask Miss Leroy for some help."

Placing another girl in my life was not what I wanted to do at this time. I had just told Theresa, two weeks earlier, that I wouldn't be over to see her any more. But I remembered how bashful this Diane Leroy was. Maybe I could meet with her in the SUB after class. But what if she had a boyfriend?

I didn't think she had a boyfriend because I was walking toward her on the sidewalk one day a few weeks earlier. I stopped her and said hello. Her bashfulness intrigued me. She smiled and looked down at the ground. I mentioned something about being hungry and was heading for the SUB. She sometimes brought a brown bag and ate at the SUB by herself.

"I'm going to a cafeteria in Duncanville for lunch today," she said. "Would you like to come?"

I was touched. She was asking me to lunch? I wanted to say yes, but I had just told Theresa that I was not going to see her for a while and I had just told Ed that I was steering away from girls.

"I'm sorry, not today; maybe another time. Listen, I need to go. See you in class."

That was several weeks ago. Now I wondered if she would remember that event and if it would get me a cold shoulder from her the next time. I headed to the SUB for lunch. When I entered into the snack bar area, I saw Diane sitting alone at a table. I dropped my books beside her.

"I'm going to get me a hamburger and I'll be right back." In a few minutes I was sitting beside her. We talked a little. I made fun of her orange that had most of the white portion of the peel still on the orange. She offered me a piece.

"The peel is where most of the vitamins are."

"Really? I thought the orange part was where the orange was." She laughed at nearly everything I said. Her politeness made me feel that perhaps she would help me.

I don't think I mentioned my Greek problems with her at this first encounter. I was afraid my failing grade might not make a good impression on an "A" student. I did begin to look for her more on campus. One day I happened to look up toward the music building. Its second floor had small piano rooms. Diane was in one of them, playing a piano. Years earlier, during my choir days at Waialae, I had purchased some sheet music of a couple songs I liked and wanted to sing someday. I wondered then if she could play them. I found them later during the week and brought them to class.

"Hey Diane, I saw you playing the piano; can you play this for me?" She looked at the music and, looking down, smiled.

"I think so."

"Great; I'll meet you in the music building Thursday and we'll go over them."

The next Thursday, I met Diane in one of the piano rooms. She played the music flawlessly and I sang. I think we met a couple times in the piano room. Finally, during one of these sessions, I made my appeal for help.

"Diane, I need someone to help me with my Greek studies. Dr. White suggested that I get with an A student to help me. Do you have any time after classes to help me?"

"I don't know; I'll have to ask my parents."

"Oh, okay." I forgot that she was just out of high school and was still under parental control. Oh well, maybe they'll let her. The next day, I saw her in class.

"Well, do we have a date?" She blushed, smiled, and looked away.

"My parents want you to come over to my house tomorrow morning to meet you. They said I could help you at my house."

"Sounds great! Give me your address and I'll be over at ten. Is that okay?" She agreed and I made plans to be at her house the next day. I was also scheduled to go back to Forney that Sunday for another youth fellowship. Ed's youth fellowship had given me a perfect game plan the week prior, so I was pumped.

Diane lived in East Dallas, off Grand Avenue. The houses in the neighborhood were beautiful. Her house had a white picket fence around its yard and a large picture window in front. I pulled up in front and made my way to the door. Diane greeted me.

"Hello, John," she said. "Come in."

"Thank you. My, you have a beautiful house."

"Thank you. I'll go get my parents. You can sit here on the couch."

I think we were both a bit nervous, but somehow we managed through the introductions. Her parents were very nice and talked much more than Diane. I was wondering where she got her bashfulness. Mrs. Leroy began to tell me all the things Diane was capable of doing as a musician. For about an hour I was entertained by the family's singing ability. Diane could play the guitar and the banjo. She had also written and copyrighted a song entitled, *There's a Reason*. She sang it to me on her guitar.

The thing that got my attention the most was her willingness to comply with every directive from her parents. She never hesitated at their wishes and was diligent with every request. I finally got to speak.

"Wow, I'm amazed with all this talent and really appreciate all this, but I'm afraid this is not helping my Greek grades."

With that statement, Diane's parents excused themselves to their bedroom while she and I retired to the dining room table. For about an hour Diane and I reviewed the fundamentals of parsing Greek verbs and memorizing Greek word endings. She had developed a system that helped me tremendously.

At lunch, Diane excused herself and began preparing us a meal. This was not just a sandwich, but a full course meal, with dessert.

"You didn't have to do this for me. I'm imposing on your time."

"No, it's no problem," said Diane. "We eat at this time every Saturday."

"A full course meal?"

"Yes, this is the healthiest way to eat. Mother is a nurse and she sees to it that we eat properly."

"Okay." Her next request was even more interesting.

"I'm fixing us some milk to drink. Do you want a full glass or eight ounces?"

Now this was a new request for me. "What's the difference?"

She responded with a puzzled look. "Let me find out." With that statement, she headed back into the kitchen. Moments later, she returned with a Coca Cola glass with water in it.

"This is eight ounces. It's at the bottom of the word, Coca Cola."

Now I began playing with her. "And where's the full line?"

Again, she responded with a bit of puzzlement. "I think it's at the top of the words on the glass. Let me find out." She started to turn around again, but I stopped her.

"No, No; I'm not a big drinker. Just give me eight ounces, please." I gave her a big grin, trying to get her to relax a bit, but I don't think it worked.

Her mother joined Diane in the kitchen as they completed the preparations for lunch. It was an amazing meal, full of all the nutritious items you would see on a television food show. I was impressed.

During the meal, I was able to introduce myself fuller as well as discover more about Diane's family. Diane's father, Bob Leroy, was a computer data entry man at Arco Oil Company in downtown Dallas. He showed me a couple of his computer pictures, like Snoopy, the dog, lying on his doghouse. The computer printout would use certain letters of the alphabet and arrange them on the paper to outline the pictures.

Mrs. Leroy was Diane's stepmother and later on, through a large writing Mr. Leroy had written, I discovered she was his third wife. She had been his nurse in an ICU ward where he was recovering from a heart attack. Both she and he were very aggressive in controlling the conversations and activities around them. It seemed neither wanted an opinion about anything discussed, just an acknowledgement that their opinion was the correct one. I found myself having to agree to all their wishes and opinions.

Diane, however, was different. She remained bashful and never made eye contact with me, except for a brief glance. This was a challenge for me, since my personality is one that never meets a stranger. I was intrigued with her personality and her politeness. I think we studied Greek for a few more hours, and then I left for home.

The next few weeks found me involved in moving from Fort Worth to Dallas, meeting with the pastor of First Baptist Church in Forney, and studying Greek at Diane's house. I also quit working at Tarrant Road Baptist Church and got a job working in the back of a large UPS truck, stacking parcels for delivery in the west Texas area.

It was early November and First Baptist Church, Forney still had not hired me. The pastor, Jerry Griffin, apologized and said they should move on this decision soon. He said it wasn't me that was causing the delay.

Meanwhile, my Saturday visits with Diane were getting friendlier. She mentioned enjoying playing basketball, so I challenged her to a friendly game of one-on-one. There was a park at the northeast end of Vivian Street, so we walked down there with a basketball. It didn't take long to realize that whatever Diane focused on, she did so with the intent of excelling. She made a few moves on the court that allowed her to outscore me for a while. I decided that if I was to beat her, I had better get serious in this "friendly" game. It was fun and I really enjoyed being with her when she wasn't around her parents. I began to see a young woman that had a heart for God and a determination to excel in life. As we walked back to her house I asked her for a date.

"Say, since you like basketball so much, how about us taking in the game at DBC tonight?"

"I'd like that, John. Let me ask my parents." Mr. and Mrs. Leroy agreed and we headed out for Dallas Baptist College. It was a fun night and I found that I really enjoyed being around Diane. She laughed at every joke I told and I was full of one-liners. I bought her a Dr Pepper that evening, something that she wasn't allowed to drink at home. She really enjoyed it.

On campus, my buddy, Ed, was now taking a second position with me, one behind Diane. I began to walk with her to class whenever to opportunity arose.

"What's with this, Jonesie?" he asked. "I thought you said you were through with dating until you finished college."

"Well, Ed, this is different. I mean, not only is she smart and helping me pass Greek, but she's also a lot of fun being around. She's different, Ed."

"I've heard that line before. I think it's more than just 'liking' her."

"You think so?" I smiled.

"Jonesie, what I see is a young woman who would be devoted to you and your ministry. I don't blame you one bit for pursuing a relationship with her."

"I just don't know if I can handle all the things that are going on now."

"Listen to me, college is temporary; ministry will come and go, but finding and marrying the woman God wants you to marry is the most important decision you'll ever make this side of getting saved."

Ed's approval gave additional sanction to my spending more time with Diane. During her piano practice time at college, I would meet with her in the studio and we would sing some songs together. We also ate together regularly at the SUB and other places off campus.

In Greek class, I managed to move up a few rows and sit beside her. She helped me understand each chapter as Dr. White explained the basics of the language. It looked like there would be hope for my failing grade.

Pastor Griffin finally gave me a call.

"Johnnie, the church is asking you to come out this Sunday evening for a question and answer time, and then they plan to call us into a conference time to vote on you. Can you come?"

"Sure; I'm honored for the consideration. Is there anything I should do in preparation for this?"

"You might want to have a short devotional planned, just in case."

"Anything else?"

"No, but do remember that you're the first youth minister our church has considered, so don't be alarmed if there are a lot of questions."

Wow, this was great! I called Diane later that evening.

"Guess what? I finally got that call from Forney about the youth minister's position."

"Oh that's great John! Congratulations!"

"Thank you, thank you. Just pray that I'll say and do the right things this Sunday evening while I'm out there."

"I'm sure the Lord will be with you and I will continue to pray for you."

The next person I called was Ed.

"Get ready, Mister Ethridge, you're going to be calling me Youth Pastor Jonesie, soon."

"Oh yeah? When's this happening?" I gave Ed all the details about the upcoming Sunday evening Q&A, and then the vote afterwards.

"What does Diane think about it?" That question startled me.

"How'd you know I called her?"

"Jonesie, I've been married a few years now, so I think I can read your situation pretty easily."

"Well, in fact I did call her first and she was elated. And you know what? She said she would be praying for me. I think that's a first in any relationship with a girl."

"Based on what you've said and what I see, Johnnie, I think she will make an excellent pastor's wife. Maybe in a week or so, if I have the opportunity, I'll visit with her and ask her a few questions about ministry."

"Well, let's get me into the youth ministry first."

"Oh you needn't worry about that. You're as good as in that position."

Ed was a very confident man. He knew what God wanted in his life and was pursuing it. But he, like me, had a few struggles with class assignments. We decided to try and work our schedules together as much as possible in order to help one another.

On the other hand, Diane seemed to grasp college very well. She was very organized and dedicated to her work. She had been helping me for about six weeks now and next Sunday was mid-November. I was at her house that Saturday. We studied a bit, and then went to the park to play "horse" with the basketball. After lunch we settled down on the couch for the afternoon study session.

"I'm tired of studying. Could we just talk for a few minutes?" I asked her.

"Okay."

I immediately closed the Greek books in her lap and sat right next to her. Because of her bashfulness, I had to be very careful and patient.

"May I hold your hand, Diane?"

"I guess so."

As soon as I grabbed her hand, I turned and looked straight into her face. "Diane, if we're going to advance in this relationship, you're going have to try and look at me in the face." She looked down and blushed. "Now look at me right now." She tried and it was an improvement, but only for a few seconds. "That wasn't so bad was it?"

"No, I guess not."

"Now look at me again." She did. "Up, up—where're you going with that head?" I touched her chin to keep it up in front of me. "Keep looking."

For the first time, Diane was able to maintain eye contact with me for nearly twenty seconds. We were both smiling.

"Good, good." I said. I began to play with her a little. "Hi, my name is Johnnie Jones and I'm so pleased to meet you." She laughed and lowered her head.

"Oh, John."

"Wait—wait a minute. I want you to call me 'Johnnie'."

"Why? I thought 'Johnnie' was a bit boyish."

"Maybe, but 'John Jones' is just a bit too common and boring. I like 'Johnnie'."

"Okay, Johnnie."

"All right, now that we've introduced ourselves, I'd like to say a few more things to you. First of all I want you to know that I like you—not as a Greek mentor, but as a person, but not just a person. I want to be your boyfriend and I'd like for you to be my girlfriend. Is that okay?"

This time I let her look down. I knew this was new territory for her.

"Johnnie, I like you a lot and I think it will be okay. I should ask my parents, though."

This was new territory for me as well. "That's fine. Do you think they like me?"

"Oh, I think they do." When she said that, she squeezed my hand and, without prompting, looked me straight into my eyes. I moved in a little closer.

"May I kiss you?" I asked.

"Yes, you may," and we kissed.

It was a simple kiss, but a kiss of purity, innocence, and sincerity. It was also a kiss of commitment. Her permission for me to kiss her meant to me that a new level of commitment was agreed upon. And in my mind my decision to ask for the kiss was a decision to commit more of my life to her.

Just prior to mid terms, when I made the decision to break away from dating, I had prayed that, later on in my college years, God would send someone into my life that would feel the same calling as I to serve Him in ministry. I specifically asked Him for a woman who could play the piano. Those were my only two requests, but God had much more in store for me when He allowed me to begin my Greek studies with Diane Leroy. He gave me so much more than I could ever imagine possible from a young woman.

After the kiss, we smiled and talked a lot. Then it was back to Greek, but now it was handholding Greek! A couple hours later, Diane excused herself and went into her parent's bedroom. The three came back out together. They were all smiles. Her stepmother, Laura, came over and hugged me and her dad spoke up.

"Well, I suppose this means that you'll be staying for supper as well." It was more a statement than a question.

"Oh, that's not necessary," I replied. "But I would like to be able to call Diane each night on the phone, after work."

"We'll discuss it further over supper," he responded with a smile.

"You bet!"

I did not take Diane to First Baptist Church, Forney the next day. I didn't want to complicate the deliberations at the time. She and her parents were members of First Baptist Church of Dallas. They were also attending a small fellowship in east Dallas, called First Indian Baptist Church of Dallas. A young Asian Indian, K. P. Yohannan, was the pastor. The Leroy's had befriended K. P. and were supporting his overseas missions ministry in India. K. P. and I would team up later on in my life for several ministry opportunities.

First Baptist Church of Forney had two youth Sunday School departments that I would serve over. There were about sixty 7th through 12th graders who were regular attendees. The total church Sunday School attendance at the time was around 350. The staff comprised of a full time pastor and secretary, a part time music director, and a part time education director. Forney was a small rural town that was transitioning into a bedroom community for the Dallas metroplex.

I simply attended the Sunday School and a.m. service as an observer. I believe a member of the youth minister search committee sat with me and explained a few things. I ate lunch with a youth family, a Dallas attorney, Don Cates. His wife was also the church pianist. Later that afternoon, I sat with the committee for further questioning. Our discussions and visions about youth ministry went well.

During the evening service, I was allowed to give my testimony about becoming a Christian and my call into the ministry. I also discussed what the church could expect of me. I suppose everything went well as I was voted unanimously to become their youth pastor. It was a great experience for me and it was especially a confirming moment in my life as to what God was going to do with me.

My wages would be $50 a week with no benefits. That was okay with me, since I had a part time job with UPS and received some extra cash from my veteran's benefits. I was offered a small lakeside cabin to stay in on Saturday nights or Sunday afternoons, as needed, by a church member. I decided to travel to Forney on Saturday afternoons, stay overnight, and leave late Sunday evenings. I also wanted to lead a youth Bible study on Wednesday evenings, but knew my UPS job would be a conflict. That desire would come later.

My time with Diane became a higher priority in my life. I would call her every night after work, around 9:00 p.m., and we would talk for at least an hour. It would cause us both to struggle to maintain our college grades. She was struggling to maintain an A average and I would struggle to maintain a C average. Our Saturday schedule changed a little due to my church ministry. I would see her on Saturday mornings, study, and eat lunch. Then I would drive out to Forney to visit youth and plan outings for them. Instead of staying in Forney, however, I would return to Diane's house for the evening.

The UPS company did not break for Thanksgiving Day, but Diane's parents wanted to introduce me to her stepmother's family in Jacksonville, Texas. It was a tight schedule, but we managed to go to Jacksonville that Thanksgiving Day morning. I remember it as a delightful time. The family was sizing up Diane and me as a "would-be" married couple. There were some tall pines about a quarter mile behind the house. I was missing the woods of Virginia, so I asked Diane if we could go walking.

"Hey, I want you to hear something," I said to her. When we got into the grove, we got real silent. You could hear the wind blowing through the pine branches. It always produced a smooth sound that I used to hear when I was younger.

"When I was a kid, I used to lie on my back and look up through the pines as the wind blew them back and forth."

"They sound very relaxing."

"Yeah, they do. Did you ever live in the country?"

"No, just Dallas."

"Really? What about grandparents?"

"I don't remember much on my dad's side. His parents lived in Brownsville when I was young. My real mom's parents lived across the street from me in Dallas. I visited them a lot."

"Tell me about your real mom. I read in your dad's handout that she was very ill for about seven years?"

"Well, it was a progressive illness. She taught English at SMU (Southern Methodist University) and played the piano. I think I was about seven or eight when I began to notice she was not able do things around the house. My dad and I began to care for her as much as we could. She had severe arthritis that began to cripple her. Somewhere along the way she developed shingles, which settled in her brain. This caused her to be totally incapacitated. We had to start feeding her and cleaning her each day. It got to where she did not recognize us anymore."

"Wow, I bet that hurt."

"Well, she had been this way for so long that you really don't know any other life. I grew up as a preteen and teenager caring for my mother."

Time was running out, so we began to leave the pines. But before leaving, I grabbed her and kissed her. This time there were no possible onlookers or interruptions. It was our first embrace. I held her close to me for a few moments. I could sense that she was a bit uncomfortable.

"I'm sorry, Diane, but I just had to kiss you without fear of your parents bursting into the room."

"That's okay, Johnnie. It's just that I've never had a real boyfriend and I'm not sure how to respond to you or how to keep my feelings in check."

"Have you ever kissed a boy before?"

"I did in fourth grade, once, and at a birthday party once; but it was nothing like this."

"Have you ever liked a boy?"

"Well, I had a crush on my youth minister at a church, but my parents said I could not like him."

"So I'm the first?"

"Well, kind of."

"What do mean, kind of?"

"There were boys in my school I liked, but most were real mean to me."

"Well I'm happy to hear that, but why were they mean?"

"I think it was because it was a private school in North Dallas (Greenhill) and I wasn't the same as most of the kids there. Most were from wealthy families. We weren't poor, but due to my mother's health, I had to move to a public school."

We began walking back to the house, holding hands.

"Tell me about your faith in Christ."

"My family was Methodist. During my mother's illness, my dad watched a Billy Graham crusade on television. At the end of the televised message, he committed his life to Christ. After that, he had me sit down and watch several Billy Graham crusades on TV. At several invitations, I would pray and ask Christ to save me."

"Several times?"

"Yes."

"How many times did you do this?"

"I think about a dozen times for over a year or two."

"Did it ever take?" I asked jokingly. Diane lowered her head and smiled—"Hey, look at me," I said. (This phrase, "Hey, look at me!" became our special phrase.)

"Yes, I was saved one of those times, I just don't know which one."

"Why did you do that?"

"I'm not sure, but I think it was because of my Methodist background. We didn't believe in eternal security, so if I sinned again after my asking Christ to save me, I thought I had to do it over again."

"Wow...do you feel that way now?"

"No, my dad became disenchanted with the liberalism in Methodism, so we switched over to Baptists. We were baptized at Royal Haven Baptist Church. My dad began to study the Scriptures a lot and he taught me things about salvation and eternal life."

"And what do you think God wants you to do now?"

"For several years I have felt God wanted me to become a youth minister."

"Really?"

"Yes, but I'm open to do His will."

That was about all the time we had for our personal, private conversation. We returned to Dallas in just enough time for me to drive over to my jobsite. I spent most of Friday and Saturday at Diane's. We were sitting on the couch reviewing for a Greek quiz.

"Can we take a break?" I asked.

"Yes; can I get you some milk?"

"A Dr Pepper would be better."

"We don't have soft drinks. Would you prefer some water or juice?"

"Water will be fine. Hurry back, I want to tell you something." I had to be careful what I said to her because Diane took every statement as a command that had to be fulfilled immediately. She was back in no time with my water.

"Thanks. I'm sorry, I really didn't mean for you to hurry up, like speed up. I just wanted to share something important with you."

She relaxed, since she thought that she had not been quick enough with my drinks previously.

I took a sip of water and then held her hand. "Diane, this may seem strange to you and I know we've only known each other as friends for about two months; but I want you to know that I feel God wants me to marry you. I have come to love you and believe God wants us to get married."

I was not sure how she would respond. I was thinking, at least she would need some time to think about it. Her response proved me wrong.

"I, too, feel the same way Johnnie. I believe God wants us to get married."

"So, is that a 'Yes'?"

"Let me ask my parents."

"No, not this time. I'm going to go ask them."

"Okay." We hugged and kissed, and then we walked together into her parent's bedroom.

"Mister and Misses Leroy? I've come to ask you if I may marry your daughter?"

They turned the television off. Mister Leroy became the spokesman. "Well Diane, is this what you want?"

"Yes," she said looking down. But as she looked down, she grabbed my hand and held it.

Mr. and Mrs. Leroy were a hard couple to read sometimes. They were a very lively couple and had a strong Christian conviction about witnessing and living healthy lifestyles. But sometimes they argued because they were very headstrong. I found myself walking very carefully around them, just as Diane did.

They looked at each other without a smile, and then turned toward us. Diane's dad spoke.

"Sounds to me then that we've got a wedding to prepare for." A big grin came over their faces as Diane screamed and jumped over on the bed to hug them both. I reached over to hug Mrs. Leroy and to shake Mr. Leroy's hand.

"So when's the big day?" he asked.

"Uh, I don't know. I haven't thought about it," I responded.

"You haven't thought about it?" said Mrs. Leroy with a grin. "Then I think Diane and I need to go look at a calendar right now." With that statement, they both jumped up off the bed and scurried into the kitchen. This left Mr. Leroy and I alone…for the first time.

"Johnnie, Diane has been through a lot of pain growing up. You have brought joy and laughter back into her life and I'm happy for the both of you."

"Thank you, sir. I want you to know that I really love her and will commit my life to making her happy and fulfilled in serving the Lord."

"Bob, June 1st is on a Saturday. What do you think?" asked Mrs. Leroy as she and Diane reentered the bedroom.

"Oh, that day is about as good as any I've heard so far," he said, smiling.

"We'll be out of school then as well," I piped in.

"Then June 1st it is!" we spoke together, as June 1, 1975 became our target date for our wedding.

"Can your parents come down for the wedding?" asked Mrs. Leroy.

"I doubt it, but I'll ask." I called from Diane's house. My mom answered the phone.

"Mom, I've asked Diane Leroy to marry me." Mom was elated, but I could sense pain in her voice. She was about to go to the doctor for more tests. She feared another ruptured disk in her back. She had fallen several times going up and down the stairway to the basement of the rock shop. Her days in the cotton mill may have been over, but the effects of climbing onto dozens of industrial-sized weaving looms, repairing picks, had taken its toll on her body.

"Oh, Johnnie, I'm so happy for the both of you. I know she must be something special. When can we meet her?"

"The wedding is scheduled for June 1st." Can you, Dad, and maybe Ricky come down?"

"Oh, Johnnie, I don't think my body can let me go anywhere anymore. It's so worn out. And you know how the cotton mill is here. If there's work to be done, your daddy has to work."

"I understand. I'll talk with Diane about it and I'll get back to you."

We traded our love to each other and then I hung up.

"I don't think they can come. She's in a lot of pain right now."

"What's her problem, Johnnie?" asked Mrs. Leroy, a L.V.N.

"She's had several disks removed in her back, due to her job. She thinks it is another slipped or ruptured disk."

"Oh, then she shouldn't travel in a car that far."

"Plus my dad is a loom fixer in the same cotton mill. He would lose his job if he came down during a workweek. The mill usually closes down a full week in August so that everyone can get a vacation."

It was now the first week of December 1974. Finals were a week away. Diane and I were inseparable on campus and she was working hard to help me pass my Greek exam. I was working five nights a week for UPS and living a rented room in Oak Cliff in Mr. Lovelace's house. Things were going well in Forney at First Baptist. It sounds like a Cinderella story, but 1975 would be a year like none other for Diane Leroy and me.

My mother was sick. She would have to go to the hospital for more back surgery during the Christmas holidays. I felt I needed to go to Virginia, but to do so would cost me my job at UPS. I prayed. Then I went to see Diane.

"Hi sweetie-pie!" It was now okay to kiss Diane in public, but she still had her guard up at her home. I kissed her as I entered the house, but she didn't respond very well. "Hey, what's the matter?"

She looked back at her parents' bedroom. The door was shut. "They had a fight last night. Mother and I had to drive around the neighborhood to find Father. We finally found him at Samuel Park, but he wouldn't get in the vehicle with us. We drove along the road as he walked back home."

"Are they okay now?"

"I don't know; I hope so."

"Listen, can we talk about the holidays?"

"Okay, but let's stay in the front room."

"I want to ask you an important question. Can you travel with me to Virginia for the Christmas holidays?"

"What?"

"Yeah, I know it sounds a bit farfetched, but let me explain the situation. My mom is going into the hospital for surgery on the 20th. We will finish classes on the 18th. I know my folks cannot come to our wedding, so I want you to go with me to meet my folks. And don't forget that I have a ring in Virginia that belongs to your finger."

"I don't know if my parents will agree to it."

"Will you go if I get their permission?"

"Oh yes! I'd love to go! But I don't think right now is a good time."

"Okay, you decide on the time I ask, but it can't be at the last minute. I will have to quit my job at UPS, because it is the worst time of the year to leave them. I want to give them a week's notice."

Diane and I studied for finals together during that first week of December. Her parents seemed to be back to normal that Saturday. We played a lot as we studied. She laughed at all my jokes like she had never heard them and I had hundreds of jokes. At lunch, I got the "green light" from Diane to ask her parents the big question.

"Mister Leroy, Misses Leroy, I have an important question to ask you."

"Sure, Johnnie; what is it?" he asked.

"Well, I need to return to Virginia during the Christmas break because my mother is having surgery on the 20th. With your permission, I want Diane to accompany me so that she can meet my parents. They will not be able to come down for the wedding, so I feel it would be most appropriate for them to meet Diane before we marry."

There was a bit of silence as we continued eating. Mrs. Leroy spoke up first. "What about your job?"

"They ask for a week's notice, so I would work until the 18th and quit. I can find another job when I return from Virginia."

"Is your vehicle in good condition?" he asked.

"Oh yes. I do my own oil changes, tune-ups, and brake jobs. Plus, I drove my Cutlass from Danville to Texas. It handles great."

"Where will you stay during the trip?"

"Well, I figure we could stay in separate rooms in a hotel going up and coming back. We can ask for rooms next to each other."

"And the costs?" he asked.

"I still have money in my checking account that was not needed for college this semester. It should be more than enough." It got quiet again.

"We need to think this over. We'll give you an answer tonight."

"Yes sir."

I left for Forney after lunch. I arrived at church about 1:30 p.m. Pastor Griffin was waiting for me.

"Let's go for some coffee, Johnnie." Jerry was a seasoned pastor. He was well organized and well respected in the community. I wanted to spend time with him, but did not try to push it. Today was different, however. We went to the local café for coffee and sat in a booth.

"Johnnie, I want to be here for you to help you in any way I can with our youth program."

"Thank you, sir. I appreciate the offer."

"To have a youth minister is new for us and many of our parents have stepped in to keep the youth ministry functioning. I want to suggest to you to keep these parents involved. Let them chaperone the kids or be sponsors on events; just keep them involved and you'll go far in this ministry."

"Pastor Griffin?"

"Please call me Jerry."

"Okay: Jerry, I need a favor. My mother is going to have surgery over the Christmas holidays and I want to go home to be with her."

"Oh. That's understandable. I'm sure the church will understand your request."

"Yes, but there is more. I've asked permission from my girlfriend's parents to take her with me. Jerry, I've asked her to marry me."

"Wow. This is serious. How long have you known Diane?"

"Just this semester. But I'm very certain this is the woman I want to be my wife."

"Have the parents agreed to this trip?"

"They're discussing it this afternoon. I should know tonight. Please know that we'll have separate hotel rooms and will not do anything to jeopardize my ministry."

"I trust you in that, Johnnie. I just can't see her parents letting her travel that far with you. I have two teenage daughters myself and I know I wouldn't feel comfortable making that kind of decision."

"Well, the problem is that my parents cannot come down for the wedding in June. I really want them to meet Diane before we marry."

"Let me know the outcome. I'll help you in any way that I can."

With that statement, we finished our coffee and Jerry drove me back to the church. I left there for some youth prospect visits.

Diane's parents agreed to the trip. I turned in my notice to quit UPS and we left on December 20th. We arrived in Danville on the 21st. My mom was in the hospital for disk surgery. Diane and I went to her room to visit her. Mom's first words about our marriage were, "Johnnie, I just knew you would marry someone like her. She is so pretty and look at her rosy cheeks."

Diane did have naturally rosy cheeks and a smile that lit up her whole face. I can't remember all that we did on this first trip, but I'll never forget our trip to Ben David Jewelers. I retrieved my old engagement ring from Mom's jewelry box. We took it in to Ben David's for an evaluation and a trade. After a few displays, Diane picked a new flawless diamond out. We also picked out some matching wedding bands. After that, we walked a couple doors down to a cafeteria to eat lunch.

"Well, are you going to put the ring on?" I asked.

"Oh, don't we have to wait for the wedding?"

"Not for the engagement ring. That goes on at the proposal and I've already proposed to you."

Diane was reluctant because she thought we were supposed to wait. Finally, I got her to put the ring on her finger. It was beautiful and sparkled with her every movement.

"Now when are we going to get married?" I asked.

"June 1st."

"Why June 1st?"

"Well, I wanted the date to be on the first day of the month, to symbolize the first start of our new life together; plus June 1st is on a Saturday."

I pulled a small calendar out of my wallet to view the months in 1975.

"Well lookie here, March 1st is on a Saturday," I said.

I pushed the calendar in front of Diane. She investigated it for a minute then replied: "February 1st is on a Saturday also." I laughed and she smiled. As we continued eating we began talking about moving the wedding up.

"Diane, if you want my opinion, the sooner the better."

"I don't know if we can put everything together in a couple of months."

My naiveté kicked in. "What's there to do? Just send out some announcements, buy some clothes, and secure a church. I bet we can use First Baptist, Forney."

"I don't know; do you think we can do it?"

"Sure we can. Let's finish eating and when we get back to my parent's house, we'll call your parents."

I called Diane's parents and told them the new plans. They wanted to speak to Diane.

"Johnnie and I want to move the wedding up. Is that okay?"

"When do you want to get married?" her dad asked.

"Well, we were looking at some months that the first fell on a Saturday and both March and February do. We want to choose February 1st."

Her stepmother broke in the conversation. "Well if we're going to get everything done for February 1st, we'd better get started right away. I'll start making some calls, Bob," she said to Diane's dad.

"Well, if that's what you want to do, Diane, it's okay with us."

"Yes sir, it is."

"Diane, I'll start looking in the paper for a dress and for someone to get a cake made."

"Thank you Mother, and thank you Father."

With that settled Diane hung up the phone. For a moment we both looked at each other, trying to let this all sink in.

"Isn't February 1st about forty days from now?" I asked.

"Yes; is that okay with you?"

"Sure, I'm ready!" And with that statement, I hugged her. "I love you Diane Elaine Leroy, soon to be 'Jones.' Mrs. Diane Elaine Jones sounds good, don't you think?"

"I think Mrs. Johnnie Ray Jones sounds better."

"Wow. My name never sounded so good as that."

My mom came home from the hospital on Christmas Eve. We had a great Christmas Day and Diane and I prepared to leave the next day. We arrived back in Dallas the evening of the 27th. I got Diane home around 6:00 p.m. Her parents were in their bedroom.

"You two come in here please," said her stepmother. Mr. Leroy had a notepad in his lap and a small adding machine, called a calculator. It was some new-fangled thing that had red "L.E.D." numbers.

"Laura and I want to help you two get off on a good financial start, so we think Johnnie should move into our house for the next month. I figured it would save him at least three hundred dollars."

"Are you sure?" I asked.

"Why not?" he responded. "We hardly know you and feel like this would be a great opportunity to get to know you. You also need to save some money in order to rent a place to live when the right time comes."

"You mean I could live here for awhile?"

"Yes, until your financial situation changes. Remember, you quit your job before your trip."

"Well, I figured we would move into an apartment over near the college." Mr. Leroy was not good with objections, so I began to notice he was a bit agitated with my line of thinking.

"Listen, I've put a few numbers together and as I see it, Diane will not be able to continue her college work until you finish, unless you live here." He then began to read out a bunch of expenses Diane and I would have if we lived on our own. Although I did not like the idea, my passive nature was no match for Mr. and Mrs. Leroy's persistence.

I looked at Diane. "What do you think, Diane?" I forgot Diane did not have a "say-so" in her house.

"It's okay with me," she said, looking toward the floor.

"Then it's settled," said Mr. Leroy. "Johnnie will move into your room, Diane, and you can move into the spare room here beside our bedroom."

I did not object because I felt the conversation was one-sided and it appeared Diane was very nervous with my "challenge." I said nothing else until Diane and I were alone again.

"Diane, are you sure about this?"

"Well, Johnnie, I'm afraid what may happen if my parents get upset with you."

"That's exactly why I do not like this idea. I'm afraid my independent nature will clash with your parents' domineering attitude."

"I don't think we have much of a choice at this time. Let's try to make it work for this month."

"Okay. I'll do my best to keep them happy." Diane smiled and we headed to the park to play basketball.

Marriage Derailment?

January 1975 began with a bang. Diane and I were very busy preparing for our February 1st wedding. She and her stepmother were running around town shopping for a wedding dress and other wedding paraphernalia, while I was busy getting back into college and looking for another job. My friend, Ed Ethridge, was also looking for me a job. We were in several classes together and relied upon each other for studying and completing class assignments.

"Jonesie, I think I found you a job."

"Really? What is it: washing your VW?"

"No, you can do that for free; but Judy's bank is looking for a man to work nights in bookkeeping."

"What do they want a man for?"

"I don't know, but sounds to me like you would qualify, being a man and all."

"Oh, glad you noticed. Where is this bank?"

"It's called Midway National Bank and it's over on Pioneer Parkway, near Highway 80. Tell me when you can go over there and I'll have Judy introduce you to the supervisor."

The next day, after classes, I met Judy who introduced me to the evening shift supervisor. The job had two purposes. One was to run a proofing machine and the other was to be a male presence for the evening tellers and bookkeepers. My only problem was that I could not run the proof machine with a ten-key numerical pad by memory. The supervisor did not think that was a significant handicap and hired me for the job.

Diane was excited that I found a job that quick, but it didn't seem to go well with her parents.

"We wanted you to be around the house more, so that we could get to know you," said Mrs. Leroy.

"I'm sorry, but this was a great opportunity for me to find employment that would fit my schedule. This will help me and Diane get on our own sooner."

By mid-January, I managed to keep peace between Diane's parents and me. During that time, we had a family wedding shower and had most of the wedding plans finalized. We would marry at First Baptist in Forney, and then spend our honeymoon in North Dallas at the Marriott Hotel for one night. Two more weeks and we would be married.

During the next week, there were a lot of decisions being made to finalize everything. I can't remember what happened that triggered a family meeting but on Saturday morning, just prior to my trip out to Forney, Diane's parents called us into their bedroom.

"Johnnie, we do not like your lack of respect toward us," said Mr. Leroy.

"What do you mean?" I asked.

Mrs. Leroy gave me an ear full. Then it was Mr. Leroy's turn.

"According to the Bible, you're supposed to do what we say and you are making too many decisions for you and Diane without consulting us or getting our approval," he said. "Your attitude and your actions are disrespectful toward us."

"I'm sorry, I didn't intend to be disrespectful. I thought I was doing what was best for us."

They did not see things as I did and it was no reason to argue the point, so I apologized again and excused myself. Diane was crying during the whole event. Once we were alone again, I tried to comfort her and then I left for Forney.

In Forney, I made a few visits to some of our youth homes. I returned to the church for some planning time. There was a note on the church door from Brother Jerry. It simply said to call Diane.

"Hello, Diane?"

"Yes." She was crying.

"What's wrong?"

"My parents want you to come home and get your stuff out of the house. They don't want you here any more."

"Why?"

"They don't like you and do not want you around me." She was really hurt. "They're calling me now; I have to go."

"Okay, I'll be there soon. Bye."

I headed back to Dallas and to Diane. When I arrived, all my belongings were outside on the sidewalk. I went to the door and rang the bell. Diane came to the door.

"Can we talk?"

"They said I couldn't come out. I'm sorry, Johnnie. I don't know what to do."

"Do you want to marry me?"

"Yes."

"Then I'll be back tonight. I'm going back out to Forney and see if Jerry will return with me. You hang in there, okay?"

"Okay," she said while crying.

As soon as I returned to Forney, I found Brother Jerry. I discussed the problem and asked if he would go back to Diane's house with me. He agreed and after supper we headed back for Dallas.

When we arrived, I rang the bell. Diane came to the door. I asked permission to come in.

"Can we speak to your parents?"

"Let me go ask."

Jerry and I sat down. Diane's parents came into the dining room and sat at the table. Jerry and I got up from the couch and walked into the dining room. I began the conversation.

"I'm so sorry I've made you angry. Please forgive me."

Both Mr. and Mrs. Leroy began to rehash all the disrespectful things I had done. I stood there and listened to them. Again, on my knees before them, I apologized, but it just didn't seem to be helping. Jerry tried to offer some reconciliatory statements.

"Mr. Leroy, Johnnie is sorry for what wrongs you feel he has committed. Next week, they plan to marry and I'm sure you want them to have your blessings on their marriage."

"I really don't care," he responded. "And I'm not even sure there's going to be a wedding. He's a bad influence on her and I don't want him around her anymore."

"But I love her," I piped in. "And, again, I'm sorry for hurting you. I will try to be more sensitive to your wishes."

"I don't want to hear anything more from you," he said. "Please leave now."

For the first time Diane spoke up. Although she was crying loudly, she had the last word.

"I don't want him to leave," she said, in tears. "I don't want him to leave."

"I'll be back Diane, don't worry."

"No you won't," said her dad.

"Then I'm leaving with Johnnie," she said. "I'm not staying here; I want to leave with Johnnie."

This was a defining moment in the life of Diane. She had never gone against the will of her parents. They sat there in a state of shock, dumbfounded. Jerry spoke up.

"Diane, I think you should stay here and work this out with your parents. I think it's important to have them involved in your wedding." (Her parents said nothing.)

"I agree with Jerry, honey," I said. "I think it's best that we work this out with your parents."

"But they won't listen to you or me! They will do something to stop the wedding. Please don't make me stay; I don't want to stay."

"We won't stop the wedding," her dad said. "You're eighteen and we can't stop you from marrying him."

"Diane, it's best that you stay here," I said. "Your parents need to be a part of the wedding. You need to trust your dad's words."

She was still crying, but managed to squeak out an "okay." Jerry then turned to her dad.

"Mister Leroy, this will pass and I'm sure you'll not regret being a part of Johnnie and Diane's wedding and their future."

"I'm doing this for Diane and not for him. Once they're married I don't care if I ever see him again."

I immediately walked over to the front of Mr. Leroy and got down on my knees. "Mister Leroy, I am so sorry to have offended you in this matter. Please forgive me."

He stared into the room as he said, "I'll forgive you because that's what the Bible says to do. But I don't condone what you've done."

"What have I done, sir, to be disrespectful?"

"I don't want to talk about it now."

After that statement, he and Mrs. Leroy retreated into their bedroom. Diane walked Jerry and me to the front door.

"Hon, don't worry; we'll get through this. The week will pass and we'll be married. And I bet your parents will be okay for the wedding."

"I don't think they'll get over this," she said.

"You call me if you have any problems whatsoever, okay?"

"Okay."

We hugged and I left with Jerry. On the road back to Forney, Jerry and I briefly discussed the situation.

"I've never seen a couple respond like that before," he said.

"Yeah, they're different. Mister Leroy was shot up in World War II and left behind in a barn. I think it affected his emotions."

"It may have."

"Jerry, this is not the way I envisioned my wedding. I don't want it clouded under a conflict. Do you think I should put it off until Diane's parents change their minds?"

"Johnnie, based on what I just observed, I would not leave Diane under that authority. If you love her, I think you need to proceed with your plans."

"Oh, I do love her and I want to marry her."

"Well, she is a great person and I think you're doing the right thing to marry her now."

"Thanks, and I appreciate so much you coming with me tonight."

The night was long, but morning finally came, so I headed out to DBC. I met up with Ed at the SUB (Student Union Building).

"Hey Jonesie, what's up with you? Looks like you got ran over by an 18-wheeler."

"Don't get me started." But I began to tell Ed everything that happened. He was now my best friend and also to be my best man in the wedding.

"Well I think you're doing the right thing to get her out of there. Something's not right, for them to not want her to marry you."

"Yeah, I'm the greatest thing that's ever happened to her," I said grinning.

"I was thinking the other way around. Her being able to play the piano may be the only way you get to become a preacher."

"Thanks for the vote of confidence."

"No problem, Jonesie."

Later that day, I called Diane. She answered the phone.

"How's it going?"

"Oh, it's very quiet. They're not talking to me."

"Are you okay?"

"Yes, I'll be okay. My mother gave me the name of the shops for me to pick up the cake and decorations. She said I would have to finish all the wedding plans."

"Do you need me to help?"

"No, Debbie will help me." Debbie was her cousin and her Matron of Honor. Debbie's sister, Donna, and one of Diane's friends were to be the bridesmaids.

"Okay, Hon. I'll check on you tomorrow. Call the Griffin's if you need me."

"Okay Johnnie. Please call me tomorrow."

"I will, I promise. I love you."

"I love you too."

In my heart, I wanted to go and get her right away. Diane was such an innocent victim of what I considered very harsh treatment. Her temperament was one of complete obedience to anyone over her. It frightened me what her parents could do, if they so chose.

Tuesday came and went with no problems. I managed to find a furnished apartment on West Illinois Avenue in Dallas. I placed a deposit on it. On Wednesday, I went to pick her up to show her the apartment and to take her to church in Forney. Although the apartment complex wasn't too pretty, it was cheap and near the college. Diane didn't seem to mind it.

"Tomorrow, after classes, I'm coming over to load your stuff. We'll take them to the apartment. Do we need to take your car over then?"

"No. My dad said I could not keep the car. After I drive out to the rehearsal, tomorrow, he wants my keys."

"He doesn't need your car. That's cruel."

"It's okay. We'll manage."

"You bet we will. My Oldsmobile is your car now. It's time you got out of that Toyota anyhow."

She smiled. "You make me feel so special, Johnnie."

"That's because you are special, so very special to me."

Thursday came without any problems with Diane's parents. They remained in their bedroom as we loaded my car with Diane's belongings and all the gifts we had received from a prior wedding shower. I think we made several trips to the apartment. We spent most of Thursday evening setting up our first home. It was a special night.

Friday was rehearsal day in Forney. After classes, I called Diane.

"You ready for the rehearsal?"

"Almost. My parents are not coming out, so I'll have to drive out myself."

"No way! I'll come by and get you."

Diane was not used to someone helping her. She was a hard worker and did many chores around her house. Her parents did not like a free-thinker, such as me. They had Diane doing everything they asked her to do. I think they realized that they were about to lose a tremendous helper around the house.

The rehearsal went well in Forney. Brother Jerry informed us that there was a sports banquet tomorrow night at the high school; therefore, many of the church members—especially youth—were not able to attend the wedding. There was also a chance of rain all day tomorrow.

February 1, 1975 – Wedding Bells

I awoke to rain. It had begun raining early. In fact, it rained nearly all day. There was some flooding reported in low areas around Dallas. I had moved into our apartment on West Illinois Avenue in Dallas. I called Diane.

"Good wet morning, Mrs. Jones." She laughed.
"Good morning to you Mr. Jones. Did you sleep well?"
"Oh yeah, but nothing like tonight!" She muffled her laugh this time.

"You'd better watch what you say, Mr. Jones."
"Oh, that's right, we're not married yet. So what are you doing today?"
"Well, Debbie and Mother are checking on the cake and stuff for delivery to Forney. I suppose I will help them."
"And how will you get to the church?"
"Mother and Daddy will bring me."
"Remind them, if you can, that all this rain may slow traffic out of town. I don't want you to be late."
"I'll have to wait and see if they're talking to me today."
"If there's any hint of a problem, please call me. I plan to arrive at the church at five. You should plan to do the same thing." (The wedding was at 7:00 p.m.)
"Okay. I love you, Johnnie Ray Jones."
"And I love you, Diane Elaine Leroy Jones." She laughed again.
"I'll see you tonight."

The day was long. I went over to Ed's house and hung out with him most of the day. The rain was torrential at times. I wondered if anyone would be able to get to Forney tonight.

Finally, at about four, the rain let up. I was back at the apartment and getting my suit into the car. The drive out to Forney was a bit slower, but fortunately there were no road closures on my route. The church was open and decorated. A friend of Diane's family had come out earlier to set up the church for the ceremony and the reception. After the reception, Diane and I were to change clothes and drive out to North Dallas to the Dallas North Marriott at LBJ (I-635) and Central. We had a honeymoon suite reserved for us.

At 5:30, I was dressed and ready. But there was no Diane. They had not arrived. Everyone was arriving, but at six, there was still no Diane. I began to pace the foyer floor.

"It'll be okay, Johnnie," said Brother Jerry. "I'm sure the wet roads have traffic going pretty slow this way."

"I sure hope everything's okay."

"You think her parents kidnapped her, Jonesie?" asked Ed.

"Don't get me thinking such thoughts."

At 6:30, Debbie burst through the foyer doors. "They're here!" she hollered. "Johnnie, get out of the foyer! You're not supposed to see her."

Ed, Bill Cates, and I left the area. Bill was a Forney youth who was my second escort. Ed was my best man. Word came to us that the Leroy's had some problems getting out of Dallas. But, thank God, they were there and now the wedding was a definite go!

The ceremony began a few minutes late, but that was okay. Diane's parents did their part in the ceremony and the pictures afterwards, but refused to stand in the reception line in the fellowship hall. But it was such a busy and happy occasion that their absence didn't seem to affect the crowd. The important thing was that there, beside me, stood a beautiful, bashful bride. She was dressed in a beautiful white wedding gown, headpiece and all. As often as I could, I squeezed her hand to let her know that she was beside someone who loved her and was committed to making her the happiest married woman in town.

After we changed into street clothes, we headed out to the car. Everyone was waiting with bags of rice to throw on us. Ed had borrowed my keys earlier to pull the car up and, true to tradition, rice and shoe polish was everywhere, inside and outside the car. We pulled away from the church with Ed and his family following right on our tail, blowing his horn. We headed out to the freeway, but instead of getting on it and heading for Dallas, I decided to see if I could shake Ed off my rear. For a few streets he stayed with me, but my knowledge of the area finally won out and I lost him. Diane was laughing and having the time of her new married life. Little did she know that she had married a guy who was committed to making her laugh.

After stopping for a few minutes, we made our way back to the freeway entrance ramp with no sign of Ed. *Good!* I thought. We merged onto the freeway and was about to begin a peaceful trip into Dallas when, lo and behold, there was Ed parked on the side of the freeway. He saw us pass him and then proceeded to catch up with us. I didn't resist this time because I was anxious to get on down the road. After a few minutes of Ed driving alongside of us and honking his horn, he finally sped on ahead and disappeared into the night traffic.

About thirty minutes later we pulled into the North Dallas Marriott on I-635, near Central Expressway. We checked into the hotel and then we went to a restaurant to eat. When we came back, we decided to bring to the room the extra gifts given to us at the wedding. It was a beautiful beginning of a marriage made in heaven.

The next day, we left the hotel and headed for our apartment on W. Illinois. On the way, we stopped at a Kroger's for some basic food. Diane had said she was going to cook for us. She had a new cookbook for the house, so it wasn't too bad. I do remember her first attempt at cooking pinto beans. She was so proud of herself for having cooked those beans most of the day. We sat down for supper to enjoy them, but after several bites I bit into a rock.

"Ouch! What is this?"

"I don't know; it looks like a small rock."

"Didn't you pick the rocks out of the beans before you cooked them?"

"Oh no, I didn't know I was supposed to do that. I'm sorry." She began to cry.

"That's okay, love. We can eat around the rocks." I got up and held her tight as she cried. Then I began to carry her around the room awhile, swinging her and making her laugh. We got through this and ended up going out for pizza.

Diane's life with her dad and stepmother imbedded into her mind a fear of worthlessness. She shared things with me that her stepmother had said and done to her that was very inhumane and disgusting to me. Her step mom had developed an intense jealousy of Diane. Diane tried and tried to please her, but she seemed to never win the love and acceptance of her stepmother. I was happy to have gotten her out of that environment. Things would be different for her now.

Our first few months of marriage had its ups and downs. Diane contracted "mono" and I received a speeding ticket while taking her to the doctor. I was in school full time and still a youth minister at FBC, Forney. Diane and I drove out to Forney every Wednesday and every Sunday, meeting with and ministering to the youth. I also continued my Saturday trips to the church for visitation purposes.

Our finances were very low, so Diane decided she would find a part-time job as a secretary. She applied at the Frozen Food Express (FFE) on Cadiz Street in downtown Dallas and was hired as an entry clerk. She was an excellent, meticulous typist, so it wasn't much over a month that she was promoted to be a secretary for one of the supervisors. The only problem she incurred was a persistent cough from the intense cigarette smoke in her area. And her clothes smelled like cigarettes…ugh!

Summer came with a bang. Diane was not feeling well. We went to the doctor again and he referred her to a gynecologist, Dr. Godat. After some tests, he confirmed that she was pregnant and would be due in February…February 12th was the expected date. This brought new concerns. Diane was afraid to continue to work in a smoke-filled environment. She did not want to hurt the baby. I agreed, so she quit FFE. I mentioned it to Brother Jerry. He saw no reason why I couldn't work an additional part-time job, as long as I could be in Forney on Sundays.

"Brother Jerry, I will be here more than that, I promise you."

"I know you'll do the right thing, Johnnie. Let's just take care of Diane."

"Yes sir, I will."

On Wednesday nights, I was doing a Bible study with the youth. We were discussing what makes a local church function. On one particular Wednesday evening, I decided that the youth should go downstairs into the adult meeting because they were going to have the church's monthly business meeting. We came in while Brother Jerry was teaching on spiritual gifts. At the close of the lesson, we had prayer and then were called into order for a business meeting. Reports were made, old business attended to, and then the new business came up. A deacon stood up for a recommendation.

"I move that we increase our youth minister's salary from fifty dollars a week to seventy-five." A second was given and the voice vote carried its approval. Afterwards, I received a bunch of pats on the back and congratulations. It was all a surprise to me, as I did not know they were going to make this motion prior to the meeting.

Our apartment complex on West Illinois was a bit on the cheap side. Diane and I listened to several fights above us and numerous occasions of glass being broken and sometimes thrown down onto the cars outside our door. Because of the screams, we had to call the police several times. One time, the upstairs apartment toilet overflowed into our apartment. It was bad.

I talked it over with Ed and he helped me find an apartment in Grand Prairie, not too far from his rented house. The Grand Prairie complex also needed someone to clean out abandoned or evicted apartments. I received a hundred dollars off my monthly rent, plus an additional twenty dollars credit for each cleaned out apartment. This would allow us to make it financially.

To this day, I have never witnessed such filth that some people lived in. I remember one abandoned apartment where a motorcycle apparently had been overhauled in the living room. Oil and grease were on the walls and large oil stains were in the carpet. Graffiti was painted on the interior walls. Old cycle parts lay all over the floor.

Our apartment, however, was located above the offices, so we had a very quiet and up-front area. Ed would come by every school morning, honk his VW beetle horn, and I would run off to school with him. Sometimes I would play "hooky" and just motion him on when he blew his horn.

As 1975 came to a close, Diane was beginning to show her pregnancy very well. It was an exciting time for us, as a couple, but her parents would call us occasionally and we would go see them. It was a difficult thing to do because every time we visited them, Diane would revert back into her old self. Her parents did not understand (or chose not to understand) that the emotional scars they put on her would be permanent. I cooperated with the visits, but I—we—certainly did not enjoy them. We also had to "perform" for them; we could never be just ourselves.

February 6, 1976 – Welcome Jenny Carol Jones!

February 1st, 1976 was our first anniversary. Diane was about to "pop" with her pregnancy. Her due date was still the 12th. On the morning of the 6th, as I was getting ready for school, she was feeling some contraction pains. I had her call the doctor's office. The nurse told her to sit in a hot tub of water and if the contractions subsided, that usually meant that it wasn't time yet. This seemed to help some, so I left for school and returned early afternoon.

Diane was still having lots of contraction pain, so we called the doctor again. This time they asked us to come in to the office. Dr. Godat examined her and announced it was time and sent us over to Baylor Medical Center next door. I think it was about 4 p.m. when we arrived in Baylor. She was placed in a holding room to wait for delivery. The doctors and hospitals were now allowing the husbands to stay with their wives during this time, if they wanted to. Man, I was pumped and ready for the birth. I think Ed and Judy were in the waiting room and Diane's parents also.

Seven o'clock came, and then eight and nine. During the nine o'clock hour things got real tense in that holding room. Dr. Godat would come by and check Diane. He and the nurses would give her breathing instructions and tell her to push with her abdominal muscles really hard. That was a command that Diane gave with every ounce of her strength. She pushed so hard that she nearly passed out once.

Finally, at ten o'clock, Diane was rolled into the delivery room. I sat beside her as Dr. Godat prepared for the delivery. We did not know whether the baby was a boy or a girl and really didn't care, as long as it was healthy. A mirror was strategically placed where I could watch the baby being born. Then came the commands again.

"Diane, I need you to push when I tell you," he said. "Okay?"

"Okay," she responded with a frightened look. I held her hand and talked to her, telling her she was doing a great job.

"Now push Diane," said the doctor. "Push much harder." She groaned as she pushed with all her might. I saw the top of the baby's head.

"It's coming, honey, I can see the head."

"Push again, Diane. You've got to give me a good one this time." Once again, she gave it her all and out popped the entire head of the baby.

"Okay Diane, we've got the hard part finished, but you've got to give me one more long push. Do it now!" Diane groaned out loudly as she clenched my hands and gave it all she could. This time the baby's body came completely out. I couldn't see through all the afterbirth if it was a girl or a boy. Dr. Godat began to inspect the baby.

"Oh, looks like you have a fine looking girl."

"It's a girl, Diane," I shouted. "Did you hear that? It's a girl!" We were both crying and thanking God for a beautiful baby. The nurse began to wipe off our little girl as Dr. Godat cut the umbilical cord and began to sew up Diane where he had previously cut. I went over with the nurse to watch her clean up our new baby.

"What's her name?" she asked.

I looked over at Diane. "Jenny Carol Jones, right?"

Diane managed to squeak out a "Yes." She was shivering badly.

"What's wrong with Diane?" I asked the doctor.

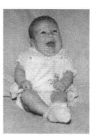

"It's the epidural," he responded. "It'll go away later tonight. She'll need to rest as much as possible. Congratulations Johnnie and Diane."

"Oh, thank you so much, Dr. Godat. You were great."

"Diane did most of the work. I'm just a coach."

"Yeah, she's the greatest," I responded, as I looked over at her. She was not asleep, but had her eyes closed. In a moment the nurse handed Jenny Carol over to Diane. It was a precious moment as we both cuddled over next to our precious gift from God.

"Mr. Jones," said the nurse. "We need to move Diane over to recovery. From the waiting room, you go down the hall and turn left. Press the button and they will let you in. Now I think you may have some folks out in the waiting room who need to hear from you?"

"Oh, yes indeed. I'd better get out there. Hon, I'll be with you in a few minutes. You rest now, okay?" Again, a nod was about all Diane could muster. I hurried out to the waiting room.

"It's a girl!" Loud shouts and congratulations came from all as I made the announcement. "Jenny Carol Jones was born at 10:16 p.m., weighing 8 pounds and 8 ½ ounces, and 20 ¼ inches long."

"And Diane?" asked her stepmother.

"She's shivering a bit, due to the epidural, but the doctor says she'll be okay. She's in recovery now and will be moved upstairs later on in the early morning. The doctor says she needs to rest as much as possible."

"The epidural should begin wearing off in a couple hours," said Mrs. Leroy. "She'll be very thirsty, but be careful how much fluid she takes in. She could throw it up."

"I'll remember that, and thanks for coming."

"Come on, Bob. We'd better go home. We'll call and speak with Diane tomorrow evening."

"Oh please come to see her and your new grand baby."

"Jenny Carol; that's a pretty name, don't you think Bob?"

"Yes, a pretty name," he responded.

With that bit of communication, the Leroy's left. Ed and Judy hung out to go by the nursery with me to see Jenny Carol. After a few minutes they left also. I hurried back to stay with Diane. When I found her, they had already given her a cup of ice chips. I fed her some as her shivering began to decline.

About an hour later, we moved Diane up to a private room. The nurses were all congratulating us as they arranged Diane in her room.

"Is there anything you need, Diane?" they asked.

"I'm very hungry and thirsty. When can I eat?" I had forgotten that Diane hadn't eaten since breakfast.

"Oh, you can have something right now, if you wish."

They brought her a sandwich and a Sprite. She gobbled it up as if it was a gourmet meal. Then she rested.

I went down the hall to the nursery to find Jenny. After a few maneuvers, the nurse brought her basinet over to the window for me to look at. I stood there in awe. I could not fully comprehend this miracle of life that God allowed Diane and I to produce. As I stared at her, I began thanking God for her and telling him that I needed His guidance in bringing her up in a godly way. I dedicated her to Him right then and there.

Jenny was brought to Diane a few hours later. Diane would try nursing her. Neither of us knew what to do or what to expect. The nurses coached Diane a little and we agreed that maybe Jenny would need some formula as well. It was a difficult process for Diane, as she had never been around a family with a newborn baby.

Jenny was born on a Friday. Our youth Valentine's banquet was the next evening. A couple from Tarrant Road Baptist Church, Ed and Sherrie Laymance, were our banquet guests. Diane was feeling well enough to allow me to attend the banquet. Ed was a great communicator and played the guitar. It was a special night, especially when he led us in the song, "Because He Lives." Tears welled up in my eyes when the second stanza was sung, "How sweet to hold, a newborn baby, and feel the touch and joy it brings..." I received a few pats on the back from those around me.

We brought Jenny home to our apartment on Tuesday. It was raining and cold, but nothing was going to dampen our spirits. Diane attempted to nurse Jenny, but was unsuccessful; so Jenny had to start early on formula. Judy Ethridge came over to help Diane adjust. She and Ed brought food over for us. We have thanked God many times for the Ethridges. They were like family to us.

I had to go back to school. I didn't want to, but I left Diane alone with Jenny. Diane had to learn a lot on her own. Childcare was all so very new to her. She cried a lot those first few weeks. And Jenny cried a lot as well. We made arrangements for a couple in our church, Bill and Gwen Smith, to keep Jenny for a few hours while Diane and I went out with the youth to our monthly Youth for Christ rally. Diane fed her just before we left, and we didn't leave any formula for her because we knew we would be back in a few hours.

When we returned, Jenny was sound asleep on a pallet on the floor. Gwen was anxious to talk to us.

"I'm sorry, Diane, but Jenny began to cry right after you left. I had Bill and Ricky (her son) run to the store to get some milk. She drank over six ounces and then fell asleep. She cried and cried and I told Bill, she's hungry and we need to feed her. After she ate, she feel asleep and has been sleeping ever since."

That was when we realized that we were not feeding Jenny enough. We called Dr. Godat's office the next day. He told us to increase her formula and they would send out some pills for Diane to take to help her dry up her milk supply. After putting Jenny on more formula, she stopped crying as much and life got a lot more peaceful at home.

Ed and Judy Ethridge were a Godsend for Diane and me. Ed's boldness opened many opportunities for me to meet and make new friends. Anyone who hung out with Ed usually hung out with a group of three or four more. Judy came over to the apartment to help Diane with Jenny. Diane had no childrearing training, as her real mother was basically an invalid during her childhood years. After her death, came her stepmother who maintained a jealousy with Diane so much so that there was no relationship established between the two. But the beauty of Diane's personality was that once she had a project or duty to perform, she gave it a 100 percent in doing it perfectly.

I was in my third semester at DBC and was growing in my knowledge of God and His word. I was also gaining beneficial experience in pastoral duties at First Baptist in Forney. Brother Jerry was a busy pastor, but managed to sit with me over coffee occasionally and give me ministerial tidbits that would add depth to my ministry. I was given an opportunity to preach for him on several occasions. I really enjoyed the youth at Forney. We had two youth Sunday School departments that kept me running back and forth to each during the opening sessions. The summer found Diane and I planning many activities with our youth "congregation."

In the fall, Ed and I signed up for our classes. We weren't able to sign up for the same classes because I was attending summer classes and he wasn't. But we managed to have several together each semester. About mid-semester, Ed came to me with a proposition.

"Jonesie, Dr. Trammell asked me if I was interested in pastoring a small church south of Dallas. I'm pretty much satisfied helping Chris Leibrum with the youth at Fairview (Baptist Church in Grand Prairie). I gave him your name."

"My name? Really?"

"Yeah, I figure you can handle it."

"Oh yeah, how many are attending?

"About a dozen."

I stared a bit at him, wondering if he was actually doing me a favor. But I really felt a calling to teach the Bible in an in-depth way and pastoring seemed to be the ultimate position to teach.

"Where is this church?"

"I think he said it was in a town called Wilmer. That's about all I know about the place."

"Wilmer, Texas…sounds okay, don't you think?"

Ed laughed. "Jonesie, you don't go by sounds, unless it's God speaking to you. Anyhow, Trammell may not even call you."

Dr. Trammell didn't have to call me because I was in class with him the next day. After class, he asked me to stay behind for a minute.

"Johnnie, your friend, Ed Ethridge, suggested I consider you as a recommendation to a church that I am currently serving in as their interim. I hadn't thought of you, but as I thought it over I feel compelled to recommend you. Are you interested in preaching in my stead?"

"Wow, Dr. Trammell, I'm honored to be considered, but I'm not sure I'm ready for the position just yet. I've only been a youth director for a year."

"Do you plan to stay in the youth ministry?"

"I sure do like it and it's really all I've ever done in church service. I don't know."

"Well, the youth ministry is certainly a noble task, but perhaps you should open yourself for other types of service and let our Lord guide you in it."

"If you think I'm capable, I'm available."

"I've got to be out of town Sunday after next. Let me give the man in charge of the Pulpit Committee your name and phone number and we'll go from there."

"Yes sir!" I have to admit, I was excited about the possibility. But I was not aware of any requirements for becoming a preacher. Later, that day, I met with Ed and, together, we formulated some ideas as to a schedule I could keep as a "preacher."

Monday came and I went to school. No word yet from the church in Wilmer. Dr. Trammell said it was called, North Wilmer Baptist Church, and it was located on the southbound feeder of Interstate 45. After school, I went to work, and then came home for supper. Diane had supper waiting on the table.

"A Mr. Henderson, from Wilmer, called you. He wants you to call him tonight."

This was it. Diane knew about it and we had begun praying for God to reveal His will in the matter.

"What do you think?" I asked her.

"I'll go wherever the Lord sends us as long as I'm with you." Diane was a willing and submissive servant of the Lord and of me. It reminded me that every decision I made involved more than just me. Now I have a wife and a baby girl to think of.

"I don't know. I enjoy the youth ministry, but I certainly don't want to tell God what I can and can't do."

"Well, I think you'll make a good pastor. You love people and want to help them grow spiritually."

That was one of my strengths. At Forney, I was already dissecting the Gospel of John and developing my own study sheets for our Wednesday evening Bible studies. But could I do this for adults?

I called Don Henderson after supper. He asked me if I would come and preach at North Wilmer in Dr. Trammell's absence. I accepted the invitation.

On Wednesday, I informed Brother Jerry. He was okay with it and told me to be sure others covered the youth announcements.

Sunday came and Diane and I headed for North Wilmer. There were about three elementary children, two youth, and about eight adults in Sunday School. Two of the adults were teaching the children and youth. Diane stayed with Jenny in the nursery. For the morning service, another family of four came in, plus another young person. Seventeen was a bit smaller than the hundreds I was accustomed to at Forney. But it was a start.

I think Don's wife usually played the piano, but when they found out that Diane played, Mrs. Henderson didn't show up for the service. I think it was planned that way. So Diane played while a Mrs. Sealey held Jenny. Mr. Henderson led the music and I preached. After the service, Mr. and Mrs. A. E. Sealey had us over at their house for lunch and a place to rest for the afternoon. He was a deacon—the only deacon—and the treasurer of the church, and she was the children's Sunday School teacher. They also served as volunteers at Baylor Hospital in Dallas. It was a pleasant afternoon. After lunch, while I prepared for the evening service, Diane visited with Mrs. Sealey. We also managed to squeak in a guided tour of Wilmer. Mr. Sealey had a small accountant's business in the town. They also showed us the church's house, called a "parsonage." It was located at 223 Thorne Street.

The evening service had similar faces as the morning with a couple faces missing, but an equal amount of new faces present. I preached again, but had no idea if I was doing it right or to their liking. Diane and I left for Grand Prairie after the service.

"Well, what do you think?" I asked first.

"I don't know. I think you did okay. I hope I wasn't too loud on the piano."

"Oh you did just fine. I think they liked your playing more than my preaching."

Diane smiled and squeezed my hand. We both played with Jenny, who was seated between us in a little car seat.

Don called again on Tuesday.

"Brother Jones, our committee met last night and we want to meet with you and Diane to ask you some questions about becoming our pastor. Could you come back out next Sunday and preach again?"

I looked over in Diane's direction. She was already nodding a "yes" with a smile on her face. "Yes sir, we would be delighted!"

"Okay, I guess I'll see you then."

"Yee-hah!" I screamed. Jenny started crying. Diane started hushing me as she went to pick up Jenny. "Can you believe this?"

"I guess they liked you after all," she said.

"I guess so. Oh, I've got to call Ed" I picked up the phone: "Ed, guess what?"

"You're going to be a pastor, that's what!"

"How'd you know?"

"I can tell it in your voice. I guess things went well for you?"

"Yep; it wasn't me as much as it was Diane's playing."

"I figured that."

"They want me back out this Sunday for preaching and a meeting with the committee. I'm going to need some help from you, cause I haven't the faintest idea what to say or ask."

"I'll check with Brother Duncan at Fairview. He'll have some good ideas. And remember, Jonesie, you owe me!"

"Yeah, yeah; gotta go, see ya!"

It was now Wednesday. I spoke with Dr. Trammell, after class, and told him. He smiled, already knowing the setup for Sunday. I also met with Brother Jerry after the evening services and told him.

"I kind of figured that was going to happen. Study the word and love the people, Johnnie, and you'll go far in ministry."

"Thanks. I'll cover my youth bases for Sunday."

I preached for North Wilmer again. This time, there were about twenty-two in the morning service. After service, the committee met at the Sealey's for lunch and the meeting. On the committee were Mr. Sealey, Mr. Henderson, and a Mrs. George. It was a good meeting. We traded a bunch of information. On the physical aspect, they were offering $100 a week, plus the parsonage and utilities. I was excited and Diane was excited to be able to move out of our one-bedroom apartment into a three-bedroom house. Jenny would have her own room!

The Sunday evening service went smoothly and we left thereafter. On Tuesday evening, Don Henderson called me.

"Brother Jones, the committee has met again and wants to extend an invitation for you to come in view of a call to be our pastor."

Diane and I had previously prayed about our ministry and agreed that if the phone call came, we would go.

"Yes sir. When do you want us to come?"

"Is this Sunday okay?"

"I suppose so. I think my church in Forney realizes it is just a matter of time."

"Well, I hope so. We'll hear you preach both services, and then we'll ask you and Diane to be dismissed as we take a vote. Then, you'll both come back into the meeting for the announcement. Do you have any questions?"

"Nope. Sounds great to me."

It was obvious that Diane and I were excited about our first pastorate. I could not believe that I was actually being considered as a pastor. My thoughts took me back to my former pastor in Hawaii, Bill Smith. He was a giant of a man to me. I loved him and hung my spiritual life on every word he preached. Then there was David George at Tarrant Road in Fort Worth. David was studying for his doctorate and was in training as a counselor at the seminary. When David preached, he never planned his illustrations for his sermons. I was amazed at his ability to preach and to make the sermon so relevant.

"Me? A pastor?" The thought frightened me. I talked to Brother Jerry the following Saturday about it.

"Jerry, I'm nervous about preaching every Sunday. Where do I find topics for every week?" He smiled.

"Johnnie, there's two ways to plan to preach. You can choose themes and find plenty of books to prepare from, or you can take your Bible and preach through a book of the Bible."

"You seem to favor themes."

"Right now, I do; but many times I go through a Bible book and pull out the themes of each chapter or paragraph. You can do it either way as long as you make sure the Bible passages are driving the messages you preach."

"What about my nervousness?"

"I can't help you there. I've been preaching over twenty years and I still get nervous."

"Really? You, nervous?"

He smiled. "Sure; and I'd be really concerned if you weren't. You have to learn to commit yourself to God for the deliverance of His word. You're simply a messenger with a message from God to His people. Learn to trust Him and His word to do the work of converting souls and teaching the believers."

North Wilmer Baptist Church, Wilmer, Texas

It was now April of 1976. With Jerry's and Ed's encouragement, Diane and I prayed much and prepared for Sunday's "call" from North Wilmer Baptist Church. The services went well. I think the George family had us over for lunch. They had a charming daughter, Ruby. She loved Jenny and played with her most of Jenny's waking hours. The vote was taken and it was unanimous for me to come and be their pastor. I accepted, of course.

I would spend one more Sunday at Forney, and then move over to Wilmer as a pastor. There was a farewell party for us at the church and many young people and their parents came to send us off. Although I was there for only a year, we had made numerous friends among the people.

I remained at North Wilmer for two years (1976-1978). First Baptist Church of Forney ordained me on May 9, 1976. FBC Forney was transferring from a large school bus for transportation to two smaller vans. I asked Brother Jerry about purchasing the large bus for our church because we had a large area of low income housing in Wilmer and I had a man in our church that was interested in helping me bring more children to our Sunday

School. A few weeks after my ordination, I received a call from Jerry to come and get our new bus.

"What? Jerry, how much are you asking for it?"

"Nothing; it's a gift from our church to yours. You just come and get it and take care of all the transfers and it's yours."

Wow, I couldn't believe it. And my bus "pastor," Brother X, was elated. His dad worked for the City of Dallas and had access to a paint barn for large vehicles. "I'll check with my supervisor to see if we can use it one Saturday during off hours," he said.

The church grew from a beginning Sunday School average of twelve to forty-nine the first year. We had a few adults to join and I baptized a few young people, but by and large, our growth came from our bus ministry.

One Sunday, we had a bright idea to take all bus children to the Dallas Zoo if they came to Sunday School. The Saturday prior, we visited our usual twenty or so bus children's homes and invited them to bring someone with them for tomorrow's hotdog lunch and zoo trip. The next day, over 80 children rode the bus to church! We had to have Sunday School outside and make most of them sit on the floor during church.

With only four adults as chaperones to the zoo, we stuck masking tape on the back of each child and wrote a number on each, starting with number 1. Then the children had to line up in sequence by their number and hold the hand of the next child in line. Watching a line of eighty children wind through the zoo was quite a sight, but we managed to do so with no one getting lost. That was the first and the last time we tried to do something like that!

Because of her stepmother, Diane was not allowed to keep in touch with her family on her birth-mother's side. She still had a living grandmother, Bess Qualls Knight, who we found in a nursing home in Omaha, Texas. Diane and I talked about it several times and decided we would drive up to Omaha to see her grandmother. Mrs. Knight, or "Mama" Knight, could hardly believe her eyes when she saw her only grandchild. It was like a dream come true for her. Also, she could hardly keep her eyes and hands off of Jenny.

We tried to go see her occasionally, as time allowed, but it wasn't enough for Mama Knight. A few months after visiting her for the first time, she arrived in Wilmer, in the front seat of a friend's car. She had taken it upon herself to relocate to another nursing home in neighboring Lancaster, a town about five miles west of Wilmer. Thus, she became a part of our weekly routine.

Mama Knight had mentioned she had some money for Diane and that she wanted me to go to her house and get all her furniture and belongings. She was renting a house from a brother-in-law, Mr. Clyde Knight, in Omaha, Texas. (Later, we discovered many of Diane's relatives, the Ragland family, were buried in Spring Hill Cemetery, near Omaha, on US Highway 259.)

"I'll have to wait until I have some money and time to go up there, Mama Knight."

"Oh yes, I understand. I told Clyde I would have it cleared out by the end of the month. Please use some of Diane's money to move your new furniture out. Her grandfather, Jesse, built the bedroom suits. I'm sure she'll remember them when she sees them."

That gave me about two weeks to plan for this move. And what about the money? After she and her friend left for Lancaster, I queried Diane.

"Did she tell you anything about money?"

"No, nothing more than what you heard her say."

"Oh well, I hope it's enough to move her stuff—I mean YOUR stuff," I said with a smile.

"What will we do with it?" she asked.

"I don't know...have a yard sale? It sounded as if some of it is worth keeping. Did your grand-paw Knight build furniture?"

Diane began to tell me of his house-building and carpentering business in Dallas. He built many homes, including their own and the one across the street that she grew up in as a child. They were located on Satsuma Street in Dallas. He also built a lot of play furniture for Diane, his only grandchild.

A few days after Mama Knight's initial visit in Wilmer, Diane received a letter from a savings and loan office in Dallas. We had given Mama Knight our address when we visited her in Omaha. The cover letter simply stated that Mrs. Jesse (Bess) Qualls Knight had transferred two certificates of deposit into the name of her granddaughter, Mrs. Diane Leroy Jones, effective immediately. It ended with instructions on renewal and penalties for early withdrawals.

Diane handed me the cover letter and looked at page two, the statement of her new account.

"What!? Oh, Johnnie, this can't be right." I took it from her hand. One CD was approximately $6,000, and the other was $20,000!

"Oh my, we'd better call this place to confirm." Diane did so and, sure enough, she was the sole possessor of $26,000. (In 1977, that was well over a year's wage, about two years my wage earnings.) We sat at the kitchen table, both dumbfounded, nearly afraid to speak.

"What are we going to do with this?" Diane asked.

"I don't know. She mentioned something about using it as a down payment for you a house."

"Yeah, but we can't just go and buy a house. Plus we have immediate needs that are more important." One such need was our debt to Baylor Hospital and Dr. Godat for Jenny. We had no medical insurance at the time.

"But first, we need to pay Mama Knight a visit," I said.

"Why?"

"Because, if there are any strings attached to this money, it goes back into her name."

Diane agreed this was the right thing to do. Our financial condition at Wilmer had worsened due to our growing family. Diane began to give piano lessons to Ruby George each week. This helped some, but my Texas Rehab grant had ceased due to some law changes. I had previously discussed with Diane my need to find a part-time job. We only had one automobile and I did not like leaving Diane at home without a vehicle when I went to college. Perhaps this money was the answer to our current financial needs? We drove over to Lancaster to see Mama Knight.

"Mama Knight," said Diane. "We received a letter about the money you placed in my name."

"Oh, that's wonderful. I wanted you to have it so that someday you may have a little home of your own."

"Well, thank you; but Johnnie and I have other needs we want to talk to you about." With that statement, Diane turned it over to me.

"Mama Knight, you know that I'm in college and my church ministry is part time. I was about to have to find another job to work alongside my church work and my college work. Diane also needs to have access to a car while I'm in school or at work."

"Oh my," she responded.

"We really appreciate your concern that Diane has a home later on, but this money will help us survive right now and this is what we want to use it for."

"Oh, I don't know. Diane, are you sure this is what you want to do?"

"Yes, Mama Knight. I don't want Johnnie to have to work another job. He has a large load right now with the church and full-time college."

"Well, it's your money now and I trust you'll do the right thing. I just wanted you to have something nice later on."

"We will, Mama Knight. The Lord will take care of us."

"And you have become a vital part to that care," I interjected. "I will have better control of my time and Diane will have access to a car while I'm away."

"A car?" she asked. "Oh, you will come to see me often, won't you Diane?"

"Yes, Mama Knight, I'll come when time allows."

With Mama Knight's approval, we transferred the smaller CD into a regular savings account and broke the larger one into several smaller CDs. We paid off our debts and I bought a used VW Beetle for my drives to Dallas Baptist College. I also declined a raise at the church, since it was not needed. Ed and I traveled to Omaha and picked up a truckload of furnishings. The bedroom suits were made of pine and were something  Diane would remember. The rest of the furniture was not worth replacing what we already had. Most of it was given to another college student who was helping me as our music director at North Wilmer. The money was a Godsend for us financially and prevented me from having to seek another job.

My ministry continued to develop and my college classes were very demanding. Ed and I would study together way into the early hours of the morning, then ride over to the Waffle House for some coffee and an early breakfast. Although no classes were a "give-me," philosophy classes were extremely tough. We had heard that a couple guys dropped out of the ministry-track curriculum because of philosophy. That news was about all Ed could take.

"Come on, Jonesie, we're paying Mr. Braidfoot a visit." He was our philosophy teacher. Upon arrival in his office, Ed began to share his concerns with Mr. Braidfoot and how he was going a little too far with his views of philosophy. I was there for moral support. Mr. Braidfoot was kind and listened to Ed's presentation.

"There's nothing wrong with sharing all these philosophical views out there," said Ed. "It's just that you have a tendency to present them without a Christian rebuttal. It really messes with a man's mind when you do that, and some of our classmates are dropping out of the ministry because of your philosophy classes."

"I see what you mean," said Mr. Braidfoot. "I'll try to remember that." With that statement, he apologized and said he would reevaluate his emphasis in his lectures. After this encounter, we became good friends with Mr. Braidfoot and he began to incorporate some Christian rebuttals to many of the philosophical views of life in the world.

Diane became pregnant again in early '77. We, of course, were excited about this. Jenny would have a new sister or brother. Diane's morning sickness was about as regular as with the pregnancy of Jenny. I felt so bad for her, but there was nothing I could do about it. Dr. Godat was informed and appointments were made. Again, Mama Knight's money would pay for this child.

In the spring of 1977, I put together a Bible conference at our church. It would coincide with our state convention's "Living Proof" promotional theme. I asked all my religion professors and our current college president, Dr. Thorn, to come to North Wilmer and preach one night each. Dr.'s Fletcher, Trammell, White, Bell, and Thorn accepted the invitation. I bring this conference up because it became pivotal to my future role as pastor of North Wilmer.

I believe it was on a Wednesday night that Dr. White preached on the assigned theme of the Bible. He did an excellent job, but made one statement that caused a problem. He was discussing the different translations and downgraded the King James Version as the only English version.

"We should not use only the King James Version in our reading of the Bible," he said. And with his trademark chuckle remarked, "You need to remember that it has a few flaws and there wasn't a single Baptist on the translating committee."

That remark caused the X family [name withheld] to stop attending our church. I heard about the issue a few days afterwards when Brother X and his dad said they were not going to do the bus route anymore. I called Mr. Sealey and told him about it. He, being my treasurer and only active deacon at the time, went over to visit the X-family. Sunday came and our attendance was literally cut in half, because of the X-family, their children, and their children's children. I was heartbroken. Mr. Sealey and I visited after church.

"Johnnie, I went to speak with Mr. and Mrs. X. I told them that Dr. White didn't mean any harm about his view of the Bible, but that there were indeed other Bible translations that are very enjoyable to read. I also told them how my wife and I support the American Bible Society by sending out a Good News Bible overseas once a month."

"Did they listen?"

"I'm afraid not. In fact, one son in the X-family called the Good News Bible, 'Bad News for Lost Sinners.' I didn't realize they were that sensitive about using only the King James Version."

When I was first saved in Hawaii, I was given a New American Standard Bible at Waialae. It was when I met Diane that I learned, through her dad, that the King James was the preferred version of Baptists, according to him. Mr. Leroy gave me a bunch of articles to read and subscribed me to *The Sword of the Lord* periodical to help me understand conservative Baptist views. Although this periodical was written mainly by independent, fundamental Baptists, Mr. Leroy was a Southern Baptist. He had bought me a New Schofield Reference Bible and I was preaching from that Bible. First Baptist, Forney had also given me a King James Version for my ordination Bible.

I decided to go to the X-family on Monday. It seems that they blamed me for Dr. White's statement, even though I had no previous knowledge of what he would say, or any of the others for that matter.

Mrs. X was crying when I entered the house. She just couldn't believe that her church would attack the King James Bible. I tried to reason with her and tried to assure her that I would preach from the King James Version. But my words didn't seem to reach her heart.

"I never knew someone would say from the pulpit of my church that my Bible had mistakes in it."

"I'm so sorry, Mrs. X, I'm sure he meant that there were various interpretations of certain passages. Take Hebrews 4:8 for example…" I had studied the similarity of the two words, "Joshua" and "Jesus," in the Greek and had preferred the context as referring to Joshua, even though the King James Version used Jesus' name. It wasn't a big deal to me, but made me realize the value of reading the original languages of the Bible. But I didn't get to give my "example."

"I don't want to hear it," said Mr. X from his ice cream bowl in the kitchen. I wasn't aware he was listening. "You're just a man and you can't correct the Bible."

"I'm not trying to correct the Bible, sir, I'm just trying to give an example of why some Bibles have different words from the King James Version." Mrs. X got out of her seat.

"I want to show you something," she said, as she was walking past me toward a closet. I remained seated as she pulled out a paper sack. She was trembling as she brought me the sack and began to reveal its contents. It was an old Bible.

"This Bible belonged to my grandfather," she said, while still sobbing. "It's all I have for remembering him. He passed it down through our family, telling us to believe every word of it as the Word of God. We do believe every word of it, and my children believe every word of it."

"I believe every word of it too, Mrs. X. It's God's Word."

"That's not what your teacher said," shouted Mr. X from the kitchen.

"Mr. X, I don't think he meant to discredit the Bible as God's Word. He was only mentioning the translating of certain words from the Greek to English. It's difficult translating from one language to another."

"I'm not interested in the Greek. What I want to know is if you believe this Bible (pointing to the heirloom in his wife's hands) has any mistakes in it?"

"I believe God has preserved His word for us to have an inspired copy of it, but I can't agree that the King James is the only English version we should have."

That statement basically drove a wedge between the X-family and me. I could not agree that the King James Version was the only English version for the English-speaking world. For the first two hundred years, all King James Bibles had the apocrypha books in them, books not recognized by non-Catholics as inspired. So it was hard for me (and most Protestants) to see the KJV as a perfect—or the only—English translation.

The X-family, however, did not see it that way, so they began attending church elsewhere, which caused our church a loss of teachers and attendees. I called Mr. Sealey and explained the results of my visit with the X-family. The next day, Mr. Sealey came to my study in the church. In his hands, he had a large stack of papers and a business-sized checkbook.

"I talked the situation over with Mrs. Sealey and we decided that we would resign our positions in the church and leave so that the X-family would come back. They're a much larger family than we two and we don't want to see our church fall apart over us."

I was somewhat stunned as he placed on my desk all that was in his hands.

"What is this?"

"It's the church checking account and all the legal papers of the property. You can come by my office tomorrow and I'll transfer all my names off the account and property deeds and you can put them in your name or someone else's."

"No sir!" I said with a raised voice as I stood up. "You and Mrs. Sealey are not the problem. The X's rejected me as well and they're not returning as long as I'm here."

Mr. Sealey managed a smile as he continued to offer his resignation.

"Mr. Sealey, if you and your wife leave, then I can assure you that what you said you didn't want to happen will indeed happen. You two are the only leadership I have now and you're not giving in to those who oppose us and you're not handing this church over to me."

"But we don't want to hinder the future of North Wilmer."

"You're not, but you will if you leave."

He looked at me as I grabbed the papers and checkbook, and handed them back to him.

"I believe these belong to you," I said as I handed the stack back to him.

"Are you sure?"

"Absolutely."

That event made me realize how fragile church ministry can be and that I had to be careful with my choice of words. I realized that I couldn't just say anything to my members without weighing the ramifications of each statement. I also learned that the church needed to be taught the need to tolerate some differences of opinions that each person may have.

The Sealey's remained faithful and another gentleman began driving our church bus. Although a few of the children continued to ride, it was never the same.

In May of 1977, I completed my requirements for my college degree. I received a Bachelor of Science degree with a major in Religion/Philosophy and Psychology. I wasn't trying for a double major, but apparently my extra classes in psychology and sociology qualified me for both majors. Ed did not graduate until the end of the fall semester of '77. He had not attended summer classes as I did. He was now a pastor in Grand Prairie.

By the third week of May, I entered summer classes at Southwestern Baptist Theological Seminary in Fort Worth. I carpooled with another friend in Dallas, Jerry Nichols. Jerry, like Ed and I, was a bit older than the other college students. He was also a computer technician. We would meet early at DBC campus, and then carpool over to Fort Worth for classes.

The summer classes and church ministry were difficult for me. No matter how hard I tried, I just couldn't seem to get North Wilmer to grow again. Since I was a pastor in the Dallas Baptist Association, another pastor mentioned that he thought a Dr. Paige Patterson, an associate pastor at First Baptist Church of Dallas and the president of Criswell Bible Institute, had some connections with North Wilmer. This pastor suggested I talk to him.

One day, Dr. Patterson spoke at our weekly association's luncheon at FBC, Dallas. Afterwards, I approached him and introduced myself to him.

"Do you have a few minutes to talk?" I asked.

"Tell you what, I've got to run to Fort Worth for a meeting with some TCU (Texas Christian University) execs to try to get them to move their radio station frequency down a few notches in order for us to get our new station's frequency on the air. Why don't we visit as I go back to my office and then to my car?"

"Great; that's fine. A new radio station?"

"Yes, the Criswell Bible Institute is planning to start broadcasting this fall. You be sure and tell your church members about KCBI. It'll be up and running soon."

I began telling Dr. Patterson about my frustrations at North Wilmer and how I could not seem to get it moving again.

"How long have you been there?"

"February will be two years, sir."

"Well Johnnie, let me say this. You have been there more than most have stayed. I know some things about that church. It is a church for student pastors to go to, to get a taste of what a challenge a church can be. Do not let it drag you down; learn from your experiences there and I will pray for you, my brother, that God will have his sustaining hand upon your ministry."

By this time, we were at his car on a side street. He unlocked his door and got in.

"Thank you, Dr. Patterson. And I will pray that your trip to TCU will be successful."

"Thank you, brother, and don't forget to listen to KCBI. We're trying to get a frequency around the 88 FM range."

I prayed much about my effectiveness at North Wilmer from that time on.

Welcome Timothy Aaron Jones! – September 29, 1977

Summer ended and I passed all my classes. I began fall classes in late August. Diane's pregnancy was in full bloom. On September 29, 1977, Diane woke me up around 5:30 a.m. Her water had just broken. We hurriedly called the doctor's office. The answering service took down the message and soon Dr. Godat called back. After answering a few questions, he told us not to panic, that the baby wasn't quite ready, but to get dressed and come to his office around 9:00 a.m.

We got ready, took Jenny over to the George's, and headed into Dallas. I had called my mom previously and told her that I wanted her to fly down to Dallas and stay with us awhile until Diane was ready to get back on her own feet. Before we left for Dallas, I secured my mom's airplane ticket and called her.

"Mom, get yourself down to Greensboro today. Your flight leaves just before 2 p.m. Ed Ethridge will pick you up at the Dallas airport."

"Okay, darling. Y'all be careful, and tell Diane I love her and will see her soon."

We arrived at the doctor's office a little early, but were ushered on ahead of the rest. Dr. Godat arrived a few minutes after us and inspected Diane.

"The baby's not ready yet, but should be delivered later on tonight. You can go back home, get your stuff, and check into the hospital later this afternoon. They'll be expecting you and will call me once you're checked in."

We left his office and, being hungry, drove to a restaurant nearby. While eating, Diane began to leak water on the restaurant seat; so we had to leave. We checked into the hospital around 4:00 p.m. Diane's parents were not happy with us at this time, but I stilled called them to inform them about the event. I knew my mom was on her way and that Ed and Judy would be here as well.

Diane's labor was slow. An intern came in to check her periodically. About 8:00 p.m., he examined her again.

"Hmmm."

"What does 'hmmm' mean, Doc?"

"I don't know, but I think this child is breach."

"Meaning?"

"Well, I feel a limb first. It must be its leg and toes I'm feeling."

"Is that okay?"

"Oh yeah, they're born that way without any problems."

The labor pains were getting more frequent. About 8:15, Dr. Godat showed up. He immediately examined her.

"We need to x-ray you, Diane, to see what's going on with this baby."

They wheeled her out of her holding room and came back a few minutes later. About 8:45, Dr. Godat came back.

"Well here's what's happening. The baby is not breach, but its arm is stuck over its head and is trying to come through the birth canal that way. If we allow it, there may be permanent paralysis involved. So we're going to take you now and prep you for a Caesarean birth."

"What does that mean, Dr. Godat?" I was a bit naïve.

"Well, you won't be able to go back this time. We'll cut her tummy and bring the baby out that way. We need to do it now, so let's go."

Diane was whisked away as I kissed her. I then went out into the waiting area. About 9:15 p.m., A nurse came into the waiting area.

"Mr. Jones, you have a healthy little boy."

"And Diane?"

"Oh she's fine. The doctor is stitching her up now."

"A boy! It's a boy! That's great!"

"Yes, he was born at 9:09, weighed 7 pounds and 8 ½ ounces, and was 20 ⅛ inches long."

"Yee-haw!!"

"And does he have a name?" she asked.

"Oh yeah: Timothy Aaron Jones!"

"Well. Mr. Jones, your wife will be in recovery soon and Timothy Aaron will be down the hallway in the nursery in a few minutes. The doctor will come get you in a few minutes."

I headed for the nursery, since I wasn't allowed to go see Diane immediately. In a few minutes a nurse began to work a few cribs around until she brought my new son up to the window. He looked absolutely perfect, except for a small piece of tape on his head, just above one of his ears. I was in awe at his presence and began to thank God for his birth.

About this time, I began to hear some familiar voices. Ed, Judy, and my mother were walking towards me.

"Let me see that baby!" my mom hollered. I moved over as they began to look at Timothy Aaron.

"It's a boy, Mom! His name is Timothy Aaron."

"Oh, he is so beautiful, Johnnie!"

"Well, JJ, now you got a girl and a boy, just like us," said Judy. (Judy called me 'JJ' because I joked a lot and her mother called me 'JJ', in reference to a current television sitcom with a Black star called 'JJ.')

Timothy looked great. My mom was anxious to hold him.

"Y'all stay here or go to the waiting room, while I try to check on Diane."

"Have you seen her?" asked Judy.

"Not yet; they were stitching her up a few minutes ago. She had a Cesarean."

"What happened?"

"Timothy was trying to be born with an arm over his head. One doctor thought he was breach, but Dr. Godat had Diane x-rayed and discovered his arm was in the way. According to the doctor, this was the only way he could be born without possible injury or even paralysis."

I left them as I headed down the hallway. Dr. Godat came out of the recovery area as I was about to enter.

"Johnnie, Diane is doing well. We had to put her to sleep quickly, but it should wear off soon. You can go back there to see her now."

"Thanks again, doc. I appreciate all you've done."

"No problem, just doing my job. Congratulations." He smiled, shook my hand, and walked away.

Diane recovered well and was released about four days later. My mother stayed with us about a month and helped Diane with the housework and with the baby. It was great to have her around. I gave her a tour of Dallas and eventually took her out to the famous South Fork Ranch, where the television program, *Dallas*, was filmed.

The rest of the fall was difficult for me in seminary. My attention was focused more on Diane and Timothy...and the turbulence at North Wilmer. I managed to finish my studies that semester, but I was not proud of my accomplishments. Also, no matter how hard I tried and prayed, North Wilmer just wasn't going anywhere. I discussed it frequently with Ed.

"Johnnie, sometimes a church will just stop growing until it gets new leadership. I don't see you with a future there. That area is slowly changing and you can't do anything about that."

"What can I do?"

"Resign and move over to our area. We'll find you a job and we'll pray for a new ministry to open up."

In February of 1978, I resigned as pastor. My family moved into an apartment in Arlington and I began looking for a job. I wasn't afraid of work, so I got a job immediately as a corrugated box builder in a warehouse. The flat sheets of corrugated paper would go through a machine that would cut the box, print on it, fold and glue it, and then tie them into a bundle. My initial job was to take the bundles off the rollers and stack them onto a pallet. Once full, I would roll the pallet onto another conveyor and start another stack. It was a strenuous job, but allowed the time to pass away. I remember getting home after work, lying on the couch while Diane was preparing supper, and falling asleep. Jenny was now two years old and Timmy was about 4 months old.

About April, I was getting very proficient in stacking heavy bundles of boxes. I played on the company's softball team and for the first time in my softball "career," I was able to hit a home run. I was known as the "preacher." With about four of these machines aligned side by side, we stackers talked loudly and made a lot of noise. Our goal was to throw the boxed bundles so hard against a steel pallet frame that the weld-joints would break. Each toss sounded like gunfire.

Our company's box orders were generally bleach, food, or cosmetic boxes. One day my machine received a new order. That was good in that it gave me a break to do some other job in the warehouse. When my machine operator was complete with the setup and test run, he found me and told me to get back to stacking. The order had already begun when I arrived, but I froze when I saw the printing on the boxes. It was a beer box order, the first our company had done.

The bundles were stacking up on my conveyer and my operator was screaming at me to get caught up. I started throwing them onto a pallet. The stacker next to me knew what was on the boxes.

"Hey preacher," he screamed. "How's it feel to be working for a beer company?"

He laughed and I said nothing. My mind was racing through my situation. *"Am I really promoting alcohol by stacking these boxes?"* I remembered a sign at the Carswell AFB main gate that warned every driver that they were about to enter the deadliest area in America, an area that had taken more American lives than all of her wars put together: the U.S. public highways. Plus, I knew that alcohol was the number one killer on our highways.

I thought some more: *"Can I support America's number one killer?"* After that thought, I knew I had to make a choice. I stopped stacking my bundles. The machine had an electronic eye that would shut its operation down, should the box bundles get backed up. Operators hated to shut their machine down during an order because of all the adjustments made and the printing variances.

The machine shut down and my operator was headed in my direction. Boy was he hot!

"What the [bleep's] going on here preacher?"

"I'm sorry, but I can't stack this order." The other machines began to shut down as all the other stackers came over to my machine. Everyone smelled a fight about to erupt and wanted to watch.

"I'm sorry, but I will not stack for a beer company."

"Oh yes you will, or…"

"Or what?" My operator had been on the job for years, I suppose, but he was way too slender to win a fight with me. He turned around, swearing profusely, throwing all the bundles off the machine's conveyer belt. Since all four machines had shut down, there was an unusual silence in our department. This silence drew the day supervisor out from his office. He came around a corner about the time my operator was throwing bundles everywhere.

"What's going on here?" My operator pointed to me.

"Jones, what's the problem?" the supervisor asked.

"Sir, I cannot stack for this order."

"What's wrong with this order? This is a new client and I want it stacked right."

"Sir, it's a beer order and I cannot, in good conscience, support America's number one killer. I am a Christian and a preacher. My primary job is to save lives, not help kill them."

"You either start stacking these bundles or go to my office."

I was about to step around him and head for his office, when the stacker next to my machine—the same one that had laughed at me earlier—spoke up.

"Boss, why don't we let the preacher stack on my machine? I'll stack this order."

The boss looked at me for a moment and then at the other stacker.

"Okay, whatever. Just get these machines back on line, pronto!" With that statement, he turned around and walked away.

"Thanks, Bill. I appreciate this."

"Just remember this favor. I'm expecting two homeruns from you at our next game." With a smile, he turned and began picking up the bundles and started stacking them. I went over to his machine and began stacking there.

When I arrived home, I shared my experience with Diane. We both agreed I did the right thing and we both began to ask God about another job or a new pastorate. Several days later, I received a letter from my mom in Virginia. In it, she mentioned her mom (Granny Burke) had a friend that wanted to know if I would be interested in preaching for her church in Ringgold (Virginia) the next time I came to visit. Mrs. Reynolds was her name and her church, Glen Hill Baptist, in Ringgold did not have a pastor. The letter had the phone number of a Mr. Roy Moore, the chairman of the Pulpit Committee.

Diane and I were amazed at the timing and the unlikely connection of this request.

"Is this an answer to our prayer?" I asked her.

"I think so," she responded.

"Well, I'm not waiting until we go on a vacation. I don't have any vacation time to begin with."

"But where will the money come from to go?"

"I don't know, but I'm calling this Mr. Moore about a preaching date."

Glen Hill Baptist Church, Ringgold, Virginia

I called him later that evening and scheduled a preaching date a couple Sundays away. Next, I wrote to my mom that I was flying up to preach at Mrs. Reynolds' church. I told my mom that if the family could help me with the plane ticket, I sure would appreciate it.

Due to the shortness of time, my roundtrip ticket was $208 dollars. (This amount was a lot of money back in 1978.) I flew in on a Saturday. The church had a supper planned for me that evening. My mom was ill, so my dad drove me over to the church and ate with me. I'll never forget that meal. It seemed every meat was fried something. I learned from Brother Jerry that I should try to sample as many dishes as possible at a church fellowship. I think I filled my plate full of food.

I was eating well until I got to a beautifully fried piece of meat. It was so chewy. I asked dad about it.

"Dad, this fish sure is chewy." An old gentleman on the other side of me caught my statement and interrupted.

"Oh, that's not fish; that's my wife's favorite chitterling recipe."

I turned back to look at dad. His ears rose his traditional one-quarter inch as he smiled. He knew I didn't like chitterlings—hog guts! I still had a couple bites left.

"I didn't get any of the chitterlings," my dad said. "Can I have some of yours?" With that request, he took the rest of mine. All I had to do was to swallow the piece in my mouth. The old gentleman next to me was watching and I think he knew how I felt about chitterlings by his next statement:

"Oh, I love my wife's chitterling recipe, especially when she leaves the corn pieces in it!" With that statement, several people laughed. I managed to keep the piece down and continued my meal.

The next day, carloads of my family came to Glen Hill Baptist Church. Most drove from all across Dry Fork and Danville. The little church was packed. During the announcements at the beginning, it was stated that a love offering would be gathered to cover my trip expenses. I had only told my mom about the cost of the plane ticket. She had collected $75 dollars for me and apologized that more couldn't be raised. I told her not to worry.

I preached a message and gave an invitation. A family of three came forward to join the church. After the invitation, a love offering was gathered. A regular offering was taken previously. What many of my family did not know was that the first offering wasn't for me. Many had contributed to the first offering, thinking they were helping pay my expenses. The love offering was taken and the amount was $131 dollars. Combined with the $75, meant I received $206, just two dollars short of my ticket expense. I felt this was a good sign about the whole event.

I preached the evening message as well. The church committee would meet later that week to see if they would recommend me as their pastor. It was an exciting day, plus the attendance was a record high for that church.

I flew back to Dallas the next day. I had previously told my boss that I would not be in on Monday. On Thursday, Mr. Moore called to inform me that the committee would recommend me as their pastor the following Sunday morning and a vote would be taken that evening. On Sunday evening, he called me again to say that I had received a unanimous vote to come to Glen Hill Baptist as the new pastor. Of course, I accepted and prepared to move to Virginia as soon as possible.

I notified my boss that I would be quitting in a week. He understood and wished me well.

"I bet you'll make a good preacher. You sure as [bleep] got our attention here when you shut down the whole production department." He chuckled.

"Christ makes the difference in my life."

"Yeah, my wife says stuff like that, but I got to have my Sundays and I got to have my beer."

With that statement, he turned and walked away from me. Although I wanted to say more to him, I never got to speak to him anymore concerning his relationship with Christ.

The next week involved my plans to move. I would rent a moving truck to haul my family belongings to Virginia. I also had a Honda Civic automobile. It was a very small car with a hatchback. Ed had a bright idea.

"Jonesie, why don't we drive your car into the back of the truck and we can load your stuff around it." Since I was planning to sell a lot of my furnishings, I figured Ed's idea would be great.

"How am I going to get my car in the back?"

"Don't they have a shipping department at your warehouse?"

"Sure, and they're loading pallets of boxes there all the time."

"There you go."

The next day, I went over to the shipping department. I found the day supervisor.

"Say, Charlie, I'm moving to Virginia next week and need to load my Honda in a rent truck. Can I come by here Saturday morning, early, and drive it in from this dock?"

"Sure, just find an empty bay and some of the guys will put the ramp down."

"Wow," I thought. *"That was easy."*

On Saturday, Ed drove the truck over to my job. I followed him in the Honda. When we arrived, I guided Ed into an empty bay. When Charlie saw me, he whistled at one of the men on a forklift to put a ramp down for me to drive onto. I ran over to my car, jumped in, and headed for the dock entrance. I drove the car up onto the dock, swung around a few pallets and drove right into the back of the truck. It was simple.

"Thanks for your help, Charlie."

"Whoa, I thought you meant a Honda motorcycle, not a car! Man, I'm glad the big boss didn't see that!"

"Oh, sorry. I thought you understood what I meant. Thanks anyway." With that statement, Ed and I left.

The plan was that Ed and I would drive the truck to Virginia, while Diane and the children would fly up a few days later. We wired up a CB radio in the truck and enjoyed talking to the truckers on our way to Virginia. We had one very interesting discussion in Tennessee:

"Breaker-breaker 1-9." Ed was driving at the time. He responded.

"You got the channel, come on."

"Yeah, I was just calling to see if my radio was picking up down below me, kick it back."

"Yeah buddy, loud and clear. And what's your 20?"

"What are you driving?"

"We be hauling stuff in a yellow rent truck, and you?"

"Yeah I see you. Look up above you and I'll be coming your way."

About that time, a small, single-engine plane flew right over us.

"Are you in the plane?"

"That's a 10-4, good buddy. Just doing a little sightseeing out here. And where you guys headed?"

"Virginia."

"Well, y'all be safe and I'm out of here."

"10-4, and maybe we'll catch you on the flip side."

"Roger, over and out."

"Can you believe that, Jonesie? We're talking to an airplane on a CB radio."

"Crazy man. Who'd of thought that?"

Ed and I arrived in Ringgold on our second day of travel. We pulled up beside the church's basement door and unloaded everything in the back, except the car. A box had fallen down and was leaning on the side of the car. It had rubbed the paint off the car, at the point of contact. Other than that, the trip was successful. I found a ramp at a construction site in Danville, drove the car out of the truck, and then turned it in.

Ed and I went to my parent's house for the night. I think Diane and the children flew in a few days later and Ed flew back to Dallas.

"Take care of yourself, Jonesie. Keep in touch."

"Thanks Ed. I appreciate all you've done for us." With that, we embraced and he got on his plane. Ed was a true friend indeed.

Glen Hill Baptist Church was as excited as I, about having a new pastor. The church had only one pastor before me. A Reverend Land was the founding pastor. He had been there for a long while. He had passed away about a year prior to my arrival. A picture of him was hanging in the foyer. His wife was still attending the church. The church had a good mix of people attending, about sixty or seventy, if I remember correctly.

Mr. Roy Moore was the song leader. He would announce the hymn number and the choir basically led the congregational singing. I was happy to be near my hometown, especially when I looked into the congregation to see my mom and dad in the audience. This was a first for them both, that is, being regular attendees at church every Sunday morning. I remember my mom had attended periodically as I was growing up, but I had never seen my dad in church, except during my testimony service at Sharon Baptist Church a few years previously. Their work shifts at the mill and work-related health problems had kept them from being regulars at church. Plus, I'm sure my dad's alcoholism had a lot to do with him not attending.

My parents attended nearly every Sunday for about six months. Then my mom took ill and dad didn't want to drive across town alone. I don't recall them attending anymore after that. My mom's work in the Dan River Cotton Mill had really messed her back up. She had more surgeries than we could count on all fingers. It hurt her to sit for long periods of time in a pew.

I still remember one of our choir members, a Mrs. Bledsoe, would always dedicate the choir special to someone or a group of folks in our church. For example, when a choir special began with its piano introduction, she would say often, "I'd like to dedicate this song to all our visitors out there. God bless them all!" Then the choir would sing. It was a neat thing and became expected every Sunday. I'll never forget one particular time, a morning when attendance was down and we had no visitors, Mrs. Bledsoe dedicated the choir song: "I'd like to dedicate this song to all our visitors out there…" Then apparently she noticed that there were no visitors, so she quickly added, "…if we had any. God bless them, wherever they are." She and her husband, Tom, were good farmers and kept my home rich with fresh vegetables, in season.

The church was part-time, so I began looking for employment. I checked with my old J. C. Penney's location, but they were not hiring. Dan River was not hiring either. Finally, I got a job as a teller at a local bank in Danville. I was in training for about a month.

The bank would close its lobby for a couple hours during lunch and reopen for a brief afternoon session. Carolyn was my trainer. She had been there for some time and was a very good trainer. I worked out of her teller window in the lobby. She eventually allowed me to take over the window as she looked over my shoulder and made sure I did everything properly.

I bring this up because one day, as we were trying to balance our daily intake of money from our window, our window kept coming up $2,000 short. I tried to balance it several times, but still could not figure it out. Finally, Carolyn took the balancing chore over herself. She ended up with the same thing: $2,000 short! We checked everyone else's window, but all the others were in balance. We checked the vault…nothing out of balance there. Then we called the branch manager over and rehearsed everything in detail.

The only thing we could not retrace was the grocery bag of money that was picked up every day from the drive-through window directly behind our window. It was kept in our window's safe, but the safe remained unlocked so that the teller at the drive-through could turn around, walk over to our window, pull the bag out, and present it to the grocer's owner.

The bank called the grocer, but he claimed there was no extra money. This was a sad day for all of us at the bank, especially for Carolyn and me. During the next day or two, local detectives interviewed us all. Then, the FBI interviewed us. We were all very nervous about this. To my knowledge, the money was never recovered and everyone—including me—kept their job.

I worked fulltime at the bank, but the bank didn't pay very well. One of my regular customers at my window invited me to a sales meeting for selling retirement plans. It was commission only. Soon, I was not only a preacher and a bank teller, but also an annuity sales representative. It was quite an experience to be involved in three different employments.

My church work didn't seem to be going anywhere. Some folks were joining, but there wasn't any spiritual revival among the folks. I felt really burdened about this. About this time, my evangelist friend from Texas, Leroy Hassler, contacted me. We talked over the phone for a while about my church. I then asked him if he would come and preach a series of messages. I could only guarantee him a love offering and a warm bed and food at my trailer. He agreed to come. I announced his coming at the church the following Sunday. Some did not like it.

"We can't afford to fly someone in from Texas," was a response.

"Why don't you get someone locally?" was another response.

My only reply was, "I have been praying for a revival meeting and I believe God has led me to bring Leroy Hassler in."

There was another grumble or two, but I assured them that Leroy was in complete agreement to come on a love-offering basis. He arrived on a Saturday and the services began the next morning. Leroy had preached a couple times for me in Wilmer when I was away on vacation or a convention, but I had never heard him in person. His morning message was good, but there was no spiritual movement. He stayed in his room (Jenny's bedroom) all afternoon. That evening, he preached again and, again, another good message. But there was still no spiritual movement. I was deeply burdened about the lack of response. Before locking up the church, I asked Leroy about praying for a while at the altar. We did, pouring our hearts out before God. We finished and headed out the rear of the auditorium to go home. But I stopped at the last row of pews.

"Leroy, we can't leave yet. I've got to pray some more."

I got on my knees at the last pew row and began to confess my sins and everything else I could think of that may be hindering God from bringing us a genuine revival in the church. Leroy prayed as well, pouring his own heart out in repentance and confession. We finished, got up from the pew, and locked up the building. In my heart, I knew that if God was going to bless this church, He would do so while Leroy was here.

Monday came as usual. Leroy slept in because he had spent additional time in prayer and study during the night. The evening service began as usual. Once again, Leroy preached a good message. He ended the service with everyone's head bowed and eyes closed. This time I crept over to the front pew and knelt.

"Oh God!" I prayed. *"For your glory, please bring revival to this church."* I wept as I prayed. Leroy continued giving the invitation. I prayed a little longer and then stood up to see if anyone would come forward. When I stood up and looked, there were about ten people standing in a line, waiting for me to receive them. Most were church members. One person after another came confessing their sins and about being lost before God. I was taken aback for a few moments, but then realized God was answering Leroy's and my prayer for genuine revival. It was incredible! Each service, after that, included many decisions for Christ. I think there were fifteen church members who were genuinely saved during that week of revival, and dozens more came to Christ during the next six weeks. In fact, among about fifty churches in our association, we were third in number of baptisms recorded that year. Only two large churches in Danville exceeded us.

God blessed the work at Glen Hill. I remember a seventy-five year-old woman, Mrs. Wall, coming to Christ during that time. The following week, she came to me.

"Brother Johnnie, I want you to come to my house tomorrow. Granny's ready to get saved."

Now for a 75 year old to call someone 'Granny' had to mean that Granny was a bit older. And she was. I found out later that Granny was the community drunk. Her grandson, Bobby Robertson, a recent convert, and I arrived at Mrs. Wall's house to see Granny the next evening. Bobby was a little apprehensive about this because he knew her history and condition. I led the way onto the front porch and headed for the door. Only a screen door was closed, so I heard some talk going on inside. I tapped on the door and began to open it.

"Come on in, Brother Johnnie," was Mrs. Wall's reply to my tapping. As Bobby and I entered, I saw Mrs. Wall in one chair and a very petite elderly lady sitting on the couch. I waited for some sort of introduction, but got none.

"Brother Johnnie," said Mrs. Wall. "This is Granny and she needs to give her heart to the Lord."

"That's right," nodded Granny. "But before I do, I've got to get rid of this." She then pulled out a small whiskey bottle from out her dress, stood up and went to the kitchen sink, and poured the contents of her bottle down the drain. Then she took her shiny metal-capped bottle, threw it in the garbage, and fell on her knees in front of me. I led her through a gospel presentation and she said all the right words as she gave her heart and life to Jesus. (I never got introduced!)

The next Sunday, Granny was baptized. A crowd showed up for this baptism because no one would have thought Granny could be saved. I believe she was about 85 years old. I remember her baptism well because she was afraid of the water. I reassured her that all would go well.

"Just walk out into the baptismal pool, grab my hand and I'll do the rest." She did just that. As soon as she grabbed my hand, she immediately folded up her legs underneath her body. I kept her afloat long enough to say a few words, and then, putting my hand on top of her head, I dunked her straight down, immersing her fully.

Granny remained faithful for another six months or so, telling folks about Jesus. I had several sweet visits with her at her home. But one of her drinking buddies came by and talked her into a drink or two. By 2:00 a.m., she was not only drunk, but was in the emergency room. Mrs. Wall called me and I went out immediately to the ER. Granny was a pitiful sight and apologized profusely as I caught her vomit in a tray. In tears, she asked if God could still save her. I assured her that if this was not to be a reoccurring thing, that God would indeed save her soul. She confessed to God her habit of alcoholism and asked forgiveness.

I stayed with her a few hours until she went to sleep. The hospital was going to check her in for overnight observation. About mid-morning the next day, I returned to her room. She had slipped into a coma during the night and would never recover. She died that same day. How I thank God for the Glen Hill revival that eventually resulted in about fifty souls saved that year.

During 1979, I had opened a Christmas Club account at the bank in which I was working. It was to be a surprise for Diane. The account matured in early November and I would have $120 dollars saved for Christmas. On the day I went to pick up my money, we were heading for a Bible conference in Charlotte, North Carolina. It was exciting to see Diane's surprised face when I showed her the money. We talked about several gifts we would get for the house.

During the Bible conference, an evangelist by the name of Manley Beasley preached on what he called, "revelation giving." I had never heard of asking God first what one should give. I always assumed the basic ten percent (commonly called a tithe) was sufficient. I knew that, as a pastor, I had to be an example in giving. But here was an evangelist that challenged us to ask God first what we should give under any circumstance. Then he had the audacity to stop the meeting right then and there and tell us to ask God what we should give at this Bible conference.

"What?" I thought. *"I've spent enough money just to come down here and spend the night for this conference. I needed to receive, not to give!"* But I began to pray. I felt I was safe because I knew I had no extra cash for this trip. Just then, I heard a voice in my mind: *"What about the Christmas Club money?"*

"What? The Christmas Club money?" I snuck a peek at Diane. She was praying as well. *"Well, if I'm going to give this $120 dollars away, she'll have to say the same thing."* I bumped her arm to get her attention.

"Is God speaking to you about giving some money to this guy?"

Diane looked at me as if she had heard a voice as well. "I think God wants us to give him our Christmas Club money."

"All of it?"

She nodded her head. I reached in my pocket, took the $120 out and placed it in the envelope provided. As a bucket was being passed around, Brother Beasley spoke:

"If God spoke to you, how about standing up and giving us a testimony."

I stood up almost immediately. "God told my wife and me to give our Christmas Club money." I sat down, almost in a state of shock.

The guy next to us stood up and said, "God told me to give you my watch." He immediately took his watch off and tossed it into the bucket. Several others gave similar testimony. Brother Beasley continued to speak:

"If God told you to do this, then you can be assured that He will bless you for your obedience."

The conference ended on a Saturday afternoon. God did bless the meeting and both Diane and I felt we had done the right thing. The ride home was very reflective.

"I wonder what we'll get for Christmas now?"

Diane squeezed my hand. "We've got each other and two wonderful, healthy children."

"Yeah, that's the greatest gift, outside of Jesus."

When we arrived home, we checked the mailbox for the last two days of mail. In the box was an envelope from a company I was working for on a part-time basis. It was not my usual paycheck envelope, so I opened it immediately. It was a letter from my supervisor: "Dear John, I checked the past few months back and discovered we had shorted your payroll check for days worked. Enclosed, please find the adjustment..." I lifted up the first page to see a check stapled to it: $120 dollars exactly! Diane and I nearly had a spell as we witnessed the truth of "revelation giving."

For a Christmas tree, we went to one of our church members and asked if he had any cedars on his property. He referred to a certain field and told us to help ourselves. We found a good tree along a fence line and cut it down. It had these tiny bulbs on it, but they looked fine on the tree. The tree served us well for Christmas, but on the day after Christmas we awoke to a problem. Throughout the living room were hundreds of baby praying mantises. Those cute little bulbs were cocoons and the warm air inside the trailer hatched them. Oh, what an experience we had trying to eliminate all those pesky creatures out of the house!

The Christmas of 1979 was full of surprises. Here's another major event that changed my life. My sister, Sandra, had married Donnie Taylor. He was a welder and got a job welding on oilrigs out in the Gulf of Mexico. They moved to Mobile, Alabama for a while. She had joined a Baptist church on the northwest side of Mobile. While in town for Christmas that year (1979), she mentioned an elderly man from England, an evangelist, had preached at their church in October. His name was Leonard Ravenhill. I remembered the name because I had read his book, *Why Revival Tarries*.

"You heard Leonard Ravenhill preach?"

"Sure did, and boy did he preach! His sermons were about an hour long."

"Man, I'd love to hear him. I've got one of his books and it is good!"

"I think our church tapes the services. I'll check and see if I can get you a copy."

"Wow!" I thought. *"Hear Leonard Ravenhill preach?"* I couldn't believe my sister had heard, in person, Leonard Ravenhill. About a month later, I received a package from Sandra. It contained twelve recordings of Ravenhill preaching at night and teaching a lunch Bible study. These tapes would become one of my most cherished possessions. I listened to them so much that I wore some of the originals out. (I did manage to copy them years later and still have a set today on CDs, but in poor condition.)

1980 – Gospel For Asia Missions – Back to Texas

Sometime after that, our old friend, K. P. Yohannan, called us. He had met Diane's parents in Dallas and had gotten our address. He wanted to visit us in Virginia to discuss his expanding missions ministry in India. He came to visit us in early 1980.

K. P. was a world traveler. He had gone to places I only dreamed about. Every year, he traveled to India to help start a new church or to get several Indian believers on the field as evangelists. This was K. P.'s passion and ministry. We were friends, but I had no idea what was behind his urgency in visiting Diane and me.

"Johnnie, my ministry is expanding beyond the borders of India. I'm changing the name from 'Gospel For India' to 'Gospel For Asia'."

"That's great, K. P. It sounds as if God is using you well."

"Yes, but I have a problem and I believe God has sent me to you to help me solve it."

"What's that? What can I do in Virginia to help you in Asia?"

"I need someone I can trust to run my national headquarters here in America while I travel around the world. I must stop in many countries now because the demand for missionaries is coming from every part of the world."

"But how can I do that from here in Ringgold? It sounds like a big responsibility to me."

"It is Johnnie. Please listen to me. There are dozens of men who can pastor your church, but there is only one man in this world that I can trust my organization to, and that man is you."

"Whoa, wait a minute. You're asking me to resign my church and run Gospel For India?"

"Asia…Gospel For Asia, and yes, that is what I'm asking you to do. I have too many office responsibilities and not enough time to keep up with all the letter writing and missionary assignments. I want you to pray about it and plan on joining me."

"But I know so little about India and the other Asian countries. What do I say?"

"You will begin immediately, in Virginia, to raise your own support and you will travel with me to India in the near future."

"Raise my support? Do you mean there is no salary for this position?"

"No, there's no salary. Even I do not take a salary out of the mission support contributions. You must learn how to go to your fellow pastors and ask to show a slide presentation of the work and ask for financial support for you and for the missionaries."

"Man, I don't know, K. P. You know Southern Baptist churches support missionaries through the Cooperative Program. They frown on independent mission support."

"Johnnie, if God is in this, He will open doors for you to go to more than the Southern Baptists. Trust me when I say that the slides of India and your personal testimony will get you started. Plus, you will need to write to all your friends about your decision to become a missionary for the lost millions in Asia."

I agreed to pray about it. K. P. was very convincing. He preached for me on Sunday and received a "cool" reception by some because of his dark skin. Blacks and Whites were still very segregated in the rural areas of Virginia, especially in churches. I mentioned this to K. P.

"This is another reason I need you in my organization. You can go to many churches in this area that I cannot."

"K. P., I'll only commit to praying about it for now."

After he left Virginia, Diane and I committed this to prayer...a lot of prayer. We prayed much about this and asked God to show us what to do. In the next few weeks, there would be several events to help us decide.

One thing that happened was the continued complaint of my allowing a "Black" man to preach in our church. Several influential families were calling other members demanding my resignation. I explained to some that K. P. was Indian, but even if he was a Black man, that still should not prevent him from preaching God's Word in our church.

My explanation did not satisfy some, and to show their disapproval, the "nay-sayers" began to withhold their regular offerings to our church. It did not matter to them that we were having some of the greatest growth in our church's history. Within a month, there began to be a financial strain on the church's budget and my salary began to be held up until the funds to cover my check were in the bank.

Some of the church members who supported me asked me to consider starting a new work down the road a couple of miles. They felt the opposition was too carnal and controlling to change the attitude and spirit of our church. *"A church split?"* I thought. *"Am I ready to do such a thing? Lord, is this the 'sign' Diane and I are praying for concerning Gospel For Asia and K. P.?"*

Another thing occurred at this time as well. I received an unusual phone call one evening, the following week.

"Hello?"

"Johnnie? Is that you?" I immediately recognized the voice.

"Dana? What a surprise. What's up?"

"Oh Johnnie, I didn't know who to call. My mother is in the hospital and I'm so worried about her. Would you be willing to go see her?"

I got some basic information from her and hung up the phone. Diane came in the room.

"Who was that on the phone?"

"Oh, no one important...just my old girlfriend, Dana."

"Dana? What's with her?"

"I don't know. She was crying about her mother being in the hospital and asked me to go see her."

"Are you?"

"Not without you going with me." We talked a while and decided to go.

The next day, Diane and I went to the Danville hospital and visited Mrs. Monk. She was her usual, happy self and did not appear to be suffering.

"Oh, I'll be just fine," she said. "How did you know I was here?"

"Dana called me yesterday. She seemed very upset. Is everything okay with her and her family?"

Mrs. Monk proceeded to tell me about Dana and her husband, and their little boy. And she told me about Dana's brothers and sister, Douglas, Robert, John, and Moriah. (Mrs. Monk's husband died in a gun accident, but I can't remember if this had already occurred.) After a brief visit, Diane and I left. I figured I might get another call from Dana and, sure enough, I did that evening. She thanked me for going and asked me how I was doing. I kept the conversation cordial, but felt a bit uneasy talking to her.

That night about midnight, the phone rang again. The phone was on my side of the bed.

"Hello?"

"Johnnie, is that you?" It was Dana again. She began to laugh.

"I'm so sorry. I was trying to call a friend, but I must have dialed your number by mistake."

"That's okay; goodnight."

"Oh wait! Don't hang up. Can we talk?"

"About what?"

"Oh, anything. I'm so bored and lonely; I just need someone to talk to."

"Dana, I'm in bed and it's midnight."

She giggled. "You go to bed much earlier than you used to Mister Jones."

"It's Reverend Jones now and I'm a happily married man. Now goodnight and don't call me again." With that statement, I hung up the phone.

"Who was that?" Diane asked. Apparently the phone call awakened her.

"It was Dana."

"What did she want this time?"

"I think she wants me, but I told her not to call again." Diane said nothing else. She rolled over in my direction, hugged me, and then fell back asleep. I continued to rehearse the events of the past few weeks.

"Lord, I do not like the situation that is developing here. My church is about to split and now I'm afraid Dana is going to start showing up in my life. I haven't finished seminary and I don't think I'm ready to split a church. I love my wife and children and do not want Dana to interfere. I believe You are answering my prayer about my future ministry and I am going to act on

this answer. If I'm misreading this, please give me an indication in my conversation with K. P. Thank you, Lord; in Jesus' name I pray, amen."
After the prayer, I fell asleep.

The next day, I discussed my feelings with Diane. She agreed with my concerns and promised to go wherever I felt the Lord leading us. I then called K. P., who was living in Eufaula, Oklahoma at the time.

"K. P.? This is Johnnie."

"Hello, Johnnie. And how is my new director feeling today?"

"How'd you know I was calling to accept the position?"

"The same God that spoke to you, last night, spoke to me as well."

That was all the confirmation I needed. I immediately began the process of preparing for a new ministry. I resigned at the church a week or two later so that I could be available to go to other churches to announce my new missionary status. As predicted, there were only two SBC churches that allowed me to speak to their congregation about Gospel For Asia. But, in Virginia, there were many independent Baptist churches. And since I was a seminary student at Jerry Falwell's Liberty Seminary in Lynchburg, I had an instant rapport with a number of Baptist ministers.

I had a large singlewide trailer house to sell as well. Although K. P. lived in Oklahoma, he felt the national GFA office should locate in the Dallas-Fort Worth area, near the international airport. This meant I had to move back to Texas.

Things had changed in Texas, since I moved. Ed Ethridge was now a pastor in Pasadena, a suburb of Houston. That meant I could not stay with him during the transition. Mama Knight had passed away in '79. Prior to her passing, Diane's parents had found Mama Knight and had moved her into another nursing home. We had spoken to her several times from Virginia and we knew that she was getting a bit senile. Diane's parents had requested all of Mama Knight's money be returned to her. We did as requested, even though there was no legal reason to do so. At the time, Diane and I felt that to be a good testimony to her parents, we would do as told.

Preparing for deputation for Gospel For Asia, 1980

I began to share the GFA story to numerous churches throughout southern Virginia and northern North Carolina. One large church in Danville, Gateway Baptist Church, had a young and vibrant preacher, Delton Agnor. He liked the GFA presentation and promised to support our work. Gateway also had a private school of about sixty students. Diane and I visited the church often, during our transition. Delton was a good, solid preacher.

For about four months, I did my deputation as a missionary for GFA. About $300 a month began to come in from churches and friends. Not enough to support a family, but enough to allow us to prepare for the move. An elderly lady responded to our trailer ad as well. She eventually purchased it in April and allowed us to stay in it until we moved in May.

About a week prior to moving, I was driving up 58 West to visit my parents. I saw Brother Delton outside in the church's parking lot with the church van hood up. I pulled in to see what was the matter. He was frustrated at the van.

"I've tried everything, Johnnie, and the thing just won't crank. The battery is not that old."

"I used to be a mechanic, Delton. Let me take a look."

I inspected the connections from the battery to the generator. There was corrosion on the battery cables, so I gave them a very tight twist. The positive cable broke loose from the battery post. I took Delton's screwdriver and scrapped the cable and post a little. Then I twisted the cable back on the post and held it tight.

"Try it now Delton." He did and the van engine fired right up.

"Well I'll be! Thanks Johnnie."

"You're welcome. Now this positive cable needs to be replaced. I had to hold it real tight to get the connection."

"I understand; I'll take it to the shop. Say, listen; I'm losing my principal of our school. I sure could use a man like you here to run our school."

"Sorry Delton, I just sold my trailer and we're moving back to Texas next week to relocate the Gospel For Asia headquarters."

"Are you sure you're doing the right thing?"

"Well, right now I'm pretty sure, but I'll be praying for God to send you the right man."

"Do that, and thanks again."

Our final week in Virginia was a busy one. We rented a truck for our belongings. With a truck full of our belongings, our family of four piled into the front of that truck and left Virginia for Hurst, Texas in May of 1980. My evangelist friend, Leroy Hassler, lived in Hurst and offered to let us stay with him for a while. When we arrived, he had received a lead on a nice house for rent nearby. It was posted at his church in Euless. A missionary owned the house and was returning to South America. We went and spoke with him.

The house was a brick home. It was beautiful, but I felt it was not affordable. Leroy felt the arrangement was of God. It did seem interesting, so we agreed to move into the house. It happened so quickly that we didn't even have to unload the rented truck before it was due back.

That Sunday, we visited Leroy's church, First Baptist Church of Euless. Dr. Jimmy Draper was the pastor. Diane had known Jimmy as the associate pastor at First Baptist in Dallas when she and her parents were members there. I had met Jimmy at one of our DBC Ministerial Alliance meetings. So this was a plus for us.

On Monday, K.P. came down from Eufaula to visit us and to scope out the area for the ministry headquarters. We drove around the DFW airport area for about six hours, picking up business rental phone numbers and making numerous phone calls. In 1980, the inflation rate was in the double digits, which made business leases very high. K.P. left for Eufaula that evening, very discouraged. Diane was anxious to hear about the day.

"So how'd it go?"

"Oh, okay I guess. K. P. wasn't too excited about the rental prices around the airport. Everything's so high."

That was about all I could say at the moment. The next day, I received a call from K.P.

"Johnnie, I have decided to wait on moving the ministry to the DFW area at this time. I don't think it's the right time."

"Well, K.P., I'm already moved in down here; what am I supposed to do?"

"I suggest you go out to the airport and apply for a good paying job. Maybe next year the prices will be better for us to move the ministry."

As I hung up the phone, I was stunned at what K.P. had just told me. I did not argue with him, nor did I remind him of the cost of moving and sacrifice I had put my family through by moving. It cost well over a thousand dollars for moving expenses and to lease our house. All for nothing? I told Diane.

"What are we going to do?" she asked.

"I don't know what to do about the ministry, but I've definitely got to find a job."

I bought a paper and began searching the employment section. Every ad seemed so impossible for me to check into. I basically had no previous experience in anything except as an aircraft electrician and various odd jobs, part time. I called my quality control supervisor whom I had worked for in Virginia. Mr. Smith informed me that Texas did its own quality control and, therefore, there were no job openings for me. I contacted several of the aircraft industries around Fort Worth, but nothing seemed to match.

An ad for a quality control inspector at the Shasta recreational vehicle construction plant, in Grapevine, caught my eye. I headed to Grapevine and applied for the position. Several days later, I received a phone call from them.

"Hi, this is John Deventer, and I'm the supervisor for the plant. I've looked over your resume and think I can use you. Can you come in this afternoon for an interview?"

"Sure, I'll be up right after lunch."

"Make it after two, because I never know when I can stop for lunch."

At 2:00 p.m., I walked into the Shasta offices. Mr. Deventer was on the grounds somewhere and eventually responded to the pages. He was a tall and slender man with a polite smile. We exchanged greetings.

"Johnnie, I have two positions that you might fit into. You responded to the quality control position and I'll show that to you first. But I really think you will prefer the other position I have which is in the repair shop. Let's go look at them both."

Mr. Deventer took me out on the assembly line where the RVs were assembled. At the end of the assembly line, there was an area out on the lot where a quality control inspection took place. The temperature in North Texas had already reached the 100-degree level. 1980 became the record year for 100+ degree days in North Texas. We went inside a trailer.

"Johnnie, here's where you'll spend most of your time, outside the building and inside a trailer. You will look for any blemishes and red tape them."

"Wow, it's hot in here." My eyes were also burning from the glue used on the trailers.

"Yeah, it's hot in the summer and cold in the winter. Look at this thermometer; it's showing 110 degrees already in here and it's only mid-June. But let me show you another job opening in the next building where we do our repairs."

We proceeded to walk over to another building. There were fans blowing, a little music playing, and about six trailers parked around the fans. Two men were on top of a trailer laying a new metal roof on it. It was definitely a much more comfortable setting in which to work.

"In here, you will do miscellaneous repair jobs. Sometimes we have to fix a leak; other times, an owner will back into something and we'll fix a dent or two. The rest is usually appliances and fixtures that we remove and replace. It's really a much better job than quality control and it's inside."

"I see your point. Is the pay the same?" (The ad had mentioned $6.50 an hour for the Q.C. position.)

"Actually, it's a little higher than the Q.C. position. Let's go inside and look at the job description."

The maintenance position started at $7.50 an hour. It was a no-brainer.

"I'll take the maintenance position."

"I thought you would," said John with a smile. "Now it does require you to purchase a few tools, but we will reimburse you for half the cost, if you do not have them already. They'll remain yours to keep."

I left Grapevine a bit encouraged. I thought $7.50 an hour was a great start (1980 wages). The following morning, I arrived at the shop ready to go. It was a very relaxed atmosphere and the men were very patient with my training time. In fact, there were plenty of menial tasks inside the trailers that they did not particularly like. Inside the units, many of the thermometers were broken.

"Yeah," said one of the guys. "They only register 120 degrees and then they pop the tops off."

"Oh, I see." Although there were fans in the building, there simply was no way to cool the inside of the trailers. The temperature outside was over a hundred every day and the inside building thermometer showed about ten degrees higher than outside. I estimated the temperature inside the trailers to be about 120-125 degrees. The unit thermometers were registering a little higher and that's why they were "popping" the tops off of them. (Two consecutive days in late June was officially 113 degrees in Dallas.)

After about a month, working for Shasta, I received a call from K.P. He was just checking in on me and told me there was no new plan for moving the ministry. He encouraged me to start visiting the local churches to see if they would allow me to show the GFA missions ministry. I discussed it with Diane.

"I don't know, Hon; I just don't know how I can present a ministry that I'm not even sure I'm going to be a part of."

Usually, Diane had something to do through my church's pastoral position. But now, it was just she and Jenny and Timmy at home. I had our only vehicle at my job site.

"Maybe I can walk around the neighborhood and advertise for piano teaching?"

"Well, it's kind of hot; and what will you do with the kids?"

"Oh, we'll take water bottles and rest in the shade."

It was July now and the temperature continued to exceed 100 degrees. One Saturday evening I was sitting in the house and thinking.

"Diane, do you remember me telling you that Delton Agnor, at Gateway, asked me to consider becoming his school principal?"

"Yes; why?"

"I don't know, but I think I'm going to call him to see if he's gotten someone."

"Doesn't school start in a month? Surely he has someone by now."

"Well, it only costs a phone call to find out."

"Sounds great! I'd love to work in a Christian school!"

I made the call to Delton. "Hello, Barbara? This is Johnnie Jones in Texas. How are you?"

"Fine Johnnie; it's so good to hear your voice! Just a minute and I'll call Delton."

"Hello," said Delton in his usual deep voice.

"Delton? Johnnie. How are you?"

"Fine. And how are you and Diane doing?"

We're hot down here in Texas."

"Yes, I heard it on the news."

"Listen, I'm calling to say that Gospel For Asia is on hold for a while. K.P. isn't moving the headquarters down here for some time. So, I guess I'm calling to see if you have a principal for your school?"

"Yes, I sure do."

"Okay, I understand. I was just calling to see."

"Well, I think you know him. His name is Johnnie Jones and he's living in Texas now, but I'm expecting him to move back to Virginia in a few weeks."

"What?!" I screamed. "Are you serious?"

"Yes sir! When can you move back?"

"Well, I guess in a week or two. But don't I need some training?"

"Yes. I'll call the training center in Texas to see if I can get you in next week. By the way, do you live near Lewisville, Texas?"

"Hold on; Diane, get me a map of Texas."

Diane had already sensed, through the conversation, that Delton wanted me to come back. She ran to the closet and returned quickly with a map. We looked and discovered that Lewisville was the next town northeast of Grapevine.

"Lewisville is right next door to where I'm working."

"Great. You stay put and I'll call them Monday morning."

"Thanks, Delton. Wow, I can't believe this is happening."

"The Lord knows what He's doing, Johnnie."

I hung the phone up. Diane and I could not believe that we were actually discussing plans to move back to Virginia. This was crazy, but it felt so good to know that I was heading back into a real ministry.

Delton called the house Monday and told Diane that I was registered to begin my A.C.E. (Accelerated Christian Education) Administrator's training next Monday morning. It was their last class for the summer. I was elated! I called Delton that evening. He was mailing a check to A.C.E. the next day. He also told me to keep a record of my expenses for going to training and for traveling expenses and he would reimburse me.

I turned in my notice for employment termination Tuesday morning to Mr. Deventer.

"So you're staying with me until this Friday?"

"Yes, and I'm so sorry for the short notice, but I have to begin training next Monday morning for my school administrator's job in Virginia."

"Oh, I'm fine with that. With this heat, I'm surprised you plan to stay till Friday. Most folks just up and leave without any notice. I'm sure you'll make a good school principal. At least it should be cooler in Virginia."

I called K.P. and told him of my plans. He wished me well and said he would contact me later when things were right for moving GFA to Texas. I wrote to my supporters and told them not to send any more checks. I think I had about six individuals and two churches supporting my plans to administrate the GFA headquarters. About $250 a month was coming in for the ministry when I stopped it.

The following week, I arrived in Lewisville for a week of intensive training on the A.C.E. educational system. It was truly an amazing system of training booklets, called "Paces," that every student uses to acquire a formal education, from kindergarten to twelfth grade. By the end of the week I was pumped.

Gateway Baptist Schools Administrator – Back to Virginia!

Diane had called for a truck rental and even set up a garage sale to get rid of the non-essentials so we could rent a smaller truck. We still had a piano, though, and that would go with us. When we had arrived in Texas, only Diane and I were around to unload the truck. We managed to get the piano off the truck by ourselves. I wasn't sure about putting it back on though. The truck ramp wasn't very wide and the incline was about 30 degrees. Somehow, though, we managed to push that piano back onto the truck.

The next problem was our lease agreement. I think we had signed a year's lease and had put a $500 dollar deposit down. The missionary couple was already in South America, but he had a man who was in charge of the house's maintenance and rental payments. I called him.

"Mr. Truman, I regret to inform you that I need to move back to Virginia. The ministry here did not develop and I have a ministry opportunity back in Virginia. I know I'm breaking my lease and don't deserve to receive any of my deposit back."

"It's funny you should call. We had another couple in our church who really wanted to move into your house, but just couldn't get the money together. They called me yesterday and told me that they had their money together and wanted the house. I told them it was rented, but let me call them back and see if they still want it. I'll call you back."

Mr. Truman didn't call back. Instead, he drove over to the house.

"Brother Jones, the other couple wants the house very much. Let me inspect it and see how much, if any, of the deposit I can give you back."

After walking through the house, he came to me.

"It looks as if the house has not been messed up at all. In fact, it looks better now than when you moved in. I'll contact Pastor Caldwell in South America. If he's okay with it, we'll give you your deposit back, because, with this couple in waiting, he won't miss a single day of rent."

"Oh, that'll be great! We need every penny for this move and resettlement."

"I'm sure you will. Have a good day, Brother Jones, and may God's blessing be upon your ministry in Virginia. By the way, what's the temperature in Virginia?"

"My pastor told me the other day that they had a high of 89 degrees."

"Oh I wish you hadn't told me that!" We both laughed.

"It's a tough place to serve," I said. "But somebody's got to do it."

The following Monday, our family of four was back in the front of a rental truck, headed for Virginia. The truck had a large gas tank, but I noticed the gauge was not moving very fast. I mentioned it to Diane, but somewhere in Louisiana we found out, the hard way, that the gauge was broken. We were about a quarter mile from the next interstate exit. Diane and the kids stayed with the truck while I began walking. It wasn't too long before a man in a pickup stopped and picked me up. The nearest gas station was about 3 miles south of the exit. He drove me down there and helped me get some gas in a can. He also drove me back to my truck and stayed until it restarted. We lost about an hour, but were grateful for the gentleman who helped us. After that experience, we stopped frequently for gasoline.

In Danville, Virginia, we unloaded the truck into Delton's basement, leaving just enough room to set up two beds. This would be our living quarters for a couple of weeks. We went back to the mobile home dealer where we bought our first trailer. They were happy to see us and made us a sweetheart of a deal on another trailer. We checked on a trailer park on Old Mount Cross Road, near the Danville city limits. It was just above Joe Eanes' old place (Larry's dad). The park sloped down a hill with a dumpster at the bottom of the hill. The owner had lot 13 available.

"Nobody wants this lot because it's number thirteen. The post office says I can skip the number or, as you can see, it's was previously marked as Lot 03. So I have a Lot 3 and a Lot 03."

"Thirteen is fine with us. We're not superstitious."

"Makes no difference to me."

By the time school started, we were happily settled into our new home in the trailer park.

Gateway Baptist School had about 60 students and nine adults serving as facilitators and assistants. I began my day by arriving at 6:00 a.m. This would give me time for a devotional and to prepare a staff devotional. My work day was at least twelve hours long. There were a lot of responsibilities in administrating the school.

Diane would be an assistant as well. Although only four years old, Jenny was tested for kindergarten. She ranked second in class scores, so we allowed her to enter school early. (Her birthday was February 6th.) Timmy stayed with a church member during the day.

The school year was fun and very educational for me. It's hard to imagine it, but I was also our school's football and volleyball coach. We played flag football and were undefeated that year—not because I was the coach, but because one new family happened to come into our school with three boys: an eighth grader, an eleventh grader, and a twelfth grader. The two older boys were previous flag football players. Our girls' volleyball team did great and, although we didn't win all our games, it was a great experience coaching the team.

During the school year, our church also lost its song leader. I had a college course on music; so with Diane's help, I began to lead the music at our church. Diane was primary pianist as well. Together we directed and presented two major cantatas to the church.

The youth were developing Scripture songs, led by our youth director, Calvin Hines. For a fund-raiser, he decided to record the youth on cassette tape and sell them. Since he only had enough songs for one side, he asked Diane and me to sing songs for the other side of the tape. We did about six songs for the other side. I mention this because Mr. Hines took the tape to a local radio station, and it wasn't long before people began commenting how nice Diane and I sounded on the radio. I don't think I ever personally heard us on the station. The youth did sell a bunch of tapes though.

As the school year ended, there was a problem developing. Gateway was an independent Baptist church. Delton, being of an independent Baptist background, held on to some strict interpretations to certain Bible doctrines. I can't remember exactly what the issue was, but one day he talked to Diane about a certain doctrine. She could not agree with him. That should have been all there was to it: a simple disagreement to an interpretation of a nonessential biblical teaching. But Delton felt that, as a part of the church's leadership, she should agree with his interpretation. That was not going to happen. We decided then that we would resign at the end of the school year (May 1981) and that we would return to Texas, where I would try and start my seminary education again.

It was a tough decision because we were experiencing a revival among the students. Many students were getting under conviction over their sins and asking Christ to save them. It was truly amazing to see students sitting at their desks and begin to weep as conviction sat in. I recall two high school boys (Toby and Bobby) leaving their desks together and going into the restroom. Since they left without permission, I followed them. When I got inside, I heard one of the boys weeping loudly.

"What's the matter, guys?"

"Bobby just gave his life to Christ, Mr. Jones, and he can't stop crying."

The revival soon swept into the church itself. Numerous people were giving their lives to Christ and the testimonies given were nothing short of miraculous. One Sunday, Mr. Hines' wife, Barbara, went to the altar to pray and to testify. She said that as she watched the children change, and heard their testimonies about salvation, she realized that she had never experienced genuine salvation. She then gave her life to Christ. This occurred just prior to our leaving.

This time, leaving was difficult because I had no job to go to. The trailer wasn't sold, but a man to replace me at the school was going to rent it. We also had no money in which to move. Diane's grandfather had made some of the bedroom furniture that we had acquired from Mama Knight. We didn't want to leave it behind, but had no other recourse. My mom and brother took a couple of pieces of the furniture. We then made the difficult decision to sell the rest. This was primarily Diane's decision because I didn't want to make this decision.

We had an estate sale and, of course, everything sold quickly. We made enough money to rent a small trailer. I had purchased a Plymouth Horizon earlier in the year. It was a small car, but enough, I figured, to handle a small trailer attached to it. Diane and the kids got on a commercial bus and rode to Texas to stay with her parents while I drove down in the Horizon with all our belongings.

When I left the trailer, I remember having loaded it facing downhill. I left going downhill, but when I tried to drive up the hill, the car's standard transmission would not pull it up the hill. The trailer load was too heavy. I backed the car up the backside as far as I felt reasonably safe and took off as fast as I could around the bottom curve. The first try was unsuccessful. I backed back down to the bottom, maneuvering the trailer back up the slope on the backside again. This time I gave it all the gas it could take. I sped around the bottom as fast as it would go. The car and trailer slid a bit around the bottom's curve as it headed up the slope. The clutch was slipping but I continued to keep the engine's rpm's up. This time I made it, burning clutch and all!

1981 – Back to Texas, Again!

When I arrived in Texas, I found that Diane had left her parents and was living with a friend of ours from Dallas Baptist College, Jerry and Jeanita Nichols. It seems her parents were getting on her case again about something, so she decided to leave.

The Nichols lived in Grand Prairie and were gracious hosts. I arrived two weeks behind Diane. We immediately began looking for an apartment to move into. We had no jobs, so the apartment selection was very small.

We decided to attend the First Baptist Church of Dallas, where Dr. W. A. Criswell pastored. Although Diane's parents attended there and were so very controlling, I still felt an obligation to try and have some sort of relation with them. Mr. Leroy wanted me to attend The Criswell College (at that time it was called, The Criswell Center for Biblical Studies, and Dr. Paige Patterson was the president). The first Sunday we attended church, we witnessed Diane's parents re-joining the church. We went down to the front to see them. They were excited to see us and immediately, at the altar, began to tell us of a new job they had for us. This job would make us a lot of money and keep us very healthy. (No, it wasn't Amway; it was Shaklee, a vitamin supplement selling business.)

Under Mr. Leroy's prompting, I visited the Criswell school's administrative office. I recognized a Forney, Texas man's name listed as Director of Student Affairs. Dub Henry was his name and I think he had a son in the youth department at Forney when I served there as a youth minister. He was delighted to see me. I discussed my current situation and that I was interested in the school's master degree program. Mr. Henry gave me a bunch of informational pages on the school.

"This should get you started. Where are you staying?"

"Right now, I'm staying at a friend's house in Grand Prairie. I have no job, so it is difficult to find an apartment."

"Oh, let me refer you to a set of apartments in South Oak Cliff. They're government subsidized, but there are a number of Criswell students and their families living there. I bet you could even carpool to school with some of them."

I did not understand how the government subsidy worked, but Diane, the children, and I drove down to the Leigh Ann Apartments, near the corner of the I-35E feeder road and Wheatland Road. The apartments were very well groomed. We stopped at the office and introduced ourselves. The manager was delighted to see us and showed us an available two-bedroom, upstairs apartment. A white elderly lady lived below us and a Black grandmother lived beside us. The grandmother had grandchildren living with her. Some were Jenny and Timmy's age, which delighted them.

Although I had no employment, the manager allowed us to sign a leasing agreement, giving us the lowest possible rent, which I think was about $280 dollars a month, all bills paid. This was a Godsend and we moved in within a few days. I remember having kept our bunk bed for the children, but we had sold the rest of our furniture, including Diane's piano. Bits and pieces of furniture were given to us. A small 13-inch, black and white television was given to us. It had no on and off switch, so we had to pull the plug out of the wall socket to turn it off. I remember seeing Jenny and Timmy lying on the floor right in front of the TV screen, watching some children's programs. Later on, Mr. Leroy's mother, Munno, would contact us and send us a used piano.

I began job searching through the classifieds. I was trying to find a job with flexible hours so that I could possibly sign up at the Criswell Center in the fall. We had some money from our estate sale for our first month's rent and we still had a car payment. But I had to find something quickly. Since I was a people person, I naturally looked into the sales ads. I found an ad on selling Britannica encyclopedias in the Oak Cliff area. I responded to it and was invited for an introductory meeting in North Dallas.

There was a little bit of start-up expense and the company provided leads for prospective customers. Within a week, I was driving throughout the Oak Cliff area, making pitches for the purchase of encyclopedias. The company had a few bonus incentives for top salesman of the month. I became the rookie top salesman for July. My commission check was to be $1,300! Everyone congratulated me and I think I received a toaster as a bonus. However, when my check was given to me in mid-August, it was only $350 dollars. I went to the manager.

"Mr. Jarvis, I think there's a mistake with my commission check."

"Let me check on it, Johnnie." He pulled out a large sheet of paper. "It shows here that headquarters rejected most of your sales due to credit risks of the buyers."

"What? I thought when I turned in the order, that it was a done deal. I went by the checklist that qualified each sale."

"You may have, but Britannica has been in business for over two hundred years and they have a point system that qualifies or disqualifies each order. The only thing you can do now is to go back to each rejected sale and ask for a money order or cashier's check for at least half the sale."

I was so disappointed. My gasoline costs were high due to the amount of traveling in selling. Now, I have to back-track and try to resale my orders? This did not sound good and, sure enough, none of the previous sales were closed. Everyone that I had sold a set of encyclopedias to was upset and angry with the company and me. I apologized, but it seemed to be a waste of time. Plus, we had no money for our family.

Diane and I eventually joined First Baptist Church, Dallas. The Sunday School department and class was our "church" because the complete church was so big. Ed Rawls was our teacher. There was a couple in the department who befriended us, Scott and Margie Dill. Scott worked in Arlington for General Motors. They lived in Arlington also and had two children similar to Jenny and Timmy's age. They invited us over to their place for lunch a few times. I believe Scott had attended Arlington Bible College some and was debating whether or not to transfer to Criswell Center. I told him that I knew Dub Henry and to go talk to him. In fact, Diane and I were going to visit with Dub the next day, so I told Scott I would drop his name on Dub.

The next day, our family went to visit Dub. I explained my sales job failure and asked if he had some suggestions. He immediately pulled out his personal checkbook and wrote me a check for $50 dollars. He then gave me a phone number for a security guard company that hired a few students. Then he took us over to another part of the church grounds and introduced us to their food pantry. After he left us there, we were able to acquire several bags of food for our family. Diane had purchased a book that taught her how to live on a food budget of $16 a week. I remember one thing she did, and that was to mix powdered milk with regular milk in order to stretch it out further.

I contacted the security guard company (William C. Dear Security Services, Inc.) and set up an interview. I was trained and hired as a commissioned security guard for a downtown Dallas bank. "Commissioned" meant that I was qualified to carry a weapon. I remember the training well. The company had supplied me with a .357 pistol for training. On the firing range I kept shooting the target to the left. I knew something was wrong, so I told my instructor. He handed me his gun and told me to try again. This time my shots were perfect. He tried my pistol and shot to the left as well.

"You tell Mr. Dear this pistol needs replacing."

Since I would be working downtown, I decided to leave my car with Diane and start riding the Dallas transit bus to work. As long as I was in uniform, I could carry a pistol on the bus. I did receive a lot of stares because I carried a gun. My main security station would be at a drive-through bank near the northwest edge of downtown Dallas. My station also had a pump-action shotgun. When the armored truck was due at our station, I was instructed to stand outside with both weapons.

Mr. Jarvis, at Britannica, allowed me to continue selling encyclopedias, on my non-security days, until he could find a replacement for my area. He also gave me a few leads further south of Dallas, toward Ennis and Italy, Texas. In order to continue working the area, I had to follow up on these leads. It meant more gasoline expenses, but I continued to try and make sales. I closed on a number of them, but the home office continued to kick back over two-thirds of my sales. It was such a frustrating experience.

I could not enter college because we were broke, financially. Diane's parents paid for all our Shaklee expenses and encouraged us (forcefully, at times) to continue selling vitamins. The trouble was that all our close friends were primarily students who had no money to purchase expensive vitamin supplements, no matter how "good" they were for our bodies. We couldn't even afford them! But the Leroy's continued ordering us bottles for us to sell, plus their up-line couple was driving me around to visit some of my older friends in the DFW area. It was a waste of my time, though, because no one I knew could afford the prices of the products.

Diane offered to help earn some money. She baked an apple pie and allowed me to take it to the bank for the tellers to sample. She made up an order form and took orders from the tellers for the upcoming holidays. The pie was an instant success and I think she received a pre-holiday order of about eight pies.

Although I was working two jobs, we were still in a financial pickle. One early morning, as I was riding the bus into Dallas, I began to ask the Lord what I needed to do in order to get back into ministry. I was broke and it seemed as if the security job was not the answer. (I had been informed that Dear might lose the bank security contract in January.) It was then that I looked up at the bus ads and saw an employment ad for driving a bus for the Dallas Transit System. It mentioned excellent benefits and overtime opportunities. I called that day for an interview. The next day, I took an extra long lunch break and went to the transit system administrative offices to fill out an application. The following week I received a call to come back to the office for possible employment. I arranged a late interview and went after work. I was hired and told to be back in two weeks for a training class.

The timing was perfect because when I went to give my employment termination notice to my security supervisor, he informed me that I was to be laid off in about a month anyhow. He told me that Mr. Dear would try to find me another security job in the metroplex area, if I was interested. I declined the offer.

The Dallas Transit System

Training for the Dallas Transit System was fascinating. I had a number of classes to attend on driving and safety. But most of the time, I rode around on a city bus, taking turns driving the thing. The biggest problem was trying to stay in your lane and off the curb. The pay was about $3 dollars an hour more than I was making as a guard. Plus, there was no limit to the extra hours you could work. Due to our finances, I remember working between twelve and sixteen hours a day, six days a week. Diane could ride free and sometimes, on weekends, she and the children would catch my bus and ride with me a few rounds through Dallas.

My family began to spend a lot of time in downtown Dallas. We were members of First Baptist, Dallas, which was downtown; plus, through a series of grants, Jenny was allowed to attend First Baptist Academy at a very low cost. My city bus line-up area was in downtown Dallas, a few blocks from the church. Downtown Dallas became an intricate part of our lives.

The Leroy's were continuing to try to tell me what to do, as far as my educational goals were concerned. They wanted me in Criswell Center. Although I had initially returned to Texas to pick up where I left off at Southwestern Baptist Theological Seminary in Fort Worth, I saw no harm in attending Criswell. I signed up to attend one class for the fall semester. I figured I could attend midday, since most bus runs had a midday break time of about three hours. I was on, what DTS called, the "extra board" as a bus driver. That meant I arrived at the bus "barn" at 4:30 a.m., signed in, and then waited for a route to drive when someone called in sick or was running late to get the bus out for its scheduled appearance.

I was never paid under nine hours on the extra board, even if I didn't set foot on a bus. But it was rare not to drive at all. If I didn't go out on a morning trip, I had to return to the shop around 2:00 p.m. for the afternoon runs. I could write a book on the experiences I had while driving a bus, but I'll keep it to several events, just to give you an idea of the life of a bus driver.

A Knife in My Back…In the Grips of Death #5?

It was during my early days as a driver that I was in the downtown line up for the afternoon runs. I was headed out on the west side on the Commerce

Street viaduct. At a signal light, I noticed the two buses ahead of me were not allowing a rather big Black man to get on their buses. He was pounding on their doors to get on, but to no avail. The light turned green and the buses ahead of me began to leave. The man then ran to my bus and nearly ran out in front of me. I stopped and opened my door. Since I was into the intersection, I proceeded forward. No sooner had I cleared the intersection, this man began to scream at the top of his lungs and began blowing snot out of his nostrils onto the bus floor. I pulled the bus over to the side of the street and ordered the man off the bus. He screamed again, as if in terrible pain, and tried to sit beside a black lady at the front. She jumped out of the seat and ran to the back of the bus. There were about ten black ladies in the rear of the bus. This man began to address them in a sexual way and proceeded to walk to the back of the bus. As he did, I began calling for route supervisor assistance. One lady grabbed her purse.

"You don't want to come back here mister," she said as she stuck her hand in her purse, implying she had a weapon.

Meanwhile, I was getting no response from any supervisor.

"Control, this is 356 Jones; I have a large Black man disrupting my bus and threatening my passengers. I need help and I need it now!"

"Supervisor Three, are you near Commerce? Robert's on the bus."

"Nope, I'm on Oak Lawn."

"Supervisor Four?"

"Not me; I'm headed for Second Avenue."

"Is there a supervisor downtown that can go get Robert off of a bus?" No response. "356 Jones, you're just going to have to drive on. There's no one in your area."

By then, "Robert" had turned away from the women and was walking back up to the front of the bus. He sat immediately behind my driver's seat.

"Mister bus driver, if you don't get this bus moving and take me home, I'm going to stick something in your back!"

That's when I'd had enough. I locked the brakes down on the bus and put the transmission in Park.

"Control, this is 356 Jones, my bus is locked down and we're not moving until you get this man off my bus!" That's when I turned the engine off and stood up beside my seat. "Sir, we're not moving until you get off the bus."

He screamed again, cursing at the top of his lungs. "You are going to move this bus and take me home or else!"

Some of the women began talking to him. Others were praying aloud to Jesus. It was enough to divert his attention away from me. He moved down a few seats and began talking to one of the women. Although it seemed like an eternity had passed, in about two minutes, three Dallas Police squad cars came sliding around the bus, along with two transit supervisor cars.

I opened the front bus door and two officers came on board. One of them looked at the man.

"Robert, you ready to go?"

Robert quietly stood up. "Yes sir, officer; I'm ready." He put out his hands to allow the officer to handcuff him and they escorted him off the bus. A transit supervisor came on the bus.

"You okay, Jones?"

"No! There's snot all over the floor and on these two seats!" I was visibly shaken and extremely upset.

"Calm down, Jones," he said, as he pulled a rag out of his pocket and began to wipe the seats and floor. "Robert's a regular. He's on drugs and gets a little wild."

"Wild? Listen, he threatened about six of these ladies and he threatened to stick something in my back if I didn't drive him to his home. And tell me this: if you guys knew about him, why on earth did you not warn me about him?"

The supervisor did not respond, but advised me to restart my bus and help these riders to get home. I sat back into the driver's seat and wiped the sweat from my face. I closed my eyes momentarily, wiped them dry, and restarted the bus.

"Thanks, Jones; you'll be okay," he said as he got off the bus. I began to pull back onto the street as several of the women thanked me and encouraged me. I learned that day to watch for people acting abnormal and that I did not have to help everyone that came my way. (In fact, several months later, I heard a distress call from another driver who had picked up Robert. This time Robert had broken out several bus windows and managed to crawl out through one of them. The driver was calling for help, but once again each supervisor was turning down the request.)

Occasionally, I would get a drunk or a glue-sniffer on my bus. I physically removed one drunk off my bus and tried another time to get a supervisor to get the glue-sniffer off. Once again, I received no help from the supervisor pool. I finally managed to get him off as well.

In Oak Cliff, there was a Black man who always carried a golf bag with him. He rarely rode a bus and when he did, he never said anything and never paid his fare. His look indicated that he was probably mentally retarded. I think he may have ridden my bus a couple times. One day, he got on a bus (not mine) and sat down. Some teenagers began to taunt him and made fun of his hat and golf bag. He was seated in the back during this taunting when all of a sudden he pulled a shotgun out of his golf bag and began shooting. The news reported that people were jumping out of the bus windows. The driver was wounded in the leg and several others were injured by buckshot or by jumping out of the bus.

I think it was around March of 1982 when I began to struggle in my spirit. I was trying to understand the purpose of the current status of my family. Although I was enrolled in a class at Criswell, it seemed as if everything pertaining to the class was all wrong. Dr. John Burns taught the class and it was a study of the Book of Revelation. He was a great teacher and the subject was fantastic, but I just couldn't get my mind to concentrate. I went to drop the class, but Dr. Burns talked me out of it.

"Dr. Burns, you know I need a C in the class if I want to use it for a transfer later on. Plus, my bus-driving job is so erratic that I've already missed half of the classes."

"Johnnie, you just show up when you can, take good notes, and turn in your term paper. You should do just fine."

His assurance did not help my inner feelings and fears. I felt so alone, spiritually speaking. I talked it over with Diane. I began to question my salvation. This really troubled her. She could not imagine my not being saved. But I could not figure out my emptiness inside. I truly felt I was not saved and Diane could not help me in that department.

I went into the children's room and closed the door. I got on my knees and began praying. I prayed for an understanding of why I felt so alone inside. I had a good job now, was in school, and was enjoying the fellowship at the church. So why wasn't I okay on the inside? I prayed for a while; still no relief.

"God, I don't know what else to do. If I'm saved, please tell me. If I'm lost, I confess to You right now that I repent of my sins and I ask for Jesus to forgive me and to come into my life and save me right now. Oh please, God, save me from myself!"

I got up from the floor and left the room. Diane gave me a curious look.

"I don't know. I asked Christ to save me and all I know to do is to act out the steps of genuine salvation."

Diane was crying, but she also hugged me and assured me she would be by my side regardless.

The next Sunday, I surprised the Dill's by standing up at the invitation and walking down to the front. I took a counselor by the hand and expressed my need to confess my salvation. I guess I must have told him that I was a seminary student because when Dr. Criswell recognized me he mentioned that he knew several preachers who, later on in their ministry, had gotten saved. A few Sundays later, Gary Holder, an associate of the church, baptized me.

I remember going home that evening after the baptismal service. Diane was still trying to figure me out.

"Well, do you feel okay inside now?"

I thought about it for a moment: "No."

"So, what's wrong?" She was crying again.

"I don't know, honey; I just don't feel right inside."

"What else can you do?"

"Pray some more, I guess." And pray I did. I went into our bedroom as Diane prepared the children for bed.

"Oh God, what's wrong with me? Why am I empty inside? What am I doing that's wrong?" I pled with God for a few minutes. Then I got quiet. It seemed as if my mind was rewinding back to the Glen Hill revival, the Gospel For Asia event, Gateway Baptist School, and my decision to return to school. I rehearsed every detail and every decision. Through these events, Diane and I had seen the hand of God taking care of us. I felt His presence all the way up to one decision: the decision to change seminaries. I had committed myself to return to Southwestern Seminary in Fort Worth, but to please the Leroy's I changed to Criswell. I didn't think it mattered to God what seminary to go to, especially if they were both conservative. I prayed again.

"Is this it, God? Have I messed up Your plans for me by changing schools? Oh Lord, I'm so sorry. I plead with You to forgive me. I promise I will not pursue Criswell after this semester and I will make plans to go to Southwestern. If this is the problem, please give me some sign. Please restore to me the joy of my salvation. In Jesus' name I pray, amen."

I stood up and immediately I felt a restoration in my spirit. I went out of the room and hugged Diane.

"Wow," she said. "Did you get saved again?"

"Yes; but this time from myself."

I lifted her off the floor and made a few circles with her. We then sat down and I explained what had happened.

"So, you didn't need salvation?"

"That's right; I disobeyed God and it's as if He withdrew Himself from me to teach me what it is like to make decisions without Him. It was like being lost—no; in fact it felt worse than being lost!"

From that day on, I made a commitment to God to always consult Him in all my decisions and to obey His leading, as best as I could determine it. I began taking gospel tracts on my buses and would leave them in selected seats. I would pray for people who would ride my bus each day. I remember, at the end of my route one day, saying, *"Lord, I don't care if I ever preach again. If You want me to remain a bus driver, I'll be the best Christian bus driver DTS has ever known."*

I was so happy and peaceful inside. I could hardly stand it sometimes. A few days later, Dr. Burns called me.

"Johnnie, I have a problem."

"How can I help you, Dr. Burns?"

"Well, I have to be at a library conference next Sunday in New York City and I need for someone to preach for me at Western Park Baptist Church in Oak Cliff. Would you be available to preach for me?"

"Me? I don't know; are you sure you want me to do it?"

"Yes sir. I feel God wants you to fill in for me. Is that okay?"

"Yes sir; I would be honored to preach for you."

"Fine. Do you know where Western Park is located?

"Yes, I used to live on Illinois Avenue and drove by the church on my way to Dallas Baptist College. What time do they start?"

Dr. Burns gave me the time and the conversation was over. It was now June of 1982. I had not preached for nearly six months. I wasn't even sure I could still preach. *"God, is this Your plan for me? I must know or I will call Dr. Burns back and cancel."* I immediately had a peace in my heart that this was in God's plan.

The pastor of Western Park Baptist Church was Russell Cook. He was away with his youth on a mission trip. I preached that morning and gave an invitation. Several men came forward to the altar to pray and several others responded to the deacon who was standing at the altar. I was so grateful to God that He would show Me His approval by allowing some response during the invitation song. We returned that evening and I preached again. It was this service, I think, that just prior to my preaching, Timmy got sick and threw up on a pew. It was a mess and embarrassing.

After the service, I announced to Diane that we should start making plans to go to Southwestern. I would see about taking a class this summer and perhaps we could move over to Fort Worth for the fall semester. We also decided to attend Western Park again. It seemed like the right thing to do. The following Sunday we attended and joined. Again, I think it was that Sunday evening that the pastor, Brother Russell, resigned as pastor of the church. He felt led of God to go to a church in Oklahoma.

Russell apologized to me for leaving, just after we joined.

"That's okay, as long as you're not resigning because we joined!"

We all laughed and he assured me his relocation was in the making for some time. He said he received confirmation from God during his time with the youth that it was time for him to move on.

The week after Brother Russell's last Sunday, I received a call from one of the deacons of Western Park. I was asked if I would preach again the following Sunday. I agreed and consulted with God once more. My plans were to always ask the Lord about any decision that could possibly affect my directions in ministry. I did not ever want to have Him leave me as He did previously, when I failed to consult Him, on such a weighty matter.

When I preached the following Sunday, once again, many people came forward. It seemed as if God's anointing was on the messages I presented. I preached again that evening and, once again, several came forward. I was amazed and thanked God for His choosing to use me. It was the confirmation I needed to know that He was not finished with me in the preaching ministry.

Dr. Burns was called as interim pastor of Western Park. He preached some very good exegetical messages. I enjoyed his preaching thoroughly. At the August business meeting, the Pastor Search Committee reported that they had received a number of resumes and would begin the process of selecting a pastor soon. One of the deacons stood up and asked to speak.

"I think we should not consider anyone else than the man God has already sent to us: Brother Johnnie Jones."

Another man stood up as well: "I concur with that recommendation. When Brother Jones preached a few weeks ago, we had a great response to his messages. I ask that the committee review his resume first."

There were a couple of "amen's" after that statement. I felt awkward being there, but before I could dismiss myself, a lady on the committee stood up to speak.

"The committee does not have Brother Jones' resume. We were selected by the church to search for our next pastor and you should at least give us time to review the resumes we've received."

After that statement, the men sat down and the meeting was concluded. One of the men came to me and asked me to send him my resume.

"Brother Standford, I appreciate your voice of confidence, but do remember that I plan to attend seminary in Fort Worth."

"Yes, I know. All of our preachers have gone to the seminary. I want you to be considered as our pastor because you have an anointing in your messages."

I thanked him again and promised to send him my resume. As we drove home, I spoke to Diane.

"I didn't know that was going to happen!"

"Yeah, it was awkward. I wish those men had warned us so that we could have left."

"Well, I appreciate their enthusiasm, but I felt the lady on the committee was feeling some undue pressure to consider me."

"What do you think?"

"I think I will not be considered, due to the way it was presented."

And I was correct. In a matter of a couple weeks, the committee presented a former associate pastor to the church for consideration as the new pastor. Since he already owned a house in the community and had several teenage children who were close friends of other teenagers, it was obvious that he would be selected as the new pastor. It was far from unanimous, but enough for a majority vote.

After that, Diane and I decided that it would be best, for the church's sake, for us to move on to another place. We were looking to move toward Fort Worth, so I began to look at churches in that direction. That's when I discovered that my pastor from Hawaii, Bill Smith, had relocated to Bellevue Baptist Church in Hurst, a city on the east side of Fort Worth. I couldn't believe it!

"Diane! Guess what? Bill Smith, my pastor from Hawaii, is now in Hurst. Oh, we've got to go there."

"Sounds great, but how long will it take to drive over there?"

"I don't know, but I used to drive half way across Oahu to get to his church."

We decided to attend the next Sunday. I didn't realize that he had been there only a month. It took us about 30 minutes to travel to Hurst. When he began the service, he greeted everyone by saying, "Aloha!" Some of the people responded with "Aloha," but others just chuckled. He said it again, a little louder: "ALOHA!" This time he got a stronger response. "Folks, I may have left Hawaii, but I was there over seventeen years. So be patient with me and help me feel at home. 'Aloha' means 'hello' and 'Aloha' means 'I love you.' It's a word that spans across many Pacific dialects, including English."

Bill preached as Bill had always preached. I had forgotten his style, which was more homiletical than exegetical. Since 1979, I had chosen to preach more exegetical than homiletical, because I felt people needed to understand the context of the verses. I also began to realize that exegetical messages produced their own application, if given a chance.

But I loved Bill and couldn't wait to talk to him. After the service, we went to seek him out. When he saw me, he screamed with delight: "Johnnie Jones! What on earth are you doing here?" We hugged each other.

"I had to bring my wife to let her hear my pastor preach!"

I introduced Diane to Bill and he hugged her as well. Then he met Jenny and Timmy.

"Oh you have such a beautiful family, Johnnie. God has been so good to you. Diane, I want you to meet my wife, Ruth. She's around here somewhere...Ruth! Ruth!"

Ruth came walking down an aisle and saw me.

"Well Johnnie Jones, what a pleasant surprise. What are you doing in Texas?"

"Ruth, this is Johnnie's wife and kids," Bill interrupted. "Diane, Jenny, and Timmy."

"We live in Dallas now, but hope to move in this direction to return to Southwestern Seminary."

"That's great, Johnnie," said Bill. "When are you planning to join here?" He smiled and looked at Diane. "Diane, I have some things I can tell you about this man."

"Am I being blackmailed here?" We laughed.

"Seriously Johnnie, I need some guys like you to loosen up these folks. I want you to head up my greetings group next Sunday morning. I've ordered some Hawaiian seed leis that I want our visitors to receive when we recognize them, just like we did at Waialae."

"Oh, I don't know, Bill. It's a long ways over here."

"Diane, did I mention the girl that Johnnie dated in Hawaii?" Again, we laughed.

"Okay, okay; I'll talk it over with Diane and we'll try to be here next Sunday morning."

We left and headed back for Dallas. Diane was quiet.

"Well, what do you think?"

"He's okay, I guess."

"You guess? What do you mean, 'you guess'?"

"Oh, nothing; he's just a little too friendly for me."

Diane's quiet temperament did not feel comfortable around Bill's outgoing personality. But I managed to get her to agree to give him a chance. My enthusiasm around Bill gave her enough leeway to allow us to attend for a while.

Bill recognized me the following Sunday morning and presented me with the new seed leis he had specially flown in from Oahu. I had a few of the younger men and ladies to watch how I greeted a few visitors, then handed them some of the leis with instructions to do the same. It was a fun experience for me as it took me back a few years to the early days of my Christian life.

We joined Bellevue a week later and attended there for a few months. While there, I visited with Bill a few times in his office. Bill was still Bill: very outgoing and truly interested in my affairs.

"Bill, I plan to return to Southwestern seminary next semester. I really need a part-time job over here somewhere and a place to live near the seminary." While I was talking to him, his phone rang.

"Bill, Dr. Draper is on line one," said his secretary.

"Oh great! Thanks." He picked up the phone and winked at me. "Jimmy, how are you today?" They discussed some Baptist issues while I scanned Bill's office. Next to me, on a coffee table, was a large portfolio of Bill's stay in Hawaii. The front picture was one I immediately remembered. It was Waialae's adult choir in the Honolulu television studio with Tennessee Ernie Ford singing in front of it. There I was, on the back row, singing in the choir. It was during one of our many specials that our choir sang for Bill's television show, "The Good Life." I began thumbing through his portfolio as Bill continued talking to Jimmy Draper, then pastor of First Baptist Church of Euless, Texas.

"Jimmy, listen, I have a young preacher friend of mine here in the office with me. He needs a job and a house for his seminary days, starting this fall. Do you have any positions open over there at your church? Oh, he's one of the best."

I couldn't believe what Bill was saying in my behalf, but it sure felt good to be around someone who knew me well enough to say stuff like that…even if he was stretching it a bit. After he got off the phone with Dr. Draper, Bill pulled out a phone book, searched for a moment, and then handed me a number.

"I want you to call the seminary in a couple of days, Johnnie. Give me enough time to make a few calls first. I'll find you a place to stay."

I loved Bill. He was a man I deeply admired. But things had changed since I was living in Hawaii. I felt I needed to speak up.

"Bill, what happened in Hawaii? You're not supposed to be here." He looked at me with his deep, penetrating eyes.

"Johnnie, it's a long story. I've got to meet with Jimmy in a few minutes, but is there a day you can come over and I'll buy you breakfast?"

"Sure. How about this Saturday?"

I told Diane about the meeting. She decided not to go, because of the children. So I met with Bill at a Waffle House on Loop 820.

Bill sat and shared his heart with me. Bill had some extreme events to occur in his life that caused him some times of physical pain. Prior to my being in Hawaii, he had been involved in a small plane crash between two of the islands. He had suffered many headaches, not to mention the time he passed out the night I gave my life to Jesus.

"Johnnie, I was at the end of my rope, so to speak. A friend of mine had a house on the beach in Molokai. He sent me over there for some R and R. I had a fire lit on the beach one night. I was praying and wrestling with God about my physical pain. I felt like the apostle Paul, as he requested God to relieve him of his pain.

"I heard from Him that night, Johnnie. He told me to write down every sin and every pain that I was presently struggling with. I did; it was a long list. Then He told me to fold the paper up and to toss it into the fire. I didn't understand at first, but as I watched that paper burn, God said that my life and my sins were to be as that piece of paper: totally consumed in Him. He told me to trust Him for the future."

Tears were in his eyes as he tried to continue the story. "That night I told God that I would resign my church and start all over with Him. There were too many things tied to Waialae that I had to let go of in order to trust Him fully for the future. I could not continue there under the pressures I was going through. So that is why I'm here now."

"But you don't seem to fit here, Bill," I responded. "I mean, you're...you're so outgoing and so polished..." He broke in with a laugh.

"You think it's rough on me, you should've seen Ruth crying for weeks. I thought she was going to divorce me for Hawaii!"

From there, the conversation passed on to me, Diane, and our future plans. Bill was uncomfortable talking about himself. He was still a pastor—my pastor—in his heart and was concerned about my future. I explained a few things that had led us to where we currently were.

"Bill, I've come to the place that I told God that I will do whatever He wants me to do. I told Him I would remain a city bus driver if that was what He wanted. That's when He confirmed to me that I needed to go back to Southwestern."

"Oh, I don't think He's through with your ministry, Johnnie. You're one of a few men that has been under my ministry that I sensed God wanting to do some special work in and through you. Stay close to Him, Johnnie, and don't make any decisions without His leading. Keep your prayer time with Him; it is essential."

I left that meeting with Bill with a fresh determination to trust God for our future.

Southwestern Baptist Theological Seminary, Fort Worth, Texas

During the next few weeks, I contacted the seminary and had all my transcripts forwarded to Southwestern. Dr. Jeter Basden, formerly at Dallas Baptist, as a recruiter, was now a part of Southwestern. He remembered me from our DBC days and got to work on my transfer. It wasn't long before he had some good news and some bad news.

"Johnnie, I have a house here on campus that you and your family can live in."

"That's great, Jeter!"

"But I've got some bad news: the classes you took at Liberty Baptist Seminary in Lynchburg won't transfer."

"What?"

"Well, Liberty is not accredited by the Association of Southern Colleges and Universities. So that won't work here."

"Hold on Jeter. That's ten semester hours of hard work. They didn't cut me any slack in those classes."

"It's not about the work performed, Johnnie, it's about the degree being recognized as an accredited degree."

"Well, if I remember correctly, I was told by Liberty that they were accredited by the American Theological Association and were under current review for the one you mentioned."

"Oh yeah? Let me check further. We might be able to appeal this to the board."

I hung the phone up and looked at Diane.

"Are you ready for another adventure?" As usual, she smiled, embraced me, and kissed me.

"I'll go wherever you go as long as I'm with you. You are my husband and if God says 'Go,' then we go."

I loved Diane's willingness to drop all the comforts of our current dwelling to join me in following the Lord. It really placed a heavy responsibility on me to make sure I was following His leading.

Within a few weeks, we were moving to Fort Worth. We moved into a small two-bedroom house on Townsend Blvd., just a block from the seminary president's house. I resigned my position as a bus driver for the Dallas Transit System, and once again moved to another city with no job to go to. Jeter Basden had told me to write a letter of appeal to the seminary board, detailing every class I had taken, and attaching a transcript to it. By the first or second week on "Seminary Hill," I received a letter from the board, accepting all ten hours from Liberty. I was excited and called Jeter.

"Congratulations, Johnnie; you pulled it off. Let me tell you, you will be the last person that they do this for, because they reformulated the requirements for future transfers."

"Just because of me?"

"Yep." Jeter laughed. "You're special, I guess."

"Yeah, that's what my wife says all the time. Thanks Jeter."

It was August of 1983 now. Jenny would begin third grade and Timmy would start Kindergarten. I checked the employment board on campus and found several job possibilities. My first one was in Arlington, working in a furniture warehouse. Before I started I had to take a lie detector examination. I wasn't worried about it, but did have one "lie" detected.

"Have you ever been intoxicated while working?" the examiner asked.

"No ma'am," I responded. She hesitated.

"Are you sure?"

"Yes ma'am!" She looked at the graph and marked on it.

"What's it saying?" I asked.

"It's saying that you're not telling the truth. What are you thinking about when I ask that question?"

"Well, two things come to my mind when you mention the word 'alcohol': one is my dad and his constant drinking, and the other is my drinking days before I gave my life to Christ."

"How long ago was that?"

"About twelve years ago." She was watching the graph as I spoke.

"Okay; so let me rephrase the question: In the past ten years, have you ever been intoxicated while on the job?"

"No ma'am." I smiled and she smiled back.

"You passed it that time."

"You mean it didn't catch that time last year when I was drinking while driving a city bus?" I smiled while she laughed.

"Now you're lying again!"

"Ah, man, I forgot I was still wired to that thing!" It was a good laugh, but a subtle reminder of the power of the subconscious.

I got the job and began working. The hours would be after school each day and about twenty hours a week. It paid $7.00 an hour, I think. Diane put a pencil to the finances and shook her head.

"I don't see how we can pay our bills on your salary."

"Well maybe a church nearby will call me and hire me as a youth minister or something."

"I don't know; I bet every man here is thinking that same thing."

"Oh yeah; I forgot I wasn't the only worker bee in the beehive here. Any suggestions?"

"Well, I could work."

"Yeah? And when could you find time to do that?"

"It won't hurt to look at the employment board again."

"Just remember that we have only one vehicle, and I work, and I'm going to need your help typing my papers. Oh, and we have two children in school."

"That reminds me, I'll be driving them to school each morning, but in the afternoon, I'll have to walk to get them."

"Is that okay?"

"Sure; it's only about six blocks away."

I went to work that day with a new burden on my heart. *"Lord, I don't know what You want me to do, but I cannot allow Diane to suffer while I sit in a classroom. Please tell me what to do."*

When I arrived home that evening, Diane was excited.

"I think I found me a job!"

"Doing what?"

"Throwing papers on a paper route!"

"Really? Tell me more."

"Well there was an ad on the board for a paper route for *The Dallas Morning News*. I called a man this afternoon and left a message on his answering machine. He's supposed to call me back."

"Sounds interesting. I wonder what the hours would be?"

It didn't take long to find out. The next morning at 6:30 a.m., we received a call from Mr. Howard Hutsell. He was the Fort Worth district manager for *The Dallas Morning News*.

"This is Howard Hutsell. Is Mrs. Jones available?"

"Sure," I replied. "Just a moment."

Mr. Hutsell set up an appointment to meet Diane at 9 a.m. near downtown Fort Worth. I went to school and then hurried off to work at the furniture rental store in Arlington. I arrived home that evening around 6 p.m. After a few minutes of wrestling and playing with Jenny and Timmy, I caught up with Diane in the kitchen.

"Well, how was your interview?"

"It went okay." She didn't seem too excited about it.

"What's the problem?"

"Well, I would have to meet a delivery truck at the hardware store on James Avenue at 2:30 a.m. and travel around the south side of Fort Worth and a small town, called Everman, throwing papers. He said I would probably be finished around 6 a.m. every morning except Sundays. It would take longer on Sundays."

"Wow, you're talking seven days a week?"

"Yes, but he mentioned I could make about a thousand dollars a month, even more if I went out and worked the neighborhoods for subscriptions."

I did my usual quiet period after that statement and began running the scenario through my mind. It didn't last long because Diane would interrupt my thinking process with the answer to my perceived problems about her proposed paper route.

"Mr. Hutsell doesn't think I can do the job. He says it could be dangerous for me and that the paper on Sundays is extremely heavy. I would have to get out of the car at each house on Sundays and carry the paper to the yard. But he wants to talk to you about the job."

"Me? I thought I already had a job."

"Well, your job will pay about $750 a month and this one pays about a thousand. I've thought through the schedule and I think it will be much better for both of us if you did the paper route than work at the furniture store in the afternoons."

As usual, Diane's analytical mind had worked a schedule up showing me how much better the time would be for me if I did the paper route rather than drive to Arlington each day. With the paper route, I could be more flexible with choosing my class schedule as well as doing my research at the seminary library. It really was a no-brainer. So, after a couple weeks at the furniture store warehouse, I became a full-fledged paper carrier for *The Dallas Morning News*. This occurred in the fall of 1982.

The paper route was grueling in that it was a 7-day-a-week job, but the pay was actually better than a thousand a month. Plus, Diane did find a job as a Tupperware party representative. She did so well, in fact, that in three months, her supervisors promoted her to a district manager. Not only did she set up parties, but also she trained other ladies to do the same. And, best of all, she was given a Mercury station wagon to drive. It was a used one, but a new one had been ordered for her. So, in less than four months at seminary, I was probably one of the highest paid students on campus and we were driving a new car. I even hired a student to help me on Sundays. I concluded that God was indeed answering a simple prayer for my family and me.

That fall, I had found a two-cycled lawnmower that had been refurbished. Our yard was small, but it did require mowing. Our house was on Townsend, a couple blocks south of the seminary campus. I always walked to school. One house that I walked by had some tall grass. I wondered about it, since it was much closer to the seminary, and nearly in the backyard of the president's house. One day as I walked home, a mower was in that yard. It had mowed a couple rounds of grass and was stopped. A young man and his preschool son were on the porch. I walked past him and waved.

"Howdy!" I shouted. He smiled. "Something wrong with your mower?" I began walking through the tall grass toward the young man, a student of course.

"Yes," he replied. "It doesn't run but for a few minutes and then stops."

"Hmmm." My mechanical brain began to evaluate the situation. "Have you checked the air and gas filters?"

He smiled again. "No. I'm not much of a mechanic."

"Well let me run down to my house and get my tool bag and I'll take a look at it." He smiled again.

I hurried down the road and found my canvass tool bag, a battered old bag that I used in the air force, and also pushed my mower back up the street to the man's house.

"Here, you can mow while I investigate your mower's problem. My mower has a two-cycle engine, which means it has only one speed and it smokes a little. It runs on an oil-gasoline mixture. By the way, I'm Johnnie Jones, a student here at the seminary."

His name was David Cranfield. His wife was Connie and their son's name was Jeffrey. They were from Anchorage, Alaska. David began mowing while I proceeded to take his mower apart, searching for the problem. The gas line appeared to be okay. The air filter was a bit dirty; so I beat it out a bit. I removed the spark plug and noticed that the tip was bent too close together, preventing a spark to ignite the combustion chamber. I reopened the plug, cleaned it, and set it at a gap similar to what I figured was adequate for a lawnmower spark plug. I put the mower back together and fired it up. It began to run and I helped David finish his front yard. As time allowed, my family and David's would visit and have supper together. He and I would later cross paths again.

My degree plan at Southwestern changed from a Master of Divinity (MDiv), to a new Master of Arts in Religious Education (MARE). David George, my old pastor from Tarrant Road Baptist Church had told me that I would get a much fuller education and a better "hands-on" training for leading a Southern Baptist church, than the typical MDiv, especially since I had majored in Religion at Dallas Baptist College.

"If I had it to do again," he said, "I would do the MRE (Masters of Religious Education; it was replaced by the MARE) and take all my electives in theology. Trust me, Johnnie, the MRE will train you how to grow your church through the Sunday School and other ministries."

And so I did; I listened to my friend and switched degree plans. One thing he warned about, however, was that the research paper load for an MRE was much greater than for the MDiv.

"In the MDiv, you will take a lot more tests; but in the MRE, you will make up for the tests in research papers," said David. And he was not kidding. The MRE classes were much more demanding outside the actual class time than the MDiv. This meant I had to spend hours in the library and Diane had to spend a lot of hours typing my research papers, using a small portable typewriter, foot-noting all my references in accordance to the seminary's specifications.

This was a time in our lives that we had to remain extremely focused on the larger picture. Diane and I had to rely heavily on our conviction that God had led us back to Texas and back to Southwestern. Our schedules were beyond comprehension.

I worked from 2:30 a.m. (woke up around 2:15) until about 6:00—sometimes 6:30, depending on the arrival of the delivery truck. When I got home, I took a quick tub bath (we had no shower), ate breakfast, and was in class by 8:00 a.m. My classes usually lasted until about noon. I took a lunch with me and then studied at the library until about suppertime. After supper, I slept until 2:15 a.m.

Diane would take the children to school, do house work, and go out into communities and either try to set up Tupperware parties or train others to set up their own parties. She would sometimes go door-to-door and ask to set up a party. After that, she would go and pick up the children from school, see to their school assignments, and type my research papers. When she had Tupperware parties, I would watch the children some, or a neighbor would watch them until Diane got home, so that I could get some sleep.

In accordance with her training, Diane sometimes double-booked parties. This meant she would schedule two parties on the same day at the same time. This practice was common because many of the party hosts would cancel at the last minute due to conflicts or because they just didn't do the legwork and get their family and friends to attend. If both parties did indeed hold on to their schedule, she would give one of the parties to one of her representatives. Several times, however, even this did not work. That's when Diane would give me this large round blue button to put on my shirt, stating: "Your Tupperware Lady is a Man!" Diane trained me how to run a party, and then we went our separate ways to both parties. In every occasion, the host was gracious, and after getting to know me, they always had a successful party. One night, my party out-sold Diane's! It was fun and I was happy to help my wife who worked so hard to ensure our family's financial stability.

First Baptist Church, Roxton, Texas

In February of 1983 I was contacted by a pastor search committee from First Baptist Church of Roxton, Texas. I think it was in May that I became their pastor. Roxton was a nice town, primarily a bedroom community for the greater Paris, Texas area. Once again, God confirmed that I was to be a pastor and that there was still some ministry for me to fulfill.

I continued my seminary education by arranging my classes on Mondays and Tuesdays. We moved to Roxton, so that meant I had to travel about two and a half hours to school. I slept in the men's dorm on Monday nights. I discovered that there were a group of men who did this. One man was Barry

Beames, the pastor of First Baptist Church of Blue Ridge, Texas. We became friends and had breakfast together a lot. He and I would cross paths again later on in my ministry.

I finally finished my seminary education in July of 1984. It was tough doing so as a pastor, but with Diane's help, we managed. She began teaching piano again and started a *Paris News* paper route in the afternoons. This was something she really enjoyed doing. Glenn and Georgia Goggins were members of FBC, Roxton, and became very close friends of ours. Glenn was a farmer, so I thoroughly enjoyed going out to his farm and helping him do stuff, like combine wheat or barley. It reminded me of my farming days on Ben Payne's farm in Dry Fork, Virginia. Diane and Georgia had great times together as well.

I remember one episode when Diane shrieked at a moth in Georgia's house. Diane did not like flying insects of any kind. But, amazingly, she was not afraid to chase down a snake and pick it up. She was braver than I, in that department. Anyway, we were headed out to the Goggins' farm when a small snake slid across the road in front of us.

"Stop the car!" Diane shouted. I did as commanded, and she went chasing that snake. Fortunately, for the snake and for Georgia, it got away. Diane had planned on bringing that critter to Georgia. Georgia was equally as fearful of snakes as Diane was of flying insects. I, for one, was glad she didn't catch the thing!

Our ministry at Roxton was not an easy one. There were a lot of conflicts between me and the men there, concerning their allegiance to our church. I challenged them a few times, concerning their priorities, and got labeled as a troublemaker.

However, there were some good events that occurred there. Both Jenny and Timmy made their commitments to Christ in Roxton. Jenny's came during a Vacation Bible School week and Timmy's came during a revival with Leroy Hassler. I also began my writing career for the local Roxton paper.

During a revival, Leroy brought in a friend of his from Euless, Chuck Reynolds. Chuck was a former NFL player for the Cleveland Browns. His salvation testimony was very captivating and caused many to seek the Lord for salvation.

Chuck would eventually come back to Roxton for several meetings. One time, he came for a weekend and we went out into the community to witness to teenagers. His size and his enormous NFL ring would nearly swoon the kids, but he was always telling them that his ring and his NFL career were no match to what Jesus did in his life. Several teenagers came to Christ as a result of Chuck's testimony.

Another event was the appearance of Miller McClure in the services. He and his family lived nearby in the High community. He was the manager of the Radio Shack in Paris. Miller had become a Christian in earlier years, but got involved in an acid-rock band and the drugs and alcohol associated with the music. His wife was more of the spiritual guide in their house. They had two children at the time, and were living on his parent's farm.

On the Sunday morning he attended, I dealt with alcohol and drugs. Miller thought his wife had conspired with me to get him there that particular morning. I knew nothing of his coming, but apparently God did. According to his testimony, while driving back home after the morning service, he began complaining about my message. His wife remained quiet for a while, and then responded.

"Do you think that you may be under conviction?"

That's all it took for Miller to realize that it wasn't me or my preaching that was causing him his problems in life. It was his run from God. I visited him at his store that week. He tried to sell me a Commodore computer, but I was there to encourage him to return to the Lord. He later said he was upset with me for coming to the store to talk with him. But, as it turned out, the Holy Spirit was revealing how far he had gone from the Lord.

The next time he came to church, he came forward to make his re-commitment to Christ public. As soon as I discovered that he could sing, I asked him to lead our music at the church. It was obvious that he was gifted in music. He had a way of presentation that made you feel you were in the very presence of God in worship. Miller and his family became a great asset to our church. Miller would eventually announce to our church that he was responding to a call into the ministry. He eventually enrolled in East Texas Baptist University and moved to the campus. (He later became a music and education minister and, eventually, a pastor.)

In spite of the decisions being made and the numerical growth of the church, the opposition to my ministry grew. It wasn't long that I felt in my heart that I had to leave Roxton. I resigned the pastorate in September of 1985 and moved back to Dallas. Ed Ethridge was a pastor in Dallas and came out to Roxton to help move me. Since we had nowhere to go, Ed had a family in his church that brought us into their home temporarily. We managed to set up the children's bunk bed in their converted screened-in porch that served as a green house for them. I went to work for a job-temp service and Diane cared for the children, as well as cleaned the house that we were living in. The couple was very grateful for her help.

North Star Baptist Church, Anderson, Alaska

I remember Diane and I were praying about going to another church where I could pastor. We told the Lord that we would go anywhere that He wanted us to go. The seminary had sent my resume out to "anywhere." About a month later, I received a call from a church in…ALASKA!

"Alaska?" Diane asked.

"Yep, Alaska," I responded.

"I don't know," she said.

"Well, we did tell the Lord 'anywhere,' didn't we?"

"Well, yes; but Alaska? What about the children? What would they do?"

"I guess they would bundle up under the covers just like us and survive," I responded jokingly. "Look, let's get some more information before we turn it down. Who knows, it may be better than we think."

The church was called North Star Baptist Church. It was located in Anderson, Alaska, a bedroom community for Clear Air Force Site, an early warning anti-ballistic radar site that could give the continental U.S. about a fifteen minutes' heads-up should a missile be launched over the western North Pole area.

Anderson was located about 85 miles southwest of Fairbanks and had a population of about 350 people. It had a real nice school that was equipped with all the latest technology, including computers in every classroom. We discovered later that Alaska boasted of having the richest school districts and highest paid teachers in America.

North Star was a previous mission church of the Home Mission Board (now North American Mission Board) of the Southern Baptist Convention. To go there, as pastor, I would have to qualify as a missionary. It meant a lot of tests, physically, emotionally, and spiritually. North Star had also started a mission church in Healy, Alaska, about 30 miles south of them, and contributed to a mission in Fort Yukon along the Arctic Circle.

Diane and I once again prayed to ask the Lord if this was His "anywhere" for us. I was intrigued by the location as well as the mission history of the church. Finally, we both agreed to talk further with the committee. They set up a conference call where everyone could be on the phone at the same time. Some of the committee members were in the church, some were in the church parsonage and one was at Clear AFS, who was arranging the conference call through military connections.

The conversations were delightful and Diane and I were deeply impressed with what they had to offer. The school activities were especially attractive to us. They had numerous sports programs and traveled across the state, playing other school districts. I was to be the Air Force site's chaplain as well, giving me a little more income. This would be in addition to the church's salary and the supplement from the Home Mission Board.

I was "sold" on the deal, but knew Diane would have to have peace about it. The church could fly just one person up to Alaska to see the situation first hand. I told them that if I came, I would like to have a three-day revival set up so that they could hear me preach a few more times than is customary. The committee agreed, but also asked that I not come unless I was pretty sure about the move. The church could not afford to fly a bunch of prospective pastors up there. I would be their first applicant. (I discovered later that I was one of 80 resumes.)

"Well, Hon, what do you think?"

Diane was quiet momentarily. "I'm not sure, but I am committed to go wherever you feel the Lord would have us to go. I will support your decision."

This laid the responsibility squarely on my shoulders. It was a major decision. I knew my resume was in a dozen churches, but this was the only church that had contacted us. I prayed.

"Lord, I am not worthy to be a pastor. I don't deserve this position and will only consider this if it is Your will. Please show us what we should do and give us peace about going to Alaska if it is Your will."

The next day, the couple in whose home we were living, had a little disagreement. For whatever reason, it spilled in on us. It seems the lady did not like the way Diane arranged some of the kitchen. In Diane's fashion, she was always trying to be helpful. She cleaned cabinets and drawers in every room, including the kitchen, which appeared to be in disarray. But the lady asked Diane to leave things alone, because she could not find her kitchen stuff.

When I arrived home from a job, I found Diane in the bedroom crying. We talked awhile and prayed some. After the prayer the confirmation I was seeking came:

"So how soon can we go to Alaska?" she asked with a smile. I hugged and kissed her.

"I'll call them tonight!"

Arrangements were made for me to fly to Alaska in early November. I would hold a revival, meet with the committee, and have a question and answer time with the church body. The church had about 35 in attendance, with only 25 members. There were only two churches in the community: a Baptist and an Assembly of God church. Therefore, all the non-charismatic Christians congregated with the Baptists.

A week later, the church would vote on me. I believe there were twelve or thirteen actual votes with only one being a negative vote in calling me as their pastor. We accepted the call and began arrangements to move our belongings, by air and sea, to Alaska, compliments of the Home Mission Board.

I think when the lady of the house realized we were leaving, she began to see Diane in a different light. She apologized for her behavior and insisted we eat Thanksgiving dinner with her extended family in Pleasant Grove, a Dallas suburb. We accepted and ended our stay with this couple on good terms. They had helped us tremendously during our time of transition.

We arrived in Alaska in mid-December of 1984. Alaska was cold, but it was beautiful. The Northern Lights were visible from the airplane as we neared Fairbanks. Timmy was the first to see them from the airplane. He thought he was seeing the Milky Way. It was winter, dark, and cold. The church had arranged to pick us up at the airport and drive us out to Anderson.

The road wound through a very mountainous area before leveling out toward the Alaska Range, south of Fairbanks.

Mount McKinley would be an impressive icon just south of Anderson. Although the tree line prevented you from seeing the mountain from the town, a short walk to the river levee would reveal Mt. McKinley in all its beauty and majesty. We discovered later that the closer you got to the mountain range the less you could see McKinley. It somehow hid itself behind the lesser peaks around it until you drove into the actual Denali Park. Denali was the original and local name for Mt. McKinley. Much could be said of the beauty of Alaska, but this story must press on with the trek of the Jones family.

After arriving in Alaska, I soon discovered that the "temporary" chaplain of Clear AFS was not going to relinquish his position to me. That was okay, but it did cause our financial status to change a bit. We needed to buy a vehicle. The church had an old van, but the drive to and from Fairbanks required a certain level of trust in the vehicle. All the major shopping had to occur in Fairbanks, so we eventually purchased a new 4-wheel drive Dodge Colt Vista station wagon. We did this by faith, believing God would honor our need for a safe, reliable vehicle.

The people of North Star were very nice folks. I can't remember them all, but among the adults were the Mackarnesses', the Brewer's, the Carter's, the Wilkes, the Phillips, the Weaver's, the Thornton's, the Woolard's, the Holcomb's, the Lovejoy's, et al. These, and many others, contributed to an exciting ministry for my family and me.

I could write several chapters of many events that took place in Anderson, but I will state briefly of several milestones that affected my family. One was that my first cousin lived in North Pole, Alaska. Larry Steve Pruitt was my daddy's sister's boy. Steve was more my brother Gary's age. He was Danny's older brother and Ronnie's younger brother. (You'll remember them from my early days, previously written.) I visited Steve a couple times. He was living with his girlfriend and her daughter. I had the privilege to officiate his wedding to her.

Adjunct Professor for Wayland Baptist University

Another event took place the spring of 1985. As previously mentioned, the temporary chaplain maintained the chaplain position. I, therefore, needed some financial assistance, due to the very high cost of living in that part of Alaska. I spoke with our area Director of Missions and the state convention office about the situation. They offered prayers in my behalf, but had no resolution at the time. As summer neared, I thought of perhaps selling my new vehicle and getting permission to drive the church van as needed. This was risky, but it would relieve the financial burden. Once again, I was driven to some serious praying.

"Lord, you know where I am and how You will have to intervene with some sort of miracle to keep me financially stable. I need some sort of sign to know Your will in this matter..."

As I was praying at the altar of my church, I heard an unusually loud creaking of the back stairs that led to the sanctuary level of the church. I knew it was someone, but this someone was new to the sounds of others that normally climbed those stairs for church services. As I peered around the pulpit, I saw a very large man open the back door. He came in as I stood up.

"May I help you?"

"Yes sir," was his reply. "I'm looking for a Johnnie Jones. Mr. David Baldwin (our D.O.M.) said I would find him here."

"Well, you've found him; I'm Brother Johnnie" We shook hands.

"I'm James Finegan, director of field operations for the extension division the Wayland Baptist University in Plainview, Texas."

"Plainview, Texas? Wow, I'd say you're really extended from there!"

"Yes," he said with a smile. "So it seems."

"So, why are you in Anderson, Alaska looking for me?"

"Well, I need your help. Wayland offers accredited liberal arts classes in business administration in two locations near Fairbanks: one in North Pole at Eilson Air Force Base, and the other in Fairbanks at Fort Wainwright. We're short a professor and David said you were one of only two pastors in the region with a Master's degree."

"Well, I don't know about that, but I do know that I can't teach business administration."

"Oh, I don't need a business admin teacher; you see, every student who gets a degree from Wayland must have at least two religion courses from us. I need someone to teach the New and Old Testament survey courses, plus maybe a few additional side courses in theology."

"Oh, now that makes better sense. And you drove 85 miles out of Fairbanks to search for me? Wasn't that a bit risky?"

"Well, my wife's in Fairbanks shopping. I told her that I had to get this need settled by the end of the week before we fly out. I just prayed, *'God, if you're in this, make this Johnnie fellow stay home today.'*" He presented a big grin. "Say, what were you doing when I came in?"

"Well, I was asking God to show me what to do to keep my vehicle."

"Oh, you're going to need a good vehicle to drive back and forth to Fairbanks. Did I tell you that each course pays $1,600 each and lasts 12 weeks during the regular semester? We have summer classes as well."

Before he left, I had Mr. Finegan join me in praise to God for answering our prayers. We both knew that God had met both needs simultaneously. It was awesome to see how God could take a man out of Plainview, Texas, bring him to Alaska, and find me on my knees asking for a "sign."

Diane and I drove into Fairbanks the next day to meet Mr. Finegan and his wife for lunch at the Royal Fork. He gave me an application and informed me that a Mister Harvey Angel, the director of Wayland's Alaska Center, in Anchorage, would mail me some textbooks and a syllabus for each class being planned for the next semester. Once again, Diane and I saw God's hand in fulfilling our financial needs.

Another event occurred that summer, during our Vacation Bible School. Most trees in Alaska are dwarfed, due to an underground layer of ice, called perma-frost. This layer of frost made many trees tall, but skinny. Timmy and a few other boys and girls were out by the church parking lot climbing up into the trees. Diane didn't like that.

"Timmy, don't go up too high. You might fall."

"Awe, Honey, don't worry about him. When I was his age, we used to climb the tall pine saplings near our house and sway them back and forth until we rode them down to the ground. It was fun!"

She looked at me and then up at the kids. "You be careful, Son."

We went down to the house to prepare for lunch, but it wasn't too long before Jenny come screaming inside.

"Mommy, Mommy! Timmy's fallen out of the tree and he's not moving!"

We both darted out of the house and ran toward the church. Timmy was on the ground twisting and turning in circles as he was gasping for breath. There was blood on his face and clothes and pieces of his scalp were missing. I grab him as he continued struggling and crying. Diane just stood there crying.

"What are we going to do?" she cried.

"Go open the car doors!" I responded.

We ran down to the car. Our neighbor (Sharon Mackarness) saw what we were doing. Her daughter had been there also, with her baby brother, who just happened to be crawling right underneath Timmy's tree. Timmy fell right beside the baby, missing him by inches.

"I'll take care of Jenny; you get him to a doctor right away!" Sharon hollered.

We headed up the road. There's a clinic at the air force site, so I headed there first. The gate security officer alerted the clinic that I was headed in. The attendant took him in and laid Timmy on a table. Timmy was more subdued now, but still curled up in a fetal position and gasping for air. The attendant looked him over and removed a couple pieces of scalp.

"Looks like he hit a few tree limbs while falling. I don't see any broken bones, but I can't tell if there's any internal damage. I'm sorry; this is all I can do. You need to take him to the emergency room in Fairbanks."

"Fairbanks?!" I thought. *"That's 85 miles away!"*

"Thank you, sir. Diane, let's go!"

He carried Timmy out to the car for us while we jumped into the car. Diane sat in the back with Timmy as I drove off the base. Timmy was still gasping for breath and groaned occasionally. I determined that I was going to get him to the hospital as soon as possible. There was only one problem. During the summer, highway crews methodically tore up long strips of the main highway to remove the buckling effect of the spring thaw. The highway from Anderson to Fairbanks was under a lot of "one-lane" traffic repairs. This meant that a guide truck would lead a cluster of vehicles for up to ten miles one-way. Sometimes, the highway was on the edge of a large crevice. At other points there were bridges.

"Lord, please help us," I prayed.

As I passed the town of Nenana, on the other side of the Tanana River, there were the road repair signs. A lady with a temporary stop sign stood up to stop me. I had flashed my headlights a couple of times as I approached her. She still wanted to stop me. I slid up to her, rolling the passenger side window down.

"Ma'am I've got a medical emergency here and I can't wait!"

With that statement I continued my speeding vehicle toward Fairbanks. I think she said something to the effect that there was a group of vehicles headed my way. There, along the river side, was no room for passing oncoming vehicles. Just ahead, about a mile, the road would turn upward from the riverbank into the hills. About a half-mile ahead, I saw the guide truck coming down from the hill with about a dozen vehicles behind him. A few more yards and one of us would have to stop and back up. I began flashing my headlights, traveling about 85 miles per hour. The truck had his flashers on as well.

"C'mon, Mister, STOP!!" I said to myself. The riverbank was to my left and the damaged highway was to my right. I knew I couldn't go left, so I began to prepare mentally to run my vehicle through the temporary barricades up onto the older, damaged road. I had no idea what the transition, from one lane to the other, would do to my car, but I had no choice. I continued flashing my headlights and grabbed a lower gear, about to convert my car into 4-wheel drive, when the approaching guide truck began pushing into the soft pile of dirt between the road and the riverbank. As he knocked down the small berm, he was giving me just enough room to clear the procession of cars, if they would follow his lead. I maintained my speed and continued flashing my lights. As I approached, each car seemed to take the lead of the one in front and cleared the way for me to pass.

We arrived at the emergency room in fifty minutes. They were waiting for us and took Timmy right in for evaluation. He was still groaning. It wasn't too long that a doctor was telling us he needed to do exploratory surgery to ensure Timmy's spleen had not ruptured. There was no other way of telling. The doctor left and prepared for the surgery. One of the nurses said that he was Fairbanks' finest surgeon and we were fortunate that he was on call. Timmy's surgery went well and his spleen was okay. The liver was bruised a bit, but the doctor said there should be no complications, just some time to heal. This was on a Saturday. The church would have VBS Family Night without us on Sunday evening. Things went well and Timmy survived this scary ordeal.

That same summer, Andy Mackarness and I took the youth to an evangelism conference in Anchorage. We had previously arranged to sleep in Glenview Baptist Church in Anchorage. The evening services went well and we headed over to the church to sleep in sleeping bags somewhere inside. The church was built on the side of a hill and had three levels, including a basement. On the upper level was a choir room with risers. We chose the choir room and I slept on the top riser. During the night, a smell woke me up. It smelled like furniture polish or something. I wiped the sleep out of my eyes and looked around. We had a small light on and all I could see was a bit of a haze in the room. I stepped out into the hall. Andy woke up and followed me.

"What's that smell?" he asked.

"I don't know. It's not as strong out here in the hall, but something is burning."

We looked up and down the hallway, but found nothing. We looked back into the choir room and once again saw the haze and the smell was much stronger in there.

"Let's check the rest of the building," I said.

Andy went in one direction and I in another. We entered the sanctuary on the second level. We not only could see nothing, but neither could we smell anything. We proceeded to the lower level, the basement. Again, there was no odor and nothing to be seen. Andy was checking rooms at one end of the hallway and I was at the other. I was in the hallway, scratching my head, trying to figure out what on earth was it that we were smelling? That's when I heard a gas-powered water heater light up in a closet next to me. I opened the closet door and immediately found the source of our mysterious smell. A large dust mop was propped up next to the heater. The mop fibers were close enough to the heater to catch fire when the heater lit up. Some of the fibers had burned to the metal brace and for some reason were extinguished. Some were still smoldering. I called out to Andy and pulled the mop out of the closet. I began stomping on the smoldering fibers. We stood there for a moment and looked at the mop and looked at each other.

"Man, Someone was definitely looking out for us tonight," said Andy. "Do you think we could have jumped out of a choir room window had this place caught on fire?" The choir room was about two levels from the parking lot.

"I don't even want to think about that scenario," I responded. "Let's check this closet real carefully." After further inspection, we decided not to call the fire department or the church's pastor. The next day, however, we did show our discovery to the man in charge of locking up after we left. I gave him good counsel on why dust mops should not lean against gas-fed water heaters. He agreed and we thanked God there was no fire.

I taught during two summer semesters for Wayland. I thoroughly enjoyed teaching these military folks who were trying to get a degree while serving our country. I couldn't believe God was using me in such a position. I taught men and women of multiple faiths, and even a few with no faith, what God was saying and doing through the Bible. I would take extra books from my library with me, challenging guys to know why you believe (or not believe) what you believe. There were some tremendous discussions within the group.

I remember one man, who had stated that he was a Jew. I had him in my New Testament class. I took my Josh McDowell, *Evidence That Demands a Verdict* book and read excerpts from it to the class. At the end of that particular semester, this same man came to me and spoke with me.

"I am a converted Jew," he said. "I once was a Southern Baptist, but saw so much hypocrisy and hatred among the church that I didn't want to have anything to do with that kind of 'Jesus'. You've shown me a different side of Christianity I've never witnessed before. I plan to take your challenge and study this *Evidence* book more carefully."

"Please do, my friend. Because if Jesus is who He says he is, then you will have a decision to make that will affect you for all eternity."

He shook my hand and left. After another class, I had another man come to me.

"Mr. Jones, I used to feel the way you do, but I've done some things in the past few years that make me wonder if God can really forgive me of my sins."

"Yes, He can. The blood of Jesus is as powerful today as the day He shed it on the cross. The question is not, 'Can He?' The question is, 'When will He?' Only you can answer that. When will you go to Him and ask for forgiveness and take Him at His word?"

The following week, after class, that same gentleman came to me, all smiles.

"I did it!"

"Now, what did you go and do…join a church?"

"No, Mr. Jones. I asked Jesus to forgive me of my sins and He did!"

"Oh really? And how do you know that He did?"

"Just like you said, I went home and read John's gospel and the Book of Romans. After that I got on my knees and took Him at His word. Man I feel great now!"

"Great! Now where do you live?"

"Right here on Eilson, sir."

(I saw another student nearby that I knew.) "Hey Joe! Come here. I want to introduce you to a forgiven believer." I looked at Charlie. "Charlie, Joe here, is a deacon at First Baptist in North Pole. He's going to come on base this Sunday morning and take you to church. Ain't that right, Joe?"

Joe put out his arm to embrace Charlie. "You bet, Mr. Jones. You can count on me!"

"You'd better. I still got some grades to turn in," I said smiling.

My experiences in these classes were extraordinary. I taught a Catholic relations director in one class. I taught numerous captains and lieutenants. Once, while driving up onto Fort Wainwright, I saw numerous airplanes unloading dozens of troopers as they parachuted down onto the ground. About thirty minutes later, one of the troopers arrived for class, with his flight gear still on.

As the winter of 1985 began, I encountered a problem that I didn't know how to fix. Darkness comes early in October, along with many inches of snow. By December, the sun peeks out above the Alaska Range at about 10:30 a.m., and then goes back down around 2:30 p.m. The children would leave home for school in the dark and return home from school in the dark. For many, especially women who stay at home for their children, the darkness creates a problem. It is called "Cabin Fever." The enclosure and isolation can get to a person. It becomes like a prison.

Diane was catching Cabin Fever. My trips, back and forth to my classes each week got me out of the house and Anderson regularly. But Diane had to stay at home and wait for the children to get out of school, and then tend to their needs. In the summer, she and the kids would come to the base and/or fort with me and go shopping or play on a playground. But during school, Diane had to stay home. This wasn't good.

For many days, she came into my church office, sometimes in tears, begging for release from the isolation. I didn't know what to do. One of the ladies of our church (Juanita) came over occasionally and they made cookies or baked things, but this was not enough. Diane was more accustom to a city environment, not to snow drifts, dark days, and isolation.

It was at the end of the semester, just prior to Christmas, that I realized I could not allow her to continue under her condition. I told her we would leave after Christmas. I resigned as teacher of Wayland and as pastor of North Star. It was difficult for me because of my love for teaching and preaching, but my love for my wife and children were greater. So, in late February of 1986, we sold nearly everything we possessed and flew back to Dallas, Texas.

Back to Texas, Once Again

Once again, Ed Ethridge had someone at the airport to meet us. David Kirby was there with a church van. We loaded up the van and tried to leave the airport. But the van battery had died and we were going nowhere. Finally, a cab driver gave us a boost and we headed over to another church member's home for the night.

50/50 CHANCE TO LIVE   266

Prior to leaving Alaska, Ed had given my name to a personnel director at Marazzi Tile manufacturers in Sunnyvale, Texas. They were looking for college-degreed leaders to come in and help the morale of the company employees. I had spoken with the director once from Alaska and told him of my planned arrival back to Dallas. He told me to call him as soon as I arrived. I did.

Marazzi Tile was a huge plant. The parent headquarters was in Italy, and all sorts of foreigners headed the management at the Sunnyvale plant. Perhaps they were having a hard time keeping good middle managers? I don't know; I knew nothing about ceramic tile, but I was in need of a job and, as usual, here was an opening staring right at me. The amazing thing about it was that they made me an offer and I countered it with a greater amount. They gave me what I asked for and I still was not sure what I would be doing.

We moved into an apartment in Balch Springs, a suburb of Dallas. It was a nice complex with several bedrooms upstairs for the kids. Diane decided that since we were between churches, she would home-school Jenny and Tim. (Timmy preferred Tim now.) She also applied for a breakfast job at a local McDonald's. The children would sleep in each morning and she would be home about mid-morning to give them their assignments and chores for the day. The schedule worked out just fine.

My job at Marazzi Tile began in the glaze department where many chemicals were weighed and mixed into a large cylinder (some were 7-8 feet in diameter) with a ceramic lining filled with ceramic balls of various sizes. With the proper amount of water added, the chemicals would rotate in the cylinder to become a liquid glaze. Once tested, the glaze would be transferred into smaller tubs to be placed on the assembly line. It was a precise procedure that required a working knowledge of metric measurements to the one-thousandth degree.

I had to learn how to maneuver a forklift between assembly lines, transporting tubs of very heavy liquid glaze. I also mixed a lot of chemicals and tested the formulas for accuracy. Because of the potential of lead poisoning, our department had to wear charcoal-filled breathing masks and rubber boots. The warehouse was not heated or air-conditioned.

One of the large mixing cylinders was contaminating the glaze mixture due to some of the inner ceramic lining chipping off. The company had tried to hire someone to come in with an electric jackhammer to chip out all the inner lining. The only opening into the cylinder was about 26 inches in diameter. No one wanted the job because of the enclosure and the deafening sound a jackhammer would produce in an enclosed ceramic-lined steel cylinder. To me, it became a challenge; so I volunteered for the job. With earplugs, a facemask, and ventilation, I worked two or three days inside the cylinder until all the inner lining was hammered loose and removed. The noise level was indeed louder than any jet engine I worked around in the air force, but I received a hero's congratulation from the upper-level management for a job well done.

About the only other incident worthy of mentioning was the day I was cleaning out some of the tubs that held the finished glaze compound. My supervisor, Fabio Borda, had instructed me to check some of the smaller tubs to ensure the mixture had enough water in them to keep the glaze in a liquid form. Each tub had a large mixing wand in the middle to keep the glaze stirred. As I was checking the line of tubs, I noticed a smaller tub was having some difficulty. The tub was probably no more than 30 or 40 gallons in size. The glaze compound appeared to be hardening and traveling upward onto the wand and out of the tub. The wand was turning rather slowly, so I proceeded to add a little water. Okay, so far. Next, with my rubber gloves on, I proceeded to encircle the wand shaft with my hand to try and force some of the liquid glaze back into the small tub. What I couldn't see was a small metal protrusion on the wand that was causing the glaze to accumulate. When I tried to squeeze the glaze downward into the tub, that clump of glaze with the hidden metal extension, grabbed my hand and literally lifted me off the floor and threw me up against the wall next to it. It occurred so quickly that my hand was still wrapped around the wand. In a split-second the wand ripped the glove right off my hand, allowing me to release it. I looked at my hand and saw all my fingers still attached, but for a moment it felt like they were all dislocated. Fortunately, no physical damage occurred to my hand or the equipment, and I continued to work.

In three months, I was appointed as lead-man for the day shift. I began to see that they wanted me to advance into a mid-level management position. The former lead-man was pretty vocal with foul language and quit rather than take orders from me. Others quit as well when I passed them in this so-called "promotion." But the company was managed rather loosely and the English used by so many different nationalities caused a lot of communication breakdown. It was very frustrating at times when I would have to go back to my supervisor and ask him to repeat the assignments for the day. The personnel director had voiced his concern to me about loosing many potentially good managers. I was beginning to see what his frustration was about.

Ed Ethridge was an evangelist at this time in his ministry. He lived nearby in Mesquite. He had sold me his truck for $25 because "the Lord told me to." (He later gave the $25 back to me.) One day, I was at his house changing out the shock absorbers on my "expensive" truck, when he received a call to fill in as a preacher for a friend at First Baptist Church in DeKalb, Texas. He already had a meeting for that Sunday, but told his friend about me. Ed handed the phone to me and I spoke with Tom Edwards, the pastor. I was to preach the following Sunday while Tom was away on vacation.

When we moved to Balch Springs, we had joined Robinwood Baptist Church in Seagoville. A "Pulpit Committee" from Robinwood had contacted me years prior when I was pastoring North Wilmer Baptist Church. They were looking for a pastor and had my resume. At that time, I had no peace about leaving North Wilmer. Jim Everidge was the pastor now. He was a fireball of a preacher and was a soulwinner. I really enjoyed his preaching and went out with him witnessing on Sunday afternoons, before evening church. Even though I was working 50-60 hours a week at Marazzi, I rarely missed church on Sundays and Wednesdays.

One incident at Robinwood must be mentioned. The associate pastor, Bobby Bryan, had received a call about a "Johnny" who was cheating on his wife. Bobby misunderstood who this Johnny was. Bobby called our house to try and talk to me. Diane answered the phone and told Bobby that I wasn't home at the time. He then proceeded to tell Diane how sorry he was to hear about the way I was cheating on her and that he was going to try and knock some sense into my head. Diane was clueless as to who Bobby really was and what he was talking about. She thanked him for the call and told him Johnnie (me!) would be in touch with him. I called him later that day and cleared up the mistaken identity. He was so apologetic and it has become one of his favorite stories spoken of, even to this day.

Jim Everidge had given me an adult Sunday School class to teach, because the regular teacher was having a series of surgeries and felt she could not physically handle the responsibility. I, of course, enjoyed the class of about 20 adults. The class enrollment was actually more than the size of the entire church attendance at North Star, so I felt right at home.

Jim wanted me to stick around and help him build Robinwood to a new level in the education department. He set up an appointment for me to visit with the Education Minister Search Committee to discuss the possibility of me filling the position. I wasn't sure if that was what God wanted me to do, but as usual, here stood an opportunity for me to minister to hundreds of people. The committee liked my credentials and the report they were receiving from some of the adults in my Sunday School class.

Once again, I was driven to the same prayer of my past: *"Lord, here I am; I am willing to serve you in any capacity You see fit. I will be a witness to the employees of Marazzi Tile or serve here at Robinwood as educational minister. It is in your hands. Please show me what I am to do."*

I was interested in the education position because I love to teach the Bible. The following Sunday, however, I was to preach at DeKalb. The committee had already given Jim the "green light" on me as educational minister, so he was all fired up about the future of Robinwood. In his style of preaching, he walked down the aisle of the church and put his hand on me and said something to the effect that here sat the church's future educational minister. It was an honor to be considered; however, I did have that commitment to preach in DeKalb the next Sunday. I told Jim that it was to fill in for a vacationing pastor. He had no problem with that and prayed for me to preach with power.

Diane and the children remained in Balch Springs as I drove a couple hours northeast to DeKalb. I preached a message that morning and played softball with the church's two teams that afternoon. In the evening service, I preached again. There were some who came forward during the invitation to seek counsel about something. As the church dismissed, one of the members (Jeanita Pruitt) introduced me to a group of folks visiting from a neighboring church, the Spring Hill Baptist Church. Spring Hill was in need of a pastor and Jeanita lived out in their community. This group was the search committee and their spouses. In the foyer of First Baptist, they asked me a few questions.

"We need a pastor; would you be willing to consider the position?" (I liked the direct approach.)

"Well, to be honest, I'm being considered as an educational director in my home church in Dallas. I'm not real sure if God wants me to remain as a preacher or not."

"Oh, He's definitely called you to preach," one of them responded. There were several "amen's" to that statement. "Can you come to our church next Sunday?" They kept looking at each other and nodding their heads in approval of Tommy Barnett's questions.

"Well, let me pray about it and I'll call you in a day or two."

"I'll need to know by Wednesday so that I can tell our interim not to come."

"I'll let you know by Tuesday night."

Jeanita was beaming. "After hearing you this morning, I told my husband, Larry, 'I'm going to call those folks at Spring Hill and tell them their future pastor is down here preaching today and they better get down here and hear him tonight!'"

I thanked them and headed back home. For two hours I prayed, and I thought through my sermons. I wasn't even aware of a committee's presence. *"Lord, is this Your answer to my previous prayer?"*

I was late getting in and Diane had to be at work at 5:00 a.m., so I didn't bother her about all this information until the next morning. The truck had a flat tire the next morning, so I walked Diane down to McDonald's. I told her of all the things that occurred in DeKalb.

"Do you know anything about the church?" she asked.

"No."

"Is the position full time?"

"I don't know."

"Do they have a parsonage?"

"I don't know."

"So we don't know anything about the church at all?"

"All I know is that they want me to come preach next Sunday and I've got to give them an answer by tomorrow night. I think we had better pray about it today and discuss it further tonight."

That evening, I received a call from Ed. He had heard about the committee meeting in the foyer of the church through its pastor, Tom, who had received a call from his vacationing spot.

"Jonesie, it sounds like the Lord wants you back into the pastorate."

"I don't know, Ed. You know Jim wants me to be his educational director. I like Robinwood and there are hundreds of folks I could minister to here."

"Well, the decision is yours to make, but let me remind you that there is no comparison to the effect you'll have as a proclaimer of God's Word. Our convention needs every conservative preacher available to guide our churches in believing and preaching an inerrant Bible. I know you, Jonesie, and I think you have an opportunity here."

"But Jim's already introduced me to his church."

"Oh, he'll get over it. He knows what it's like to be called as a preacher. You follow the Lord in this decision. Let's pray right now."

And so we did. And so did Diane and I. And on Tuesday I called Mr. Barnett to tell him I would be there that Sunday, with my family.

I spoke with Jim on Wednesday, in his office. He was somewhat disappointed, but quickly responded that I must follow the Lord's leading in this matter. He took it much easier than I had anticipated. We prayed together and then I left his office.

The mid summer's drive to Spring Hill Baptist Church was awesome. The northeast area of Texas is loaded with pine trees. Everything was so green and beautiful. Diane and the kids seemed to really like the area. The church was about eight miles north of the town of DeKalb, a couple miles west of US Highway 259. The sanctuary was a bit small, but could handle about 120…much larger than North Star! The facility included an educational wing and a fellowship hall, with a small, framed parsonage on the backside of the church grounds.

About 75 people attended the services. C.D. Jackson, a deacon and house builder, led the music. Diane filled in as piano player. I don't recall if we sang or not, but the services went well and the people were very hospitable. I don't remember where we ate lunch, but the committee did show us the parsonage, with a hint that the church was planning on building a new one soon. That was an encouragement, since the existing one was very old.

I felt at ease in the pulpit once again. I was always amazed at how God seemed to confirm His message through me by allowing folks to get things out of His Word when I preached. Diane also looked like she was at home whenever seated at the piano. Jenny and Tim also loved the large yard surrounding the parsonage. Plus there were two abandoned cats living under the house. They were a bit wild and did not come out, but a member was feeding them from the back porch.

After the evening service, we drove back to Dallas. The kids were all excited about moving out of the apartment. Diane and I rehearsed the day and discussed our feelings about it. The committee was planning to meet that week and make a decision. I always listened to Diane's feelings about our ministry because she had good discernment about people and situations.

I looked at her as I narrowed the discussion. "Well, what do you think?"

"I liked it. It's a nice place and there seems to be many people in the area. They spoke highly of the school there in DeKalb and someone mentioned the school had a marching band."

"Sounds good to me," I responded.

"Yea," was the response from Jenny and Tim.

"Now don't get your hopes up too high, kids," Diane responded. "The church has to meet and ask Daddy to be their pastor."

"Oh I think they liked Daddy," said Jenny.

"Yeah," responded Tim. "One of the kids thought he was funny."

"Oh, so that's why they want me, huh?" I reached back to try to grab a leg from someone.

"Well, someone needs to go there and take care of the cats," said Jenny. "And there's plenty of room for a dog! Can we get a dog? Please, Daddy?"

"One step at a time here. Let's see what the week brings, okay?"

I think it was Thursday when Tommy Barnett called. "Johnnie, the committee is unanimous in asking you to come back Sunday after next, in view of a call to be our pastor. Will you accept?"

I began nodding my head to Diane as she nodded "okay" back to me. "Yes sir; I'd be happy to come back in view of a call."

"Okay. We'll hear you preach in both services and maybe have a question and answer time in the evening service. Then, we'll vote at the end of the evening service."

Jenny and Tim were screaming their approval as the news circulated in the house. It seemed to be the next ministry that God had for us as a family and we were all excited.

I notified Jim that I felt this was of God. He acknowledged it as well and spoke of how he would miss my leadership in the church. Bobby Bryan was also supportive of the decision.

"If God has called you to preach, you'll never be satisfied doing anything else," said Bobby. "I think the timing of this was very significant for you, and you're doing the right thing."

"Yeah, and as long as I don't get caught cheating on my wife, I'll do just fine."

Bobby started laughing. "Oh, Johnnie, you'll never let me forget that one, will you!"

We both laughed and hugged. "My wife still can't believe I called Diane and told on you."

"Yeah, and I'm going to send you the marriage counseling bill when we're finished."

"Johnnie, don't tell me that!"

"Just kidding, Bobby; just kidding."

Spring Hill Baptist Church, DeKalb, Texas

The next trip to DeKalb was very joyful and exciting. I preached that morning. At the invitation, Larry and Jeanita Pruitt came forward to join the church.

"We just know this is the Lord's will for us and this church," Jeanita said. Larry shook his head in approval and I think C.D. got a voice-vote of approval to receive them into the fellowship. There was a fellowship meal held at the church and a special time for members to ask Diane and me questions.

After the evening service, we were escorted to a room in the back while the church voted. It was a unanimous vote of approval and we, of course, accepted it.

"So, will you be back next week?" Tommy asked.

"I'd love to, but I need to give my employer a two-week's notice and my Sunday School class a 'goodbye.' If you don't mind, I'll start here in two Sundays."

"That's fine. This will give us an opportunity to get the house readied for you and to say our goodbyes to our interim pastor as well. Whatever's the cost to move you here, we'll pay for it."

"I'll get a rental truck and get my friend, Ed Ethridge, to help me move. He can drive the truck back."

"Whatever; you just let me know when, and we'll meet you here at the house to unload you."

Spring Hill Baptist Church, in DeKalb, Texas, would be a phenomenal work of God while we were there. It wasn't full time, but this allowed me to work as a substitute teacher in the DeKalb ISD and in the neighboring Avery ISD. It would be through my substitute employment that I would reach many teenagers for Christ. I recall one year when I baptized 26 or 27 senior high students from the Avery high school. I never had so many teenagers respond to the gospel as then.

Because of the youth growth, we had to redesign our educational wing to make larger youth classes. Our youth Sunday School attendance tripled. On Wednesday evenings, just prior to prayer meeting, the youth met with Diane and me in the parsonage. We fed them a meal, sang praise songs, and I gave them a Bible study. We had more youth attending the Wednesday evening session than adults attending the prayer meeting.

Youth growth also caused adult growth. Many folks from the DeKalb and Avery towns were driving out to Spring Hill Baptist Church. I had the privilege of leading several Mormon family members to faith in Christ. It was amazing to see this small rural church packed every Sunday morning. Sometimes, extra folding chairs were brought in to accommodate the attendance. The church also built a new parsonage. With C.D.'s guidance, we were given the freedom to help design the new home.

Jenny was now a pre-teen and was getting involved socially with the other kids. Tim had his friends as well. Diane had tried to keep both children involved in piano lessons, but she was losing the battle. She finally gave up on Jenny as she began playing the clarinet and was getting more involved in the marching band. Tim still had piano lessons, but he, also, was practicing with a trumpet for the school band. Diane did have other children and adults as piano students.

I taught a lot as a substitute during the school year. I also helped C.D. build houses throughout the area. I became his paint and stain detailer, although I also assisted with roofs, studs, and sheetrock. I just did whatever I was told. But one year, C.D.'s house-building business began to wither. He had to lay off his regular workers, including me. I helped him some on minor repairs, but it just wasn't enough. To help our income, Diane began cleaning a few homes in the area.

One evening in Texarkana, Diane and I were eating in a restaurant and discussing our financial needs. A couple of men across the aisle began talking to us. One of them was Charlie Gibbs and he was interviewing the other man for a possible "Mom and Pop's" business in the area. His pitch sounded very interesting and when he asked for our phone number, I gave it to him. His business was expanding and he was looking for some other partners. It also required very little investment up front. It sounded good to us and we were looking forward to a future interview with Charlie.

Several weeks later Charlie met us in our home. He presented to us the Amway sales plan that involved us purchasing home-use products and selling them to others. He also explained that with as few as six more people purchasing an average $100 a month, we could become financially independent and wealthy. All it required was six more who would find six more who would continue to find six more. The sales chain would become endless and we would get a percentage from everyone who sold items underneath us.

We had been introduced to the Amway plan through a lady in Virginia at the Glen Hill Baptist Church. She had a man come to our house to draw six circles on a chalkboard, explaining how that would make us rich. I did not understand his presentation at all. He left us and we never heard any more about it.

"Isn't this the same thing we heard at Glen Hill?" I asked Diane.

"I don't know; I think it may have been."

"Well, do you understand how it works?"

"Well, it appears that you have to buy their products, use them regularly, and then try to get others to do the same."

"Will it work?"

"Well, maybe. I think I bought some of their cleaning stuff from Mrs. Land in Virginia. It worked okay, but I believe it costs a little more than what I could get at K-Mart. So I quit ordering it."

"Okay, so the price increase is probably making up for the bonus checks we get. I see now. So, if everyone doesn't mind paying a little more per item, then we will all be helping each other get rich. Hey, that doesn't sound so bad, does it?"

"For you it may not, but don't ask me to sell anything."

"I understand, Love, but would you object to using the products?"

"Some of them are okay, but I still like to go shopping and I think we still have just a certain amount of money we can spend on household products."

"Okay; but you do you mind if I look into this further?"

"No; you go right ahead."

I was cautiously optimistic about the Amway plan, but I still could not quite figure the sales pitch. One of Charlie's "down-line" associates was pitching the plan in Texarkana next week. I went to hear it one more time. This gentleman did a great job explaining it and I was pumped! I went home all excited.

"Diane, this thing really works! All you need to do is purchase about a hundred dollars a month of cleaning products and find six more who will find six more who will continue to find six more. It's incredible!"

"But a hundred dollars a month of cleaning products is a lot of cleaning products. We don't buy a third of that amount now."

"Yeah, but there's also shampoo, toothpaste, vitamins...the list of products is endless. You can even buy car tires and get points! They have a water and air treatment system. The list is endless!"

"It sounds like we're going to buy an additional one hundred dollars a month of more products than we are currently buying. Where do we find an additional one hundred dollars from our budget? Remember, we were discussing how short we are from our current budget. We were looking for ways to either cut our budget or get more income when we met Mr. Gibbs."

Diane's objections didn't seem to stick with me. All I could envision was helping church members, friends, and family members become financially wealthy by buying products they could use and do use every day in and around their homes. I was sold on the concept and notified Charlie that I was in.

Charlie lived in North Little Rock, Arkansas, but he began traveling to DeKalb to set up meetings in my house and in others' homes if they were interested. My job was to get folks to attend the sales meetings. Charlie was a Baptist deacon and had considered entering the ministry once, himself. But, in his words, "When I saw what they paid a preacher, I decided I could help preachers more by getting them into this business."

Charlie was a talker and he knew exactly what to say to get me pumped. I loved people and I loved the prospect of helping people get out of financial difficulty. So I began talking to everyone about this concept. Charlie said to not mention the word "Amway," because it had been around for decades and others may have a negative connotation about it. "It's changed a whole lot in the past few years," he said. "Some people need to rediscover how it works."

"Well, I'm not going to lie about it, but I understand your point."

I had meetings at the parsonage. I brought in church members, friends, and folks I knew in DeKalb from the school and from working through C.D. I had dozens of folks listen to Charlie and, surprisingly, within about six months I had ten folks in my own personal down-line. *"Wow!"* I thought. *"This is too easy!"*

But it wasn't working financially. Everyone who signed up was not able to find a hundred dollars' worth of products each month to purchase. Some of the men who bought into it were complaining that their wives didn't want to stop shopping at Wal-Mart. Shopping was their "get-out-of-the-house" relief and nobody was going to take that away from them. Others said they like to have options when they shop.

In addition to the complaints, Charlie taught that to be a good example, I needed to attend all the group meetings sponsored by my up-line. He had me (and Diane and the kids!) traveling to North Little Rock for numerous sales meetings. He even paid my hotel bill for a trip to Fort Lauderdale, Florida. We went, but it was still a costly endeavor.

The bottom line for me became time. The more I invested into the plan, the more time I had to spend promoting or supporting it. And I soon discovered that the bonus checks do not become substantial until your down-line develops depth. My ten were not finding their six who would find their six who would continue to find their six. It was like spinning plates on sticks. I had to go to each member of my down-line to get them "spinning" again or they would quit. The products were okay and the plan seemed okay; but the time needed to invest in the plan and the bonus checks were not okay. I had to find another job.

Charlie, of course, was disappointed that I was backing off, but he continued to contact me and encourage me to bring others to regional meetings. I thanked him for his energy and time invested in me, but I never went to another meeting. I wrote to my down-line, encouraging them to make their own decisions about their involvement. I explained to them why I could not invest the time needed to make the plan work. I even offered to buy back any products that anyone had that they felt they could not use.

In the meantime, Diane found me another paper route with the *Texarkana Gazette*. Once again, I was out every morning, very early, seven days a week, throwing papers throughout the DeKalb/New Boston area. It wasn't easy, but it did help pay the bills.

Vacations were rare for our family. We did discover Beaver's Bend State Park, north of Broken Bow, Oklahoma. It was about a 45-minute drive from

Spring Hill and was loaded with hills, trees, active creeks, and wonderful hiking trails. It became our haven for rest on my day off, when I had one.

In the summer of 1990, we planned a vacation to discover the Houston and Galveston Island area. The children had never been to the beach and, although Galveston Island didn't have the cleanest beaches I'd ever seen, it was near other attractions. Plus, Jenny and Tim had never seen another beach by which to compare Galveston with. We all enjoyed the beach and the thing we talk about most concerning this trip was the pizza we ate on the beach, under the umbrella! And, not so surprising, the hotel's swimming pool was a high attraction for the kids. Once in the pool, they did not have a desire to go anywhere else. (We could have stayed at a Texarkana hotel and saved a ton of money!)

In Houston, we visited the NASA Space Center, the Astroworld Amusement Park, and attended an Astro's baseball game. Houston had a lot of attractions for us to see. The two things Diane and I did not like about the Houston area were the hot temperature and the extremely high humidity. There was also a refinery-type of odor in many areas we visited.

Upon returning to Spring Hill, I stated on the following Sunday that, although we had a very good time in Houston, I would never want to live there: "God would have to hit me in the head with a two-by-four before I would move to the Houston area!" The folks laughed and life went on in DeKalb, Texas.

We were at Spring Hill from September of 1987 to March of 1991. Although we were having a lot of growth, the financial situation of the church and of my personal needs became a hardship. During this time, our nation was experiencing a slow-down in its economy. I knew that C.D. and Tommy Barnett's house-building jobs were slowing down. (Tommy was a house builder as well.) Diane had lost a few piano students, but she continued teaching and she still had a couple houses to clean.

I continued throwing papers every morning. It was okay, but Sunday mornings were tough. I would get to the paper drop-off point at 2:30 a.m. and throw papers until about 6:00 a.m. I then came home and slept for about two hours, before preparing to go to church. I didn't like the setup, but really didn't know what to do. I shared my concerns with the deacons once, but they offered no solution.

Another area of concern was an attitude from at least one deacon who voiced concern about people joining our church from the towns of DeKalb and Avery. In his opinion, people should not be driving past several Baptist churches just to come to Spring Hill. "I think they should support the churches of their community and not come all the way out here," he said.

No one else seemed to want to counter his objection. I responded that people would go to a church where they felt like they were being fed with spiritual nourishment. "It's like taking your family out to eat," I explained. "You probably will pass several local restaurants to go to the one you like best. The closest eating-place to us is the Dairy Queen in DeKalb. The next time you take your wife out to eat, see if that's where she wants to go."

We had several solid families from DeKalb and Avery that got wind of this "concern" and discontinued attending our church. I tried to bring them back, but to no avail. It was frustrating for me, to say the least.

1990 – Alta Vista Baptist Church, Pasadena, Texas

In the late fall of 1990, I received a call from a pastor search committee in Pasadena, Texas. Of all places, a suburb of Houston, bordering the refinery ship channel! The church was Alta Vista Baptist Church where Ed Ethridge had pastored in the late 70s and early 80s. The chairman of the committee, Louis Ely, had contacted Ed asking him to consider returning. Ed was still in evangelism and did not feel led to return to Alta Vista. He did, however, recommend me for the position. Louis called me and asked for my resume. I obliged and sent it.

Diane and I discussed the possibility. We knew the church because Ed had us visit it in 1979, during the SBC annual meeting in Houston. At that time Ed needed a youth minister and wanted me to consider the position. I was a pastor in Virginia and really had no desire to become a youth minister, but because of our friendship with Ed, Diane and I agreed to visit with the youth committee during the trip to Houston. It didn't work out.

Alta Vista, in our estimation, was a large church. It had a large sanctuary, educational facility and even a full-court gymnasium. I could not envision my being considered for such a church. At this time, they had a fulltime youth minister, music minister, and secretary. The associational records listed Alta Vista as having several hundred active families with an average Sunday School attendance of 175 each week. That's about a hundred more than Spring Hill.

But Houston? I remembered the vacation trip: the humidity and the smell—especially near the ship channel! Surely this was not going to happen. God really didn't have a spiritual "two-by-four" propped up beside His throne, did He?

About a week later, Louis called again. He wanted to talk further to Diane and me. The committee was interested in me, but felt like they needed to explain the current "problems" at Alta Vista. Ed had already filled me in on some of the current difficulties at Alta Vista. I told that to Louis.

"Well, Ed probably could detail our particular need right now better than I could," he said. "Does this mean that you're still interested?"

"Louis, I want to say 'No,' but let me have a few days to pray and discuss it further with Diane. Do you think the church is willing to make some major changes, if I came?"

"Johnnie, let me say this. If we don't make some major changes, we will not survive our current leadership problem."

"I'll be back in touch." I hung up the phone and had a serious talk with Diane. We knew the church was having a leadership problem. We knew the church was dead-locked in a transition from a deacon-led ministry to an elder-led ministry. The former pastor had taken some of the church's men to John MacArthur's Shepherd's Conference in California and, later, the church had rewritten the church's constitution in order to allow an elder-rule form of church government.

This new constitution required an annual two-third's vote approval of each serving elder. The church was functioning well under this new constitution, although, some were not agreeable to it. The current crisis occurred after the pastor resigned to go to another church. The new form of government was still in its infant stages when he left. The interim came in and allowed the church to continue to try and find another pastor without interfering or offering suggestions for the church's leadership instability.

In a nutshell, the current status of the church was that it had no official legal leadership. The annual renewal vote for the current elders had failed to get a two-third's approval. The constitution only allowed the deacons to simply serve the church and assist the elders. The staff had no powers either. According to the pastor search committee, the church was deadlocked in its preference of leadership style, about 60/40: 60 percent favored the deacon-led form and 40 percent favored the elder-rule form.

I, personally, had no problem with the elder-rule form of church government. It could be proven as biblically sound as the Baptist's more common deacon-led, congregational form of church government. But I had no experience with the elder-rule form and had no desire to "re-tool" my understanding of it. Diane and I discussed the issues thoroughly. We both understood the complications involved, but we both felt that my particular style of leadership would help ease the tensions at Alta Vista and save the church from imploding. We prayed.

I called Louis back a few days later. "Louis, I must tell you that I am open to this possibility; however, the church will first and foremost hear me say that I will not continue to lead the church under the elder-rule form of church government. If I get called to pastor Alta Vista, it will also be considered a vote to rewrite the church's constitution. The church will appoint a church constitution revision committee right after I accept the call."

Louis promised to get back to me as soon as possible. A week passed before he called again.

"Johnnie, it's not unanimous, but a clear majority of the committee wants you to come and preach for us and to meet with us for some specifics as to your style of leadership. We have arranged for you to preach at a church nearby in South Houston. Will you come?"

After discussing it further with Diane, she agreed that we should at least pursue it further. A date was set and I told my deacons at Spring Hill what was going on. As expected, my deacons had mixed feelings about this. Some did not want me to leave; others saw it as a fresh start in a new direction for the church. This was the easy group to announce my intentions. Now it was time to tell Jenny and Tim.

"No, Daddy! We can't leave DeKalb!" exclaimed Jenny. "I'm a line-leader in the marching band. All my friends are here. I don't want to move!"

Tim was a bit easier to deal with. He didn't seem to mind it very much.

In January of 1991, we drove down to a small church in South Houston, where I preached for the Alta Vista committee. They took us out to eat and we met at Alta Vista that afternoon. Jenny and Tim got to play in the gym, while we met. The discussions were long and thorough. I think we covered just about everything under the spiritual sun. I pulled no punches on my style of preaching and church leadership. They, likewise, said that there would be opposition to the reversal of church government. I agreed and said that I would expect some opposition.

"The main thing, however, must be that the church body forms the revision committee and will draft the constitution. I will simply be a guide for understanding the congregational form versus the elder-led form of governing the church. This must be seen as a church proposal—not Brother Johnnie's."

I preached again for the committee and then we headed back for a late-night arrival in DeKalb. Things were a bit quiet in the car. Tim said he liked the church and the gym was especially nice. Jenny didn't say a thing for a while. Finally, while we were discussing the largeness of the church, Jenny piped in: "Will you be full time there?"

"Yes, Hon, I will be."

"Will we have a house?" she continued.

"They mentioned that I would have to purchase a house. They would pay me a housing allowance."

"I want first choice on the bedroom selection."

"That's not fair!" Tim hollered.

Jenny's positioning for first rights in the bedroom selection was enough of a remark to tell me that she would go along with this possibility of moving. She still didn't like the idea, but at least she had opened the door for the possibility. (She had a boyfriend in DeKalb.)

The next week passed with no word from Alta Vista. The Spring Hill folks knew what was happening. This is always a difficult experience for a pastor and his church family. They could be thinking, *"Does the pastor not like us anymore?"* And the pastor may be thinking, *"What if I don't move; will the church still follow my lead? Would they still listen to me the way they used to?"* It is a difficult time, but this is the Baptist way of trying to follow the Lord's leading.

The next Monday evening, Louis called again.

"Johnnie, the committee is unanimous in extending to you an invitation to preach before our church body in view of a call. Will you accept?"

"Yes, sir; I will." Diane and I had already discussed the idea and how that it needed to be a unanimous invitation from the committee. We also believed that the church vote should be at least an 85 percent approval. Two Sundays later we were in Pasadena again, at Alta Vista. We were overwhelmed at the large group of people attending. The parking lots were full and people were everywhere. There were several nurseries with a paid staff and Sunday School classes were bustling with adults, youth, and children. Jenny and Tim were immediate celebrities and received a lot of attention from everyone.

I preached both services, as well as led in a question and answer time just prior to the evening worship hour. There were some tough and straightforward questions from the congregation. This was good and I answered everyone's questions to the best of my ability. After the evening service, the vote was cast. Diane and I had already asked the Lord for an 85 percent affirmation. The vote was counted and it turned out to be 84.7 percent. It was rounded up to 85. We looked at each other and agreed by our look that it was close enough. We accepted the call.

I resigned at Spring Hill the following week and we moved two weeks later. Diane and Jenny would drive our Oldsmobile to Pasadena while Tim and I took care of the rental truck. I had previously driven my Geo Metro car down to Pasadena, looking for a temporary apartment for us to move into. I did find something over on Edgebrook Street that looked like a possibility. I would wait and allow Diane and the kids to approve.

Alta Vista Baptist Church was spread out, both in its physical plant and in its membership. Some lived as far away as the Sagemont community of Houston. There were some who lived north of the ship channel and south in the Clear Lake area where NASA was located. Membership occupations varied as well from medical doctors and NASA engineers, to blue-collar laborers for the refineries. We had schoolteachers as well as private business owners. The church was very diverse.

The church was very aggressive in its ministry to children. On Wednesdays, they had a large AWANA Clubs ministry and during a.m. church services, they had a puppet town called, Caraway Street. On Wednesday nights, there were home "cell" groups for Bible study and fellowship. Those adults not working in AWANA would meet in homes for Bible study. The church also had two softball teams. The activities available for everyone made it very difficult to see any "leadership" problems. I mean the church was so busy doing good things!

I loved playing softball, so I got on one of the teams. It was a great release from all the daily chores of work. I remember one particular game in which I was the catcher. We were playing a Hispanic church team that was considered the best team in the league. They knew it too and were real "hotdogs" while playing. They were winning rather decisively, but in one inning, I made a historic play. There were no outs; one runner was on second and another on first. The batter hit a ball that dropped down in far left field. All three runners were running at top speed. The batter was catching up with the other two runners, hollering, "Go, go, GO!" They were all headed for home base. Our left fielder just happened to swoop the ball up and, without missing a stride, ran forward as he wound up throwing the ball in. I stepped up in front of the home plate, moving just enough out of the way of the baseline. The throw was as straight as any I had ever received at home plate. I caught the ball just as all three runners ran past me. I tagged them all! The umpire danced backwards on one leg, pointing one hand at the home plate and pumping the other hand as if cocking a gun to fire it, as he cried out, "Yer OUT, yer OUT, and YERRRR OOUUTTTTT!!!" Three outs in one play! Even though we lost the game, that was some inning.

I attended the first scheduled elder/deacons meeting. It was there that there seemed to be a notable division among the representatives. There was no clear-cut directive as to what to do. I announced to them that I wanted several deacons and several elders to volunteer as representatives to a new constitution revision committee. I also planned to open the floor at the next church conference for the election of two additional members for this committee who were not elders or deacons. There was no negative response to this plan at the meeting. Right after the meeting, one of the men entered my office and shut the door. He began arguing with me that I should not allow just anyone to be voted on to fill such an important position on this constitution committee. I disagreed.

"When the election is made, it will be stated that this is an important position and that no one should allow their name to be placed on the ballot who does not feel gifted or capable of contributing to this project."

His face turned red. "Well [so-and-so] said that he would not let this very thing happen and he sat there tonight and didn't say a word!"

"Listen to me," I responded. "We have a great church here and an even greater responsibility to allow God to lead us out of this conflict into a unified body that would represent the body of Jesus Christ. Now let's give Him a chance to do so."

I put my hand on his shoulder and assured him that I would do my best to help lead our church back together. He calmed down afterwards and we prayed and went home.

During the transition from Spring Hill to Alta Vista, the youth minister had resigned. I didn't know him very well, but he seemed like a really nice guy and I was saddened to hear of his resignation. I felt every position needed to remain as stable as possible during this time.

The Constitution Committee was formed and we went to work immediately. There were some tense moments when the move to demote the ruling authority of the elders was brought up and a shift back to a more centralized deacon-servant ministry was proposed. I reminded the committee that prior to my vote, I had stated that this would be the direction our church would follow.

"I am not saying one form of church government is more biblical than the other. But I am stating that as it currently stands neither is operating in our church and we must take measures to break this deadlock."

I presented to the members several constitutions made available to me by different churches of our local association. We used these as well as our existing one to form a new constitution. The new constitution would elevate elders to the minister level (pastor or ministerial staff) and the deacons would become spiritual servants over the flock to tend to the physical needs as needed. The elders were stripped of their power to approve items apart from the congregation. Decisions would be congregationally approved. The elders objected to that provision. They felt the congregation did not have the spiritual discernment to decide on such matters.

I countered: "When have you ever seen a spiritual recommendation turned down when it was properly discussed, prayed over, and presented?"

"That's not the point," one man responded.

"Then what is the point?" I responded.

"Our lay-membership should not be expected to have to make spiritual decisions that impact our entire church."

"Are you saying that some of the members of the body are not as important as other members?"

"Well, in certain areas, yes."

I pulled my Bible over to the man. "I really need your biblical references that state the levels of church body importance." I began flipping pages of my Bible. The pages just "happened" to fall on First Corinthians, chapter twelve. He knew where I was going with my line of reasoning and chose not to participate.

The committee worked for about three months on the new constitution. It wasn't a unanimous document and we stated so before the church body at a church conference. The elders on the committee held their ground as to their preferred form of church government. Others spoke for and against it. We decided to spend a couple weeks in prayer and to circulate the document before voting on it. If I remember correctly, a copy was mailed to every active family of the church, encouraging everyone to one final discussion meeting and vote.

Prior to the voting date, one of the elders came to me stating his desire to speak against the document just prior to the vote at the called conference. I gave him permission to do so. But his next statement really troubled me.

"Pastor, if this document is approved, I want you to know that I will resign all positions of leadership in this church, including Sunday School teaching."

"I'm sorry to hear that. I was hoping your input on this document would allow some compromise on your convictions."

"No sir; I am convinced that the elder-rule church form of government is the most biblical and I cannot compromise that conviction."

"I have no battle to fight against your conviction. If you can change the wording on our church sign and eliminate the middle word, 'Baptist,' off of it, then your form of leading will work here. But as long as this church is a Baptist church and it stands in good relations to the Southern Baptist Convention, then you should honor the vote of the majority of its members. That's all I ask; let the majority vote and let's move on in evangelizing and discipleship."

The church's called conference was well attended. The afore-mentioned elder spoke against the recommendation of the committee to adopt the new constitution. Several others spoke as well, some for and some against. The vote was cast by ballot. The new constitution was approved by a 93 percent approval.

"The church has spoken," I said. "Now let's throw this piece of paper in a drawer somewhere and get on with the mission and ministry of this church." There was a hearty "amen" to my statement. The die had been cast and we now had a working constitution with a permissible leadership: the church body.

As promised, I had a letter of resignation on my desk the following morning. As it turned out, the major teachers of our adult Sunday School classes were the elders. In the next few weeks, three of them would resign as teachers and leave the church. The cell-group leader would resign as well. I expected some of this to happen. What I did not expect was the fall-out from the "followship."

Two separate groups began leaving our church. One group was the more solid core of the church. For some reason, those who had held the church together for the past few years began to retire and move away. I couldn't foresee this happening and I'm certain this group did not conspire to do so, but all of a sudden, about six couples moved out of the Pasadena area, including several who were on the pastor search committee. Several more, who were looked upon as the shakers and movers for the future of our church, and who loved me and thought the church was now doing the right thing, left as well.

The other group was couples—mainly young married couples—that were dependent on the elders for their spiritual growth. The teaching elders were devout students of the Bible and just another adult teacher was not going to suffice. Our Sunday School Director quit as well. What began to occur is what I call the "domino effect." One couple would leave, and then the next couple would leave because the other couple left. It was a crazy year.

Our church's attendance dropped from the 150s to the 70s in the Sunday School in less than a year. And, as you might expect, our finances went "south" as well. I had managed to purchase a house prior to the fall-out, but the Treasurer came to me with some hard facts and decisions that had to be made based on these facts.

"Preacher, I hate to say this, but we're going to have to get rid of some staff."

"What do you mean, Clayton?"

"Our staff is consuming most of our income. We can either have staff and sit in the dark with no air conditioning or we can reduce our staff. That's the only two variables that we have."

"We don't have a youth minister and our custodian is part-time. That leaves me, Harper, and our secretary."

"And your nursery staff."

"Oh yeah, I forgot."

"I would suggest you go back to a volunteer-only nursery first, and then put Harper on part-time. Then we'll re-assess the damage."

Clayton left as I sat there mulling over the choices. *"No nursery staff? Harper* (our worship leader) *part-time?"* Neither choice sounded good to me. I had already given Harper and his wife, Marty, some extra youth responsibilities. They didn't mind and were working hard in the church.

The nursery program was already a delicate situation. I had already fired a lady due to some complaints from a couple of parents. This lady's son had already stated that he was going to beat me up for firing his "mama." I didn't know that I had a "price" on my head and went down the following week to visit the lady. (She told me later that she had to restrain her son from coming out in their yard and making good on his promise.)

The "exodus" continued. I prayed. *"Lord, what is happening? I can't seem to get this church to stop spiraling downward. Is there something I'm missing?*

Eventually, my Treasurer, Clayton, retired and moved away. Again, the retirees did not conspire to do so, but so many familiar, stable families left that year that it seemed as if we had an entirely different church body. I had no choice in the matter. I immediately reduced our paid nursery staff to one elderly lady who would be in charge of setting up a volunteer system. And then I had a meeting with Harper. You need to understand that Harper was my number one cheerleader. He supported me 100 percent. I felt as if I were consulting with a surgeon about cutting off my right arm. This was a difficult consultation.

"Harper, I'm afraid your position must become part-time for now." He sat at his desk, working a pencil through each finger.

"I figured it was just a matter of time, Johnnie."

"I'm so sorry. You kept things going during this horrible transition of finding a pastor, and now that pastor is demoting you."

"I don't know what to say. I...I don't even know if I can work at another job. This is all I've ever done."

"Didn't you say you were a teacher, prior to the ministry?"

"Oh yeah, but things have changed. I don't know...just give me some time alone, if you don't mind."

"You bet." And so I walked out of his office and shut his door.

In my heart, I wished it was I having to go part-time instead of Harper. But I knew the church would never allow that.

Later on, Harper came to my office.

"When will this change occur?"

"In two weeks."

"Will you support me in an attempt to find another full-time music ministry?"

"Yes sir; you have my absolute support and I'll be your number one reference, I promise."

"Thank you, Johnnie. Now, if you don't mind, I need to go home and speak with my family."

"Go right ahead. Take the rest of the day off...with pay, of course."

He managed a slight smile, but my usual dry humor didn't seem to help much this time.

In the meantime, I was busy trying to establish some new leadership. We needed some new deacons. The church had recommended several men and the current deacons and I were going through the process of selection. There were a number of potentially good candidates, so it took some time interviewing all candidates selected. Only the two receiving the highest number of votes would be selected at this time.

Then we incurred another problem. Termites had invaded the buildings—even the newer Glory Building. A company came out and gave us a spot bid of $5,000, or for the whole complex, $7,000. This included drilling under the foundation of all the buildings. We decided to do the entire complex.

We also had another problem. Our air conditioning system was a very old water-cooled tower system. It had boilers tied to it also, I guess, for the heating side of the system. This thing was leaking and malfunctioning continuously. It needed replacement. There was only one HVAC company in the area that would service our equipment. Their replacement bid was $20,000 to remove the old and replace it with all new equipment.

I began walking through our current facilities. It seemed very logical and appropriate to me for us to move our Sunday worship services into the Glory Building. It had three middle rooms with partitions that were used for fellowships and receptions. With a little platform at one end, it could easily accommodate all who were currently attending, plus save us at least $400 a month in utilities. I kept this idea in the back of my mind for the time being.

Harper pursued and acquired a new full-time position at another Baptist church south of Pasadena. Another church member began leading our music as a volunteer. This helped us financially, but it seemed every step we took to address the downsizing problem created another problem. People needed people, and with each departure of the familiar, it seemed to cause additional departures.

Our secretary tried to explain the problem. The former pastor who built up the church led autocratically. Everyone in the church was used to him making all the decisions. He led and the people followed. It was as simple as that, according to her.

Trying to read between the lines, I understood her telling me that I needed to be more aggressive in my leadership style. My style, which involved more of the congregations input, was foreign to our folks and they interpreted my style as weak.

"You need to tell us what to do and just get out there and do it!" she said.

Sounded good to me. But since arriving at Alta Vista, I was constantly doing things to "plug" the membership drain. The only thing I had thought of that I had not followed-up on was moving the church services into the Glory Building. Okay, here goes...

"We're going to move the church services into the Glory Building," I announced to the deacons. "This will save us approximately $400 a month in utilities. Any questions?"

"Who's going to set up and tear down each week?" asked the AWANA director? "I need these rooms for AWANA Clubs."

"We'll do a rotation among the deacons," I responded. "We'll group ourselves into two's and get it done."

"What about a sound system and a piano?"

"We have a portable system that we use in the gym," said someone.

"Okay, and I'll ask our sound man if he'll set it up each Sunday morning," I said. "And we'll look into renting or purchasing a new keyboard."

"Any other questions?"

"Yes: when?" asked the Treasurer.

"We'll announce it this Sunday and start the next. Any other questions?

Again the Treasurer: "Pastor, you say this will save us about $400 in utilities? I believe you're about right. However, our books say if we don't find another thousand dollars a month in savings, we're going to deplete all our accounts in five months."

"Well, I don't know of anything else to do except cut the remaining two full-time salaries back to meet your projections. I can't speak for the secretary, but I know how to work outside of the church and pastor it as well. I'm not afraid of working. Plus, maybe we could put our secretary on two-third's time. I'm just throwing out some ideas for you to consider."

No decision was made concerning the salaries at that particular meeting. The secretary's husband, however, was one of our newest deacons. That meant that she would know of my comment very quickly; and she did.

The next morning, the office area was much quieter. And her door, usually open, was shut with her inside her office. I didn't feel up to an immediate confrontation, so I went to my office and thought things over again.

"Lord, I still don't understand where we're headed in this church. What am I supposed to do here? Why is the membership still going down? What other decision do I have to make?"

I was uncomfortable in this autocratic position. This simply was not me. I knew it and God knew it. But Alta Vista wasn't buying into the new paradigm. More and more, in the sight of some members, the problem became my problem. And I had no answer to the problem.

The Treasurer was preparing a new budget for the new church year, which began in September. As predicted, my salary was cut about one-third. The secretary's was also cut. When this news got out, she was very unhappy and voiced her disapproval. Therefore, her salary was re-established to its previous status. For the time being, I agreed to leave it alone. I went out and found a job as a sales clerk for the Baptist Book Store, on South Main in Houston. My hopes were to work enough hours to make up for the budget cuts. This occurred during the fall of 1992. We also hired a part-time music director, Jim Hamblen. He was a salesman for the H & H Music store in Pasadena. I also knew his uncle, "Ham" Hamblen, at Forney, during my youth minister days. Jim had another uncle, Stuart Hamblen, who was in several movies with John Wayne, and had written a famous praise song, *"It Is No Secret, What God Can Do."* Jim did a tremendous job in leading our condensed congregation in worship in the Glory Building.

Then, another problem popped up. This time, it wasn't financial, but "image." It seems some of our folks were not adjusting to having their pastor work in the bookstore. There were numerous complaints about me working outside the church. The deacons and I met to discuss the issue.

"What else can we do?" I asked. "We've trimmed the budget in every possible way. Everyone wanted a music minister and we got one. What else can we do?"

Someone mentioned cutting the secretary's position to part-time and re-establishing my position back to full time. Her husband was quick to respond: "That's not going to work. She will quit before she works part-time."

Another countered: "So what we're saying is that the secretary's position is more important than the pastor's position? Is that true?"

The husband responded: "I'm just saying that if you touch her salary, not only will she and I leave, but several other families will leave as well."

I interrupted: "Guys, I do not work well under threats. In fact, I will not serve as a slave to anyone but my Lord and Savior, Jesus Christ. This rhetoric is not God-honoring and anyone—including our secretary—who is not willing to help us through this crisis is not serving here for the betterment of the church or His kingdom.

"I do not particularly enjoy driving to downtown Houston three days a week. I do this only to help our church. Had I known this crisis was coming, I would never have purchased a house. But what is done is done. I now have financial obligations to keep and the only way for me to keep them is to either work part-time or to have my original salary re-instated."

"I think we need to re-instate your salary and cut our secretary to half-time," the same guy, as before, said.

Before her husband could respond, I interrupted again: "Let's don't go down that road again, please. Let's cool our jets here, pray, and dismiss. We'll meet again Sunday evening and see if there are some other solutions that come to our minds."

I left that meeting very dejected. It seemed as if God's Spirit had left the meeting and I was trying to figure out if he had even left me. I went home. Diane knew there was a problem.

"What is it this time?" When she said that, I realized that nearly every day, I came home with a new set of problems. It was a confirming statement as well that this church situation was not going to be remedied by me. Someone else, with a new set of ideas would have to handle this. My ideas and decisions were not getting us anywhere, except deeper in ungodly discussions.

"This Sunday morning, I plan to call the church into conference. I will state that if we're going to survive this current crisis, the church will have to make a decision. The decision will be for them to give me the authority to make some hard budget and staff decisions. If they approve, then they are saying that they have confidence in my current style of leadership. If they disapprove, then they are saying that they do not think I am the pastor they need to get our church through this crisis. That's the only solution I have to remedy our current crisis."

Diane looked at me and then she hugged me. "You could not have stated it better. I will follow you wherever you go. I am your wife and I support your decisions."

That was also a confirming statement. My wife made me feel that I was once again getting control over our ministry and mission in life. And once again I knew God had a hold of this situation.

I called our chairman of deacons and notified him to have the deacons meet with me early on Sunday. In that meeting, I informed the group of my intentions. The secretary's husband said that he, also, would like to speak before the vote was taken. The chairman stated that anyone else who wished to speak, for or against the pastor's proposal, would be allowed to do so.

The music service went well. We even had some visitors. When I stood up to preach, I recognized our guests and apologized that this morning's usual message would be interrupted with some church family business and that they were free to stay or leave. They chose to stay, stating that they were new in town and felt this meeting would help them feel the heartbeat of the church.

I presented my case for leading our church through our current crisis. There were several who spoke in favor of my style and how that I had come into an existing problem situation and needed more time to get us through the "storm." Others felt that we were not progressing, as we should, and that we lacked the faith to go forward. The secretary's husband got up and stated that if I got my wish, then his family and friends would be leaving. He also stated that he had contacted my previous church and had spoken with a deacon there. According to that deacon, I had led my previous church into financial disarray and had personally borrowed money from the church without paying it back.

I looked at Diane and asked quietly, "What is he referring to?" She shrugged her shoulders and said, "I have no idea. We've never borrowed money from the church."

When he finished his talk, I asked, "Who was the deacon who told you that?"

He would not give me the name.

"Well, I asked Diane about it and we do not know of any situation where we asked the church for money and did not pay it back. I do not think it is proper to bring this issue up in this meeting, especially since I do not have the opportunity to respond to hearsay."

The discussions ended and the vote was cast. Seventy percent voted against my proposal, which was a vote of no confidence in my leadership. I looked at Diane and then stated, "Your vote this morning is too great for me to be effective in leading our church out of this crisis. You have problems here that need to be resolved, but I'm finishing my statement by telling you that I am not your problem. I offer you my resignation and officially give you my two-weeks notice. I have not used any vacation time, so if you can help me through this transition I would appreciate it."

Jim Hamblen spoke next. "Folks, I came here to help Brother Johnnie. I do not feel led to stay any further than his stay, so I will be leaving as well."

The former volunteer music leader was in the audience as well. He spoke next. "Don't come to me either. My family plans to attend elsewhere."

The service was dismissed and we left. Although I had no clue what was going to happen to my family and me, I felt a great burden lifted off my shoulders. I preached that night from my verse-by-verse study in 1 Corinthians, which happened to be on carnality. I was careful not to insinuate anything from the message. I figured I would preach two more Sundays and then be released, but I received a call on Monday night from the chairman of deacons.

"Johnnie, the deacons met tonight and decided to let you go immediately. You don't need to show up Wednesday night or next Sunday. We'll get someone else to preach in your place."

"That's your decision, but I really need some time to make this transition financially. Will the church help me?"

"Yes. We plan to pay you for your next two weeks, plus give you a month's severance. We only ask that you be patient in receiving the money. It may take a couple months, but you'll get it."

"Thank you. That will help tremendously. I will come in tomorrow to begin clearing out my office."

I was disappointed in this abrupt ending, because I wanted to preach a message to encourage the folks to press on in recovering the mission of reaching the community for Christ. But I was denied that privilege. I went in the next day and cleaned out my desk and bookshelves. The secretary was cordial and kept her door shut most of the time. Another deacon's wife was there with her.

I continued to work, part-time, at the bookstore. I asked the manager about full time, but he explained that he could not do so. It was a company policy thing. One of the church members from Alta Vista came by the house and gave me a phone number of a job lead in sales that he did part-time, alongside his full-time job.

"I've worked for Doug Endsley a long time. He's the joint-owner of the McDonald's I manage here in Pasadena. He also owns a coupon advertising company that I think you can do well in. I'll let him know of your situation."

"Thanks, Dave, I'll give him a call tomorrow."

I walked Dave out to his car and he left. I stood there, looking at our brick home on Zuni Trail. It was like a dream to be living in my own home. Besides our two singlewide trailers in Virginia, we had never owned a home like this one.

About a year and a half had passed since we purchased our "dream" home. The previous owners were the Surley's, church members at Alta Vista. They wanted to move toward San Antonio, but were having a difficult time selling this home. We had looked at it when we first moved to Pasadena, but the price was out of our budget range. After about five months of searching, we still had not found a house to purchase. The Surley's contacted us for a meal out at Kemah. We accepted. While eating Rick made a proposal:

"We feel like the Lord wants us to help you purchase our house, if you're still interested in it."

"Oh man, it's a beautiful house; but you know we cannot afford it, Rick."

"We know, but what if we reduced the price and paid all your closing costs?"

"I don't want you to take a loss on it just for us."

"Johnnie, the Lord has blessed my business. We're not going to be hurting by reducing the price. We'll still get enough equity to make our transition, plus it'll help you and our church to get on with the mission and ministry God has for the both of you."

Rick and Carol were a fine couple in our church. I knew they had a desire to move to Bourne, Texas, and had been trying to sell their home for nearly a year. Diane and I loved the house and the location was awesome, but we also knew that our mortgage needed to stay at one-fourth of our monthly salary.

We accepted their offer and began the process. The Surley's were feeding us numbers to give to the mortgage company. The mortgage price was still a little too high. Rick then came to us with another idea.

"You close on this deal and then I'll write you a check to cover the difference between the mortgage and your budgeted amount for two years. That should give you enough time at the church to get it growing and by then you should have a raise to cover this difference. What do you think?"

"I can't believe you're doing this, Rick."

"Well, we believe it's a God-thing."

"I am so glad it is. I cannot thank you enough for the sacrifice you are making that will allow my family to live in such a nice home."

The above happened about sixteen months ago. Now I was staring at a beautiful home, wondering, *"Whose would it be in a few months? Lord, who's house is this? Is it still yours?"*

Register Tapes Unlimited, Houston, Texas

The next day, I called Register Tapes, Unlimited (RTU). Doug Endsley was not in, but I spoke to the sales rep manager, Peter Gross.

"Oh yeah, Dave said you would call. He's a fine guy and a great salesman. Can you come into the office this afternoon, say around two o'clock?"

"Sure thing. I'll see you this afternoon." RTU was located on the west side of Houston, one exit west of Beltway 8, on I-10, the Katy Freeway. On a good traffic day, it was about a 55-minute drive from my house.

Peter Gross was something else. Very jovial and a mental wizard! This guy had memory retention like no one I had ever met. He had worked in McDonald's with Doug in the past. When Doug bought RTU, he brought Peter in to keep the sales and sales reps going. Peter explained all the ins and outs of register tape coupon advertising. The coupons were those small ads on the back of the register receipts that customers received when they purchased items in major grocery stores. RTU had contracts with all the Houston-area Randall's, Rice, Apple Tree, and a few smaller chains and independent grocery stores. Peter wanted me to go out with another sales rep for training the next day. I had to work at the bookstore, so we set it up for the following day.

The sales job paid commissions only. That meant if you didn't make a sale, you didn't get paid. I had been in sales before, selling annuities and encyclopedias, so I knew it was a risky profession. But the potential for sales seemed open-ended. I accepted the position. After several days of training, I was given the new Randall's store in Texas City. According to Peter, a new store, with its grand opening, would be an easy sales area for me. It was south of Pasadena also, which helped in the expense department.

There would be nine slots on the register tape for ads. Peter said that meant I needed to present the ad concept to at least 180 business owners. I had 3 weeks to do so. Then I would be assigned to another existing store in south Houston and, if I did well, he would give me an additional store to work around. The directions seemed easy enough, so I went to work. I worked like a Trojan around that new store, from daylight to sundown, trying to get an appointment to sit down with business owners. During the morning hours, I tried to catch the early morning businesses, such as donut shops, restaurants, and dry cleaners. In the afternoons, I went to every daytime business, and then in the evenings, I tried to catch some of the evening businesses as well.

I made a couple quick sales, but they were rejected because Randall's policy would not allow a coupon for anything that they themselves sold. So the donut ad was rejected and the flower shop ad was rejected. I continued to work. I think I visited every legitimate business in this town…168! I sold 5 ads. Now many of the ads were paid on a monthly basis and I had the responsibility to collect the money as well. This meant a lot of business miles and a lot of gasoline. RTU paid no travel expenses. I continued working the next area in south Houston. I was given two stores this time. This particular area of Houston was a bit run down, so the businesses did not seem to have a desire for advertisement. I continued working the area as much as time allowed, but once again I only sold about five ads.

The first month's commission check was about $450. That was about two-thirds of my mortgage payment. The second month's commission check was about $400. Diane and I had a long talk and decided that it was time to put our house on the market. It would be a "For Sale – By Owner" attempt. We put an ad in the paper and put flyers out in a tube in the yard. Believe it or not, we actually had a couple interested in the house for the price we were asking.

The kids did not like it, however. Jenny was especially vocal about how bad an apartment was and how she hated the church and the way it treated me. Tim was a little less vocal, but he did not like the apartment idea either. I felt bad for them. I did not want to disappoint them, but I knew we had to make a financial change. Alta Vista's severance was trickling in and it was for only four weeks' pay, not the six weeks I had thought we agreed upon. We did receive a few anonymous gift checks from Alta Vista members during this time. That helped a bunch, but it was still not enough to afford our house.

I gave RTU another try. This third area was a bit more affluent, with several attractive stores for me to work around. I was getting much more proficient in my time and sales pitch. I worked extra hard this third month, hoping that my previous two month's work, plus this new area, would boost my commission check somewhat.

Once again, my commission check was $450 for three months of non-stop labor and three months of driving all over Houston for about a fourth of my previous wage. I had to stop this job and I had to stop now! I headed for Doug's office. He came out of his office and proceeded in my direction as well. We stopped at the conference room. Doug spoke first.

"Hello Johnnie. Could we talk for a moment?" We stepped inside the conference room.

"I was about to come and speak with you, Doug."

"Yeah, I noticed your commission checks have been very low since you started with us."

"Yeah," I responded. "I don't know what I'm doing wrong. I'm visiting all the businesses and making the pitch just as I was taught to do, but no sales."

Doug smiled. "Yeah, sometimes it can be a little rough at the beginning."

"I was just now coming to see you to tell you that I cannot continue doing this. I'm sorry, but I cannot survive on $450 a month."

He smiled. "Who can? Listen, I like you and I like your personality. This type of business needs people like you working with our clients. We have what we call 'in-house' accounts. These are large accounts that are pretty secure. The commission rates are less, however. Peter normally handles all of these accounts, but due to our growth, I need to feed these out to someone else.

"Johnnie, how much salary will it take for you to come into our office every day and service these in-house accounts? You would still have to go out and collect on them and try to expand the existing ones. We'll also feed you all the phone inquiries, at the 'in-house' commission rates."

Doug was serious. He was offering me a secured salary, based on the projected in-house account commissions. I gave him my bottom-line, monthly salary need, which would be about $30,000 a year. He accepted it.

"It's a deal. It'll be reflected in your next check."

"No, Doug. I can't wait another month." He looked at me and then grabbed my commission check and went to his office. He came out with another check to make up the difference.

"Now go to Peter and he will explain all the schedules and procedures for these new accounts. And I want to see them grow as well," he shouted as he disappeared out of the office area.

I stood there staring at both checks. I could not believe what had transpired. Ten minutes ago, I was headed down a dark and uncertain financial future. In two days, we were to close on the house sale and I had an apartment that was waiting for a deposit. Now, it seemed as though everything had changed.

Peter began dumping a bunch of files into my care, describing each client and the schedules involved. Their locations were all over the Houston area: from Galveston Island, northward to Conroe, and from Katy, eastward to Baytown. I would be traveling a lot and working to expand these solid clients. These clients were the core of RTU and Doug wanted to make sure they were well-attended to.

I went home with a new feel and an excitement about our future. I could hardly wait to tell Diane. When I told her the news, the next question was anticipated.

"So, does this mean we get to keep the house?" she asked.

"I think so. You'll still need to get a few more piano students, but I think we can make it work."

With that statement, we called off the closing of the house and made a commitment to live on Zuni Trail, mainly for the sake of keeping our children's environment stable. At this point in our lives, we felt having a solid home base was a more important testimony to the faithfulness and ability of God than anything else our children needed.

For church, we attended several places before settling down at Cornerstone Baptist Church in League City. Former evangelist, Mike Schmidt was the pastor of this new church start. A music evangelist/entertainer, Robert, was the worship leader. He was funny and exceptionally gifted on the keyboard. The church was small, but bursting at the seams with love, praise, and talent. It was just what my family needed after the experience at Alta Vista. Mike had previously visited me at Alta Vista, sharing his evangelistic ministry and his focus on a prayer ministry that he taught. I was impressed with his demeanor, but unfortunately, due to the constant troubles I was involved in, I never had the opportunity to enlist his ministry at the church.

I also had a small group meeting in our home on Wednesday evenings. This was not tied to any church, but several families from Alta Vista who left the church when I resigned, attended the meetings. I was being encouraged by some of this group to start a new work in the Pasadena area. It was considered for a while (I even drafted a vision for the "Family Bible Fellowship"), but never got any further than a plan on paper.

Jenny was two years ahead of Tim in school. Both were into their teenage years. We started them in public school, and then moved them over to a private Christian school, and then back into the public school arena, when our finances went "south." It was a difficult time for both of them, as they had to readjust in friendships, culture, and educational philosophies. It was equally difficult for them to understand the benefits of embracing the church as a haven of Christian rest. To them, the church represented discouragement and turmoil for our family. Jenny always pointed to my ministry and our frequent moves for the difficulty in personal adjustments she encountered in school and in her social life. Tim was always quieter in these type discussions, but I sensed his adjustments were equally troubling.

Diane and I wanted the best for our children, but knew we could not defend the turmoil produced by our recent church experiences. We both held on to the belief that our home stability would eventually win out on the past difficulties of ministry. We remained focused and committed to staying on Zuni Trail throughout their high school years…and we did!

I was doing well at RTU, selling ads and servicing the house accounts. As the company grew, I was given more responsibilities in delivering cases of register tapes to the stores and eventually designed and edited an RTU newsletter for all our salesmen and employees. The newsletter was an instant success for the company and I got to do something I really enjoyed doing: writing and editing.

In the fall of 1993, John Green, a former Pasadena pastor, called me to fill in for him for a preaching assignment in south Houston. He was semi-retired, and was filling in as an interim pastor in various locations. John explained that he could not preach for this church that had called him, the Garden Villas Baptist Church, near Hobby Airport. He asked if I would do so.

I was not looking to pastor again, but was being called on to preach in several churches locally, as pastors occasionally took off for various meetings and vacation. I agreed to fill in for the following Sunday.

Garden Villas Baptist Church, Houston, Texas

The Garden Villas Baptist Church is located at the end of the northwest runway of Hobby Airport, just a couple blocks from Telephone Road. When Diane and I arrived (Jenny and Tim attended Cornerstone) a large airplane flew right over the church, causing the trees to twist in their tops and produce an unusual whistling sound. We held our fingers in our ears.

"Wow!" exclaimed Diane.

"Tell me about it!" I responded. We took the sidewalk from the back to the door on the west side of the sanctuary. Locked! We then proceeded to the front main doors. Locked again! I looked at Diane.

"I guess you need a membership card to get in this place," I said.

The next set of doors on the east side of the foyer was unlocked. *"Good,"* I thought. *"The church is open."* We entered, but the sanctuary was empty. It was a large sanctuary that could easily handle 300-plus people. We walked down to the front. The floor slowly slanted downward to allow a comfortable view for everyone. Diane looked at the piano.

"I wonder if they need a pianist for the service?"

"I don't know. I wonder if they are going to have a service." I smiled and managed to get a small smile from her. We then heard another door open and shut. It was toward the east side of the sanctuary, behind the platform.

"Life!" I exclaimed. "Let's go see if they know what's going on."

"I'll stay here," Diane remarked. "You come back and let me know."

Diane was bashful toward meeting new people and chose rather to gravitate toward the piano where she always felt most comfortable. I headed east. Around the organ was another set of doors that led to an outside door and several rooms. In one of the rooms, there were voices. I knocked on the door as I slowly opened it. It was the Sunday School office.

"Hi. I'm Johnnie Jones. I think I'm supposed to preach here this morning?"

"Oh, so you're our preacher for the day!" said the lady. "Well I'm Sue Powell and this is Jeff Browning." We exchanged handshakes.

"Jeff is one of our deacons and will be in charge of you today."

Jeff walked Diane and me around the facilities. The bulk of the church use was on the east side. That was the reason the west side was not open. Also the front doors were extremely large and, due to humidity, they were difficult to open. So everyone used the east side to get into church; that is, everyone who were not visitors.

As Sunday School ended, people began coming into the sanctuary. If memory serves me correctly, they had a pianist, but the organist was missing. I mentioned Diane playing the organ, but she immediately declined. She could play an organ, but never enjoyed doing so.

"Do you play the piano?" Jeff asked.

"Yes, as long as I know the songs."

"Great!" he responded. "My wife plays, but she is limited in what she can play. She would love to have you play this morning. Would you?"

"Well, are you sure she doesn't mind?"

"Oh, I can assure you that she would love to sit out this service."

So Diane took a bulletin and recognized all the hymns to be sung. Jeff led the music as well. About sixty-five people comprised the a.m. service that morning. There were about eight teenagers and a few children, but mainly median-to-senior adults. The service proceeded well, but sixty-five people in such a large sanctuary made for a lot of empty spaces.

I had barely started preaching, when an airplane either came in for a landing or was taking off over the church. In a humorous way, I ducked below the pulpit as if the plane were coming into the building. I got a few laughs out of the move.

"Boy, you folks must really be a people of faith to sit here while those metal tubes fly over you!"

They laughed again. I started preaching my usual style. Two teenage girls, on two separate pews in the far left rear corner, were turned to each other in a lively conversation. I abruptly stopped preaching and addressed them.

"Ladies, I notice that you have something more important to say than what God may be trying to say through me to you. Would you be so kind as to share with the rest of us what is it that you're speaking of?" There was silence. Neither spoke, so I continued. "Well, if it's not as important as what I have to say, then please turn around, be quiet, and face the front." They obliged. "Thank you; now let's continue the message."

I finished the message and went to the rear of the sanctuary to greet folks as they departed. The two teenagers did not shake my hand, but did manage a small smile. A lady approached next.

"One of the girls you called down was my daughter."

I thought: *"Oh, oh; now I'm going to get it!"*

"I want to thank you for having the guts to do what you did in there. They both needed to hear your message."

"Well, thank you. I'm usually not distracted so, but I guess it had to do with the new surroundings."

Jeff's wife, Dana, was next in line. "Yes, thank you. The other girl was my daughter."

Again I thought, *"Oh well, so much for an invitation to return. I called down the daughter of the music minister and deacon!"*

I did return that evening and preached again. There was a group of about forty people there, more than I anticipated. It was a good service and everyone seemed to really pay attention. Maybe they were afraid I would call them down as well.

Several days later, John called me.

"Johnnie, Jeff Browning called and asked permission to call you directly. Is that okay?"

"Sure John; is it about my calling down his daughter for talking in church?

"Oh no," he laughed. "I think they want you to return this Sunday."

"Oh; okay. Sure, you can give him my number."

Jeff did call me later that evening and did invite me to return the next Sunday. I accepted.

"And please ask Diane if she will play the piano again."

"Okay, but she will need the hymn list prior to publishing it, just to make sure she knows the songs."

I talked to Diane about it. "Okay, but this is just temporary, correct?"

"I'm sure it is. They are way too small to afford me and I'm not sure I want to be a pastor anymore. I'll preach as requested, but I'm not going through another Alta Vista, and neither is my family." Diane showed a sign of relief as I assured her that I was not actively seeking a church position. Garden Villas was about 20 minutes away, so there would definitely be no moving.

I preached a few more weeks for Garden Villas before they asked me to become their interim. With an explanation to Diane what an interim did, and with her approval, I agreed. That occurred in September of 1993. The pastor-side came out of me as I began to visit members in their homes and in the hospitals. My RTU job occasionally brought me into the south Houston area as well as the hospital area, so it was no problem to stop and visit folks.

In December, I was about to conclude the morning service, when a member, Bruce Coma, interrupted my dismissal prayer. (The other teenager I had called down during my first sermon was his daughter.)

"Preacher, before you dismiss us, I need to speak to the congregation." Jeff nodded his head in approval.

"Sure, Bruce; go right ahead." I proceeded to sit with Diane when he asked us to step outside for a moment. We left the sanctuary and stood outside.

"What's this all about?" Diane asked.

"I haven't the slightest idea."

"They're not voting on you to become their pastor, are they?"

"How could they? They don't have my resume and I've not spoken to any committee."

A few minutes later, Bruce's wife, Lynne, asked us to come back in to the sanctuary. Bruce was still standing behind the pulpit.

"Johnnie, our church has just unanimously approved calling you as our permanent part-time pastor. (There were a couple of 'amen's.') Would you accept the position?"

I glanced at Diane before speaking: "I'm honored to be so considered; but I don't think I can do it. I have numerous financial obligations and I have a full-time job that I just can't leave now. I'm afraid I could not give you the time you need for a pastor."

An elderly gentleman stood up. "I'll tell you one thing, preacher; these past two months you have visited our people more than our last full-time pastor ever did." There were numerous "amen's" said in affirmation to his statement. He continued: "You keep visiting us like you're doing now and keep preaching the way you are and you can keep your full-time job." (Again, many "amen's.")

"Well, I really need to discuss this privately with my wife. If you don't mind, I'll respond to this invitation tonight."

That afternoon, Diane and I discussed Garden Villas in detail. I liked the idea of preaching each week, but I wanted her to feel okay about the situation. She was enjoying the opportunity to play the piano again in church, but she still did not want the kids to have to change churches.

"They would not be required to change churches," I assured her (and them, later on).

"I like their involvement at Cornerstone. They've established some new friends there and I don't want them to change again."

"They won't. They can drive themselves to Cornerstone every Sunday."

"Okay, but don't ask me to get involved at Garden Villas beyond playing the piano."

I assured Diane that all she had to do is attend with me on Sundays. Our previous church had hurt Diane and she was not ready to get close to a new congregation. It had only been about ten months since we had left Alta Vista. She was building her piano business in the Pasadena area and we were all enjoying a period of family and financial stability.

That evening, I accepted the call to become Garden Villas' part-time pastor, with the assurance that I was not quitting my day job and that my children would not be required to attend. The church was in full agreement with my terms and welcomed Diane and me with warm and grateful embraces.

How can I describe receiving a cure for a spiritual wound? And that was exactly what Garden Villas was to me. To the congregation, I could do or say no wrong. The attendees hung on every word I preached as the freshest words from God they had ever heard. It was incredible how they responded to me. And, truthfully, this type of response was exactly what I needed in order to re-establish my hope of a continued pastoral ministry, for I had already resolved in my heart that I would no longer pursue another pastorate. I was content now as a salesman for RTU.

This contentment, however, did not spill over into my children's lives. There were some real pulls from the world for their very hearts. There were some times of rebellion that I feared greatly. Jenny had gotten into trouble at school a couple times. She was rebelling against all authority, including my own. There was one time I had to give her a choice of either abiding by the house rules or leave. She left one night—but thank God, just for the night. She came back the next day and agreed to live by the rules, but it was not going to be an easy relationship. Diane and I continued to try to show her our love for her and our restrictions on her were for her own welfare. She endured us and stayed put.

Jenny had met Charles Crabtrey and they were now engaged. They married just prior to his Navy training in Orlando, Florida. She was going to Florida to be with him. She was expecting their first child as well. The baby decided to come on a Sunday morning. Diane and I had decided we would drive to Florida to be with Jenny during the delivery, but this plan was not going to happen. I preached the morning service and told the members that we were headed for Orlando.

We drove non-stop, resting briefly at a couple rest stops. However, by the time we arrived at Orlando, Jenny had already had her baby and was home that Monday afternoon.

Amber Michelle Crabtrey was born on March 13, 1994, and was our first grandchild. Of course she was the most beautiful baby we had ever seen. We stayed a few days with our newest extended family member, and then headed back to Houston. It was awesome to see our family tree begin to sprout a new limb. Amber would be the cause of several more trips to the east coast, one more in Florida, and another to Charleston, South Carolina. (My mom, in

Virginia, benefited from the South Carolina trip as well. She and my sister, Sandra, met us once.)

Later, it would come Tim's time to rebel. It was primarily during his senior year. One of his friends at Cornerstone seemed to lead Tim into some questionable encounters. Tim, like Jenny, was given a choice of abiding by the house rules or leave. He left, but not just overnight. I think his departure was over a year's time. There were times I was afraid of losing him, even physically, but he, like Jenny, eventually returned home. Their life stories are their own to detail, if they so choose. From my perspective, I pleaded with God for both of their lives, but I asked Him to do whatever was necessary to bring them back to Him. (Today, 2008, they both have wonderful families and are faithfully serving the Lord in their churches.)

In my usual tradition, I had Ed Ethridge come to Garden Villas and preach a revival. Ed had preached in every church I had ever pastored. He was like a brother to me and we loved each other as close brothers. Ed was impressed with what God was doing at Garden Villas. Attendance was now about a hundred and the fellowship was really great. He preached prophetically, how God blessed their faith to bring me in as a pastor and to take care of me as they were currently doing. And he challenged them to believe God for even more.

At the end of his Tuesday evening message, a lady stood up to give a testimony. She shared how that this past year, God had really done a work in her life and she was grateful for Him and for me. She also felt that we, as a church, should vote that very night to pay me enough to bring me into our community full time. There were several "amen's" to the testimony and several other positive testimonies to support the idea. The church's finances had been in the "red" for about six months prior to my arrival. It was now about $5,000 to the positive.

Ed was enjoying the testimony time and encouraged them to follow God's will in the matter. He then turned to me.

"What do you think, Jonesie?" I stood up to address the congregation.

"Folks, nothing would please me more than to be able to focus all my attention on growing our church. I think what God leads you to do you should act on it. However, tonight would not be proper to vote on such an important matter. This is not a properly called meeting to make such a decision. If this is of God, it will still be His will at our next church conference, which is but two weeks away. I recommend that we pray about this and if you still feel the same way at the next conference, we'll bring it before the church and I will be prepared to tell you how much it would take to bring me on full time. Agreed?"

It was agreed that we wait. This would give us all time to prepare and to make sure it wasn't just an emotional response to a powerful message on faith. Ed did a wonderful job preaching. His entire ministry has always been to stretch believers in the area of faith and trust in God.

Several weeks passed and the proposal was resubmitted to the church. The amount was given and accepted, and I accepted the invitation. I promptly informed RTU and reduced my register tape involvement to just a few local clients in Pasadena that Peter asked me to keep and service. He also wanted to keep me in the southeast area as a problem solver, should a grocery store call him with a register tape shipment problem. The church did not object, since it was virtually non-conflicting with my ministry.

Garden Villas was still a transitioning community. Although I had the privilege of leading folks to Christ, many of them would move on to other areas to live. I remember one such couple as an example. Derek and Amanda Ross were of a Catholic background. They had a fresh baby in their lives and Amanda was checking the local church for the baby's sake. I did a follow-up visit. I witnessed to her in front of Derek. She was interested in receiving Christ, so I led her through a sinner's prayer. Derek, on the other hand, was not responsive. I continued to visit their house. Finally, he opened his heart toward the gospel and received Christ. After that, neither of them seemed to get enough of God and His word.

As the baby grew, they determined to sell their house and move to a more stable community. Garden Villas was a beautiful community in Houston, filled with large pecan trees and large lots (for gardens, of course). However, it was a rough community. The Houston transit system chose to reroute their bus line around the Garden Villas/Telephone Road area due to bullets shot at passing buses. It was with mixed feelings to see several members, such as the Rosses, to leave our church. (The Rosses would eventually become missionaries overseas.) Eventually, the Browning's would move away, and then a few more.

Some of the church's teenagers were dabbling in drugs. I recall one of our boys calling our house and leaving a message on our answering machine, asking Diane for a particular recipe of hers from something she had brought to a church potluck. His home phone had "clicked," signifying someone else was calling his number. He said "goodbye" and proceeded to click over to his other line. What he did not know was that his conversation continued to be recorded on our answering machine. It was from a friend who had some drugs over at his house, inviting our teenage church member to come on over. He joyfully accepted, describing how he was going to enjoy doing some drugs after such a bad day at school. In time, we would discover more of our church kids were involved in drugs. It was scary to realize how many were doing drugs.

I remained full time for over a year. We were growing spiritually, but the physical numbers began to decline. The community attrition and the drug culture were just too great to overcome. Our church needed to consider allowing other ethnic groups to try and start a fellowship within our walls. We did manage to lease one of our buildings to a Black lady, who had a day care center at her home nearby. Her center had grown too large for a residential location, so she made a proposal to our church. It was granted, but not without some resistance.

I had recommended that we try and start a Hispanic and, possibly, a Vietnamese congregation in our facility. It would be this discussion and "vision" that would start the turn against my leadership. Not me, personally, but the elderly of the church just could not see to let go of their hold on the facility. I explained to them that we would still enjoy our services and fellowships, but that there were other groups in our community that could use the facility at other times. It was not going to happen, however. In mid-1997, the church's finances were such that I announced that I would return to part-time employment. Since many folks had moved out of the community, the objection to my decision was nil.

A Writer and Photographer for the *Pasadena Citizen*

For employment, I responded to a classified from the *Pasadena Citizen* newspaper for the position as a news reporter. Instead of going into the paper's office to fill out an application, I decided to write a mock news article: "Local pastor is hired as a news reporter." I did it up in the column style of the Citizen's newspaper and went to see the editor.

The paper's receptionist looked at the article and then looked at me. She started laughing as she read how that the *Citizen* was hiring me, based on my longevity in the community and the rapport I had with people in general.

"I'll be right back," she said as she disappeared around the corner. Soon, I was seated in front of the editor of the paper.

"Did you write this?" she asked.

I grinned, "Yes ma'am."

She laughed. "You have quite an imagination. I've never had anyone respond to a job in this manner. I like it, but you must still fill out a regular application, you know, with your experiences, etcetera."

"I have none," I responded.

"'None' what?"

"I have no news reporting experience."

"Oh…None?" I shook my head. She studied the mock article I had written. "Well, let me make another proposal to you. I want you to consider being a contributing, freelance writer for our religion page. Each week, you could interview ministers and ministries, finding out what makes them tick and how they contribute to the community."

"Sounds interesting. What does it pay?"

"It'll pay $25 an article and $10 for each picture we use in the article. In fact, if you're interested, you can be on-call for various pictures I may need. We have a full-time photographer, but she can't be in two places at one time.

A stand-alone picture will pay you $15; $25 for captioned pictures, and if it makes front page, full color: $35! Do you own a camera?"

"Sure do. Who buys the film and pays for the developing?"

"We do, of course. We have a charge account at the camera store in the Pasadena Mall. Take as many pictures as needed to get a good one. Deal?" She reached out to shake my hand.

"Deal!" I responded as I shook her hand.

"Great! Take this letter to Ritz Camera Store in the mall. It'll get you some fresh film and put you on the account. Also, let me introduce you to Michelle, our photographer. She can give you some pointers on taking pictures for the paper."

I thanked her, met Michelle, and then left for the camera store. While at the store, I received a phone call. It was the editor, Darilynn.

"Johnnie, I need a picture from you right away. Do you know where the community center is, located on Burke Street, south of Fairmont?"

"Sure do."

"Go there right away and get me some close-up shots of some construction guys laying down bricks with contributors' names on them. I need it for tomorrow's edition. Can you do it? It'll probably be a front-pager and I'll pay you fifty dollars for such a short notice."

"You bet! I'll get right on it."

"Okay, let me talk to the store manager and tell him you're coming right back for developing."

"Wow," I thought. *"That employment was fast!"* I left, took the pictures, had them developed, and into Darilynn's hands by 7:00 p.m. The next morning's paper had my picture, in full color, on the front page. It was truly an amazing sight to see.

"Diane! Look at this!" I displayed it proudly before her eyes. She was elated. "And this one paid fifty bucks!"

The number of articles and pictures I took for the *Citizen* and the Deer Park paper (handled by the *Citizen*) would eventually exceed one hundred. I wrote for the *Citizen* (and its Deer Park affiliate) for the remainder of my stay in the Pasadena area. I was privileged to write articles for various types of ministries, community organizations, businesses, and even one of a cluster of articles when President Bill Clinton visited Pasadena. Writing was a great release for my mind and I enjoyed it thoroughly.

First Baptist Church, Blue Ridge, Texas

Unfortunately, Garden Villas Baptist Church continued to decline in attendance. It was returning to the same size as when I first preached there. I knew it was a matter of time before I would have to give it up. I continued working for the paper, plus Peter had me selling a few ads for RTU stores on the southeast side of Houston.

In August of 1998, I received a telephone call from a man in Blue Ridge, Texas.

"Hello? This is Chub Johnson from Blue Ridge. Is this Johnnie Jones?"

"Yes sir, this is Johnnie."

"Are you a pastor?"

"Yes sir; how may I help you?"

"Well, our church is looking for a pastor and your name was given to us as a possible candidate."

"Uh, yes sir, I think I'm interested."

"Blue Ridge?" I thought. *"Am I going back to Virginia again?"*

"Are you talking about the mountains, Blue Ridge?" I asked. There was a moment of silence.

"No, this is Blue Ridge, Texas. Our church, First Baptist, is looking for a pastor and your resume was submitted to us by a lady in our church. Are you still looking for a church?"

I was still intrigued by the name. "Where is Blue Ridge, Texas?"

"We're located northeast of McKinney, about 30 minutes."

"Oh, okay…and where is McKinney?"

"North of Dallas about 45 miles."

"I'm sorry for being so inquisitive, but I didn't know my resume was being distributed to any churches. How did you get my name and phone number?"

Mister Johnson was being patient with all my questions. "A lady in our church knows a preacher friend of yours, a Reverend Ethridge? He gave her your resume and she gave it to us."

"Oh, okay, now I understand. Well, yes I'm interested in considering the position."

"Houston is a ways off for our committee to travel to. Do you plan to be in the Dallas area sometime in the near future?"

"As a matter of fact, my wife and I are attending a church growth conference in Denton, Texas in a couple of weeks. Would that work for your committee?"

He agreed it would work and together, we would see if we could find a church for me to preach at in order for the church's search committee to come hear me. I contacted Ed. He said that a couple from his church (Michael and Dee Peltier) had moved to Blue Ridge a few months ago and that Dee had come by his office wanting some recommendations for their church's pastor position. Ed had given her two resumes of two different friends. Although mine was a few years out of date (about 5 years!), he figured there was enough information there for them to consider me, if God was in it.

The church conference in Denton was in late August and I preached for the First Baptist Church pulpit committee at Cooper Creek Baptist Church in Denton. We met after the service and discussed their church and our ministry background. A few weeks later, I received another call from Mister Johnson. This time I was asked to come to their church in Blue Ridge, to meet with the committee a second time and, if that went well, to stay over on Sunday to preach in view of a call. I accepted.

The church was nearing a year without a pastor. Dr. Ray Rusk, retired state director of the South Carolina Baptist Convention, was the current interim. Members of the committee felt the church was now ready to move forward in keeping up with the growing pace of Blue Ridge and its surrounding communities.

First Baptist had about 85 in Sunday School attendance in 1998. Diane and I traveled over to the Blue Ridge community prior to the Saturday and Sunday I was scheduled to meet. We just happened to arrive on Friday as school was being dismissed. We were impressed with the number of children and youth walking down the street from the school. Diane's church specialty had always been music and children's Sunday School. She had a heart for children and seeing all these kids stirred her with excitement.

"Wow," she said. "This place has a lot of children."

"Yeah. A great future for a church, wouldn't you agree?"

Her comments and smile confirmed our hearts were together on the possibility of this new ministry. We had a great visit with the committee on Saturday. I preached both services on Sunday and the church voted on me that evening. It was a unanimous call for us to come to Blue Ridge and we, of course, accepted. We would begin our ministry on the first Sunday of December 1998.

The church had a parsonage for us to live in. It was a 1,100 square-foot frame house on Davis Street, a bit smaller than our 1,630 square-foot brick home in Pasadena. With the promise to build a small storage shed in the backyard, we saw no problem in fitting into our new home.

Our house in Pasadena would need to be sold as soon as possible. We decided to sell it ourselves instead of listing it with a realtor because we needed every penny we could save to go into the upgrading of the house in order to sell it. The major things that had to be upgraded were a complete new roof, a new privacy fence around the backyard, and new carpet. The main bathroom floor had to be replaced due to a water stain underneath the linoleum and the central heating system had to be replaced. It would require some tight financial maneuvers, but we figured this was the only way to sell the house.

The house did not sell immediately. We put it on the market in October, but by the time we moved to Blue Ridge, there was only one family interested in the house. He would happen to be the pastor that replaced me at Alta Vista. He needed a home, but wasn't sure if he could arrange the financing for ours at this particular time. We arranged a one-year lease with him, with an option for him to buy at any time during the year. A year would allow me enough time to fix the major repairs of the house. This pastor was also a carpenter by trade, so he did some of my house repairs in lieu of rent.

We moved to Blue Ridge in December and enjoyed an icy Christmas that year. After about a month, the deacon body and I were discussing the need to build a larger sanctuary to accommodate the expectant growth of the area. In February, 1999, a Planning and Steering Committee was formed by the church. The initial committee included Jim Bowling, Lana Carter, Martha Isham, Chub Johnson, Michael Peltier, Johnny Williams, and Robert Todd as chairman. *Ex Officio* members included me, as pastor, and the current treasurer, who was Terry Douglas, Sr. Eventually, Chub would become treasurer and Ricky Hodges would follow Chub. Chub then replaced Peltier, who had to resign due to his oil drilling business in Oklahoma, and Lori Watson replaced Martha, due to her health condition.

As a committee, we first looked at the possibilities of expanding the current facilities on West FM 545. There was an open lot on the rear side of the current facility. The Branch family had been paying the taxes on the land for many years. However, there were some "lost" inheritors of the property, making it near impossible to get a clear deed to the land. It was about a couple acres of land available. After numerous meetings and discussions, the committee felt we needed at least 10 to 15 acres for our future growth. It was decided and recommended to the church that we should relocate our church to a new site, within a five-mile radius of the center of Blue Ridge. This recommendation was overwhelmingly approved.

Meanwhile, after about nine months, my house in Pasadena was still in limbo. The pastor renting it had notified me that he could not get the necessary loan for the purchase and would have to move out at the end of his lease. About this same time a group of college singers from Dallas Baptist University came to our Friday night "5th Quarter" fellowship after a home football game. During the meal, I discovered one of the singers was from Pasadena.

"Pasadena? That's where I came from before moving here."

"Oh yeah?"

"Yeah. In fact I still have a home down there that I'm trying to sell."

"That's interesting, because my parents are looking for a house to purchase."

"Well let me give you the address and my phone number. Have them go by and look at it and if they're interested, have them call me."

That was about all that was said of the house. About three days later, I received a call from this young man's dad. He and his wife had driven by our house and fell in love with it. It was exactly what they were looking for and by the end of the current lease, a new family—another minister—had closed on the house and was ready to move in. It was God's perfect timing for all three families involved.

Back in Blue Ridge, my family had increased to having Jenny, Amber, and Kayti living with us. Jenny had divorced her husband several years earlier and was now attending Texas A & M Commerce for a teaching degree. She would eventually get a bachelor's and a master's degree in education. Diane's piano teaching business was increasing, plus she was traveling to nearby McKinney for in-home lessons.

Jenny had met and married Shawn Martin and they were both now employed at Blue Ridge ISD, she as a teacher and he as a baseball coach. In the next few years, they would bring forth two more children, Sarah and Connor.

Tim, my son, remained in Houston. He would eventually marry Marissa Mauldin. They currently (2008) have two children, Rachel and Hannah. Marissa is a school teacher for Pasadena ISD and Tim works for a large law firm in downtown Houston, helping to maintain their computer systems with up-to-date technology. Tim completed his Bachelor of Science degree in Computer Science in December of 2007 and plans to pursue a Master's and PhD in computer science.

First Baptist Church of Blue Ridge continued to research and plan for a complete relocation. The committee had about twelve different parcels of land in which they were interested. The one that rose to the top was a 40.7 acre plot on State Highway 78, near the FM 981 intersection. The owner gave us two options: we could buy 20 acres for $85,000, or purchase all forty for $120,000. That was the lowest priced per acre highway property offer we had. We decided to recommend the purchase of all 40.7 acres to the church. Again, the church overwhelmingly approved the purchase.

After many meetings, much prayer, and a few financial "hurdles" to jump, we held a dedication and ground breaking service in October of 2003. We financed the building of the facilities through a bond program that allowed our membership, their extended families, and friends of the church to purchase savings bonds over a twenty-year period. There were a few concerns on whether we would find a million dollars among us for the investment, but when the sign-up Sunday came, over a million and a quarter was entered in the registration.

Lana Carter's son-in-law, Tommy Pulliam, was hired as our general contractor. Between him, Robert Todd, and me, we managed to have a building erected and ready to move in, the second Sunday of July, 2004. Our first Sunday in the new facility registered over 450 in attendance, thanks, in part, to the United Methodist Church of Blue Ridge joining us in our first service. After that, the attendance settled into the 250 range. The new auditorium can potentially seat about 500, plus there is a full-court gymnasium and classrooms for about 300. There are many wonderful stories I could write about my experiences at First Baptist, Blue Ridge. It has been a blessing. There remains, however, one final, but important, chapter to be detailed.

Shingles and Post Herpetic Neuralgia

On June 8th, 2007, I was at a rehearsal for a wedding I was to officiate on the 9th. I had an ear ache that evening. I didn't feel a hundred percent, but was able to officiate the wedding okay. However, by the end of my preaching services on the 10th, I told Diane I was sick. I had a severe earache and a headache. On Monday, she took me to our general practitioner, Dr. Luan Pho. He examined me and saw no ear infection. He said I either had a sinus infection or the shingles.

"Shingles? What's that?" I asked.

He proceeded to explain that it was a viral infection from the dormant chicken pox virus in my body. Shingles create very painful lesions that form as a band somewhere on the torso or it can form across the face and head. Since I had no lesions, and due to my continuing severe headache and earache, Dr. Pho gave me some ear infection medicine and had me go for a CT scan on Tuesday for my head pain. On Wednesday, I still had an ear ache, a lot of head pain, but no lesions.

On Thursday morning I awoke to an enormous amount of lesions from the top left of my head, through the left ear, and down the left side of my face to the base of my neck. Boy did they hurt. I called my doctor and he instructed Diane go to the pharmacy right away for medication to treat my shingles.

I could not go to church the following Sunday. The lesions were so sensitive that I could not put on a shirt or let air blow on my ear and head. Shingles usually last for a couple of weeks to a month. The lesions did come and go, but my ear and head pain continued throughout the month.

Mission Trip – Back to Alaska

In July, I was a part of a 16-member mission team that was returning to my old church in Anderson, Alaska, the 5th through the 15th. I spoke with my doctor about going. He wasn't too happy about it, but I put my best face on (right side, of course!) and asked him to help me survive the plane ride. He prescribed me some additional medication that would relax and help me make it.

Diane and I, Shawn and Jenny, and her oldest daughter, Amber (our first granddaughter), were among the sixteen. I had to go in order to keep the mission project alive, because the Alaska pastor at North Star had an emergency trip to the lower 48 to care for his wife's multiple sclerosis. We made it okay, and everyone enjoyed seeing me being moved about in a wheelchair, from airplane to airplane.

I wasn't much help, physically, but my presence helped accomplish the mission. I managed to preach again from my former pulpit in North Star, although I was having numerous headaches. Sometimes the pain was so severe that it caused me to hold on to something, lest I fall.

Our mission team slept at the church from Friday through Tuesday. While there, we painted the outside of the church (two coats) and the interior entryway. We enclosed the rear entry exterior stairway and added several windows in it. We also replaced the existing shower and made it functional, and rebuilt the front exterior porch to include a ramp. Additional jobs included replacing deteriorating wood around the basement windows, dismantling the old coal/kerosene oil burning equipment shed, and re-graveling the front drive way by the new ramp.

In addition to the construction work, our ladies walked the community to advertise the Vacation Bible School to be held during our stay. About ten children came to the sessions. And the most important person of all was our in-resident cook, Janna Simants, who wowed us with her creative "Alaskan" dishes. (Not bad for a Texas girl!) Oh, the stories could go on about the wild strawberries and raspberries, and the men's fishing trip into the brush on four-wheelers.

Giving Diane the support she needs!

On Wednesday, the team left Anderson and headed back to Fairbanks for a few days of sightseeing. Our return flight to Dallas was scheduled to leave the airport a little after midnight, Saturday. We arrived back at the hotel Wednesday afternoon. This would give us a full three days for sightseeing.

While standing in the lobby, waiting for room assignments, I had another severe headache and nearly fell. Shawn's dad, Bobby, caught me and several helped me to a room where I laid down. The piercing pain shooting through my head would not stop. It was then Diane decided that I needed to return to Texas and go to an emergency room. I was in such pain that I could not argue against the idea. Thanks to one of our team members, Pam Clem, a former flight attendant, Diane and I was able to catch a flight out of Fairbanks that night and arrive back into Dallas, Thursday afternoon. As in many previous cases of my "emergency" needs, Ed Ethridge met us at the airport and drove us to Blue Ridge. Diane then took me to the emergency room, whereupon I received more medication and was told to see a neurologist.

On Friday, I saw a neurologist, Dr. Brian Joe. He prescribed other meds and asked me to return in a couple of weeks. The main medicine helped neutralize the pain in the nerve endings. For several weeks I stayed indoors. My church deacons had told me to stay home as needed. I would improve, but when I began interacting with a group of people, my head would begin to emit these deep throbs from the left side. The pain would follow a path through my left ear and then follow my left jawbone, burning the left cheek and jaw as it reached the chin down to the left base of my neck. The pain stopped at the collar bone area. Driving a few miles was okay, but if I tried to drive into McKinney (about 25 miles away) my head would begin to emit those same piercing headaches. The headaches felt like an ice pick being thrust into my head until it reached the base of my neck, sometimes causing my entire body to shake.

On August 2nd, Dr. Joe increased the dosage of my meds. The next day was a Friday and I felt better. In fact, I went outside and worked a little in my yard. I cleaned up afterwards and met Diane in McKinney for supper. We were amazed that I could drive in without any problems of pain. After supper, we met Shawn and Jenny at the cinema for a movie. It was a spy movie with lots of action. This was my favorite type of movie, so nothing appeared "wrong" to go see it. It was sort of a celebration event, celebrating my getting out of the house.

The movie was good, but as the movie became more suspenseful and more active in its dramatic car-chase scenes, my head began to pound a little bit harder. Near its end I began to grip my seat arm tighter. My eyes were now fixated on the screen, but my mind was not able to assimilate the frame sequences. I felt small tremors in my body, so I tightened up my grip to keep me from shaking. Diane looked over at me and noticed I was in trouble.

"You want to leave?" she asked.

"No, no; the movie's about to end," I managed to say. But I really didn't know what was happening in the movie. All I was experiencing was the extremely loud bangs of cars crashing, the screaming of tires, and rapid gun shots. I seemed to be feeling every loud sound deep into my body and I literally shook as if I was in the actual scenes of the movie. Diane was getting very concerned.

"Honey, let's go now," she said. "I'll help you." She grabbed my arm.

"No!" was all I could say. She obliged, but was getting upset at my stubbornness. All I tried to think was that this movie was about to end and I couldn't let Shawn, Jenny, and her miss the ending. About that time, the movie did go into its last scene and the noise level decreased significantly. I had managed to close my eyes a few minutes prior, but was still gripping the chair's arm tightly.

The movie ended, but I wasn't moving. Diane began helping me to stand, but I felt tense. My heart was pounding and every nerve in my body was tingling. It was as if I was connected to an electrical current of some sorts. Shawn had already left the movie to go to the restroom. Jenny assisted Diane as they walked me out of the theater. I was so weak in my legs that I had to sit on a brick ledge by the exit doors. As soon as I sat down I remember heaving as if I was going to vomit. Someone laid me down with my face in the landscaping. I don't remember all the details, but was told later that a nurse came by us and suggested Diane call 911. Diane wasn't sure what to do, but at the nurse's insistence, she finally made the call.

The next event I recall was a man (maybe two men) assisting me onto a gurney and putting me into the back of an EMS vehicle. I felt needles and tape being stuck into and onto me. Several men were asking me questions. I had words in my head to speak to them, but my mouth was not cooperating with my mind. There was some sort of disconnect between the two. It was frustrating. I thought I heard one of the men say to the other that "this is a fake," but I may have been dreaming.

The ER at the Presbyterian Hospital in Allen took me in and checked me out. After about four hours of IV and consult, I was released early Saturday morning, with orders to return to my neurologist as soon as possible. That would be Monday.

Once again I could not attend my church and preach. I felt bad missing, but the medications were keeping my mind and my mouth from coordinating ideas. Monday came and Diane called Dr. Joe's office. He saw us in the afternoon. I was still weak from the weekend "drama." Dr. Joe asked Diane a few questions, looked at me, and said he wanted to admit me into the hospital that day for further tests. Diane agreed, but I resisted. She won out, which was the right course of action. I think I cried like a baby not to go, which revealed just how emotionally out of balance I had become.

I spent five days of testing in the hospital. The final analysis was that I had a severe case of post herpetic neuralgia (PHN) which is a nerve damaging disease that stems from the shingles. PHN can last for months, even years, with no certainty when the pain will subside. A casual search on the internet indicates that PHN is still a mystery as to its cause and endurance. Each case is different, due to the section of the nervous system through which the virus travels and damages. My church gave me the month of August to rest and to recuperate.

During September, I had good days and bad days with head pain. My left inner ear affected my walking ability. I was now on several medications for severe pain, as needed. The medications caused my thinking and speaking processes to slow down a bit, and my walking gait sometimes turned into feet shuffling. I began preaching again, but limited my office hours to a minimum. October, November, and December remained relatively the same. Several times, I tried to reduce my medication levels, but the pain returned. I had to go back on them. Our insurance company refused to pay for some of the more expensive medicines, but we managed with the assistance of our church, our Baptist association, and the state convention. (Later, in 2008, our insurance company reviewed my appeal and decided to pay for a third of the medicines previously denied.)

The Christmas holidays would be a test for my head. Unfortunately, when my grandchildren came, I would have to go to my bedroom. It seemed to be a combination of the interaction and noise of the group that affected me most. I managed to survive, however, so it was a chance to see all my children and grandchildren together.

On Sunday, December 30th, I had a baptism to perform at the beginning of the morning service. Prior to the baptism, I had to assist in resolving a scheduling issue for the day, during the Sunday School hour, so my mind was already churning prior to the main service. I had no sharp pains, so I wasn't anticipating any problem. As I began climbing the stairway up to the baptistry in my usual gait, I had to stop near the top. I became dizzy and disoriented. I stood there frozen. One of the men who assisted me for baptisms saw me there and asked if everything was okay.

"Just a minute; I'm a little dizzy."

It was 11 o'clock—time for the service to begin. One of the men came up to help me. I felt I could continue and did so. I made some announcements and proceeded with the baptism. My mind and my voice seemed to be struggling to connect. After the baptism, both men assisted me down the stairs. I told them I thought I could continue and so I left for the platform.

There was a movie trailer promotional being displayed as I entered the sanctuary, so I sat down. Our music minister, John Salles, welcomed our guests and had everyone stand to greet each other. I stood and was planning to proceed to the platform to my usual seat, but once again my head began to throb. I turned around instead and retreated a few rows back and told my daughter, Jenny, that I was going to rest a bit in my office and to come get me during the special song, just prior to my preaching time.

Obviously, she looked concerned; so did a few more, because in a few minutes there were several at my office door checking on me. I think Jenny was at the door explaining my situation. I had my eyes closed and was leaning back in my chair as far as it could go. In a few minutes, Diane came as well. She had been playing the piano for the service and was unaware of my departure. By this time, I was lying on the floor.

"Johnnie, are you okay?"

"Yeah; yeah; just give me a few minutes to rest my eyes and head."

"Can you preach?"

"I think so. I think I can do it." About that time Jenny said it was time to go in. I got off the floor, checked my hair and necktie, and headed for the door. Diane and Jenny escorted me to the sanctuary door. Diane went on in while Jenny stayed with me. I think I told her that I could go up alone;

anyhow, as we walked in she went to her pew seat as I climbed the stairway onto the platform. Everyone was as quiet as a mouse. You could have heard a pin drop.

I think I made an apology statement, but went right into the opening of my message. Somehow, by God's grace, I managed to preach for about twenty minutes. It was then that the pain began to pierce the left side of my head. I had to put my hand on the area because it always seemed to help. But no sooner was the pain throbbing on the left side that the front lobes of my head began to shoot piercing pain across my forehead. This caused me to lose my thoughts on the message. I stared at my notes, but nothing seemed to make sense anymore. I made another statement or two, and then I closed my Bible and my notebook.

"I'm sorry folks, but I'm going to have to sit down." Once again I thought I could finish the sermon, but the pain just wouldn't subside.

"Let's everyone bow our heads and close our eyes. I want Matt to take over in the invitation." (Matt Henslee was our Associate Pastor of Student Ministries.) At that point, I think I said a prayer and turned to walk away. Several hands began leading me out of the sanctuary as I held my head. I don't remember who did what, but I was thankful for everyone's concern and help. When I arrived in my office, I lay on the floor until Diane brought the car over to my office door. I was frustrated, but really had no control over what was going on around me, and I certainly could not predict the hits of severe pain in my head. Diane drove me home.

Medical Disability or Retirement?

The spring of 2008 found me visiting numerous doctors for my Post Herpetic Neuralgia. The head throbs continued to affect my ability to concentrate and to speak in group settings. The nerve damage in my left ear continued to affect my walking gait. I still encountered difficulties in driving on most highways. Road noise and vibration affected my head and ear, causing the nerve pain to manifest itself. My neurologist said there was no cure for PHN; you just have to wait until the nerve endings stop being sensitive to movement. For most with PHN, the pain subsides. I have discovered that if I get excited or tense, the head pain returns.

For example, in late July, Diane and I were invited to join the annual Martin family get-together in Beaver's Bend, Oklahoma. (This is Jenny's husband's family.) At the time, my head was okay. I drove us to Bonham, about 40 miles away, but that was as far as I could drive. We decided to stop awhile at Walmart; this would give us a little time for me to rest. Afterwards, she took over the driving and we continued to go to Beaver's Bend. We arrived safely, but the trip made me walk rather cautiously. I had to use a hiking stick most of the time.

The next day there was a small "emergency" in our bathroom with a grandchild. I was lying on the bed and the only adult nearby. I left the room to find Diane or Jenny to help with the problem. They came running to the rescue, but the excitement increased the pain of my existing headache. I went into another tremor and had to lie on the floor. This caused me to have to stay in the cabin for the rest of the day. My medications were increased, allowing me to rest. My need for a quiet environment allowed Diane and the others to enjoy the park and the lake. I was grateful for that.

The next day, Sunday, I felt better. So Diane and I decided to take Shawn's grandmother, Granny, into the park to show her its beauty. She had never been to Beaver's Bend. We were doing well until a surprise bump came upon us in the car. I tensed up quickly, anticipating the jolt. Immediately, my head pain returned and I had another tremor experience in the car. This meant I had to stay indoors for the rest of the outing. Diane and my plan to drive to Houston to visit Tim's family was canceled.

Prior to the Beaver's Bend trip, I was called by our chairman of deacons requesting a meeting with the deacons over some "issues" that had come up. He and the deacons wanted to meet with me the next Sunday, July 27th, but I explained that we had already scheduled the Beaver's Bend trip and that I would not be in town that weekend. The meeting was rescheduled for the following week, which was the normal week for the deacons' meeting. (Because of my PHN, I had not been meeting regularly with the deacons.)

I met with the deacons on Sunday, August 3rd. I think all the deacons were present. The meeting began with a discussion of concerns from the deacons. Most of the concerns were simply issues that needed a clarification or change that would be easily accomplished. However, some concerns addressed my preaching topics and, of course, my health. I do not think the preaching issues came from a majority of the men, but we were all concerned about my continued health issues and my inability to predict my ear and head pain. I could not say whether I was improving or when I would get better. The PHN continued to be my "thorn in the flesh," so to speak.

The next day, I had another case of severe pain mainly across my forehead. Red bumps and streaks appeared on my face and forehead on Tuesday. The bumps were very sensitive to touch. Diane drove me to my neurologist and he confirmed that my shingles had reactivated. He put me on an antiviral medication and steroids. I missed a few days of work, but was back in the church office on Wednesday. The rest of the week went okay.

On Sunday, August 10th, I preached both services without a hitch, plus we had our usual monthly church conference after the evening service. Nothing unusual occurred, but the day was draining on me. On Monday, I wasn't feeling well. Sunday had taken its toll on me. On Tuesday I spoke with Diane about the continued difficulty and accompanying stress of each week. The PHN was becoming a regular weekly "hit." We decided that it was best for me to stop trying to maintain my position as a pastor. We both agreed that my continued health issue would affect our church's growth. We discussed our options and decided that I would announce my resignation on August 17th and make it effective the 31st. This I did.

Life Goes On

I began September 2008, as officially unemployed. The church gave me a severance package that would allow me the remainder of the year to heal. I thank God for a church that has been sensitive to my personal needs. This month, I have met with another specialist through the VA hospital system and I am also in touch with another specialist, Charles Crane, MD, who specializes in treating nerve damage with laser technology. I am hopeful for some solutions in the near future. I have also applied for disability through the Social Security Administration. The outcome of my new treatments and the disability decision are still pending.

As I begin to close this volume of my life's experiences, I find that each new month of my life reveals new details for this story. Will laser treatments heal my damaged nerves? Will I qualify for S.S. disability? I could go on and on with new updates, but I am ready to stop writing and to publish this work. Perhaps there will be a sequel to my story.

I became 57 years old on June 28, 2008. I know in some ways my life is very typical; but perhaps the twists and turns of this story can be a work of encouragement for others to press on in life. I have been in the grips of death many times, yet survived. Through my faith in God and Jesus Christ, I have made moves and job changes that only He could orchestrate. My prayer throughout this whole project has been to show every reader how an ordinary person (?), such as me, can do extraordinary things through a personal relationship with Jesus Christ. My life has had its ups and downs, but I am confident that it will maintain the excitement of new discoveries to come. As a minister, I've had the privilege and high honor to baptize around eight hundred people! That alone has been worth the life for which I have lived and I thank God for my hope, my eternal salvation, and for the privilege of serving Him. To Him alone I give glory for each new day.

Now allow me to tie up a few loose ends. My mother turned eighty years old on July 4th, 2008, and is living on her own in Danville, Virginia. My older brother, Gary, is living in Birmingham, Alabama. (My oldest brother, Joe, passed away in 1987.) My sister, Sandra Jones Taylor and younger brother, Ricky, continue to live in the Danville area and have growing families of their own. I have lost contact

The Jones clan, (late 90s): Ricky, Mama, Gary, Sandra, & me

with many people mentioned in these pages, except my Hawaiian "family," the Miller's. They now reside in different locations in Ohio. And I still maintain contact with some of my church friends from times past. Ed and Judy Ethridge now live in Carrollton, Texas, about a fifty-minute drive from Blue Ridge. He currently serves about ninety churches as the director of missions for the North Texas Baptist Area (NTBA) in Lewisville. He and I continue to be the best of friends. (He even mowed my yard a few months ago!)

Diane and I live in a new home in Blue Ridge that was built in 2007. It is a beautiful home and has its own miraculous story that I could write many more pages about...but I won't. I continue to edit and produce a newsletter for the NTBA association, where Ed serves. I am a volunteer chaplain for the Collin County Fire Marshall Department. I have written and published two additional books entitled, *Metamorphosis: Changes From Within* (© 2002), and *Metamorphosis 2: The Transforming Power of Intimacy With God* (© 2004), plus several workbooks on biblical subjects (*Diakonos: Deacon Word Study*; *Benefits of Christianity Study Guide*; *Children's Guide to Discovering Jesus Activity Pages*). Writing has become my favorite pastime.

I want to end with a statement about the most loving and committed person that has ever been a part of my life. Although special credit is due to my parents who loved me and sustained me during my growing-up years, I have to pay special tribute to my wife of 33 years (2-1-08). Diane has done more and sacrificed more to make these adult years the most pleasurable and satisfying of all. Her consistent and enduring love and commitment to me (and to her Lord!) has been the fulfillment of that prayer I prayed to God, during my college days (pg. 173). God knew exactly what this man needed as a companion through the many changes and decisions of our married lives. She has always had a gift of discernment and has saved us from many a failure and wrong choice. And as it looks from this moment on, she will continue to affirm me and be my positive, uplifting companion. What a blessing she is!

And so I close this portion of the story of my life with the final and two most important names in my vocabulary that I could enter. I end on the highest of notes with those two beautiful names. For the most exciting and fulfilling life I could ever imagine possible for one man, I owe it all to my Lord Jesus Christ and to my precious wife, Diane Jones.

Diane and Johnnie

To be continued...?

50/50 CHANCE TO LIVE ✦ 317

Our Growing Family
TOP: The Martin's: Sarah, Jenny, Amber Crabtrey, Connor, Shawn, & Kayti

BELOW: The Joneses: Marissa, Rachel, Tim, & Hannah

The Family Tree continues...
(next page)

✦ 50/50 CHANCE TO LIVE ✦

The Martin's

Amber (Crabtrey)

Kayti

Sarah

Connor

Shawn & Jenny

Shawn's parents are:
Bobby and Rhonda Martin
Bobby's parents are: R. C. and Lavada Martin
Rhonda's parents are: Lawrence and Mildred Dunn

(Jenny's family line follows next page.)

The Joneses

Rachel

Hannah

Hannah

Rachel

Tim and Marissa

Marissa's parents are: Bob Mauldin and
Lanny and Marsha Mikulencak

Jenny Martin and Tim Jones parents are:
Johnnie R. Jones and Diane E. LeRoy

Diane's parents are: Robert C. LeRoy & Katherine Knight
Robert's parents are: Vernon LeRoy & Arlie Yates
Katherine's parents are: Jesse Knight & Bess Qualls
Vernon's parents are: Fred LeRoy & Virginia Barlow
Arlie's parents are: Clark Yates & Etta Johnson
Jesse's parents are: William Knight & Amanda Ragland
Bess's parents are: ?
Fred's parents are: David LeRoy & Mary McCollum
Clark's parents are: Isaac Yates & Mary Ann Osboro
Isaac's parents are: John Yates (Yeates) & Polly Risley
Amanda's parents are: Burrel Ragland & Matilda ?

Johnnie's parents are: Wallace A. Jones & Mildred Ruth Burke
Wallace's parents are: Willie A. Jones & Nellie Walton
Mildred's parents are: Azzle Burke & Dola Gerrells
Willie's parents are: Bennie Jones & Lily Pulliam
Nellie's parents are: Robert Walton & Mary Ann ?
Azzle's parents are: Benjamin C. Burke & Maude Strickland
Dola's parents are: William S. Gerrells & Callie E. Allison
Benjamin's parents are: James Burke & Carrie Lou Merritt
William's parents are: Ely Fitzgerrells (Fitz- was dropped off)
      & Mandy Kinsey
Callie's parents are: Charlie T. Allison & Vonia L. Victor

Postscript

— The Christian life is a life that depicts a union between flesh and spirit. It is best described as a marriage between two entities, the Greater which brings honor to the lesser, making both equal in manifestation. I existed physically, emotionally, morally, and yes, "spiritually," without a relationship with God. This is everyone's nature and makeup. I was progressing as well as any normal person could do.

But inside me, that is, in my soul, there remained a conflict of interests in my life. I discovered during my adolescent years that I and other people around me needed to relate to one another in order to survive in the "physical" and "spiritual" realm of being. I believe everyone is looking for purpose in life, for satisfaction in "being."

I remember back—I think it was the fall of 1972—in Hawaii, when Bev was about to leave for college on the mainland, that I asked her if there was anything I could do for her while she was gone? She answered, "Yes: please find my sister, Terry. She left home to go live in the jungle. See if you can find her and bring her back."

The "jungle" was a local reference to the inner city of Honolulu where thousands of young people moved into to be set "free," so to speak. Bev was concerned for her sister's well being, as well as her spiritual condition. By a stroke of "providence," through her parents, I discovered that Terry sometimes showed up at the sailing clubhouse of which the Ashbaker's were members, to see them. Mrs. Ashbaker told me that on a particular night, a rock band would be performing at the clubhouse. She suspected that Terry would attend; and she did.

I attended that same evening. There was a lot of drinking, dancing, and socializing going on. When Mrs. Ashbaker saw me, she immediately pointed out Terry, who was dancing among the crowd. What I saw was a long-haired, hippy-type young girl, who I discovered was staying with some guys in an apartment. I introduced myself to her and told her I was Bev's boyfriend. She immediately took me in as a dear and close friend.

During the band's break, she and I accompanied them outside for a "smoke" break. We ended up in a circle inside a gutted-out VW van (I'm not kidding!), where the "joint" was passed around for all of us to smoke. I observed how satisfying it was to everyone who partook of the weed's intoxicating qualities. When it came my turn, I took the joint, gazed at its embers momentarily, and passed it on to Terry. Some of the band members questioned my reluctance, but Terry interceded for me.

"He's my sister's boyfriend and they get high with Jesus."

"Oh; that's cool," said one of the band members. So the joint continued around the circle until everyone was "ready" to finish the stint.

Back inside, I danced a bit with Terry and sat with the Ashbaker's. But I felt terrible inside. I felt that I was not being a "witness" for Christ at all and that they—the world—was being a "witness" to me. I eventually went outside and leaned against my car. I began to cry and pray. In fact I remember crying like a baby. What I did not know or see was Mrs. Ashbaker observing me from a distance. She came up to me and hugged me and apologized for the "setting." I told her that I was doing this for Bev and that I felt like I had failed her. Mrs. Ashbaker encouraged me not to lose hope and to come back in and speak to Terry again before I left.

She walked away and went back into the clubhouse. I remained outside to try and get my composure back. It seemed only a minute or two when Terry came up to me in the parking lot. She knew something was wrong with me and apologized as well. We sat among the vehicles and visited for awhile. I told her that Bev was missing her and that she was concerned about her (Terry's) condition.

"Bev asked me to find you and to bring you home." Terry laughed.

"I have a home," she responded. "And my roommates supply me with all that I need." She meant of course, food, shelter, clothing, and marijuana.

Somehow, I managed to see her several times during the upcoming weeks. I witnessed to her several times. I told her about my "high" in Jesus and how it brought me inner peace and that it was everlasting. She listened, but didn't budge, until after a little incident.

I was taking Terry to her apartment one day, when she asked me to stop at a different set of apartments. She wanted to see a friend. We walked down a corridor, climbed up several flights of stairs to the top floor, and knocked on a door. Inside was a dark room filled with a cloud of incense. The music was as deep as the darkness. The guy looked me over and spoke softly to Terry.

"He's cool," she responded. With that statement he went to another room and returned with a brown bag. When he unrolled the cloth inside, I saw dice-sized clumps of "hashish." Terry bought four clumps and we left. I didn't say a word, but I was thinking, *"Man, I am risking everything important to my spiritual and physical livelihood for this girl."* I think Terry was reading my mind. In the car, she spoke first.

"John, I'm sorry; I didn't mean to put you in harm's way."

"Terry, your merchandise is illegal and affects not only you and your health, but it jeopardizes everyone you come into contact with. My Jesus offers you more than what that little fix offers and He's not illegal. I will take you home today, but I can no longer continue this relationship."

She looked at me and knew I was serious. Somehow, I got to her. She promised that if I would sit with her, that she would come to church with me. Well, that statement "got" to me and I continued to see her and she did attend church…several times. In fact, Mrs. Ashbaker began attending as well (after our clubhouse scenario). I think it was perhaps the second or third visit that at the invitation song, Terry, who was seated with her mother (I was in the choir), went to Brother Bill to announce that she had given her life to the Lord Jesus. There was great joy and tears from so many friends of Bev's and mine.

After church, we went over to Dennis and Denise Cook's house and from there called Bev, who was still in college on the mainland. Tears of joy continued to flow as Terry was sharing her salvation experience to Bev.

I sat there and looked at a young girl who had literally changed before my eyes. She still had her hippy-styled clothing on, but she looked different. And she was different. In short, Terry moved back into her parent's home and I got to see her grow and develop in the Lord for a brief time in my life.

I interjected this little story as an example of what I mean when I say that something on the inside of a person is crying out for fulfillment of purpose, for "being." For some, fulfillment is found in a "joint" or some other drug;

for others, alcohol or sports maybe. Still others find their "high" in entertainment or in a personal achievement or hobby. Everyone has a life story to tell, an interest to get indulged in… something that gives them a "high."

But here I was, living in one of the largest entertainment centers in the world, observing people who, living on the "isle of paradise," still depended on something or someone else in order to cope with life. I compared Hawaii's fulfillment of joy and satisfaction with my own personal relationship in Jesus. And guess what? Guess Who won in my comparison, hands down? (You can read the rest of this story inside this book.)

May I kindly tell you, the guilt and weight of emptiness in my life was due to a broken relationship with my Maker. God designed me to have a relationship with Him. The first man (Adam) messed up all of mankind's relationship with God through disobedience and rebellion. I inherited this sinful nature and became a God-dishonoring, rebellious sinner in my own right.

To deal with the disobedience in my heart and to find inner peace I had to come to grips with this one issue: what have I done with God's only remedy for my sin nature? What have I done with Jesus? I could not have it both ways; I could not remain a servant to sin and maintain a relationship with God.

I was enslaved to my sin nature and it was leading me to eternal death. But God was offering me adoption into His family through the Lord Jesus Christ, if I would simply repent and turn. The choice was mine: would I choose His offer of adoption and deliver me from the penalty of my sin and spend eternity with God, or do nothing and risk spending eternity in hell, in judgment of my sins?

You know what? When your physical life is over, all the physical "highs" end as well; but if there is an eternity, and I believe there is! …if there is a Creator, and I believe there is! …what will you do?

There is a remedy to this eternal question. Just as it happened to me… if there is conviction in your heart about emptiness and isolation from God; if you can believe in your heart that God loves you enough that he gave His only Son as a payment for your sin, then you must turn away from your sin nature and its sinful lifestyle (it's called, repent) and turn to Jesus for salvation. "Repent therefore and be converted, that your sins may be blotted out, so that times of refreshing may come from the presence of the Lord" (Acts 3:19 NKJV).

If you haven't dealt with this imperative issue, seek a Bible and a Christian for counsel. I have also written two additional books on spiritual metamorphosis that can help in this matter. Look for an advertisement in this book for ordering information. – JRJ

The book that introduces the switch to Christianity as the transformational change that ignites a fulfilling, intimate relationship with the Creator of mankind.

Discover the Joy and Satisfaction of an Inner Transformation!

METAMORPHOSIS
Changes From Within

ORDER YOUR COPY TODAY!

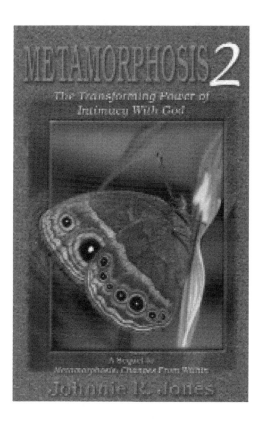

There's more to a marriage than the wedding day! Discover the beauty of a transformed life in Jesus Christ. It's called the "new and living way" of reaching your potential through an intimate, maturing relationship with Him. (Hebrews 10:19-20)

METAMORPHOSIS 2
The Transforming Power of Intimacy With God

ORDER YOUR COPY TODAY!

A Comparison of Meta 1 to Meta 2

Metamorphosis: Changes From Within (© 2002) is an introductory presentation of the initial spiritual change that occurs when one yields his life to Jesus Christ. **Meta 1** uses the fruit of the Spirit (Galatians 5:22-23) to reveal the conception stage of an inner change that can lead a person into a fully satisfied and maturing spiritual life with God through **changes from within**.

Metamorphosis 2: The Transforming Power of Intimacy With God (© 2004) picks up where **Meta 1** ends and goes into the daily encounters one can experience with God. This volume develops the experience of intimacy with God, through the Holy Spirit, and explains how intimacy is the key to reaching maturity in a spiritual relationship.

If <u>Meta 1:</u>	Then <u>Meta 2:</u>
Is conception	Is gestation
Is birth	Is life
Is a high school education	Is a college education
Is driver's education	Is driving alone
Is driving the family car	Is driving your own car
Is basic military training	Is active duty
Is the wedding day	Is the marriage
Is marriage before children	Is marriage with children
Is the "old" nature	Is the "new" nature
Is the O. T. covenants	Is the N. T. covenant
Is the 2 fish and 5 loaves	Is feeding the 5 thousand
Is the "milk" of the Word	Is the "meat" of the Word

Conclusion—For what is a birth without a life? Or what is a wedding without a marriage? There is more to a spiritual life than just to be "born again." As our physical life was designed for an intimate relationship, so our spiritual life was designed for an intimate relationship with our Creator God through Jesus Christ our Lord. Read to find out more!

ORDER BOTH COPIES TODAY!

Order Information (Retail)

Postal orders may be sent to: 316 Hwy. 78 N., Blue Ridge, TX 75424 (or contact First Baptist Church of Blue Ridge, TX for more information: 972.752.5611):

Direct Email Orders: brojohnnie@gmail.com

Make checks payable to: **Johnnie R. Jones**

Qty. Title

____   ***Metamorphosis: Changes From Within*** (© 2002)
Price per book: $11.00* (price includes shipping)

____   ***Metamorphosis 2: The Transforming Power of Intimacy With God*** (© 2004)
Price per book: $13.00* (price includes shipping)

** Both Metamorphosis books, shipped together: $20.00

____   **50/50 Chance to Live** (© 2009)
Price per book: $20.00 (price includes shipping)

** All Three, shipped together: **$35.00 (Best Price!)**
Prices are current and may be changed after 2010.
(Keep in touch for additional writing projects!)

Phone or Email:
(should there be any clarification needed on shipping)

All orders in the U.S. will be shipped U. S. Postal Service, unless otherwise requested. Additional shipping charges may be added for other locations or methods of shipping.